The Horrors of the Half-Known Life

*the text of this book is printed
on 100% recycled paper*

The Horrors
of the
Half-Known Life

Male Attitudes Toward
Women and Sexuality in
Nineteenth-Century America

G. J. BARKER-BENFIELD

HARPER COLOPHON BOOKS
Harper & Row, Publishers
New York, Hagerstown,
San Francisco, London

Designed by Dorothy Schmiderer

First HARPER COLOPHON edition published 1977

STANDARD BOOK NUMBER: 06–090539–5

77 78 79 80 81 5 4 3 2 1

To Donald B. Meyer

"Prithee, friend, leave me alone with my patient,"
said the practitioner. "Trust me, good jailer, you
shall briefly have peace in your house; and, I
promise you, Mistress Prynne shall hereafter be
more amenable to just authority than you have
found her heretofore. . . ."

"Thy acts are like mercy," said Hester, be-
wildered and appalled. "But thy words interpret
thee as a terror!"

Nathaniel Hawthorne, *The Scarlet Letter*, 1850

Contents

Contents

Introduction

The title of this book is taken from Chapter LVIII of *Moby Dick:*

> Consider . . . the universal cannibalism of the sea; all whose creatures prey on each other, carrying on eternal war since the world began.
>
> Consider all this; and then turn to this green, gentle, and most docile earth; consider them both, the sea and the land; and do you not find a strange analogy to something in yourself? For as this appalling ocean surrounds the verdant land, so in the soul of man there lies one insular Tahiti, full of peace and joy, but encompassed by all the horrors of the half known life. God keep thee! Push not off from that isle, thou canst never return!

Melville's work suggests that this psychological bifurcation, and its geographical expression, had a particular significance for American men. It suggests, too, that the relation between the sexes corresponded to the same split. Ishmael's preservation followed his determination to separate himself from "the rushing Pequod, freighted with savages, and laden with fire . . . the material counterpart to her monomaniac commander's soul." Ishmael placed his "conceit of attainable felicity" in "the wife, the heart, the bed . . . the country," even if, in some way, he reserved homosexual fantasies to himself. So Melville deplored the effects on men of the separation of the sexes, even if in his later work, especially *Billy Budd,* he showed he could not escape them.

That view of Melville was the starting point of this book. Its subject is a conventional one; it is WASP males, the physiological minority who have monopolized the attention of conventional historians, most of whom have been white and male. My focus is the nineteenth century.

The book is divided into four parts. The first provides the background for the rest of the book. It is based very largely on Alexis de Tocqueville's view of the effects of democracy on American men and on their relations to American women. Donald Meyer first drew my attention to the meaning and implications of Tocqueville's account of the uniquely extreme separation of the sexes in America. I have expanded Tocqueville's thesis (which, it is sometimes forgotten, was based on exhaustive research) to include the views of some nineteenth-century writers on childrearing and mental illness. I suggest that white American men's experience of the increasingly democratic society was one of unrelenting pressure, and that their sexual beliefs and their treatment of women were shaped very largely by that pressure; beliefs and treatment affected childrearing in ways that perpetuated and reinforced the pressure. My subject is sex roles, not family structure, although I acknowledge the arbitrariness of that distinction. I should like to point out that recent, persuasive research into the history of the family has destroyed the popular notion that there has been a single and steady contraction of the family over the last three or four hundred years in the West. In fact, there have been a variety of family sizes and structures throughout history, coexisting within the same societies, and as phases within the life cycle of single families. What I argue about sexual relations is not at all incompatible with such variety.

Part II of the book opens with a brief account of the victory of obstetricians over midwives during the first half of the twentieth century. Male domination of parturition is a remarkably American phenomenon, and is an indication of sexual beliefs. The rest of Part II provides a historical context for the banishment of midwives; it points out that the only area in nineteenth-century medicine in which the United States could claim international standing was gynecological surgery, and argues that American doctors and gynecologists shared the attitudes described in Part I. Part II includes an account of the life and work of the most famous American gynecological surgeon of the nineteenth century, J. Marion Sims, and concludes with an account of female castration in America.

Part III concentrates on the Reverend John Todd, the writer of immensely popular books telling young men what psychology to adopt under incessantly competitive conditions. Analysis of Todd's work supplies an organizing perspective for the meaning of masturbation phobia and the beliefs in "the spermatic economy" and "proto-sublimation" (terms I define in Chapter 15). These beliefs reflected men's attitudes toward women, and vice versa. And in a context of real and impending change in sex roles men interpreted any deviation in women's behavior as tantamount to social anarchy. They projected their sexual beliefs onto the political and natural worlds. The subject of Part IV, Augustus Kinsley Gardner, was an obstetrician and gynecologist, concerned with the social and political meaning of reproduction. He told men and women how to govern copulation in the best interests of the body politic.

While I do claim that in some respects the sexual attitudes I describe were uniquely intense in nineteenth-century America, I should point out that the general features of those attitudes—men's habits of dividing themselves into mind and body, arranging those parts hierarchically, with the former dominating the latter, and believing that the development of the one had to be at the expense of the other—have been limited neither to America nor to the nine-teenth century, nor to Western civilization. By definition they have been linked to man's beliefs about sex and the position of woman, and his need to separate himself from and subordinate woman be-cause she was the objective correlative of his own sexuality. Such beliefs seem to have shaped the traditional values requiring the separation of male destiny from heterosexual love and equality. One can trace them in ancient Indian and Chinese culture, in Plato's projection of his sexual beliefs onto his split world view, Aristotle's devaluation of woman and aggrandizement of sperm, St. Paul's Platonism, the "Great Chain of Being," the world view of Descartes, and Romanticism through Freud. Modern instinct theory challenges the "economy of the libido" and the notion of "sex drive."[1]*

My examination of the evidence is very largely psychoanalytical. But I have avoided running the evidence through Freud's, or Erik-son's, or anyone else's scheme (profoundly suggestive as they are): in one sense the book explains the historically limited nature of Freud's instinct theory. Instead I have used what I hope I may be forgiven for calling an existential method, explaining nineteenth-century man in terms of his own existence: it assumes that "every aspect of his being is related to every other aspect," and attempts to set "particular experiences within the context of his whole being-in-his-world."[2] I have not excluded those facts about humanity to which psychoanalysis has drawn particular attention—association,

* Notes begin on page 309.

transference, projection, the role of unconscious mental processes, the effect of childhood trauma—facts that are not historically limited or capable of reification. Such a method avoids, I hope, what Elizabeth Janeway has called "racism by chronology,"[3] by insisting that people in the past have been just as complex as we like to think we are.

This book is dedicated to the teacher and friend who inspired it.

My wife, Kathleen, has helped me more than I can say. So have Anthony West, John Callahan, and Michael Hollington.

Esther Brass, Ann Calderwood, Misha and Cipa Dichter, Lawrence and Sharon Friedman, Jack and Dianne Hart, Susan Kirschner, Randall McGowen, Ann and Charles McLaughlin, Jean Meyer, Linda and Shel Mehr, Cynthia Merman, Terence and Martha Murphy, Al and Joyce Parker, Michael and Marianne Shapiro, and other friends in America and England have given me constant encouragement. So, too, have my parents and my brother.

I should like to acknowledge my teachers and fellow students at Trinity College, Cambridge, and at U.C.L.A.

Hugh Van Dusen supported the venture from an early stage, and gave me some invaluable advice at a critical moment toward the end. I thank Martha Murphy for her patient and skillful typing.

1974   G. J. B.-B.

Part I

_____

The Sexes in Tocqueville's America

1   The American Man

Alexis de Tocqueville and Gustave de Beaumont were so moved by
the story of a French couple's flight to the American West that they
made a pilgrimage to Frenchman's Island in Lake Oneida, where
the couple had found refuge. Tocqueville embodied the experience
in *Democracy in America,* and Beaumont shaped his sociological
novel *Marie* according to the original account of the flight. There
is a sharp contrast between the "tranquil joys" and the "charms
of conjugal union" of the French couple whom Beaumont and
Tocqueville envisioned in "a new Eden," and the picture they each
presented of the relations that existed between a typical American
and his wife, whether in the wild West or in the settled East. The
imaginations of Tocqueville and Beaumont were captured, not by
the Frenchman's braving the wilderness, nor by his fleeing society,
but by the relationship, under daunting circumstances, between the
man and the woman.[1]

Tocqueville's observations of the typical American male's behavior in the face of the wilderness provide a suggestive frame for
an account of his observations of the typical sexual relations between
an American man and his wife. "Everywhere extreme civilization
and nature abandoned to herself find themselves together, and as it
were, face to face." Tocqueville was sensitive to his natural surroundings. In spite of his soul's penetration "by a sort of religious
terror" he "couldn't keep from admiring the supreme horror of the
place," the wilderness. On one occasion he and his companion were
softened into a rare state of consciousness, beyond the will to express

3

it. Open to see nature's momentary equilibrium, Tocqueville became
aware of the corresponding dimension of his own body.

> The canoe slid without effort or noise. There reigned about us, a
> universal quietness and serenity. We ourselves soon felt as if it were
> softened by such a spectacle. Our words began to come more and more
> rarely. Soon we expressed our thoughts only in a whisper; finally we
> fell silent; and lifting our paddles in unison, the two of us sank into
> a tranquil reverie full of inexpressible charm. . . . Who will ever
> faithfully paint these rare moments in life, when physical well-being
> prepares you for moral tranquility, and when, before your eyes, as it
> were, a perfect equilibrium is established in the universe; when the
> soul, half asleep, balances between the present and the future, between
> the real and the possible, when, surrounded by beautiful nature,
> breathing calm and balmy air, at peace with himself in a universal
> peace, man lends his ear to the even beating in his arteries whose
> every throb marks the passage of time which, for him, seems to flow
> drop by drop in eternity.

He presented these feelings as "the sweetest and most natural emotions of the heart."[2]

Apparently the American man did not experience such feelings;
he took the confrontation with nature in his stride. "A daily witness
of these marvels, the American sees nothing astonishing in them.
This unbelievable destruction, this still more surprising growth,
seem to him the usual procedure of the events of the world." Thoreau made a similar generalization: "For one that comes [to the
woods] with a pencil to sketch or sing, a thousand come with an axe
or rifle."[3]

The American's treatment of the Indian, Tocqueville observed,
was as ruthless as his approach to nature. He followed his account
of the Indians (whom he found pathetic after reading François-René
de Chateaubriand and James Fenimore Cooper) with a bitter
analysis of the American hypocrisy which rationalized the Indians'
destruction. He described the white American response to a drunken
Indian lying in their way in terms which we shall see later at the
heart of Tocqueville's view of American male psychology—"insensibility," "cold and implacable"—not only in connection with the fate
of the Indian but in the attitude toward nature generally and toward
the American woman. "In the heart of this society, so policed, so
prudish, so sententiously unreal and virtuous, one encounters a
complete insensibility, a sort of cold and implacable egoism when
it's a question of the American indigenies. . . . This world belongs

to us, add they. . . . The true proprietors of this continent are those who know how to take advantage of its riches."[4]

Those proprietors "understood" the land insofar as it could be turned into money. If "it's a question of gaining a dollar" the American could understand crossing almost impenetrable forests, passing deep rivers, braving pestilential swamps, sleeping exposed to the damp of the woods. "But that one should do such things through curiosity, that's something that doesn't reach his intelligence . . . that one has a high regard for great trees and a beautiful solitude, that's entirely incomprehensible to him." To get Americans to show them the way across the wilderness, Tocqueville and Beaumont had to pretend that they too were interested in a fiscal relation to it. The American, in contrast to the Indian and Frenchman, was "tenacious," "cold," and "pitiless" in his struggle against the soil and savage life. "He struggles ceaselessly against it, despoils it daily of some of its attributes."[5]

In Tocqueville's account, the demands of this struggle affected the attitude of the American male toward his wife and family. Intent "on the one goal of making his fortune, the emigrant has finally created for himself an altogether individual existence. Family sentiments have come to fuse themselves in a vast egoism, and it is doubtful if in his wife and children he sees anything else than a detached portion of himself." This is Tocqueville's portrait of the pioneer American wife "in her prime":

> time has weighed heavily on her; in her prematurely pale face and shrunken limbs, it is easy to see that existence has been a heavy burden for her. It is in fact, this frail creature who has already found herself exposed to unbelievable miseries. To devote herself to austere duties, submit herself to privations which were unknown to her, embrace an existence for which she was not made, such was the occupation of the finest years of her life, such have been for her the delights of marriage. Want, suffering and loneliness have affected her constitution, but not bowed her courage. 'Mid the profound sadness painted on her delicate features, you may easily remark a religious resignation and profound peace, and I know not what natural and tranquil firmness confronting all the miseries of life without fearing or scorning them. Around this woman crowd half naked children, shining with health, careless of the woman, veritable sons of the wilderness. From time to time their mother throws on them a look of melancholy and joy. To see their strength and her weakness one would say that she had exhausted herself, giving them life, and that she does not regret what they have cost her. .

D. H. Lawrence described the homesteader wife as a "poor haggard drudge, like a ghost wailing in the wilderness, nine times out of ten," and Hamlin Garland asserted in 1892 that such a life of self-denial (repression some would say) cost her her sanity: " 'Oh, the fate of the women!' 'Yes, it's a matter of statistics . . . that the wives of the American farmers fill our insane asylums.' " Eighty years earlier Benjamin Rush suggested that the solitude of a country life in America predisposed women to madness.[6]

According to Tocqueville, devotion, submission, courageous resignation, and self-denial were also characteristic of American wives back East. Their husbands shared the psychology of the American male out West. "The man you left in New York you find again in almost impenetrable solitudes . . . same clothes, same attitude, same language, same habits, same pleasures . . . the spirit of equality has spread a singularly even coloring over the inner habits of life. Now, note this well, it is precisely these same men who each year go to people the wilderness." The acquisitiveness, the constant motion, and the excited pursuit of chance characterized the American democrat, at home and on the frontier, and as we shall see, it was the anxieties generated by American democratic conditions that shaped a common view of women. According to Tocqueville, this "unknown man is the representative of a race to which belongs the future of the new world." It was a "nation of conquerors who submit themselves to the savage life without ever allowing themselves to be seduced by it." American men "shut themselves in the American solitudes with an axe and some newspapers." The typical American man left the social "bosom" that nurtured his early years, his "natal earth"; avoiding "staking" his life "on the throw of the dice or the destinies of a woman," he converted his desire "into the labours of the wilderness." He pursued an obsessive but confined ambition under circumstances that stirred Tocqueville to reverential awe. "Is a man capable of such sacrifices, a cold and insensible being? Ought not one, on the contrary, to recognize in him one of those mental passions, so burning, so tenacious, so implacable?"[7]

Tocqueville sensed that he had been led to "see the still empty cradle of a great nation." The terms accompanying the birth were violent and destructive, as one would expect, since they were in the hands of that cold, implacable pioneer. "It's the idea of destruction, this conception of near and inevitable change, which gives in our opinion, so original a character, and so touching a beauty to the solitudes of America." Democracy marched inexorably into the forest. The representative American, hard, closed off from the feelings regarded by Tocqueville as "natural to the heart," compelled himself pitilessly to the destruction of the Indian and the exploitation of nature, his wife, and perhaps himself.[8]

2   The Arena

Pioneer couples have not captured American myth. The lone hunter of Cooper's *Leatherstocking Tales*, Natty Bumppo, realized the promise of total mobility because he was free of women. Lawrence represented Natty's life style as the "wish fulfilment" of a man otherwise shackled by the obligations of marriage and work. Arthur Moore, too, links the fantasy to the mundanity of settlement: the creation of "playful savages" "appears to owe quite as much to the dark irrational content of the metropolitan unconscious as to the physical frontier." Indeed the frontiersman was largely a creation of the eastern imagination.[1]

Cooper's lone hunter could not be integrated into ordered society. According to Lawrence, "Natty had no business marrying. His mission was elsewhere. . . . A philosophic old soul, he does not give much for the temptations of sex. Probably he dies virgin." He asserted that "childless, womenless men . . . are the new great thing . . . the inception of new humanity. . . . The essential American soul is hard, isolate, stoic, and a killer." Lawrence, child of a dominant mother and weak father, rootless, dipping for energy into woman and nature, shared this mythology.[2]

American history is in several ways the interplay between male activity construed as free with the heterosexual obligations of settlement. The bachelor in the nineteenth century was a more genteel version of the hunter, and one that perhaps could sit more comfortably on the civilized knee of the reading public. Cooper's *Notions of the Americans* retained the form of his Leatherstocking novels, a dialogue between unattached males and married society. The

"Notions" were "Picked up by a Travelling Bachelor," who wrote letters describing them to members of an all-male club. The sole qualification for membership was bachelorhood. It was this sexual definition that made the narrator an outsider, traveling beyond heterosexual society, just as Natty did. To marry was to "fall," to destroy the freedom of autonomy: marriage was a "malady," showing "symptoms." That is, it represented a threat to a man's body. It shackled and humiliated; according to the bachelors, sexual union was a painful and permanent form of subordination and women were perennial dangers.[3]

One way of keeping woman at arm's length was to make her an abstraction, and go through the motions of manifesting "a proper spirit of homage to the loveliness of the sex," and in that way avoid any real contact, any consideration of a woman as an individual person. Homage to the sex was one fantasy the bachelors could play with; another had the respective elevations reversed: "There is a good deal of Caesar in my composition, as respects the sex; unless I could be first with the Houris I believe I should be willing to abandon Paradise itself, in order to seek pre-eminence in some humbler sphere." They explained the form of their sexual lives by "ambitious temperament," which "has been our bane, and has condemned us to the heartless and unsocial life we lead." They said they had banished settled heterosexuality to the imagination: "alas! what is the testimony of one who can point to no fireside, no household of his own but the dreaming reverie of a heated brain."[4]

The bachelors were both attracted and repelled by the idea of marriage. The narrator in the introduction to the second volume of *Notions of the Americans* explained that he had just escaped having to give up his bachelor chair in the club, from "a cause so fatal as marriage." He claimed a triumph in not being married: most "other [than English] husbands consider matrimony, more or less, a convenience; but these downright moralists talk of its obligations and duties. Obligations! There is our [American bachelor's] triumph." Leslie Fiedler has pointed out that "the typical male protagonist of our fiction has been a man on the run . . . to avoid . . . the confrontation of a man and woman which leads to the fall to sex, marriage and responsibility."[5]

The ambivalent attitudes of Cooper's bachelors toward women and marriage, their susceptibility to reverie, travels, and encounters with a variety of women only to part from them, were all characteristic of the theme of bachelorhood in nineteenth-century literature. Characteristic too was the group identity of bachelors in a club, drawn together as "brothers," perhaps by the construing of sexual relations as a war. Sexual conflict was intensified in America by the hypostasis of sex and race in place of class identification or at least by the much greater emphasis on physiological identity.

Reveries of a Bachelor by Ik Marvel, pseudonym of Donald Mitchell, was one of the best-selling novels of 1850. By 1859 it had gone through thirty-nine printings. The autobiographical bachelor, claiming to be the "only safe and secure observer of all phases of married life," sat poker in hand before a fire, enjoying the good fortune of "sober quietude," in contrast to his tenant's "multiplying contrivances with his wife to put two babies asleep." Moreover, his companion to bed was the fire, his disturbance only the rattle of windowpanes, that is, not the troublesomeness of a female body. The bachelor compared the qualities of the mates he conjured up to the differences between fires built with sea coal ("sparkling," "coquettish," "teasing," when poked "breed[ing] a tornado of maddened action, a whirlwind fire that hisses . . . send[ing] out jets of wild, impulsive combustion") or with anthracite ("open" "glowing" "strong," "it hurts the eye," "it might scorch"). He then went off on his travels to meet a series of women and part from them in characteristic fashion: "she is beautiful, but I am strong; the world is short; we—I and my dog, and my books, and my pen, will battle through bravely, and leave enough for a tomb-stone." In the last chapter the bachelor appeared to marry and settle down with all the ends tied. But in the book's final paragraph heterosexual end-tying turned out to have been just another fantasy. "I took my gun from beside the tree, and my shot-pouch from its limb and whistling for Carlo [his dog] . . . I strolled over the bridge, and down the lane. . . ."[6]

Bachelorhood lived astride the question: "Shall a man stake his independence, and comfort upon the die of absorbing, unchanging relentless marriage?"—a question Tocqueville's typical American male avoided. Life was already too full of unavoidable gambles on which democratic selfhood had to be staked. Moreover, "freedom" in America could be readily translated into sexual terms: "Shall a man who has been free to chase his fancies over the wide world, without lett or hindrance, shut himself up to marriage-ship?" His interior reveries corresponded to geographical mobility: once married, the bachelor would have "no more room for intrepid forays of imagination—no more gorgeous realm-making. . . ." The bachelor's choice lay between fantasy and actual woman. In either case, he regarded her as his resource. Unmarried, the bachelor's brain could "feed on long vagaries." The idea of marriage "could serve . . . as a mine for teeming fantasy." On the other hand, a wife could be a "second self," a phrase similar in meaning to Tocqueville's representation of the American's viewing his wife as "a detached portion of himself." When "a glowing thought comes into your brain . . . you could tell it over as to a second self," the putative wife, and watch the thought go on to reproduce itself, "catching that girlish mind, illuming [*sic*] that fair brow . . . far better than going out, heavy, lifeless, and dead, in your own selfish fancy." Was it not better, he asked, to be caressing a wife than "patting your glossy coated dog . . .?" and as we have seen, his answer was no. The bachelor's fantasy also drew sustenance from other men's fantasies. One of his favorites was Melville's *Typee* (1846), like *Omoo* (1847), a runner-up to the best sellers of their years of publication. Both are accounts of the lusty wanderings of males torn between autonomy and the obligations of settled heterosexuality at home.[7]

I want to draw attention to the terms Marvel used in his study of the psychology of reverie. The male mind penetrated the idea of marriage as if it were working a vein of ore, and converted it to prolifically "teeming," self-generating fantasies in the same way that he fancied his glowing thought could be doubled by entering his "second self." The bachelor's brain could breed in sexual and economic terms. "Can any children make less noise than [those] . . . who have no existence, except in the *omnium gatherum* of your own brain? . . . Can any family purse be better filled than the exceeding plump one, you dream of, after reading such pleasant books as Munchausen, or *Typee*?" A single man was self-sufficient. Whereas a tangible wife would empty your purse and the body for which Marvel makes it stand as a metaphor. "She will be provokingly silent when you hint to a tradesman that you have not the money by you for his small bill;—in short, she will tear the life out of you. . . ." A man's being, given a specifically sexual identity, was a receptacle drawing on, or being drawn upon by, powers outside itself.[8]

The bachelor's sentiment at this point (and in his *Reveries'* resolution) was identical to that of Lantern-Jawed Bob, a wandering Kentucky hunter. "Darn the gals! . . . They're pooty enough to

look at, as picters! but to marry one on 'em, an' have her around
all the time, huggin' an' sich like, would be too much for human
nater—turn me into a skeleton if it wouldn't."[9]

The deeper meaning of the vulnerable flow of a man's being was
perhaps closer to the surface when Marvel turned almost directly to
the physiological and moral implications of his metaphor for the
reverie process.

> I know not justly, if it be a weakness or a sin to create these
> phantoms that we love. . . . If this heart is sick of the falsities that
> meet it at every hand, and is eager to spend that power which nature
> has ribbed it with, on some object worthy of its fulness and depth,—
> shall it not feel a rich relief,—nay more, an exercise in keeping with
> its end, if it flow out—strong as a tempest, wild as a rushing river,
> upon those ideal creations, which imagination invents.

"Spend" in the nineteenth century meant to reach orgasm. It was
the shortened form of the more refined term "expenditure." Reverie
was commonly held to lead to masturbation, the uneconomical expenditure of male creative power. "Hand," "spend," "fulness,"
"relief," "exercise," "end," and "flow out" are connected in a context
of self-sufficient sexual fantasy.[10]

On the other hand, the bachelor wonders, "will dreams satisfy,
reach as high as they can?" Humiliating as it may be, shouldn't a
bachelor, like Ishmael, "lower or at least shift, his conceit of attainable felicity" from "squeezing that sperm" by hand?

> Are we not after all poor grovelling mortals, tied to earth, and to
> each other; are there not sympathies, and hopes and affections
> which can only find their issue and blessing in fellow absorption? Does
> not the heart, steady, and pure as it may be, and mounting on soul
> flights often as it dare, want a human sympathy . . . to make it
> healthful? Is there not a fount of love for this world as there is a
> fount of love for the other?

Perhaps a wife would not be too absorptive after all, and at least
replace what flowed into her. "How would not all that boyhood,
prized of enthusiasm, and quick blood, and life, renew itself in such
presence!" And at best "that . . . fond look of hers . . . has power
in it to nerve your soul to high deeds. . . . Your heart, beating large
with hope, quickens the flow upon the brain," a flow we saw to be
construed in sexual and economic terms. The man asserted control
in the teeth of the uncontrollable power of the female deity, and in
the same physiological terms. "In God's name,—thought I, puffing

vehemently,—what is a man's heart given him for, if not to choose where his heart's blood, every drop of it is flowing? Who is going to dam those billowy tides of the soul, whose roll is ordered by . . . Venus?"[11]

Finally, this self-pitying bachelor, ambivalent toward marriage and sex, unendurably repetitive in his nostalgia for childhood and schooldays, must be characterized as an errant son; and therefore the final characterization of his putative wife was as mother, tolerant, constant, and forgiving.

> A home! . . . it is the Presence. The Lares of your [i.e., the man's] worship are there; the altar of your confidence there; the end of your worldly faith is there; and adorning it all, and sending your blood in passionate flow, is the ecstasy of the conviction, that *there* at least you are beloved; that there you are understood; that there all your errors will meet ever with gentlest forgiveness; that there your troubles will be smiled away; that there you may unburden your soul, fearless of harsh, unsympathetic ears; and that there you may be entirely and joyfully—yourself!

Clearly outside the world of woman, a man could feel that he could not be loved, forgiven, or mistaken—in short, could not allow himself to be who he really was. In his autonomous frame of mind these values were reversed, his hunting, pipe smoking, reverying world safe from the fatality of marriage. And if the woman viewed from that position was harsh, unsympathetic, and "frozen" then there was only one characterological slot in which to put her: she must be a man: "what a happy careless life belongs to this Bachelorhood, in which you may strike out boldly right and left; Your heart is not bound to another which may be full only of sickly vapors of feeling; nor is it frozen to a cold, man's heart under a silk boddice—knowing nothing of tenderness."[12]

The possibilities for men who wanted to experience autonomy, to leave home, and go not only to a new place for them but a new place for anyone, were enormous in nineteenth-century America: no checks on movement horizontally, and formally, none vertically for white men, together with a typing of life style that strenuously encouraged motion, from country to town, job to job, ambition to ambition, and the most striking area for this motion was the West. To go West (or to go to sea), whether literally or figuratively (to sense oneself in a sea of chances), posed the issue of how to connect the parts of one's life, before and after the going West.[13]

There was a particularly disturbing dimension to this problem. The individuals who could grasp these chances were men. Life back home, in the past, the future, or at both ends of the day, was the part of existence that contained women, and the men's relations with them. Natty's problem of connection, between possibilities and responsibilities, was there for many Americans. More men than women could and did leave settlement, and Cooper was among many to notice the preponderance of women in the settled East.[14]

The sex ratio (the proportion of men to women) was high everywhere in the first century of settlement in North America. During the eighteenth century this ratio was reversed in New England. In eastern Massachusetts, Rhode Island, and Connecticut there was an appreciable surplus of women. Male surplus in the sex ratio moved West. Kentucky, focus for frontiersman ideology, had the highest sex ratio of all regions covered by the 1790 census. J. R. Potter divides his recent compilation of American population statistics according to geography and place of birth (foreign, outside state, and inside state). In 1850 there were "surplus women" only in New England (20,000), the Mid-Atlantic states (19,000), and South Atlantic states (19,000), all of them grouped as "born inside state." By 1860 the number of surplus women in New England had climbed to 49,000. The only other figure representing a surplus of women in 1850 is 3,000 "born outside state," but again in New England. In all other divisions and areas there was a surplus of men. In "East North Central" (Ohio, Indiana, Illinois, Michigan, and Wisconsin) in 1850, there were 75,000 "surplus men" born outside the various states but in America. In California at mid-century the corresponding figure was 57,000. By 1860 these figures for East North Central and California had swollen to 260,000 and 161,000 respectively. There were 342,000 men out of a total California population of 380,000 in 1860.[15]

While the figures for "surplus" men and women were quite small in relation to total population, their distribution does seem significant. The overall figures for the U.S. in 1850 show a surplus of 262,000 men among those born outside the state in which they were counted, and 11,000 women among those born inside the state (the 1860 table does not give the corresponding breakdown). The significance of these figures is dramatized (as it was for contemporaries) by the two exceptionally large imbalances: long-settled, civilized New England "overpopulated" with women, and raw, frontier California dominated by men. Areas most recently settled tended to have a very high sex ratio, even if the population was small. So the mountain states showed a surplus of 46,000 men out of a population of 175,000 after the first decade of substantial settlement (1850–1860).[16]

These figures may explain the uprooting of the hedges Puritans had attempted to place around bachelorhood to preserve the coherence and stability of their communities against the potential anarchy personified by Thomas Morton. But New England soon had to face the regular loss of its young men. The censuses of 1850 and of 1860 suggest a fall in the incidence of marriage in New England, postponement of marriage, and consequently a rise in the age of marriage, all of which may be related to the currency of bachelorhood in popular books and to the "alarm about spinsters." That alarm should be put in context with the anxieties our bachelor displayed about women in general, which left him (and his "brothers") bachelors, which left more spinsters, and so on. Ideas clustering around frontiersmen and bachelors may be associated with the high sex ratio moving West, and more women, more heterosexuality, left behind.[17]

The activities of men seeing themselves operating in such an arena expressed the kind of psychology Tocqueville described. Lantern-Jawed Bob and the hero of *Reveries* left women in order to preserve body and mineral-mine fantasy respectively. Tocqueville's representative male was out West to line his pocket more directly; he was the advance guard in the conquest of nature, the ineluctable march of American democracy. For Cooper the planning of the Erie Canal exemplified American progress: "In . . . the circumstances under which the New York canal has been made, we may trace the cause of the prodigious advance of this nation."[18]

The transportation revolution was the central achievement in the economic history of 1815–1860. Unique opportunities for risk taking and profit were ferociously pursued by American men. George Rogers Taylor suggests that it was the same psychology—"spirit of adventure," "aggressiveness," "willingness to make sacrifices"—which drove settlers, merchants, and businessmen. It is very close to Tocqueville's characterization.[19]

Competitiveness was one of the most wasteful characteristics of this life style, and it was the enormity of the resources in the West that absorbed and masked the effects of such waste. "Each new method of transportation had to establish itself in a bitter competitive battle against previously existing devices, and each new traffic

route had to meet competition from established ones." The terms
that Taylor uses for the initiation of each new "device," are: rage,
mania, boom, craze, fury, fever, and orgy. And the words that frequently describe the economic accomplishments themselves are:
triumph, growth, movement, enthusiasm, energy, tremendous accel-
eration, drive, pace, and pursuit. The particular industries (geared
above all to "speed" and "size") are: extractive, exploitative, and
productive. The historian's language here imparts the mood of its
subjects, who expressed themselves in the same terms.[20]

Canal building, for example, was haphazard and crazy, a prodigious expenditure of energy. Canals, like roads, steamboats, and
railroads, opened magnificent vistas to male energies. They linked
the settled round of home with the seas of freedom and recklessness.
According to Taylor, "The success of the Erie Canal provided the
spark which set off a nation-wide craze for canal building. . . . a
veritable canal-building fury gripped the country from Maine to
Virginia, and from New Jersey to Illinois. . . . [In the] 1820's, Erie
fever inflamed men's imaginations and loosed the strings of their
pocketbooks." Three states brought themselves to the edge of bankruptcy; between 1816 and the Civil War more than $200 million was
invested in canal construction. In the end, most of the country's
canals would succumb to insuperable railroad competition.[21]

Railroad boosters appealed to local ambition and to a vision of
what Henry Nash Smith calls a "Passage to India." Their rhetoric
also conjured up a sexual motif. At the Chicago Railroad Convention
in 1847, William M. Hall described the coming of the railroad in
this way: "They saw him pluck out the forests, tear up and fling
aside the seated hills, and with the rejoicing sound of progress in his
train, made way into the body of the continent with the step of a
bridegroom going to his chamber, or a prince to occupy his throne."
That metaphor recalls bachelors' alternatives, and the "implacable
egoism" of Tocqueville's pioneer, absorbing land and family. In
1856 the Marietta and Cincinnati Railroad's Annual Report decried
"the dangerous tendency, with mere local interests, to combine in
construction of unnecessary lines which must divide or destroy the
traffic of existing routes" just as the railroads had done to the
canals.[22]

The steamboat had been the first large agent to connect the male-
dominated frontier activities with settlement. Eventually it was put
out of business by the railroad. The style of riverboat and canal life,
the setting for so much southwestern humor dominated by fighting,

transient, manly, womanless men, has passed into folklore. The correspondence of steamboat life to the haphazardness and heedlessness of the construction of roads, canals, and railroads is more apparent, perhaps, in the incidence of steamboat explosions and accidents, and the dilatoriness of anyone doing anything about them. Nearly a third of all western steamboats built before 1849 were lost in accidents, and the average life of a steamboat in western rivers was five years. Congress failed to pass effective legislation until 1853, "following a period of disastrous explosions."

Whalemen were, perhaps, the apotheosis of the insensible, haphazard, self-righteous, extreme, ruthless expression of male energies. Ahab articulated the temperament and took his image for his mad hunt of the whale from the most dramatic of the economic exploits of the society of which the *Pequod* was a microcosm. "Swerve me? ye cannot swerve me, else ye swerve yourselves! man has ye there. Swerve me? The path to my fixed purpose is laid with iron rails, whereon my soul is grooved to run. Over unsounded gorges, through the rifled hearts of mountains, under torrents' beds, unerringly I rush! Naught's an obstacle, naught's an angle to the iron way!" More than 12,000 men were engaged in the whaling industry in 1860, and in some years between 1816 and 1860 the value of whale products (including sperm) may have equaled that of the rest of the fishing industry. In Nantucket, the nature of the separations between whaling husbands and their wives passed into cliché. On upper Main Street the houses of whaling captains and merchants were fitted with walks which came to be known as "widows' walks," where wives watched for returning ships and husbands.[23]

The arena, then, for the ambitions of the American male imagination was divided between the free, exploitable resources of the West and the seas, and the obligations of heterosexual settlement. Into this arena, men drove crazy, feverish, short-lived ventures: "men are generally led to attach an excessive value to the rapid bursts and superficial conceptions of the intellect, and on the other hand to undervalue unduly its slower and deeper labors."[24] We shall see in the next chapter that men within settlement (where, after all, most of them were) divided their world in a way similar to western heroes, and similarly, too, pursued their objectives in it.

The economic growth in the first half of nineteenth-century America was generated by a particular kind of human behavior. Economic historians may decide on the necessity for recklessness as the fulfillment of economic "function"; or that later industrialization, and railroad networks were made possible by the legacy of the canal era. But self-evidently, they are not historical explanations, not the perspectives men had on themselves in their recklessness. Why did men go about their enterprises in the way that they did? The rest of this book will suggest that the answer was linked to the way men saw their sexual relations—and their own sexuality.[25]

3   Work and Sex

As for myself, I do not hesitate to avow that although the women of
the United States are confined within the narrow circle of domestic
life, and their situation is in some respects one of extreme dependence,
I have nowhere seen woman occupying a loftier position; and if I
were asked, now that I am drawing to the close of this work, in which
I have spoken of so many important things done by Americans, to
what the singular prosperity and growing strength of that people
ought mainly to be attributed, I should reply: To the superiority of
their women.[1]

According to Tocqueville, the "superiority of their women" lay
behind the most notable achievements of the American people. This
"people," to whom the possessive pronoun "their" and the "women"
it qualifies belong, were men. Tocqueville's devotion of a few chapters to women in the second volume, and only a few specific references to them in the first, emphasizes that, for him, it was the men
who exhibited the phenomenal workings of democracy and equality
in America. Women were usually ignored. "In the United States, except slaves, servants, and paupers supported by the townships, there
is no class of persons who do not exercise the elective franchise and
who [the sense is: and who *therefore*] do not indirectly contribute
to make the laws."[2] Or else they were subsumed under "men."

But Tocqueville did not assume the general terms that so often
cover men and women when he came to consider the relations
between the sexes. "In no country has such constant care been taken
as in America to trace two clearly distinct lines of action for the
sexes and to make them keep pace with one another, but in two

19

pathways that are always different." There was an apparently total contrast between the world outside and home life. It was the difference between "turmoil" and "peace"; between chance, competition, anxiety, vicissitudes, restlessness, and innocence, calm, moderation, simplicity, order; between materialism and passion for gain, and religion and passionless domesticity; between immorality and morality. According to Tocqueville there was a uniquely extreme distinction between sexual roles in America, which appear to have been imposed by parents not only in very early childhood but from birth.[3]

As Tocqueville saw, the separation of spheres coincided with another kind of separation. After the Industrial Revolution, industry left the home on an increasingly significant scale, the "working" member of the family followed it, and activities which from time immemorial had been joint were carried on separately by husband and wife. Work was conclusively detached from residence, with extensive social and psychological effects. At the start of America's economic takeoff, men left women at home. The changing relation between men and the "bosom of nature"—men's mastering of distance and resources on the scale of railroading and whaling—coincided with the separation from the household of male enterprise within society.[4]

This alteration in the age-old relation between man and wife could have presented an array of new opportunities to women who wanted to leave the domestic round, or even take over the chief breadwinning role within it. Or a woman could have stopped working altogether; with her man out earning essential bread money and more, she was relieved from necessity. Donald Meyer has pointed out the significance of this change. At the beginning of the nineteenth century in America these possibilities were embryonic, and were not to be realized fully for nearly a century. To a large extent, women continued in their old style, although this was modified and woman's attitude toward her role changed in the light of the freedom which could be grasped in the cities. But the urban, trend-setting women, the "women of the future," were placed in a difficult position, caught between new possibilities and the need for a response to the special demands that men made of them. Industrial growth and the phenomenal shaping of American history in the nineteenth century were inalienable from the male attitude that demanded not only that the two styles of life, male and female, be separate, but that women should remain subordinate, and in the home.[5]

In 1870, the first year that gainfully employed women and girls were counted by the federal census, four-fifths of them were engaged in their traditional occupations on the farm or in domestic service. The labor of those who did enter industry remained cheap and unskilled. While the number of women in manufacturing rose between 1850 and 1900, the proportion of women to men dropped during the same period. It was not only that men required women to stay out of the marketplace. Women acquiesced. They would not have served an apprenticeship if any craftsman would have taken them on, as they looked forward to marriage. Whereas boys learned the whole trade of typesetting in four years of low wages, girls preferred to perform the mechanical and repetitive task of merely setting type, since they could earn more money and with luck leave to be married within four years. All the skill they needed was patience in the repeated performance of a simple task, and patience would be their main qualification for marriage.[6]

The one job men willingly left to women was teaching; it lacked the chanciness and competition of the totally manly world. At the beginning of the nineteenth century men had dominated teaching. Their leaving it coincided with the transportation revolution and the separation of sexual spheres. Catherine Beecher pointed out that it was "chimerical" to expect men to overcome their sex's "aversion to the sedentary, confining, and toilsome duties of teaching and governing young children," when they could have the "excitement and profits of commerce, manufactures, agriculture and the arts." Women and children belonged together. By 1870 two-thirds of all teachers in public and private schools were women.[7]

Tocqueville explained that the separation in America of the spheres of men and women was according to physiological definitions. Morever, this division happily coincided with the demands of "the great work of society."

> Americans admit that as nature has appointed such wide differences between the physical and moral constitution of man and woman, her manifest design was to give a distinct employment to their various faculties. . . . The Americans have applied to the sexes the great principle of political economy which governs the manufacturers of our age, by carefully dividing the duties of man from those of woman in order that the great work of society be better carried on.

The "great work of society" was presumably the dynamics of that "singular prosperity and growing strength." The "superiority" of women was connected with the separation of the sexes in the production of the great society. Moreover, as biology served economic needs, so morality was subordinated to industry; "good morals contribute to public tranquility and are favorable to industry." Both biology and morality were the domain marked out for women.[8]

All men in the American "outside world" "more or less contract the way of thinking of the manufacturing and trading classes." Their style of life outside the home, chancy, anxious, in constant motion, suggested for several reasons that they choose a submissive, ancillary woman. Tocqueville suggested that American men would not be so unbusinesslike as to choose a woman who would have threatened the peace that apparently remained to them at home, by being as chancy and competitive as the world outside.[9] He described the typical American man at home, always serious, indulging in no light conversation; begetting children, reading the Bible and newspapers. "As he finds an orderly life is the surest path to happiness, he accustoms himself easily to moderate his opinions." Did he offer opinions to his wife on politics and business? Gustave de Beaumont was explicit on this point:

> Having little happiness, she is very religious, and reads sermons. . . . In the evening the man comes home, full of care, restless, overcome with fatigue; he brings to his wife the fruits of his labor, and already dreams of tomorrow's speculations. He asks for his dinner, and offers not a word more; his wife and children do not tear the American away from the practical world, and he so rarely shows them a sign of tenderness and affection that a nickname has been made for those households where the husband, after an absence, kisses his wife and children—they are called "kissing families." In the American's eyes, the wife is not a companion; she is a partner who helps him spend for his well-being and comfort the money he earns in business.[10]

Even if the businessman was "offering an opinion" on how to bring up the children, he would be required to moderate it only according to his demands on himself. Formally, he controlled all the terms of the dialogue. Americans "do not deny him the right of directing his partner."[11]

4   Democratic Fathers and Democratic Sons

While vastly accelerated by the Industrial Revolution, separation of sexual spheres in its modern form seems to have originated as one more expression of the Reformation's centrifugalism. The emergence of dynamic individual consciousness as a potential for everyone (even women) "atomized Western Christendom." The most well-known separation was described by R. H. Tawney as the divorce of morality from economic activity, and Max Weber rooted the rise of capitalism in individualist "selfish" psychology—calculating, daring, temperate, shrewd and above all, irrationally compulsive. This chapter suggests how the emergence of such behavior was linked to the undermining of traditional sources of male identity.[1]

Levin Schücking argues that Calvinism's insistence on self-control was peculiarly adaptable to the old English characterological ideal of "sobriety." English Puritans, he suggests, developed it to the point of "moral hypochondria," which informed Puritan childrearing and pervaded social relations generally. Self-discipline came to demand that a man distance himself from his fellows and make "a withdrawal even from his own family circle." Ian Watt describes Puritan character in the familiar terms of economic individualism and goes on to connect the concomitant devaluation of traditional relationships with changes in sexual identity. Rational autonomy for steady movement upward necessarily had to keep sex down and, ideally, out.[2]

Watt argues the significance of the appeals of Defoe and Richardson to English middle-class sensibility in terms of these related aspects of Protestant culture: economic individualism and the

23

"redefinition of virtue in primarily sexual terms." It was this sensibility, this "level of English civilization," "confronting us with Defoe and Richardson," which Perry Miller suggested linked "the England of Cromwell to that of Cobden and Bright." New England, and then American culture generally, assumed a fragment of English culture for the whole. Similarly, what was a peripheral political tradition in England (or at best competing with other established views of authority) became central to American politics: Bernard Bailyn's "country vision," looking back to resistance to the patriarchal Stuarts, characterizing any central government as essentially antagonistic to the individual, an encroaching castrating threat, was grounded ultimately in a belief in individual autonomy.[3] Robinson Crusoe anticipated Natty Bumppo.

The postulate of male autonomy devalued all human relations. Thus Richardson embodied a "more complete and comprehensive separation of the male and female roles than had previously existed." Watt traces such separation back to the early seventeenth century, in the "Jacobean outcry against the decay of 'housekeeping,'" meaning the old self-sufficient medieval household under a paterfamilias. For Sir Robert Filmer, the newly risen trading and commercial classes "challenged the authority of the father over his family . . . the emblem of every other kind of authority and order." While early seventeenth-century Puritan writers bewailed the frequency of married couples living apart, such apartness was only the literal expression of Puritan behavioral emphases. Changes in the position of women and men's senses of fatherhood and sonhood seem to have anticipated the ideological realignments at the time of the Reformation, which included the banishment of women from heaven.[4]

Certainly Puritans continued to be preoccupied with their identity as sons in relation to their omniscient Father. Looking back on the Pilgrim fathers' motives for leaving Leyden, William Bradford suggested that the "most heavy" was the rebellion and departure of their children into "licentiousness of youth" and "far voyages," the latter precisely the course of action for which Bradford, the Pilgrims, and the Puritans of the Great Migration, as well as successive immigrants, might have been condemned by their parents. The specter of children modeling their behavior on rebel parents by rebelling against them haunts American history. Thomas Jefferson feared the reestablishment of a corrupt monarchy by his descendants. Perhaps the Protestants' erection of an unmediated (by hierarchy or woman) Father was compensation for their rebellion against earthly fathers—pope, king, and forefather—a rebellion that continued in its behavioral dynamic, so that even the new Hebraic totem was eventually pulled down.

Winthrop Jordan includes a similar psychological portrait in *White over Black:* Elizabethan men, breaking out of traditional forms, mobile geographically, sexually, intellectually, economically, but guilty over their mobility. Most mobile were those who came to America. They could project their dark guilt onto people who were to be eternally static, subordinate, as, perhaps, the Elizabethan migrants felt they themselves should have remained. They fixed to these embodiments of their guilt for father repudiation the marks of punishment for parricidal treason in a patriarchal state (running the gamut from a child's striking his father to king killing), that is, corruption of the blood and castration. These themes emerge in Bailyn's presentation of the struggle between the king and the sons who finally asserted their independence against what they perceived as the king's paternal threat to enslave and castrate them. Assuming the guilt that formerly they had projected onto black people, they momentarily contemplated freeing the subordinated black, and became Founding Fathers.[5]

The colonial cousins of Watt's subversive Jacobeans separated the sexes in the interests of their society's major goals, in terms remarkably similar to those of nineteenth-century American men. The Reverend Richard Mather regarded the effects of the death of his wife on him "the more grievous, in that she being a Woman of singular Prudence for the Management of Affairs, had taken off from her husband all Secular Cares so that he wholly devoted himself to his Study, and to Sacred Imployments." The Reverend Samuel Whiting's wife similarly "by her discretion freed her husband from all secular vocations."[6] "Calling" was an issue for men; Puritan women became housewives. In short, Puritans subordinated their women.[7] Man was the conveyance between God and creation, including woman. Her mind was weaker, or conversely, her more earthly ties were stronger. Those most concerned with the apparatus of election, of separating man out from earthly ties, were men, and among earthly entanglements that had to be watched was the sexual relation.[8] In his tougher-minded mood Schücking paints a devastating picture of the Puritan family: "the iron strictness which was still the real basis of all family relationships . . . rendered any personal relation impossible." One of the chief reasons for this "discomfort" in family relations was the devaluation of mother. The mass of evidence shows that the Puritan ideal was that of "masculinity, whose rough nature had little understanding for the loveliest features of the feminine character." Schücking's earlier account of the Puritan male writer's feelings toward marriage as a "most delicate craving for sympathy . . . both comfortable and warm" must therefore be counted as an expression of the "torturing dualism" of Calvinist man, between his "true self" and his discipline.[9] It may be suggested that the masculine ideal's opposition to that craving for warmth is a projection of that dualism onto the sexual relation, and of course it emerges in very similar form sexually in *The Reveries of a Bachelor.*

At the same time, the family replaced the whole spectrum of earlier social relations, and assumed their function. It had a defensive, conservative function, and became the molder of bodies and souls, the chief transmitter of psychological styles. At least, that was how some viewed it in early nineteenth-century America. "It seemed possible that the family might prove to be the central bulwark ·of stability and values. Not the family but everything else was disintegrating and the family therefore at all costs must hold." In Europe the middle class had emerged in opposition to other social classes, but not so in America. In some ways "the feudal stage of history" had been "skipped"; there were "no debased codes of law against which the bourgeois belief [could] define itself." The absence of countertraditions evidently posed problems for social and individual identity: these problems intensified with claims for uniqueness and equality, and for the overthrow of historical authority. The "juxtaposition of inequalities" which middle-class Europeans feared largely according to their sense of class identity had to be translated into different terms in America, those more exclusively of race and sex. While the new American society was, like the European middle class, "craving for identity" and intolerant of variations, forcing "each person . . . to resemble a conventional model," the intolerance ran more emphatically along a basic line, that of the body. Tocqueville observed that "hardly anything but money" remained to leveled society as a source of distinction, of identity. He defined that "hardly anything" by suggesting that as men "relinquish more and more the peculiar opinions of a caste, a profession, or a family, they simultaneously arrive at something nearer to the constitution of man. . . ." America was the freest field for the fulfillment of this tendency. White men constituted themselves the headship of American society on the basis of physiology, namely skin color and genital organs, and charted their superiority according to the differences in beings who were regarded as naturally lower down the great chain, closer to the animal, to dark passions, appetite. The idea of autonomy was aggrandized at the same time, and in America the individual male seems to have taken precedence over the family as a cultural ideal.[10]

In Tocqueville's view, the effacement of what he called "class identity" was interlocked with intrafamilial democracy in the relations of fathers and sons. Before the Reformation father had performed his role of head of the family as only one of an integrated number of roles in a network of reciprocal relations in the system. And for a while Puritan fathers appear to have retained much of their authority, since Puritanism at first took over the old hierarchic forms of social organization. But the egalitarian and individualistic tendencies in Protestantism steadily eroded these forms, including the patriarchal family. No longer could fatherhood be clearly defined with reference to an all-embracing scheme.

By the time of Tocqueville's visit, the father had ceased to act as a bridge between past and present. His old aristocratic functions, his formal representation of the whole external scheme of tradition, custom, and manners, and the power that this old position commanded over his son's feelings—respect, deference, and fear—were stripped from him. The democratic father in the eye of the law was "only a member of the community older and richer than his sons." The social context surrounding family arrangements undercut the pretensions that a father had to rule his sons. They could leave home early and hunt equal wealth and equality. Democratic men adopted the "general principle that it is good and lawful to judge all things for oneself," denying the authority of past beliefs; hence "the power which the opinions of a father exercises over those of his sons diminishes as well as his legal power." The male was exposed to the effects of equality even within the family. The father could no longer command his sons *ex officio patris*. He could, however, guarantee himself authority over his wife and daughters. The terms of social existence outside demanded that the family split along sexual lines. In America, the leveling process had intensified at the hands of men who, dissolving class barriers in any European sense, evolved a new "asocial" style. The evolution of an "ideal type" to confront a world where the old social relationships had defaulted demanded that family life be tributary to it. Men bolstered, and indeed justified, "unbearable moral solitude" by objectifying and absorbing the resources around them, including the family. The American family was defended in the interests of male domination.[11]

The more democratic the society, the more intimate and affectionate the relations between father and son: "rules and authority are less talked of, confidence and tenderness are often increased, and it would seem that the natural bond is drawn closer in proportion as the social bond is loosened." Writing about the American family, Tocqueville did not refer to mothers, daughters, or sisters, nor to relations between them, or between them and the men of the family. He did not consider heterosexual passion, yet he claimed to be dealing with "those passions that emanate spontaneously from human nature itself." In the American family, such passions seem to have been those among men—fathers, sons, brothers.

The intimacy between father and sons in America did not come about by resolution of the tensions between the generations; there was no struggle to reach a man-to-man platform. "In America, strictly speaking, there is no adolescence; at the close of boyhood the man appears and begins to trace out his own path." Tocqueville's terms suggest that in his mind this process, reaching manhood, was bound up with struggle and conflict between father and son: he found it remarkable that in America there was, apparently, none. In Europe, the "moral violence" of the "struggle" in which a son "shakes off" established authority to "wrest" his freedom from his parents involved "precipitation" and "rancorous or irregular passion."[12]

The evolution of sexual selfhood for men, at least in the modern history of Western civilization, seems to have required the successful supersession of a distinct father. But the father's role has been progressively stripped away, his traditional ideological supports knocked over, and his work separated from his home. The stripping appeared first and went farthest in America. By 1831 Tocqueville could record democratized fatherhood as a salient characteristic of the new social form. Alexander Mitscherlich points out that in agricultural, pre–Industrial Revolution days, in Europe and America, a son could know his father-in-his-world and compete with him directly. Defeat of the introjected father (or coming to see oneself no longer as child to man, but as man to man, and potentially as father), and the consequent "free choice of identification," allowed the son henceforth "full discretion in the exercise of both sexuality and aggression." Deprived of such struggle and measurement, the democratic son may have felt all his desires to be possible. On one hand, the failure to give recognition to adolescence could result in a "ruthlessly aggressive type, to whom the outside world is . . . an alien jungle" and who fails to "develop the secondary processes through which we grow into human beings." On another, the American male retained and extolled unresolved autonomy as a virtue. The autonomous nineteenth-century male existed between bachelorhood and marriage, and Beaumont's married businessman existed in similar limbo. Benjamin Franklin made it clear in his *Autobiography* that the full range of appetitive selfhood was tasted only by and after the systematic destruction of both father and the transgenerational expectations of patriarchal apprenticeship.[13]

Nineteenth-century America was anything but a social system which orchestrated "religion, law, morals and technic," from which the adolescent could "develop a sense of individual mastery from his ability to adapt." The only "coherent measure of historical identity" lay in the rejection of history. Daniel Boorstin's applause for the absence of such orchestration is of course another expression of the same rejection, the obverse of Henry James's famous lament. The young man's mythology was one of self-sufficiency, his behavioral models those of unremitting distrust of all human relationships. The responsibility for "tracing out his own path" was experienced as relentless pressure. The "embarrassment of choosing" "forced all men to pass the same ordeal," subjecting them to the "waste" of their youth and the "quenching of their imaginations," to the extent that they despaired of "ever fully attaining what is held out to them."[14] Dr. Edward Jarvis, speaking in 1851 before the Association of Medical Superintendents of American Institutions for the Insane, made exactly the same analysis as Tocqueville had twenty years earlier. In America,

> no son is necessarily confined to the work . . . of his father . . . all fields are open . . . all are invited to join the strife. . . . They are struggling . . . at that which they cannot reach . . . their mental powers are strained to their utmost tension. . . . Their minds stagger . . . they are perplexed with the variety of insurmountable obstacles; and they are exhausted with the ineffectual labor.

As a result, democratic men were more prone to insanity, in contrast to men in static, patriarchal societies. Jarvis went on to use terms similar to Marvel's bachelor's consideration of the injudicious flow of the heart's blood. In proportion to the emancipation of "new generations from the . . . old . . . the manifold ways of life are

open to all, the danger of the misapplication of the cerebral forces
. . . increases, and men may think and act indiscreetly, and become
insane." Dr. George Beard made the same analysis as Jarvis in
1881.[15]

In Europe in the nineteenth century, the possibilities existed that
a man would share more with a woman of his own class, rank, and
religion than with a man of different class, rank, and religion. Men
were not reduced to the residual physiological distinction as they
were in democratic America. In this respect sexual solidarity would
not, according to Tocqueville's logic, have been nearly so complete in
Europe as it was in America, where men had the outside world in
common, and at home shared nothing of it with their wives. From
an early age, the young man participated in the all-male, anti-au-
thoritarian world as his father did. It was a world where the father
ideal had been "diffused" (in effect as perpetually hostile, jungle
eyes). The "absence" of the father could well have contributed to
susceptibility to peer group influence in the nineteenth century as
it does in the twentieth. The fantasy of autonomy led to uniformity.
Primacy of outside world activities required that the young man
select a wife according to dictates to which his father was equally
subject. Tocqueville did not record any intimacy between the young
man and his mother. The terms of the new bond between father and
sons, the binding of brothers together, the general reinforcement
of homosexual relations that would be experienced outside the
home, encouraged a remarkable sexual demarcation within it. The
relations of nineteenth-century fathers and sons was likely to be
fraternal and antifeminine, but at the sons' level, so that in some
ways the father would have regarded his wife as his mother, as the
errant bachelor regarded his putative wife.[16]

So the absence of barriers outside the home led to the erection of
greater ones inside. "Distinct and compulsory occupations" were "so
many natural barriers" between husband and wife. While they may
have looked upon their homes as a haven from the storms of democratic competition, men retained within the family the sexual divisions of the world outside. The "natural barrier" in an American
family was likely to have run through generations, between men
and women, whereas in an aristocracy the parental generation would
have had more in common with each other, irrespective of sex, than
with their children.[17]

While the absence of the recognition of adolescence has a number of implications for the psychology of American males in the

nineteenth century, contemporaries did not ignore the primacy of earlier phases of life in psychological development. The advice of William P. Dewees (1768–1841), professor of midwifery at the University of Pennsylvania, was, perhaps, typical of nineteenth-century attitudes toward childrearing.

It requires only a little firmness in the beginning . . . to make children conform to the dictates of their parents, and to render them entirely obedient to their wills; for it is only necessary to commence sufficiently early, to make the child know it is not to think for itself. Neither its palate, nor its caprice, is to be consulted—the parent must set before it . . . such articles of food as are judged best for it; and it is to be made to understand, that it must eat them, or nothing. If this plan be followed for a short time, all trouble will cease; since, as the child has never had a wish gratified at the expense of propriety, it will soon cease to have any; or rather, it will never have any to arise. But if the parent be weak enough to consult the child's taste at table, it will soon demand a portion, nor be satisfied until it obtain it. We need not say how subversive this is of all order, and propriety.

Dewees set vulnerable parents over potentially insatiable children; parents depended for strength on the eradication of the will of their children.[18]

Breaking the child's will, rooted in Puritan tradition, was part of the general body of nineteenth-century childrearing advocacy. Parents were advised to intervene strenuously in the early development of their children. Todd (1800–1873) told his daughter that her child's education "will commence before she is six months old, and every day after that is a day of discipline." The watchwords were discipline, regularity, and the exaction of obedience; suckling on demand was wrong. Not only was "indulgence" condemned, but a "hardening" process (cold baths and plunges) considered necessary, an attitude fostered perhaps particularly in the raising of boys. "Men are made monsters by indulgence in infancy."[19]

Children were to be inculcated with habits of extreme neatness and cleanliness in the way that male experts inculcated mothers. Dewees began his discussion of toilet training by measuring cleanliness in economic terms. "An attention to cleanliness costs neither time nor money beyond its worth; for the cleanly man or woman, can make their toilet with as much despatch as the sloven, or the slattern; and they gain by it. . . ." American adults seem to have learned the lesson, since some travelers thought them the cleanest people in the world. Dewees's recommendation for the age to start toilet training has been widely paraphrased, but with varying de-

grees of accuracy. This is what he said: "Children may be so trained
to cleanliness, that, at a very early period of their lives, they will
avoid soiling themselves. A friend informed us, that the little patient of eight months old . . . had not worn a diaper since it was
a month old. . . . This, we admit, to be a rare instance of discipline,
but it is not the less worthy of imitation." The remaining terms
elaborated Dewees's own feelings on the score: aggression, pertinacity, disgust, indomitable willfulness, righteousness, and an obsessive
concern to control the eruptive child's sphincters. He continued with
a minute account of the details of cleaning a child, especially regarding the temperature of the water, in all cases "regulated by the degree of vital energy" in the child. Coping with the child's dirt had
the end of the preservation and improvement of its vital energy. In
addition Dewees associated the retention of feces and urine with the
development of the sexual instinct. "Children should not be permitted to indulge in bed long after daylight; as its warmth, the accumulation of urine and faeces, and the exercise of the imagination,
but too often leads to the precocious development of the sexual
instinct."[20]

Male experts, then, directing their advice at women (mothers),
advised them to break their child's will and to instill principles of
self-control according to adult standards. Preschool educational activities were geared to that end. Surveying nineteenth-century childrearing literature, Robert Sunley suggests that parents "forced"
their children, since precocity (of intellect) was much admired.
However, he may be deducing that from nineteenth-century experts' jeremiads against "charging the head with stores of learning" to the neglect of the control of the "feelings and emotions."
"Early training—early mental discipline—self-control—self-denial—mastery over the passions, how much of our future welfare and
happiness depend upon the steady cultivation of such habits of
mind." Again and again control is posed against total uncontrol, in
the proto-Freudian belief in the "eternal truth, that the earliest impressions made upon children have a powerful influence over their
mental and moral development, and go with them, bearing good or
evil fruit to the latest hours of their existence."[21]

These experts' accusations of parental neglect, indulgence, and
"want of judicious training" were directed specifically at control
of the body. To charge the head only was a "defective and faulty
education." A "predisposition is produced" which "renders uncontrollable the animal propensities of our nature." To interpret the

advice manuals as advocating indulgence would be wrong: the experts were concerned to expand on what they saw as only partial, disproportionate control to the "whole" unit. Mind *and* body had to be developed equally for the total mobilization of energies.[22] So it was that Dr. Amariah Brigham, in 1832, exhorted the development of mind and body together in "the production of correct and long-continued mental activity."[23] Thirty-one years later, in 1863, facing an intensifying blast of competitive, vicissitudinous democracy which produced such a "rapid consumption of the mental energies," Dr. Isaac Ray hammered away at the same object as Brigham. Crucial in meeting the demand on a boy's "vital powers" was the "early strengthening of the nervous system" to "promote the future vigor and efficiency of the mind." Ray's goal was the mass development of "a bodily constitution possessing extraordinary powers of endurance. This it is, and this only, which sustains the industry, the patience, the indomitable perseverance, indispensable to the highest success. . . ."[24]

According to Brigham, the peculiar restlessness of American men seriously affected the bodies of their children. The "fearful rapidity" of the increase of insanity in the United States was due to faulty childrearing—and faulty gestation. American fathers applied the same mad and spasmodic impatience in their expectations of their babies as they did to their own pursuit of elusive success, with a "constant search after new and sure methods" for the development of infant minds, "novel plans," even "machines invented for accelerating the progress of babes." Aristocratic privilege offered no control in democracy, and parents looked for it in their own power and attempted to develop it in their children. In spite of his claims that overdevelopment of the "intellectual faculties" was particularly true of baby daughters, Brigham's terms suggested that the contribution of the father's ambition for his child was limited to his son, as in the case of the Puritan's calling: "he aims to prepare his son for a different fortune, and aspires to place him among the most distinguished of . . . his country." Brigham applauded the goal, but pointed out that it could be reached much more effectively if the child's mind was not developed precociously, so that it burned out before the end of childhood. Ray too believed that the larger proportion of insanity in the American people was "contributed by the female sex," yet the fundamental thrust of his book *Mental Hygiene* was the advocacy of the marshaling and conservation of male energies.[25]

The medical truth both Ray and Brigham were at pains to convey was the somatic basis for the operation of the mind. The brain was an organ of the body like the stomach and must not be overloaded. It had to be "carefully and judiciously exercised" as it grew. The intellect depended on the material body for "vigor and power." Properly developed, the mind itself could stimulate the body's resources: "mental excitement increases the flow of blood to the brain." But too much exercise, too large a flow, could "enfeeble or derange the mind." In Ray's words, "a certain amount of mental activity is necessary to obtain the highest degree of mental health. Although excessive exercise of the mind is calculated to impair its efficiency, yet it is no less certain that the worst results sometimes follow excessive inactivity and listlessness."[26]

Their underlying model for the operation of "the whole man," psychological and physiological, was an economic one, the medium of exchange energy, vital force. The mind had to be so related to its material resources that its energy would be increased and perpetuated. Brigham cited several European authorities' version of this economic physiology; it was a "fundamental law of the distribution of vital powers . . . that when they are increased in one part, they are diminished in all the rest of the living economy." The premature development of the brain, according to Brigham's native contribution to the metaphor, entailed the "robbing" of other organs of their natural share of vital energy.[27]

Ray was obsessed with this "fundamental law of animal economy," the rail on which *Mental Hygiene* ran. "To obtain the highest degree of mental vigor, we require suitable habits of bodily exercise." When the "vital energies" were depressed, the "qualities of the brain" deteriorated. "Surplus energy is needed to meet the demands of a suffering organ." When vital energies have been impaired by "exhausting labors," then "stimulants may be required to supply the waste of nervous energy." Such an economy could be simplified into subtraction and addition. "It depends very much upon ourselves whether we so manage our minds, that every exercise will add something to their capacity and vigor, or only subtract from their energies." Ray's advice was for the "management" of energy, vital forces, powers, "so as to ensure the greatest possible return." The body's resources were regarded as an investable commodity. Mental activity had to be profitable: a "mind furnished and disciplined is provided with a fund of reserved power to fall back upon when assailed by adverse forces." Like other currency, energy could be "converted" and "debased."[28]

What can be claimed to be historically significant in *prescriptive* childrearing evidence is, first, the attitudes the advisers display. Dewees's toilet training advice represented his own existential "anality," and Dewees, Ray, Cook, Todd, and Brigham all assumed that the body operated according to an economy of energy. Second, the advisers were all men claiming superior expertise over a field rhetorically held to be especially woman's.

As far as the relation between adviser and mothers went, it would be unlikely that their cultural values were divergent on the issue of childrearing. Moreover, women gave way to male expertise, as we shall see. It is probable that the experts' recommendations filtered downwards in the nineteenth century just as they do today (with various degrees of resistance, according to subcultural values, geography, and literacy). Not only did women generally copy the cultural values of the trend setters in the way that Cooper and the other sources observed, but they were exposed to childrearing advice from the pulpit, since the experts were frequently ministers.[29]

It is in an existential[30] way that the importance of the sexual distinction to adults (asserted ad nauseam) must have informed adults' attitudes toward childrearing and consequently the child's feelings. A later part of this book describes the aggrandizement of the production of male babies, and the devaluation of girls. Fathers profoundly concerned to maintain distance between the homosexual world of competing men and the heterosexuality of the home would have identified their immortal ambitions with their sons, just as Brigham said they did, and thereby would have intensified the distinction between sexual roles. As we shall see, both Brigham and Todd adjured parents to foreclose the education of daughters. Dewees assumed that "girls, from necessity, can have fewer games and amusements than boys" and that boys (at seven years old) were "necessarily less under the eye of the parent than girls; consequently more vigilance is required with regard to them." Sunley suggests that little girls were precociously religious, "submissive, seemingly drained of vitality and desires, and met an early death, often by the age of ten." Harriet Beecher Stowe's little Eva is a case in point (although she is also like Hawthorne's Pearl, a subversively female Christ). They seem to have learned to anticipate the life of Tocqueville's typical pioneer wife; Tocqueville described the process whereby all young American women were educated to submit themselves to the cloister of their "honest duty"—marriage. These little girls, then, may have given in to adult/godly power, as young women gave themselves up to men.[31]

These, then, are the putative fragments of a picture of relations between democratic fathers and sons in nineteenth-century America. The father demanded babies be ordered, and demonstrate self-control, which he measured first by the baby's control of the sphincter. Presumably he would have been more concerned to discern precocity in the potentially autonomous, manly, male baby than in the female. (He probably delegated toilet training to his wife, given the general perimeters of the relationship.) In short, a Dewees son could demonstrate his precocity by early adopting his father's attitude toward "soiling" himself. Second, the father's identification with the son would evolve as they grew older together into more fraternal feelings, and the ideal of precocity would make the father view such equality as the earlier the better; i.e., the sooner the son was like the father, the more precocious the son, and the more fraternal the relation. The intensity of the father's feelings may have been spasmodic, according to father's absences and preoccupations, which may have intensified the corresponding spasmodicalness of the son's feelings toward his father. These feelings would of course be interwoven with the son's feelings toward his ever-present mother.

Bernard Wishy's recent study of childrearing in the nineteenth century suggests the emergence of the mother's parental power in default of the father's. Dr. Cook said in 1859 that some mothers "with true womanly spirit and fortitude take upon themselves the burden so thoughtlessly cast aside by the fathers . . . while many, we fear, give as little thought as the fathers to the infinite responsibilities." The absence of father in several senses (diminished authority, place of work, preoccupation with business) and the physical presence of mother suggests that the dominant influence on the American child's psychology could have been hers. This hypothesis is endorsed by the nature of the male preoccupations described below, and the ubiquity of a maternal icon in literature of all kinds.[32]

5   Freedom of Intercourse

Unique about nineteenth-century democratic men was the leveling of fathers and sons. Young democratic women were uniquely free before marriage. Tocqueville's account of the young American woman's "independence," her "singular address and happy boldness" restrained only by "reason" and "self-guidance," corresponded exactly to Cooper's in *Notions of the Americans.* The phrase which Cooper egregiously applied to this phenomenon was "freedom of intercourse." The existence of this freedom was made all the more noticeable when contrasted to the lack of freedom in woman's married state. "In no other country is the same freedom of intercourse between the unmarried of the two sexes permitted, as in America. In no other Christian country is there more restraint imposed on communications between the married." Once she was married, an American wife was "burdened" and "sobered" with "matrimonial duties." It was a contrast on which Tocqueville and Cooper agreed. And in both cases the freedom of intercourse of the unmarried turned out to be as carefully circumscribed as the life of the American wife.[1]

Unmarried women, according to Cooper, were "much more reserved and guarded in their discourse at least in the presence of our sex." A man could address an unmarried female in the "language of gallantry" only if he was prepared to marry her. Women had to be both "feminine" and "natural." Cooper challenged the world to "produce finer instances of genuine shrinking delicacy . . . greater feminine propriety," and without batting an eyelid claimed they were "eminently frank, unreserved and natural." Femininity, then, must have been second nature.[2]

Moreover, woman exercised even this restricted freedom of intercourse in a world sexually divided. Men and women existed "in different circles." Men's "inclinations and pursuits" brought them together with men much more frequently than they did with women. Yet the woman's aim during her unmarried years was to join her life to a man's in marriage, "the first, the highest, and most lovely office of the sex." Cooper asserted her possession of an "inherent right" to choose a husband: it was one she had to exercise "in the morning of life," during the period of her freedom. The consequences of such a choice had to last a lifetime. Her freedom of choice enabled Cooper to transfer a sixteenth-century proverb about England to America of the 1820s: America was, he said, "the true Paradise of women."[3]

The restraints between the married couple Cooper mentioned may have been derived in part from the husband's work preoccupations, which Beaumont and Tocqueville described. The unmarried man, early embarked on his ordeal in the outside world, was anxious to obtain a wife who would not distract him by engaging his passions, and who would conform to his expectations of women. Indeed it was this very preoccupation which guaranteed woman's "freedom of intercourse." It existed not because of woman's moral strength, but because of the absence of an army, "or any class of idlers, to waste their time in dissolute amusements." American democratic men had broken away from aristocratic time-wasting. "In a community like ours, where almost every man has some healthful and absorbing occupation, there is neither leisure, nor inclination, to devote much time to unworthy pursuits." The words suggest that perhaps work was "absorbing" the unhealthful sexual energies which otherwise would have been directed dangerously toward women. The moral underpinning of freedom of intercourse was incapable of being challenged.[4]

Under such conditions this unique "freedom" could not have meant to women what it might have meant for men—that is, personal exchange unfettered by any other than individual and interpersonal demands. In that sense "freedom of intercourse" was rhetoric. Cooper himself admitted the meaninglessness of the claim to woman's special freedom in America in his response to the warnings that would be sounded should women really be freed: "no reasonable man can suppose that a sagacious nation . . . would stupidly allow their sisters and daughters to be debauched, when their own personal experience must apprise them of the danger to which they are exposed." One wonders what this "personal experience" was; the attitude was the same as that of the American men of Tocqueville's account, who showed their respect for women by legislating against rape.[5]

The unmarried woman had to exhibit a character just as limited by male definition as a wife's. She was aiming at marriage anyway. Her "reserve," her "appealing to the generosity of men by admitting her physical weakness, [gave] strength and durability to her moral ascendancy." Her behavior in the freedom of intercourse was based on the moral character dependent on man and directed toward marriage. The "natural" female delicacy would be "extinguished" if a woman dropped her guard during courtship, and thereafter she would lose her essential "fear of man," a phenomenon to which Dr. Ray gave expert testimony in 1866. "The shrinking delicacy of the female character, the sense of right and wrong, the fear of man and the fear of God, all disappeared—utterly extinguished by the desire to be revenged."[6]

But in spite of male preoccupations, the young lady's own internal "guard" was inadequate to maintain sexual safety. So in another part of *Notions*, Cooper again explicitly admitted the hollowness of freedom of intercourse.

A young lady never goes in public without the eye of some experienced matron to watch her movements. She cannot appear at a play, ball, etc., without a father, or a brother, at least, and it is thought far more delicate and proper that she should have a female guardian. She never rides or walks—unless in the most public places, and then commonly with great reserve—attended by a single man, unless indeed under circumstances of a peculiar nature.

This was all that was left of "freedom of intercourse": "She pursues that course which rigid delicacy would prescribe without however betraying any marked distrust of the other sex." While these remarks were focused on the upper class, Cooper observed that the constant chaperoning of young women was "relaxed little as you descend in the scale of society." He expressed the need for separation between the sexes in terms which suggest that the feelings involved in such "delicacy" belonged to those who did the "permitting," that is, men: "there is something repugnant to the delicacy of American ideas in permitting a lady to come . . . in contact with the world." Men it was who dominated "American ideas," and on this score they seem to have had the psychic force of repugnance.

But such widespread rhetoric did have a function. At an obvious level Cooper wanted it believed (and to believe himself, perhaps) that women were freer in the new, American nation—and at the same time did not want an actual change in their position. Men (and one can include Cooper) liked women to play the role of "shrinking delicacy" because men were "used to no other custom." Perhaps the rhetoric was merely a different way of enforcing woman's subordinate role in a society opening up in so many other ways.[7]

Woman's greater freedom to choose a husband followed the rise of individualism. It had been accompanied by the separation of sexual spheres and the devaluation of women. Such division was a basic condition of the choice the unmarried woman had to face, in "the very station for which she was designed by nature." Democracy, Tocqueville said, had brought man and woman face to face: "equality of conditions has swept away all the imaginary or the real barriers that separated man from woman." Conversely, the sexual distinction was the only one guaranteed a man. His dire need for such a distinction was manifest in the erection of new barriers between the sexes in the democratic home.[8]

Separated from men's "sordid traffic" within the "sacred precincts of her own abode . . . preserved from the destroying taint of excessive intercourse with the world," woman could provide moral fiber for a whole people. Man retired tainted to his home in order "to seek consolation from one who is placed beyond [tainture's] influence." Consolation and correction would meet the requirements of Marvel's bachelor in his mother-wife fantasy. One wonders what exactly the wife would have corrected in her husband; or of what the moral fiber would have consisted. Perhaps the son used "the pure and unalloyed lessons" that he "received from the lips, and, what is far better, from the example of the mother" in the choice of a wife, whose unspeaking example would also be more in accord with the family relations described by Beaumont. Certainly such moral equipment would be irrelevant to the son's life outside home, in the "sordid traffic" and prosperity of building the transportation revolution.[9]

Cooper said that these assumptions regarding sexual roles and behavior were those of "the women of America of all classes." Everyone, men and women, he implied, placed the greatest significance on separating the sexes. "I saw everywhere the utmost pos-

sible care to preserve the females from undue or unwomanly employments." It was in their very separation that wives were bound
to their husbands. "Women, are literally, our better halves"—a definition echoing Marvel's bachelor's "second self" reverie, and Tocqueville's observation that the representative American male saw in his
wife "but a detached portion of himself." The ambiguity of construing one's wife as a necessarily separated part of oneself was clearly
a less open version of the bachelor's ambiguous fantasies of freedom
and fireside.[10]

Tocqueville called his description of the American phenomenon
of young women's freedom "Education of Young Women in the
United States." This title represented the results of his analysis of
her putative freedom; it was deeper than Cooper's, and Tocqueville
found the contradictions in it more disturbing. Like Cooper, he began with the assumption underlying the "freedom," namely, that
"no free communities ever existed without morals," and "morals
are the work of woman." American men came together readily and
found neither "peril nor advantage in the free interchange of their
thoughts." But some freedom was more free than other freedom.
"Such is the respect entertained for the moral freedom of the sex
that in the presence of a woman the most guarded language is used
lest her ear should be offended by an expression." In a society which
permitted free interchange it was anomalous that half the population was so narrowly circumscribed. Perhaps Tocqueville's consideration of the much vaunted self-controlled freedom of the independent woman was prompted by the expectations that democracy
postulated. But it was the existential conditions of American democracy—chanciness, competition, ceaselessly moving monotony, restlessness, ambition—all in the hands of equal males, that marked out
the terms of woman's freedom of intercourse, her wifely "circumscription," and her function as a moral repository.[11]

Tocqueville suggested part of the case against any real exercise of
freedom by women. "The tumultuous and constantly harassed life
that equality makes men lead not only distracts them from the passion of love by denying them time to indulge it, but diverts them
from it by another more secret but more certain road." We have
already seen how this effected a typing of wifehood, and that was
what the unmarried man would have in mind, even if an independent, bold, young unmarried woman were eager to engage him in
wider terms.[12]

Tocqueville continued his description of the busy American

male's frame of mind in selecting a mate during the limited amount of time he would allow himself for the purpose. Instead of running after "those violent and capricious sources of excitement" (like sea coal), which would "disturb and abridge" his own energies, the American male "procures" a wife as prepared as Marvel's bachelor's wife-mother to "support [his] vicissitudes with calm and unquenchable energy." He had to face the severe stresses of the competition between the equals of American democracy. He could "rise and sink again through all the grades that lead from opulence to poverty." Men could not afford to expose themselves to the dangers of unknown challenges from home, from woman. The equalization of relations between father and son, and the rigid separation of the sexes, ill-prepared the young American male to cope with such challenges.[13]

In contrast to the young male's perplexing sea of possibilities, the young woman had only one, and all the men and women around her pressed her in that direction. If she sensed alternatives, insurmountable odds crowded against her. Tocqueville explained that "the transition from the status of girl to married woman has no dangers for [her]," and her education permitted her great freedom. But as in Cooper's argument, the evident superfluity of such moral armor when there were no aristocratic or military layabouts to test it makes the claim suspicious.[14]

What, then, was the purpose of the unmarried girl's independence? Why did American men expose the young woman to dangers that did not exist? Instead of placing her virtue "under the shelter of prejudice, ignorance and fear," they taught her to survey "the great scene of the world . . . with a firm and calm gaze." She was not being let alone here; someone was at her elbow, preparing her for a great task. "The vices and dangers of society are early revealed to her; as she sees them clearly, she views them without fear, for she is full of reliance on her own strength, and her confidence seems to be shared by all around her." That solidarity must have added considerably to her resolution. Among the "vices and dangers," we may speculate that she did not know bad, obscene language, since men guard their language in the presence of women; talk about sex would presumably "offend her ear" too, and of course, the basis of her moral independence was that she did not experience any; in conversation women had to "contrive to manage their thoughts and language" "along a narrow path"; if their male kin consorted with some of "the great number of courtesans," it was not likely that they would offend their young women by talking about them, or introducing them.[15]

The one social danger a woman had to see was the danger of not being married. Upon her entrance into the world, a young American woman would learn, if she had not learned before, "that the inexorable opinion of the public carefully circumscribes woman within the narrow circle of domestic duties, and forbids her to step beyond it." She had to face the meaning of that inexorable opinion for her own life. She was not "slow to perceive that she cannot depart for an instant from the established usages of her contemporaries without putting in jeopardy her peace of mind, her honor, nay even her social existence." She was educated to that realization, and to bow to it; and she found the "energy required for such an act of submission in the firmness of her understanding and in the virile habits which her education has given her." In order that she understand fully the futility of any other course, she was freed to choose subjection.

> When the time for choosing a husband arrives, that cold and stern reasoning power which has been educated and invigorated by the free observation of the world teaches an American woman that a spirit of levity and independence in the bonds of marriage is a constant subject of annoyance, not of pleasure; it tells her that the amusements of the girl cannot become the recreations of the wife, and that the sources of a married woman's happiness are in the home of her husband. As she clearly discerns beforehand the only road that can lead to domestic happiness she enters upon it at once and follows it to the end without seeking to turn back.[16]

Woman had to design herself to suit her husband's pleasure, not her own. Young wives would bend "themselves at once and without repining to the austere duties of their new condition." A woman "learned by the use of her independence to surrender it without a struggle and without a murmur when the time comes for making the sacrifice." This sacrifice—and it was, according to Tocqueville, typical—was the purpose for which woman was educated.

The education of the young woman in the United States was intended to overcome her potential freedom, given society's rhetorical postulates. It did so by granting her the illusion of free choice: "no American woman falls into the toils of matrimony as into a snare held out to her simplicity and ignorance. She has been taught beforehand what is expected of her and voluntarily and freely enters upon this engagement. She supports her new condition with courage because she chose it." That is the meaning of the suggestion, "these two conditions of life [freedom and marriage], are perhaps not so contrary as may be supposed, and it is natural that the

American women should pass through the one to arrive at the other." The willing resignation of so many people into a kind of life demanded of them by another group was an awesome event, awesomely repeated. The analogies with race slavery were evident to contemporaries.[17]

Tocqueville's analysis was that the historical process culminating in American democracy had made men too weak to subordinate women directly, even as such subordination became more necessary to them. So they devised a new method.

> Under these [democratic] circumstances, believing that they had little chance of repressing in woman the most vehement passions of the human heart, they held that the surer way was to teach her the art of combating those passions for herself. As they could not prevent her virtue from being exposed to frequent danger, they determined that she should know how best to defend it, and more reliance was placed on the free vigor of her will than on safeguards which have been shaken or overthrown.

The most "absolute and irresistible" power in America championed her virtue; and her will was deliberately "invigorated" not to defend her virtue, in the face of preoccupied democracy, but to assist her "cold reasoning power" to understand that she had to submit her independence in marriage, and be pleasing to her husband. The magnitude of the act of submission was that it represented the repression of those "most vehement passions," and the willingness to repress them for a lifetime. From that moment of resignation, of sacrifice, one can look to the harrowing immediacy of Tocqueville's description of a pioneer woman "in her prime," her existence "a heavy burden."[18]

Tocqueville recognized the apparent anomaly of such a position for women in a society based on the destruction of inequality. And while, like American men, he said ideas such as inequality and politics belonged to a category separate from "nature"—that is, the inequality of the sexes was an issue with which politics had nothing to do—Tocqueville was too honest not to present woman's having to repress herself in order to maintain such an artificial distinction. His presentation belied the distinction. And as if to emphasize this subversive meaning, Tocqueville used the term "virile" to describe woman's "holiest duty," her "firmness of understanding" in submission to the distinction. Male superiority depended on a distinction based on an act by women which denied both distinction and superiority.[19]

6   Strong Men over Orderly Women

In spite of their severe circumscription, women were delegated a great moral responsibility by American men. Yet it does not seem that religion or morality (the terms are very close together in meaning in *Democracy*) could have prevailed in the unpredictable outside world. Tocqueville had large reservations about the strength of spiritual breakwaters against the tides of materialism, physical and philosophical. He did not meet a single American "whose imagination did not possess itself by anticipation of those good things that fate still obstinately withheld from him." He presented the American democrat pursuing them obsessively to the end of his days.[1]

Tocqueville presented the American home as ordered, in contrast to the incessant chanciness of life outside. Men returned from the restless pursuit of physical gratifications to a relationship they required to be ordered: "they attach great importance to procuring for themselves that sort of deep, regular, and quiet affection which constitutes the charm and safeguard of life." Their appetite for chance somehow needed order and "regularity of morals," which contributed to "public tranquillity" and were "favorable to industry." Men combined their industry with "a species of religious morality." This they did by appropriating to themselves by marriage a member of that group whose sphere morality was.[2]

While religion often was unable to restrain man from the numberless temptations of "chance," and while it could not check him at all in "that passion for gain which everything contributes to arouse," its "influence over the mind of woman" was "supreme." Women, therefore, were the "protectors of morals."[3] Tocqueville explained

that these apparently divergent sexual traits led to unique respect
and appreciation for "the tie of marriage": woman was committed
to the protection of society's morals, while in his insatiable appetite
for chance, man needed to secure his rear by the safeguard of his
private convent. Domestic order may have been the "surest path to
happiness," but it was men's addiction to chance in their world of
work that determined their courses. "Men . . . continually change
their tack for fear of missing the shortest cut to happiness." They
relegated marriage (and its concomitants, morality and heterosexuality) to the periphery of their lives, and even when they were
at home they remained occupied with the affairs of the outside
world. Women were in no position to restrain men, who nonetheless
made fantastic claims about their power.[4]

"It is the Americans themselves who daily quit the spots which
gave them birth, to acquire extensive domains in a remote region."
Given the life style of incessantly restless, accumulative democratic
men, it was essential that society expand, grow, and prosper. The
"desire of prosperity has become an ardent and restless passion in
their minds, which grows by what it feeds on." And it was not only
profit that so passionately absorbed them: they engaged in commerce, "not only for the sake of the profit it holds out to them, but
for the constant excitement occasioned by that pursuit." In whatever direction men went, commerce, industry, or pioneering, their
pursuit of riches led to that particular emotional or psychological
charge to which Tocqueville repeated the American male was
addicted. Tocqueville pointed out how perpetual and ubiquitous
were commercial passions. Evidently they were the impulse for
westering and for the transportation revolution. What would have
happened if the West had not existed? Could society have contained
itself? Tocqueville said no, and explained the irrelevance of checks
to the American passion for gain (implying perhaps that his worst
apprehensions for democratic psychology would be fulfilled).

> In Europe, we are wont to look upon a restless disposition, an un-
> bounded desire of riches, and an excessive love of independence as
> propensities very dangerous to society. Yet these are the elements that
> ensure a long and peaceful future to the republics of America. With-
> out these unquiet passions, the population would collect in certain
> spots and would soon experience wants like those of the Old World
> which it is difficult to satisfy; for such is the present good fortune of
> the New World that the vices of its inhabitants are scarcely less
> favourable to society than their virtues.[5]

The customs and laws which Tocqueville later claimed "regulate democracy" look flimsy beside that most noticeable characteristic of nineteenth-century American history, expansion, whether on the part of mythic lone hunter, entrepreneurial loner, or self-absorbed pioneer. In America "nothing seems to be more prejudicial to society" than the European virtues of "orderly manners, domestic affections, and the attachment that men feel to the place of their birth." The American state did not want such "great guarantees of . . . tranquility and happiness," much in the way that its men had no interest in the sure path to happiness that marriage could be. "American society" included activities beyond settlement which were "prejudicial" to society. By definition, it was a society on the move. "The American republics of the present day are like complete companies of adventurers, formed to explore in common the waste-lands of the New World and busied in a flourishing trade. The passions that agitate the Americans most deeply are not their political, but their commercial passions."[6] Tocqueville had already excluded from the American man's psychology the "natural passions" of feelings toward nature and toward women. If the narrowed passions for riches and emotional gain were at present useful for expansion, they could be dreadful if the area for growth were to be used up. "New wants are not to be feared [in America] since they can be satisfied without difficulty; the growth of human passions need not be dreaded, since all passions may find an easy and legitimate object."

So Tocqueville negated a value he claimed for American women, that the regularity of their affection was the safeguard of American men's lives. He suggested that domestic order was at best irrelevant and at worst prejudicial to the great work of society. Tocqueville reproduced the bachelor's ambivalence. But he was emphatic about a connection between domestic order and male activities in the outside world: "the American derives from his own home that love of order which he afterwards carries with him into public affairs."[7]

Clearly the "order" the man derived from his home was not morality. Then what was it? All along Tocqueville was describing the functions of mate training, selection, and possession as the safeguard of man's life. And Isaac Ray starkly declared that woman's special province of morality, her "christian spirit," was for the discipline of herself rather than for the protection of society's morals. Tocqueville believed that the general leveling process "will raise woman and make her more and more the equal of man." But he held that physiology made for irreducible differences between the social functions of men and women, and he believed that those differences could be threatened by attempts at equality: "by thus attempting to make one sex equal to the other, both are degraded, and from so preposterous a medley of the works of nature, nothing could ever result but weak men and disorderly women." According to Tocqueville, man's social and political superiority should not be challenged. If you attempted equality, men would be weakened by being nearer women: they were stronger, more manly in the present, unequal arrangement; and if you changed woman's position by removing her from her moral superiority, her pedestal, by blurring the line between the spheres, she would threaten order. The order would be better maintained by keeping strong men over potentially disorderly women.[8]

But the people threatening social order were men, craving autonomy, tempted to repudiate political authority as well as the ties of heterosexual obligations. Men were projecting onto women what they feared from themselves. So in a real sense women did represent order, in virtue of not being free, of not being men. The order that men derived from home was the separation of the sexes and the subordination of women. Furthermore, this order effected a peculiarly democratic sexual restraint. Sexual demarcation lessened the incidence of copulation. "All these distinct and compulsory occupations are so many natural barriers, which by keeping the two sexes asunder render the solicitations of the one less frequent and less ardent, the resistance of the other more easy."[9] It was men's "desire of prosperity" that Tocqueville described as "ardent . . . passion in their minds," which grew "by what it feeds on." Women contributed to the prosperity and growing strength of Americans by not demanding that men divert such ardor; they had to be above sex. Here the meaning of Tocqueville's balanced prose touched Lantern-Jawed Bob's fear of being turned into a skeleton and the bachelor's fear that woman could become wild, impulsive, and uncontrollable. Democratic men's bodies had to be freer of sexual demands. Fear of such demands suggests that the "women safe—men at work" explanation for democratic virtue should read "men safe—women circumscribed."

So sexual separateness in society at large and in the family was interpenetrative, a mutually reinforcing circle. Men derived their sense of order from the family, and retired home to experience order. Women were subjected to the discipline men imposed on their own bodies, covered as wives were by their husbands' "vast egoism."

Order ultimately derived from men's preoccupation with themselves, in ways later chapters will describe.

"Order" had a general and familiar significance in the large historical arena of heterosexual settlement and homosexual mobility, and the mother seems to have had considerable effect in shaping it. While men within the area of settlement could relegate woman to the fringes of the day and identify in their work with all-male freedom, their lives were actually bounded. Locating heterosexuality apart from them, like bachelors and frontiersmen, they still experienced the regular order of home, albeit reluctantly. The West in places was womanless. The University of Washington's first president complained that Seattle's predominantly male population was "almost wholly beyond the reach of feminine influence and wholesome restraints." His solution was to go East and return with a few female millworkers and Civil War widows. Catherine Beecher made the connection between woman and civilization the basis for her scheme of sending out Christianizing, civilizing women teachers, thus combining remedies for several ills, including some women's positions in the East. Women and heterosexual regularity represented civilization, which the American man resisted in the interest of his autonomy. In the frequently quoted words of Huck Finn, "I reckon I got to light out for the Territory ahead of the rest, because Aunt Sally she's going to adopt me and civilize me, and I can't stand it."[10]

So perhaps woman's presence in the settled area had the power of inhibiting Ahabian destructiveness in the male pursuit of autonomy. Much of Melville's work represents such a belief. Men, whether pioneers or businessmen, who had a continuous relation with women had to pay at least minimal lip service to the settlement that marriage and heterosexual obligations required. Such contact perpetuated the male demand that women play a single knowable role and in that way, perhaps, kept his skeletalization down. At the same time it reproduced the tensions that drove men toward separation, bachelorhood, and compulsive recklessness. American "order" generated anarchy. The famous safety valve metaphor for American expansion implies imperative pressure.[11]

The anarchic, homosexual West was "pure democracy," the natural wilderness a source of health and potency in contrast to the madnesses of heterosexual civilization. One cannot help feeling that this belief was informed by the deep attraction the idea of autonomy held for men. The image of the American Adam "contrived to embody the most fruitful contemporary ideas . . . a figure of heroic innocence and vast potentialities" was "undefiled by . . . family." His innocence in nature was that he was beyond woman.[12]

But the democratic assertion of autonomy entailed an agonizing—and inevitable—burden. The weight of choice at the outset of adult life was maintained and increased throughout the following years. The "deliberate tentativeness of autonomous choice" was experienced as relentless ordeal. A pervasive theme in the historical literature of the nineteenth century is the incessant pressure of vicissitudinous business. Tocqueville argued that American men found order essential to business, *and* that it was fundamentally a hindrance. Attitudes toward stresses on the male brain were correspondingly ambivalent: on the one hand they drove men mad, and on the other they were stimulants to success. The explanation was the same as that underlying Brigham's advocacy of judicious stimulation of the brain: success required enough, but too much led to insanity. The "mad impatience" Tocqueville saw as characteristic of democratic men and George Rogers Taylor's account of "craze" and "mania" building the American economy had literal correlatives in insanity: "the new and sometimes uncontrolled if not uncontrollable motive powers, and the new modes of travel . . . multiply the causes of cerebral disturbance. . . . Pecuniary difficulties, perplexity in business in which the mind struggles to accomplish and gain what it cannot . . . the feelings are oppressed with anxieties and fears." Melville watched his father die mad from repeated business failure. Tocqueville located the cycle of boom and slump specifically in democratic psychology: "the return of these commercial panics is an endemic disease of . . . democratic nations . . . it cannot be cured, because it does not originate in accidental circumstances, but in the temperament of these nations." The pursuit of physical gratifications, the appetite for chance, was a form of insanity "said to be more common [in America] than anywhere else."[13]

American doctors accepted Esquirol's dictum that "insanity is a disease of civilization, and the number of the insane is in direct proportion to its progress." Since America was most "advanced," doctors found there the highest incidence of insanity.[14] They attributed it to the democratic passions in men free of despotic rule. English doctors believed that the inevitable shock of fluctuation in the amassing of success predisposed commercial classes to insanity; in America this predisposition was democratized. Experts expected the depressions of 1837–1844 to be followed by an epidemic of mental illness. They asserted it was the chronic uncertainty of American life, the economic boom and slump, and the burden of choice which explained the increase in insanity. Among the reasons for the "gradually increasing predominance of the nervous system among the American people, and consequent predisposition to the various forms of nervous and mental disease which are becoming so prevalent among all classes" was a scene identical to the one Beaumont had described nearly thirty years before. "Very many American fathers are strangers to their children. . . . A hasty 'good morning,' a few moments at meals, and a weary 'good night' are as much as they can spare from the absorbing pursuit of money-getting. . . . They are far better known on Change, in their counting-rooms and offices, in the street or club-room, than in their houses." Fathers' preoccupation reflected the democratic government's. To Scheiber's account of the Ohio legislature's deference to the force of economic individualism, and to Tocqueville's point that public officers provided models of dangerous wickedness to their constituents, may be added Dorothea Dix's ascription of insanity to "capricious legislation causing commercial panics and disaster." It should be remembered that Tocqueville described the "mad impatience" of pursuit of success and chance as a characteristic of *all* democratic men, that some such madness in men was regarded as essential to progress, and that this belief provided the context for the selection of the "insane."[15] Failure, success, insanity, could all be gauged as degrees of "mental excitement." Furthermore, psychiatric experts advocated the strict training of young children in self-control and self-denial for the prevention of mental disease.[16] If the obsessive channeling of life toward the future derived in some measure from such training, this advocacy would have intensified the conditions it was intended to prevent, a circuitousness we shall see repeated time and again in the stylization of young, democratic males.

Insanity was attendant on the progress of civilization, and progress lay in the individual strivings of men: nineteenth-century analyses found men most exposed to insanity by their very commitment to progress and civilization. Yet, at the same time, insanity came to be located particularly in women, more assertively so after mid-century.

Since the eastern seaboard states were more civilized, it was logical that nineteenth-century doctors observed a much higher incidence of insanity there than in frontier settlements. By the mid-nineteenth century Massachusetts had more asylums than anywhere else. Frederick Law Olmsted warned that if people could not reinvigorate in "natural" surroundings, "serious mental disorders might well result." This was of course another version of Frederick Jackson Turner.[17]

The contrast between civilization and nature was that much clearer with the urbanization that accompanied the transportation revolution. The population of the United States increased by 226 percent between 1820 and 1860, but the urban population rose by 797 percent. Cities were swept by plagues and epidemics until late in the century and were associated with a general rise in the death rate. Jefferson's famous characterization of cities as "sores" is specifically a metaphor of disease. Cities were regarded as hotbeds of vice and "breeding places for insanity." Back East was where women were in the greatest numbers. The associations of industrial civilization were, in a significant sense, sexual. The surplus of women in New England coincided with the contemporary view of the higher incidence of mental and physical disease. Dr. James Athon believed that the "insane rarely emigrate, and consequently the number accumulates in those States which have been settled the longest time.[18]

The insane were characterized very much as women were. In addition to an "inability to resist disease," the "persons composing this class are unable to govern themselves, or direct their energies. They feel entirely indifferent to society, and seek to hold no relation to it, other than dependence upon it" (1857). In this lack of self-government, inability to direct energies (the specific meaning of which is explained in Chapter 15), and separation from/dependence on society, they failed the norms of healthy male activity set up by Jarvis, Ray, and Cooper, for example.[19]

Doctors provided a specific formulation of the general association of women with the wrong side of the social ledger, divided between the credit and debit of active and passive, progress and stagnation, normalcy and abnormalcy, health and disease, nature and unnature, country and city (and, paradoxically, morality and immorality, good and bad). I have noted Ray's assertion of women's contribution of "by far the larger proportion of insanity" in America. This was an inevitable consequence of the "lamentably patent" fact "that the health of our women has been depreciating during the last forty or fifty years" (i.e., before 1863). The "busy idleness" of "mere butter-

fly existence" of the new workless, city-dwelling "female members
of families in easy circumstances" was regarded as the cause of
insanity (although Ray noted that the overburdened toiling of the
"female sex in the humbler walks of life" could use the relief of a
"better supply of cheap and innocent amusements"). At the same
time the main thrust of mental hygiene was aimed at preparing
durable *men* for the inevitable and lifelong pressure of their competitive lives—and thereby intensifying the pressure, the need for
mental hygiene, and, I would suggest, the more desperate need for
men's distinction from women.[20]

From the outset of his *Remarks,* Dr. Brigham insisted that the
dangerous imbalance of mental labor over exercise of the body was
"more particularly true of the female." He listed four "causes" of
the great prevalence of insanity in America. His first, and therefore
the prior context for the others, was too "constant and too powerful
excitement of the mind, which the strife for wealth, office, political
distinction, and party success produces in this free country." These
were male pressures on males. It was Brigham's commitment to
this "strife" that shaped the rest of his concerns. He wanted to
persuade men to lay a foundation for staying power in the new,
free democratic world. His second cause was the too early cultivation of the mind and ensuing "predominance" of the "nervous
system"; concomitantly, neglect of the development of the body;
and fourth, the "general and powerful excitement of the female
mind." So Brigham swung from the special pressures on men's minds
to the special pressures on women.[21]

One explanation for the emphasis on women was the irrelevance
of any developing of women's mental powers, in comparison to male
needs. The women he identified specifically (although he talked
about "woman" and women-in-general throughout) were the
wealthy, living in cities; the nature of their psychology was the
result of the "general conviction" after the Industrial Revolution
that "knowledge is power." In short, they were the new workless
women, freed of the necessity to work for physical survival. They
had no jobs to go to, but faced a new kind of enslavement. Brigham
said that to make women "as capable as men" was to go against
"the dictates of nature." Such education would "suppress" her
naturally "finer sensibilities," which were (in their emotional form
only) "far superior to men's."[22]

The logic here was murky. The development of woman's mind
amounted to the suppression of her body; this seemed to be a version

of the physiological economy in man, in whom a soundly developed body was the base for sustained mental energy. Perhaps Brigham was saying that in women's case, the same process was bad. In woman, the "nervous system naturally predominates." Behind that assertion the thought may have flickered that women were effortlessly closer to the successful production of nervous energy, power. However, women's nervous energy must not be converted into "qualities of mind," but instead show itself as "sentiment" and "affection." To argue that the development of women's intellectual powers changed their "natural sensibility" or rendered it "excessive" was vague, but one can infer that Brigham would have preferred to leave women's "natural sensibility" unchanged, undeveloped, uneducated. Her superiority to man perhaps lay in her mindless body.[23]

Brigham claimed that women's nervous systems overloaded by mental excitement would have "deplorable effects upon their offspring." Unless women were directed back to a focus on the body, the United States would experience "dangerous consequences." The responsibility for social insanity shifted to women: "there may be other causes besides ignorance and vice, slowly and silently operating upon physical man, which will *as certainly lead to the ruin of the country*. The decline of the Roman empire was marked by the general predominance of a nervous sentiment, especially among the Roman ladies." It was not simply that women were driving themselves insane: "Whoever . . . witnesses their violent emotions and knows anything of the effect of excited mind upon a delicate bodily organization, must . . . fear, not only for the injury which such procedure must inflict upon the females themselves, but for that which may be entailed upon the generation to come." Brigham asserted: "No people will long hold a high rank among the nations of the earth where . . . females are generally feeble." The political nation, men, depended on women's falling back on a definition of self based entirely on body. Women were responsible (under the guidance of such experts as Brigham) for the physical and psychical health of boys and men in the future, just as they were responsible for morality and order in contemporary democracy.[24] This was in spite of the assumption of the "necessary insanity" of democratic men, and their necessarily anarchic expression of energies.

Brigham asked parents to concentrate on body as well as mind in childrearing. But he singled out females' psychology as especially disordered and reserved apocalyptic warnings about the ruin of the country for his assessment of "the female mind." A pregnant woman had a particular responsibility to American men, since she may have been carrying a male in her womb. Sanity would be preserved by distinguishing between the teaching of boys and girls, and getting women to give up their mental efforts, thereby reducing both their own tendency to insanity and that of their offspring.[25] Once more the precarious order of democratic society depended on woman's subordination of herself. And, said Brigham, if men could not believe that would work, they had either to get away entirely from women they increasingly felt to be a danger to their bodies and their society or else to find new ways of controlling them.

There remains the issue of the connection between the pressures driving democratic men insane and the assertions in Brigham and Ray of woman's particular liability to insanity. The implication in Brigham, that women were responsible for the health and sanity of American society, derived from the same assumptions as those behind the separation of spheres generally. Like those assumptions, they expressed the pressures on men in democracy and the needs those pressures generated. Men needed to assume that women were the source of their society's curable insanity. This emerges clearly in Edward Jarvis's 1850 consideration "Of the Comparative Liability of Males and Females to Insanity, and Their Comparative Curability and Mortality When Insane."[26]

Men's use of the head in a mental and physical sense was, Jarvis said, more dangerous than women's. Headship was naturally man's. Men became mentally obsessed, "bent" as they were "on the acquisition of wealth." Jarvis was to elaborate on that "obsession" in his 1852 article considering the question of the increase of insanity. The article explained the pressures driving men mad by way of the dissolution of the old hierarchy, and consequent perplexity of a variety of insurmountable obstacles. Jarvis's second "head" cause of male insanity, like the first falling under this rubric of perplexity of insurmountable possibilities, was "excess of study, excessive devotion to various interests and pursuits, and anxiety about political or other success. . . . Men are more devoted to books, and investigations, and theories. They are more ungoverned [than women] in their ambition and eagerness to accomplish their purposes of gaining knowledge or for the advancement of science." Part of women's advantage in this must have been that ungovernable men governed women for them. And third, Jarvis argued, men's headship was literally more vulnerable; they were three times as liable to injuries of the head as women.[27]

Women on the other hand were more liable to insanity from "heart" causes. "The temperament of females is more ardent, and more nervous than that of the males. Women are more under the influence of the feelings and emotions, while men are more under the government of the intellect." The last clause is perhaps wishful thinking, given Jarvis's account of men's ungovernable ambition. (The wish was shaped in the context of the need to govern women who lacked the intellect to govern themselves.) Women were more easily wounded through "affections and tender sensibilities." They were more "timid" than men and "less acquainted with the realities of the outer world, and less used to exposures and dangers." But women had been fulfilling male demands in cultivating that kind of "shrinking delicacy."[28]

According to Jarvis, part of men's difficulty in self-government was their sexual eruptibility: they had "stronger passions and more powerful appetites and propensities." A manifestation of this lack of sexual control in men, uniquely recorded in American asylums and repeated several times by Jarvis, was masturbation. If women could not govern "feeling" and "affection" by their weaker intellects, they did have an innate lack of desire, a "sensibility" that allowed them greater "self-control" than men. At the same time "all the various and manifold derangements of the reproductive system, peculiar to females, add to the causes of mental disorder." The connection between a woman's organs and her liability to insanity would later provide the basis for the century's most radical attempt to control disorderly women. "Among these causes [of insanity] females are alone exposed to those which grow out of the uterine and mammary structure and functions. The puerperal condition, lactation, and catamenial irregularities, are then so many causes of mental disorder."[29]

Jarvis felt that to determine the relative liability of each sex to insanity, "we must inquire which sex is most exposed to the influences that produce it, or which has the most power to resist them." He concluded that the "realities of the world" to which men were exposed, together with their greater "sexual passion," made them more liable to insanity than women. The sexual expression on which Jarvis dwelt was masturbation. Moreover, in accordance with Esquirol's dictum and, it may be suggested, with Jarvis's own existential sexual priorities, he concluded that these male liabilities were inevitable. That men were "more given to masturbation and sensuality . . . more involved in business . . . more interested in property, in politics, in schemes of aggrandizement, and in pursuit of knowledge" made them "more frequently bankrupt or disappointed, or overwrought with labor and anxiety." They traveled more frequently and involved themselves "in strifes and bloody quarrels"; and all of these "exciting causes" made men prone to insanity. But Jarvis was describing the restless, insatiable, vicissitudinous, and essential nature of male society, to which women were ancillary. The male tendency to insanity was ineluctable. Curability was dictated by such values. The "mental disorders that grow out of afflictions, domestic troubles and disappointments, which are among the leading causes of female lunacy, seem to be somewhat more curable than those that are produced by causes connected with property, business and poverty, which are prominent among the causes of insanity among men." The respective mortality of the sexes reflected this difference in curability.[30]

The effect of all of this was first to register the enormous pressure on men, intensified by their feeling that it was a given of their society (the instability of which was accordingly and necessarily a given too), and of their sexual role within it. The characteristic disorder of boom and slump was, as Tocqueville put it, an "endemic disease" of the democratic "temperament." The corollary of accepting such conclusions about men was to direct social/medical/psychological expertise at that area of society that was not a given, that was not held by men to be so inalienable as the nature of their own existences, and consequently was more controllable, that is, to direct it at women. And a step beyond that was to concentrate on that part of woman that made her specially liable to insanity, her sexual organs. The second half of the nineteenth century saw the rise of gynecology, the subject of the next part of this book.

Part II

From Midwives to Gynecologists

7   The Absence of Midwives from America

One of the casualties of the male drive to take control of women was the midwife. The present contrast between America and the rest of the world in the matter of the delivery of babies is an example of the extremity of the division between the sexes in America.[1]

From the time of the first settlement until their exclusion in the first decades of the twentieth century, midwives delivered the vast majority of babies born in America. The male obstetricians' campaign against midwives seems to have intensified in proportion to the spread of the male behavioral style described by Tocqueville. It began in the second decade of the nineteenth century. In 1851 an anonymous female defender of midwives suggested that the demands of men to take over obstetrics represented "the customs of a perverted society." She asked, "What motive, but a lustful or mercenary one, can induce Physicians to make frequent examinations with the finger, or the speculum, when the highest medical authorities have declared such examinations generally *unnecessary,* and often hurtful; and when, in any case an educated woman could make them as well, at least as any man?" The obvious alternative, the educated female midwife, was one obstetricians and gynecologists rejected.[2]

How was it that men became obstetricians and then gynecologists during a century when "true womanhood" was nominally untouchable? The issue reached one focus during the 1850s, in the controversy over "demonstrative midwifery." Dr. James Platt White championed "the ocular perception of delivery" in the obstetrical

education of GPs. The American Medical Association's Committee
on Education pronounced such exposure of woman's genitals during
parturition to be unnecessary for teaching purposes "and stated that
knowledge pertaining to obstetrics could be obtained from descriptions, plates, and mannikins, and the sense of touch under a sheet."
In fact both views expressed male apprehensiveness over woman's
generative power, and the desire to control it. The latter was the
older attitude of circumscription by pedestal, and the former, the
new, more intrusive approach, heralded the emergence of "gynecology." It was men's anxieties about themselves, their fear of the
changing status of women, and their desire to conquer and control
the innermost power of nature that explains the overturning—in the
controlled, medical sphere—of the traditional shibboleth. Later
parts of the book provide a more detailed explanation. This chapter
describes the most decisive phase in the elimination of the midwife,
in the period 1900–1930.[3]

The final stage of the assault on midwives was considered by
reformers as part of the general reform of medicine. Another part
was medical education, criticized by the "devastating" Flexner
Report of 1910: it assumed that medical progress went hand in hand
with the systematic domination of midwives by "obstetric physicians." And medical reform was itself part of a change in the new
middle class, which Robert Wiebe calls a "revolution in identity."
Wiebe describes specialists in many areas of work at the turn of the
century "awakening both to their distinctiveness and to their ties
with similar people in the same occupation." They were eager "to
join others like themselves in a craft union, professional organization, trade association, or agricultural association." These various
groups made their skills the source of social prestige; they formalized entry requirements and championed a national vision of
progress, desiring "to remake the world upon their private models."[4]

If doctors did win some kind of new identity, it was at the expense
of women, both practitioners and patients. The "joining" of "like
people" together had as its corollary the extrusion of unlike from
professional standing: GPs, obstetricians, and gynecologists were
alike in respect of expertise—and of sex. One of what Wiebe calls
the "family" of triumphant specialties, obstetrics, saw its success
in terms of the elimination of women rivals, the culmination of a
long power struggle in which "the midwife lost her hold upon the
practice of obstetrics, and medical men began to realize that the
work was worthy of the best efforts of the best men." The "Amer-

ican Midwife Controversy" was resolved in favor of male experts. The "family" of medicine became homosexual.[5]

Doctors and obstetricians formulated and inspired two methods for the elimination of the midwife: propaganda and legislation. Most people believed that birth was usually a natural and healthy process, and that only exceptional circumstances required an expert. Obstetricians campaigned to reverse that belief. They set out to make mothers "fear" the dangers of pregnancy and childbirth, and think of "no precaution as excessive"; and then to comfort them with the assertion of their right to the care of the only ones who could provide it, the professional obstetricians. A doctor in the mid-1920s took the fact that 75 percent of deliveries in Pasadena had fallen into the hands of obstetricians in hospitals and demonstrated that the public in California was "being educated to the advantages of hospitalization in maternity cases." Obstetricians saw themselves as "idealists," concerned with "the long term good of the American mother." They could represent their propaganda campaign as a response to the Flexner Report's demand for the "creation of a public opinion which shall discriminate between the ill trained and the rightly trained physician." The midwife should be driven from the field (and the obstetrician enabled to raise his prices to attract "able men" into it). Since birth was unnatural, it was liable to affect the "patient's" health in any number of unpredictable ways, with which only a fully trained expert was qualified to cope. By the nature of her psychology and of her "surroundings" the midwife was incapable of being fitted for such responsibility. Midwives were "hopelessly dirty, ignorant and incompetent, relics of a barbaric past." Their abolition would halve the doctor's annoying competition in obstetrical cases. From the obstetrician's point of view it would finally reveal the value and preeminence of his specialty.[6]

So one method for the elimination of the midwife was propaganda, which dried up her market by persuading women that birth was so dangerous that they had to have obstetricians. But men did not leave the issue open to competition, although they claimed to do so even as they rigged the market. Those who proposed to reform and maintain female midwifery succeeded in establishing the Bellevue School for Midwives in New York in 1911 (which lasted for thirty years). This, said the outraged Dr. George Kosmak, to be editor during the 1920s of the *American Journal of Obstetrics and Gynecology,* gave midwives enough kudos to compete directly with doctors in the matter of fees. He refused to train them in his hospital, and worked toward legislation for their licensing. Admitting that the New York State Board of Health's new regulations (enacted between 1913 and 1915) would have the effect of eliminating the midwife, Kosmak, in the same paragraph, claimed that "the element of competition would do more to eliminate their practice than anything else." In addition to propaganda, then, obstetricians worked to eliminate the midwife by legislation.[7]

Before the Rochester Board of Education in Midwifery was appointed in 1895 there had been thirty to forty midwives delivering more than one-third of the recorded births in Rochester. By 1915 there were only nine, attending 18 percent of births. To gain a license there a midwife had to show "vastly greater practical experience" than a third-year medical student: but to practice she had to have a license. Catch-22. The Rochester City Health Officer at the time, Dr. George Goler, said flatly: "We do not want midwives." The deputy commissioner of health of the State of New York in 1915, Dr. Linsly Williams, held that, ideally, "it would be better to abolish the midwife." The New York City Board of Health first tried to control the midwife in 1907. In 1913 the State Legislature established a Public Health Council, which enacted a code for the licensing of midwives, progressively stiffer in 1914 and 1915. Among the provisions were the vouching for the midwife's moral character by medical authorities; her general appearance and habits of cleanliness; the examination of her home and outfit by a doctor's nurse. It is perhaps superfluous to contemplate doctors' reactions to the application of such provisions to themselves. The midwife had to have attended, under the supervision of a physician, no fewer than fifteen cases of labor, far more than the average physician at the time of his graduation. So she might very well have been supervised by a man less experienced than she. When the code first went into effect there were 439 midwives registered with various local authorities (outside Rochester and New York City). But during the first two years of the new state provisions, only 326 midwives were licensed: 113 had been squeezed out. Of these 326, only 134 spoke English, and only 38 were American or English. The vast majority were Polish, Italian, German, Austrian, and "Slavish." The new rules were bent at the bottom of the scale, where "poor foreigners" were attended by their own midwives, who could neither read nor write, but whose services were a *pis aller*. Midwives were allowed to practice where physicians refused to go, where the customer was too poor and too alien. Once such customers were Americanized to the extent of speaking English and earning more money, the physician could move in and the midwife be discarded. Defining scientific, male obstetrics as essential to natal care, American government agencies and official American medicine made access to it a function of success.[8]

The issue of immigrants' obstetrical care manifested a profound difference between those who defended midwives and those driving to eliminate them. Of the former, a woman obstetrician, Dr. Josephine Baker, felt that properly trained midwives were essential where "immigrant women, and particularly their husbands, would allow no male attendants. They expected the simple nursing care and household help that a doctor would not provide. . . . they rejected a hospital delivery, which would badly upset the home situation." R. H. Shryock suggests that immigrant women at the turn of the century were more welcoming to women doctors in the United States because they were used to midwives.[9] A crucial difference between immigrant and native attitudes here lay in the impact of male medical ideology. Americanization came to demand a straightening out of blurred lines, the blurring representing the European families' resistance to "outside" influences. Conversely, the professional obstetricians represented the opening up of the immigrant family to penetration by "outside" male expertise as an essential part of acculturation.[10]

Obstetricians like A. B. Emmons and J. L. Huntington argued that the existence of barbaric midwives in America was somehow the fault of the recent flood of immigration. The fact was, they wrote in 1912, that midwives are

> not a product of America. *They* have always been here, but only incidentally and only because America has always been receiving generous importations of immigrants from the continent of Europe. *We* have never adopted in any State a system of obstetrics with the midwife as the working unit. It has almost been a rule that the more immigrants arriving in a locality, the more midwives will flourish there, but as soon as the immigrant is assimilated, and becomes part of *our* civilization, then the midwife is no longer a factor in *his* home.[11] (My italics.)

The only acceptable female functionary in medicine was the utterly subordinated doctor's help, the wifelike nurse, who naturally had to share her master's views: Dr. Kosmak asserted in 1915 that "our American nurses" did not want to associate with such "personages" as midwives. The first midwife in fact had come over with the *Mayflower*. But the rewriting of obstetrical history was consistent with the intentions of antimidwife legislation and propaganda. Dr. Goler joined Emmons and Huntington in purging American history of the midwife. "The whole midwife problem in America is an attempt to engraft an old continental custom upon the people of the United States." The Flexner Report had called for a "medical patriotism on the part of the Physician" and assumed such a sentiment was essentially male. The attack on the midwife on the grounds that she was an un-American interloper went hand in hand with a growing anxiety about the sterility of WASP women in contrast to the sexually fecund immigrant. Dewees (1826) and Brigham (1833), concerned for the future of America, had advocated proper breeding and the restraint of the development of girls. The assault on midwives and, later in the nineteenth century, the coterminous rise of eugenics and of drastic gynecological surgery were aspects of a persistent, defensive attempt to control and shape women's procreative power. Such an attempt may be dated according to the intensification of male anxieties by democracy and by the Industrial Revolution.[12]

The campaign against midwives succeeded. In 1908 there were 3,000 midwives in New York City; by 1914 there were 1,700 delivering 53,000 babies a year, that is 37 percent of recorded births (compared to 40 percent overall for the United States in 1914). In 1919 the approximately 1,700 New York midwives delivered 40,000 babies, 30 percent of the total; and by 1929 the remaining 1,200 midwives delivered only 12 percent. The figure dropped to 270 in 1939, two in 1957, and the last one retired in 1963. Moreover, midwives seem to have survived longer in New York City because their ranks were strengthened by immigrant midwives and customers to whom native American doctors and obstetricians could not or would not cater. In Washington, D.C., midwives delivered 50 percent of babies in 1903, but only 12 percent by 1912. The professional obstetricians' attitude became official in Massachusetts in 1913: midwives were outlawed, and those who continued to practice were prosecuted. Conversely, GPs delivered 50 percent of recorded births in the United States in 1911 and 80 percent by 1929.[13]

Obstetricians may have been aided in their campaign by the increasing tendency to limit families, the limitation made possible by contraceptive education (which, ironically, obstetricians and gynecologists had fought against for so long). Pregnancy and parturition became rarer, and the latter came to be thought of as a major operation. The terms of this change would seem to bear out the effectiveness of the professionals' strategy. Frances Kobrin suggests that woman's desire for greater obstetrical care and her turning away from the "natural," domestic scene of childbirth were functions of her emancipation. In fact, contemporary suffragists identified their own demands with the idiom of medical reform, seeing themselves able to cure society of the ills caused by entirely male control. The outcome of obstetrical reform placed women's reproductive power completely in the hands of men. Women's accession to male obstetrical expertise also should be placed in the context of another aspect of feminism during the period, that is, the change from an ideology of universal rights to one that shared the nativist paranoia of the male citadel into which women demanded entrance. Doctors succeeded in associating midwives with immigrants and branding them un-American.[14]

So it is hard to see the midwife crisis as an emancipating one for women. Kobrin herself presents it as a campaign with the deliberate tactical exploitation of fear, and the postponement of better obstetrics for an enormous number of people, not because such obstetrics were not possible, but for reasons of "status," money, and the identity of professional men. If women were, as Kobrin says, "becoming increasingly self-conscious about their own welfare," infused with "the reforming zeal of Progressivism," they were not able to overbear the vision of the male obstetrical authorities, and to insist on the involvement of more women in more skill across sexual lines, by steadily raising the standards of existing midwives.[15]

Indeed, the defenders of midwives and of the idea of natural childbirth (called "naturalists") did manage to raise their standards by establishing successful programs in several eastern cities during the period 1920–1930. Programs in Philadelphia and Newark, for example, emphasized the communal function of the midwife and respect for the "modesty and integrity of the household." The reformed midwifery program in Newark compiled a much better record in terms of infant and maternal mortality between 1914 and 1916 than obstetrics in Boston, where midwives had been banned. Midwives waited and worked in a more personal way than doctors and obstetricians, helping to run the home before and after birth. Their care seems to have represented the successful adaptation of the traditional function long associated with women everywhere.[16]

At the forty-sixth annual meeting of the American Gynecological Society in 1921, Dr. Rudolph W. Holmes found it "lamentable that

properly controlled midwives have less mortality than those [i.e.,
obstetricians] who practice a routine intervention. The proponents
of operative cults have produced no evidence to show that their systems are more worthy, less risky, and promise a higher conservation of life than carefully watched spontaneous labor." The corollary to the notion of birth as usually unnatural and dangerous, even
a sickness, was the proliferation of "unnecessary operative interference." Doctors had added to parturient dangers: the "authorities
who have fostered a method of routine interference in all parturient
women . . . have retarded the advance in obstetric care, and are
part contributors to the high American mortalities incident to childbirth." A Dr. W. H. Allport held the then "modern" view in 1912
that Caesarean section should be performed immediately when labor
"became obstructed." The midwives' defenders resisted this kind of
expert encroachment, finding that babies could be delivered "normally" after Caesareans had been recommended for them by modern-
ist obstetricians. Mothers' actions also revealed that obstetricians'
diagnoses were out of touch with physiological reality. "Quite recently in this city [Buffalo], two women delivered themselves while
the surgeons were scrubbing up preparatory to Cesarean section."[17]
  Moreover, the successful exclusion of midwives meant that the
great volume of obstetrical practice had to be assumed by the general practitioners, who by definition had less specialized experience
of parturition than midwives and obstetricians, and most of whom
were the products of the shoddy and corrupt medical education
Abraham Flexner condemned. Medical schools released upon a
"helpless" community "a horde of ill-trained physicians . . . licensed to the practice of medicine without any serious thought as
to whether they had received a fair training or not." Even after the
beginning of reform, teaching obstetrics remained "the weakest
area. . . . Poor schools with poor facilities and poor professors
were turning out incompetent products who lost more patients from
improper practices than midwives did from infection." They "hud-
dled together" since they "prefer[red] competition in some already
over-occupied place." Whatever his training, the general practitioner was as convinced of his superiority to the midwife as was his
confrere, the obstetrician. In spite of these conditions, doctors and
obstetricians preferred to exclude the midwife rather than to discipline themselves. GPs took their lead in obstetrical work from obstetricians, and so, like them, were prone to try to speed up delivery
with instruments. Few mothers could afford obstetricians, there

were not enough obstetricians to go around, and in any case obstetricians preferred "to wait in comparative idleness for a few years" until they picked up "a more fashionable practice with high fees." Beneath the midwife controversy was the large social reality of "great masses of women . . . dependent upon the midwife and the busy and often unskilled general practitioner." The male specialists could not cope with the field to which they laid exclusive claim. Even a hostile obstetrician admitted in 1915 that 25 percent of births in New York State outside New York City would be deprived *entirely* of assistance when the midwife was eliminated.[18]

In 1926 Joseph De Lee described the maternal death rate for childbearing in Detroit as "appalling," and attributed the inadequate or absent prenatal care to the family physician's neglect of the 80 percent of the population between the wealthy and the "indigent" (who attended free clinics). And as far as parturition and postnatal care were concerned, clinics, hospitals, and doctors had failed completely to respond to the need created by the destruction of the midwife. Authorities agreed that the "glaring fault of high morbidity and morality in obstetrics . . . is that the neophyte in medicine is self-taught in obstetrics." Doctors refused "team-work" with other men, let alone with barbaric relics.[19]

In fact, De Lee accused doctors and obstetricians of neglecting that gamut of unpredictable dangers to which they argued parturient women were subject. They had excluded midwives on the grounds that midwives were incapable of noticing such inevitable risks. In De Lee's view, hospital deliveries in 1926 displayed carelessness, thoughtlessness, laziness, obstinacy, and parsimony; the *accoucheurs* were insensitive to hemorrhage, dangers in anesthesia, and exhaustion factors. They even failed to diagnose the baby's delivery position. "How many men think of these things during the conduct of labor? Not many or we would not have to bewail our [American] mortality statistics."[20]

These early-twenty-century doctors requiring the segregation of their work from women displayed some of the other characteristics of nineteenth-century American men.

A well known internist once insultingly remarked that an obstetrician had nothing to do but "watch a hole." Out on the frontier men have been shot for less provocation than that, but since the author has observed the work of many doctors a little more, he believes that man was right, that a good many obstetricians do nothing else than watch a hole. Some of them do not even do that. They sit in the doc-

tors' room at the hospital, and swap stories and smoke cigarettes instead of watching the patient, and in the meantime the baby can die,
or the mother can have a hemorrhage, or labor can go on until she is
exhausted, or an occipito-posterior can become persistent, or something may happen which should not have happened, and which could
have been prevented, if the man had been on the job.

There was perhaps a limit to the extent that boring, undramatic,
natural childbirth could be made "unnatural," and, in any case,
obstetrics had long suffered from the derogatory attitude on the part
of more spectacular medical specialties. Obstetricians themselves
had recently expanded their specialty into the more decisive and
flamboyant possibilities of "gynecology" and gynecological surgery.
That way they were able to identify with the heroic, masterful male
identity represented by Natty Bumppo and Wild Bill Hickok, seeing medical rivalry in terms of a western gunfight. The obstetrician
was concerned with his standing in the eyes of other men and accepted the devaluative connotations of the labeling of his woman
patient as "a hole." The terms suggest the common ground—the
sexual one—between internist and obstetrician, while the story
swapping and cigar smoking invoked the atmosphere of the bachelor clubs.[21]

Attempts since the 1920s to revive the midwife as the "nurse midwife" have been made among the untouchables—Indians, blacks,
Chicanos, and the Appalachian poor.[22] Proponents still faced opposition from what has become the central tradition of medical authority, vigorously male.[23] A leader in the attempt to revive midwifery
in the 1920s and 1930s declared: "Medical and nursing educational
systems in the United States . . . rejected the idea of educating
and using the services of the trained midwife. . . . They have developed, instead, an ideal plan . . . [fixing] the full responsibility
for planning and for carrying out the plan for patients' care upon
the physician." A nursing textbook written by a female nurse declares that "the training of nurses in midwifery has been prevented
by the attitude of the medical profession, who have held the ideal
that every woman should be delivered by a physician."[24] The current assault on such authority by women qua women and by medical reformers has coincided with a renewed interest in the naturalist view.

In 1929 Dr. Howard Haggard pooh-poohed the ancient Athenian
law that midwives must be women past childbearing who had had a
child. He did so on the grounds that it was "in effect as if it had been

said that the requirements for a surgeon were that he had passed the age of fighting and had been wounded." The analogy of childbirth and wound was perfectly consistent with the view that parturition was normally dangerous, not only not a natural physiological process, but a condition that had to be cured. It is a view that still prevails in many official quarters. Dr. Robert B. Nelson, Jr., chairman of the District of Columbia Medical Society's Committee on Obstetrics and Gynecology, believes that having a baby is "an operation . . . a medical procedure . . . after all, the labor room is an operating room, and this is an operation. . . . No one would let a man in if his wife's uterus was being removed. I can't see that there is any difference." He equates the emergence of life with the destruction of part of it. The reporter who gleaned this admission amplified his account of Nelson's view. "For him . . . the easiest method of delivery is one in which the woman is heavily sedated, labor is frequently hastened with drugs and forceps are used, . . . a procedure in which it is quite accurate to say the woman is a patient whose condition is terminated by a medical action." "Patienthood" is of course defined, even created, by the doctor. "Delivery rooms became operating rooms, obstetricians became surgeons, not because childbirth is inherently so difficult but because . . . doctors have made it so."[25]

The century-long campaign against midwives was an expression of the struggle to establish the male specialty of obstetrics and gynecology. Before describing that development, it is necessary to describe the general characteristics of American medicine in the nineteenth century.

8   Democratic Doctors

Ben Franklin had published his model for free, democratic man's behavior, issuing "rules for mobilizing and multiplying personal energy." Once the energy came to be seen as overwhelmingly physiological, it was appropriate that medical doctors take over the democratic publication of the rules for its cossetting.[1]

In 1825 Dr. Dewees took it upon himself to tell mothers what to do "with the earliest formation of the embryo." He adjured men and women to choose mates according to the highest physical standards (defined of course by doctors) and to fulfill their "duties to society" by reproducing those same standards, the precedent for such a concern the Enlightenment preoccupation with the improvement of livestock by selective breeding. Amariah Brigham postulated the "ruin" of the United States unless body and mind were developed correctly. His reviewer in the *Boston Medical and Surgical Journal* recognized the doctor's claims to tell society what to do: "we would that it were the . . . great and sovereign guide, of every male and female in the country. . . . Were it so, the next generation would be vastly superior to the present both in bodily vigor and mental energy," terms carrying a specific meaning for each generation's bodily economy, and a vision to evolve into programs for the eugenic breeding and sterilization of humans. Confronting "the flood of moral turpitude and mental disease which is sweeping over the country," Dr. Cook assumed the responsibility of directing "American homes" to their "legitimate work" in mental hygiene, the development and preservation of mental health in concert with the harmonious development of the body. The terms of such analysis and exhortation contradicted Cook's earlier statement that the "evil is beyond the reach of the legislator or the physician." Doctors dispensed rules on the grandest scale. When social values were based on the body, doctors had good claim to social authority.[2]

The nature of the major problem Isaac Ray felt confronted America in 1860 meant its detection depended on "medical men." His book *Mental Hygiene* was designed to alert the general reader to the "appalling magnitude of the evil." This evil was that the "amount of mental power which has . . . been destroyed is infinitely greater . . . than that which has been suffered to work out its destined purpose."[3] Civilization depended on the proper working out of mental power. But the nature of democratic life led to the compulsive expenditure of energy which made American men "crave the excitement of work as something necessary to their very existence." Such appetite rapidly consumed men's energies and their "elasticity" of power to replace them; so too did the hyperestimation of speed in America which tended to precipitate the "vital movements of the brain, and consequently to consume its energies faster than they can be supplied."[4]

Ray's generalizations about democratic psychology coincided with those of Tocqueville. According to Ray, "Impulsive dashes at speculation take the place of well-matured, far-reaching plans; and reckless adventure suits the humor of the times . . . the mercantile spirit of our times leads to a fitful and feverish activity of mind." In short, Ray measured what he called the popular mind of the American social body as a whole against the fundamental law of animal economy, and found it wanting. *Mental Hygiene* supplied the blueprint for the national application of the systematic concentration of energies, in the face of the nation's own appetite to consume them.[5]

Ray's definition of "hygienic effect" was the "quickening" of "torpid energies" to prevent the "current of . . . mental life from becoming utterly stagnant." Mental hygiene had the precise meaning of mobilizing human resources to a balanced energy level, enough for success, but not to the extent that would lead to insanity (in accordance with Esquirol's view): "most men go through life with a large amount of latent power undeveloped, and utterly unable to concentrate their energies on any particular point. To accomplish the most with a given amount of original endowment is a result that can come only from a course of suitable discipline."[6]

Ray listed the kinds of people who were not economically mobilized. He exhorted all men to adopt his program, emphasizing "independent, self-originating" activity, distinct from the mass behavior controlled by what he called the "law of sympathy." The law of sympathy rested on "instinctive tendencies": in the sympathetic process the "intellect is entirely passive." It was not surprising that Ray presented women as especially liable to this mass behavior. The best girls, he was to point out in his article on insanity by way of seduction, were submissive. Women had "little power of endurance" and were not candidates for the program of mental hygiene. His parade of exemplars for the preparation for success in the world of work was unrelievedly male, as the majority of his examples of mass behavior were female. All of this suggests that the one certain way in which men could distinguish themselves from the law of sympathy was simply in contrast to the given existence of women. If a paradoxical result of Ray's advice to men would be another kind of mass behavior (all men seeing themselves as self-originating), at least it would be distinct from the mass (and non-self-originating) behavior of women.[7]

That Ray was able to adopt a "popular phrase" to characterize the law of animal economy suggests the popularity of the notion. "By insanity, paralysis, and other organic lesions, brains are now 'used up' in the popular phrase, with a frequency full of instruction."[8] Further refinement of the meaning of "energy" will explain how the movement for sex hygiene rested on the same assumptions; so too probably did the popular idea of "being spent," and of "spending" in copulation. The ubiquity of the "fundamental law of animal economy" created an audience peculiarly avid for medical expertise. American men valued themselves according to an autonomy ultimately physiological.[9]

Ray devoted a large portion of *Mental Hygiene* to the recent and "unhealthy" dissemination of "exciting" popular literature, stimulating the "prurient imagination," purposeless, evanescent in its utility to the bodily economy: "he . . . whose reading is calculated only to inflame the imagination with pictures of unhallowed enjoyment, to banish every manly thought and pure emotion, to extend the empire of passion, and induce him to fill his measure of happiness with things that perish in the using, is weakening all the conservative principles of his mind." Ray described youth's being led by vicious books to "abandon himself" to "indulge himself in secret with such means as nature has provided," that is, to masturbation. But Ray's account of the process could have had the same effect as the process it described, a problem persistently bothering those whom in their *Cyclopaedia* Evert and George Duyckinck termed "molders of their age" finding it necessary to preach "a gospel of real manhood and real womanhood." Dr. Gardner felt that the "delicacy of the theme requires some reticence of expression . . . to make the desired impression upon the minds of my readers, and yet so guardedly, as not to minister to the prurient curiosity of the thoughtless or the depraved." The Reverend John Todd took refuge in describing the effects of masturbation in Latin.[10]

The medical "molders" of Ray and Gardner's life spans (1807–1881, 1821–1876, respectively) were not nearly so confident as Rush and Franklin had been (1745–1813, 1706–1790). Medicine and politics had been permeated by the rational optimism of the Enlightenment between 1750 and 1800, when American doctors established the first hospitals, medical schools, institutional libraries, professional guilds, and state medical societies in the new nation. Doctors participated in the successful revolution as politicians and surgeons general. "Professional pride" and "patriotic emotion" had reinforced each other. Dr. Rush had signed the Declaration of Independence and had been a delegate to the Constitutional Convention and a treasurer of the U.S. Mint. As he had assisted in this implementation of Enlightenment political thought (shot through, of course, with traditionalism and historicism), so, too, he had developed a medical system representing the underlying unity of all diseases, like the coterminous belief in the unity of human psychology. Rush asserted the revolutionary and independent quality of his theory, yet it harked back to classical theory. Indeed, like American republicanism, it was in some respects more conservative than contemporary European ideas. Perhaps in his assertion of American medical identity Rush reflected another facet of that momentary assumption of that responsibility for self implied by Bailyn and Jordan's accounts of Revolutionary thought.[11]

At the same time Rush's work included themes in partial and contradictory form which would emerge full blown in later medicine, very much like the eventual distortion of his fellow Father's persona, "endless rules, regimens, exercises, resolves and drills inflating Benjamin Franklin's simple code into a mania. . . ." If, as later doctors also believed, Rush held that woman's physiology made her more prone to insanity, he pointed out that she was more easily cured. His advocacy of a *via media* between sexual excess and sexual restraint was explained (as was everything in his monistic theory) "in terms of tension and laxity in the nervous or vascular systems," which anticipated the debit and credit of bodily economy law. But Rush's version coexisted with a greater ease over sexuality, in spite of his occasional apprehensions of the weakening effects of "onanism."[12] While promiscuous sexual intercourse with women could also lead to "seminal weakness," it was "transient" compared to the effects of masturbation. But Rush was not obsessed with masturbation as his successors would be. He advised the reading of novels, with none of the qualms Ray betrayed.[13] And if the ambiguity of the bachelor of 1850 was foreshadowed in *Medical Inquiries,* Rush also advised men to engage in sexual relations in order to prick the bubble of "Revery."[14]

So Rush recommended "mixing with the sex." While, like later (and preceding) doctors, he conceived a *"furor uterinus"* in a frustrated woman and the "greater delicacy of the female sex," he also accepted the *health* of a woman with sexual appetite. One of his female patients regularly practiced "pious habits" during her derangement. "Her recovery was marked by the gradual neglect of her devotion, and by a return of the gay and dissipated practices of her middle life." That view may be compared with, say, Tocqueville's and Cooper's accounts of American women. Sixty years or so after Rush's death doctors found it necessary to apply surgery to women who displayed erotic tendencies. The later obsession with man's bodily economy inevitably demanded rigid separation of the sexes, a denial of woman's sexuality, and a very strong tendency to leave women altogether.[15]

The transition from the confidence of Rush's all-embracing system to the narrow despair, even "nihilism" of mid-nineteenth-century medicine resembled the political transition from the hierarchical republicanism of the last decades of the eighteenth century to the turbulent new politics of "Jacksonian democracy" in whichever of the first three decades of the nineteenth century one places it. It resembled, too, the change William Appleman Williams and Scheiber both describe, from the rational planning of public, governmental concern to government's capitulation to laissez-faire. Drs. William Shippen, Jr., and John Morgan had managed to submerge their bitter differences in the first medical school at Pennsylvania Hospital during the 1760s, and Rush had "urged an end to quarrels over scientific matters": yet his observation that "the whole odium of the hostility of physicians to each other" was simply a result of "competition for business and money" boded ill once such competition had been given full rein. Laissez-faire became the standard appeal against any attempts to raise medical standards, and early twentieth-century obstetricians objected to state recognition of midwives on the same grounds.[16]

The competing attempts at social reform were of the nature of Ray's mass appeal for autonomous regeneration; doctors no longer devoted their energies to political activities in the way that Rush had done, any more than they could commit themselves to a theory of universal medical truth. In fact, Perry Miller headed the second part of his outline about doctors in his projected intellectual history of the nineteenth century "The Search for Identity." Doctors' uncertainty was, in effect, the expression of the contradiction between radically opposed theories of medical knowledge.[17] The realization produced bewilderment and self-doubt, which the doctors communicated to their patients. Clients approached experts with the same Tocquevillean impatience the latter demanded of themselves. The ground was ripe for quacks, who sprang up like dragon's teeth and, in turn, intensified the pressure of expectation and disappointment in both "orthodox" practitioners and the public. All that doctors seemed capable of doing was to disprove one another's theories.[18]

The apprenticeship of seventeenth- and eighteenth-century medical training gave way in the nineteenth to the "distinctly American product . . . the commercial medical school," a process whose anxieties contemporary doctors like Edward Jarvis described, and whose possibilities Franklin represented in his account of breaking away from the traditional formulation of youth. Abraham Flexner pointed out that the deans of medical schools were more skillful at appealing to poor boys than they were at teaching medicine. The growth of nineteenth-century medical education followed the same course as Ohio or Pennsylvania canal and railroad construction.

> These enterprises . . . were frequently set up regardless of opportunity or need: in small towns as readily as in large, and at times almost in the heart of the wilderness . . . essentially . . . moneymaking in spirit and object . . . business throve. . . . Rivalry between the schools [was] ludicrously bitter . . . in attempting to monopolize the spoils.

The result was overproduction and further competition, intensified by the proliferation of quacks and, beginning in the 1850s, the "unexpected intrusion of women doctors."[19]

In both economic and theoretical senses the "speculations" of nineteenth-century doctors were unchecked. Tocqueville's explanation of why Americans were "addicted" to practical rather than theoretical science was that the "calm . . . necessary to the deeper combinations" could not be found amid the "incessant conflict of jarring interests, this continual striving of men after fortune." His account was as appropriate to a doctor as it was to any other democratic American male who "perpetually has to rely on ideas that he has not had leisure to search to the bottom . . . in the long run he risks less in making use of some false principles than in spending his time in establishing all his principles on the basis of truth . . . the daily study of the fleeting passions of the multitude, the accidents of the moment, and the art of turning them to account decide all . . . affairs" of the democratic world. Dr. Gardner described the doctor's experience of this anxiety to the readers of *Frank Leslie's Illustrated Newspaper* in 1872: the "great trouble that is met with is in the positive assertions respecting simple observations being often found to be false and valueless by more honest or competent investigators coming after." American doctors were also more subject to religious precepts than European experts (in the matters of treatment of the insane and of anesthesia, for example), and more vulnerable to the enormous power of public opinion. Medicine was often considered "stupendous humbug." Yet doctors did have power over life and death, and did persuade female patients to do as they were told, to the extent of the patients' having parts of their bodies cut off to cure nervous disorders. Women were eventually persuaded to believe that childbearing was unnatural.[20]

Not only was the doctor's expertise relative and transient, it was secondhand. What the astronomer Simon Newcomb said of science generally was abundantly true of the abundant[21] doctors. "The fact is that our science was little more than a timid commentary on European science." European models were followed, he said, as slavishly as medieval schoolmen followed Aristotle.[22] From the time of the first one (Cotton Mather's), American medical treatises had been derivative. Apart from the Revolutionary moment of Rush's native assertion, American doctors had to acknowledge with William Dewees in 1833 that "we have almost exclusively depended upon European publications for information upon almost every subject connected with medical science." Even Rush had had some trouble distinguishing his ideas from those of the Edinburgh school when he and his contemporaries were trained, and, in broad outline, the Founding Fathers' creation is a shadow of the British constitution. But between 1800 and 1840 American medicine experienced a complete swing from Rush's doctrine to the extreme empiricism generated by the Paris school: the "deluge of material" from the new French research reached America in the 1820s, and thereafter American trainees (Dr. Gardner among them) made their pilgrimages to Paris, and claims for the "superiority of American medicine were rarely heard."[23]

This was the pattern for the rest of the nineteenth century, American doctors going to Europe for any advanced medical training, and waves of European expertise succeeding each other's crossing of the Atlantic. The "really capable and energetic students" were going to Germany for their training after the Civil War. "Alienists"—doctors specializing as superintendents of insane asylums (forerunners of psychiatrists)—were similarly vulnerable to transient truths, dependent on European thought, and similarly riven by factionalism throughout the century. For them, too, the dead Rush was the only American authority comparable to Europeans. At mid-century American superintendents of asylums claimed their superiority to Europeans in that their democratically raised patients were more violent and therefore demanded the tougher restraining methods the superintendents patriotically supplied. Eventually the latter had to acknowledge their part in the interactive cycle, that the patients' violence increased in proportion to the violence used in restraining them, and vice versa. The disparity between Europe and America in psychiatric care and research grew larger during the second half of the century. In 1900 almost all the leading American philosophers, scientists, and doctors were careful to spend at least a year in a French or German university. America was culturally still a European colony. "Fully aware of the derivative nature of their formal standards of learning, Americans vacillated between asserting their own adequacy and independence and a frank Anglophilia or Francophilia or Germanophilia." The one apparent exception to the depressing dependence on European medicine lay in the area of gynecological surgery.[24]

9   The Rise of Gynecology

Until today in most of the world, and until the end of the nineteenth century in the United States, childbirth has been in the hands of women. The occasional "man-midwives" of the sixteenth and seventeenth centuries were criticized by woman-midwives and looked down on by doctors. Toward the end of the seventeenth century man-midwives began to be a little more widely accepted in Europe and America. In England, William Smellie, William Hunter, Thomas Denman, and a growing number of man-midwives concentrated on obstetrical research and established schools for the teaching of midwifery to men and women. These new experts still aimed, as their Renaissance predecessors had, at spreading their improved techniques among the general practitioners of obstetrics, that is, midwives, but increasingly they feared these agents were resistant to change and progress, and they began to emphasize the greater competence of man-midwives. The decisive encroachment on the field of midwifery by men and instruments was another edge of the mechanization of social workings, of the Faustian stirrings that would reach still greater climaxes in the nineteenth-century articulation, control, and expenditures of all kinds of power in the interests of white men.[1]

Elizabeth Nihell, a well-known midwife in the eighteenth century, recognized that the assaults by men and by instruments were sides of the same coin. In 1760 she challenged male obstetricians' arrogation to themselves of superiority and attacked the

insufficiency, danger, and actual destructiveness of instruments in the art of midwifery . . . crotchets, knives, scissors, spoons, pinchers, fillets, speculum matricis, all of which and especially the forceps whether Flemish, Dutch, Irish, French or English, bare or uncovered, long or short, straight or crooked, windowed or not windowed, are totally useless or rather worse than good for nothing, being never but dangerous and often destructive. . . . to arms! to arms! is the word; and what are those arms by which they maintain themselves but those instruments, those weapons of death.

While man-midwives competed with one another in the invention of new instruments during this "great age of obstetrics" (the latter part of the eighteenth century), "the sight of a man-midwife struck terror in the hearts of most women." Man-midwives were advised to hide their various kinds of cutting instruments in bags and pockets as they approached the pregnant patient. All of the new instruments except the forceps were for killing the fetus, for cutting it into bits and drawing them out, without anesthesia, needless to say. Even forceps could be and were mutilating in effect.[2]

But during the eighteenth century the lines between new technological expertise and the traditional practitioner did not correspond rigidly to the distinction between male and female roles. Evidence of the nonalignment between sexual role and obstetrical expertise in the eighteenth century is the teaching of male and female midwives by obstetricians in both Europe and America at that time (although there seems to be no account of women obstetricians teaching). Edinburgh created a chair of midwifery in 1739 for the instruction of men and women; the University of Paris introduced a course for student midwives in 1745, and William Shippen did the same in Philadelphia in 1762. It was not until the nineteenth century that the alignment of scientific medicine and sexuality would become a central tenet of the characterological ideology most fiercely articulated by those whose job it was to grasp sexuality scientifically, that is, by gynecologists. Even then, rigid role alignments themselves hindered such gynecological claims and added a dimension to the problems of the authenticity of nineteenth-century medical authority. Man-midwives continued to endure the opposition of other physicians even after the establishment of their specialty.[3]

By the time of the American Revolution, obstetricians were established in Europe and America, with publications, museums, prestige, lying-in hospitals, and considerable acceptance of the authority of their teachings by midwives. The discovery of childhood and victories of middle-class notions of familial and sexual values, both associated with the rise of the modern industrial and commercial economy, provided the conditions for the obstetricians' success. The picture must not be overdrawn: midwifery was still in the hands of "ignorant women dominated by inveterate prejudices." Obstetricians remained dependent on the desires of rich women throughout the nineteenth century, and these customers were the last to want to clutter themselves with unwanted babies and the first to learn about new effective contraceptive techniques, facts which nineteenth-century obstetricians bewailed; they made their expertise irrelevant. Most people continued to rely on midwives in the belief that birth was a natural process. What was of significance was the establishment of a male bridgehead.[4]

During the late nineteenth century obstetrics expanded into gynecology; the great obstetricians were invariably gynecologists. Just as the specialists expanded their mastery from a phase of woman's generative process to the exploration and mastery of its entire ebb and flow, so abdominal surgery developed largely out of gynecology, and then in some sense, psychology out of gynecology: women provided the guinea pigs for modern surgery and psychology. Advances in pathology, cellular theory, embryology, bacteriology, and other aspects of physiology and anesthesia were applied to gynecology, and that focal point of nineteenth-century medicine benefited enormously from the discoveries of Joseph Lister. The gynecologists increased their armamentarium in the age of the railroad. An aspect of this development was the opening of hospitals and similar institutions for the isolation of diseased women and children, and their treatment by the men who wielded the powerful new knowledge.[5]

A striking aspect of gynecological history in the nineteenth century was the appearance of American gynecologists onto an international medical stage. This was consistent with the unique place of gynecology in the history of American medicine. The origins of formal medical education lay with William Shippen's course of lectures on midwifery. The first specialized medical journal (if the *American Journal of Insanity* can be discounted) was an obstetrical journal. This originality lay in sheer operative daring, not in theory or laboratory research. Some of the operations which Americans pioneered—ovariotomy, hysterectomy, and the repair of the vesicovaginal fistula—were hazarded under the most primitive conditions, and American triumphs in this particular area of medicine are all the more intriguing in that research facilities were almost nil at the time of the operations. No American city was a research center in the way that Paris, London, or Vienna was. Yet by the second half of the century, New York was a gynecological leader, exchanging teachers, practitioners, and discoveries with Edinburgh, Paris, and London.[6]

Ephraim McDowell first performed ovariotomy on a pioneer wife on a plank on the Kentucky frontier in 1809. The American J. Marion Sims (the subject of Chapter 10) was held to have launched "the new medical specialty" of gynecology, and Sims, the brothers Atlee, T. Gaillard Thomas, and Thomas Addis Emmett led Europe in operative gynecology for years. The peculiar preeminence of American gynecology in nineteenth-century medicine was an expression of the hypostasis of sexual identity at the same time by men bent on controlling women, and the campaign against midwives conducted by gynecologists was a variant of the separation of the sexes in society at large.[7]

In 1848, the year of the first Woman's Rights Convention, Dr. Charles Meigs had indicated the direction that post–Civil War gynecologists would take. He had advised his pupils that their study of female organs would command an understanding of woman's whole being. Woman's

> intellectual and moral perceptivity and forces . . . are feminine as her organs are. Beyond all these, you shall have to explore the history of those functions and destinies which her sexual nature enables her to fulfill, and the strange and secret influences which her organs, by their nervous constitution, and the functions, by their relation to her whole life-force, whether in sickness or health, are capable of exerting, not on the body alone, but on the heart, the mind, and the very soul of woman. The medical practitioner has, then, much to study, as to the female, that is not purely medical—but psychological and moral rather: such researches will be a future obligation lying heavily on you. . . .

Meigs's analysis here was consistent with that in Brigham (1832), Jarvis (1850), and Ray (1863), all of whom had emphasized woman's especial liability to insanity by way of her body's peculiar dominance. In 1866 Ray stated expressly that all women hovered on the verge of hysteria, insanity, and crime. "With woman it is but a step from extreme nervous susceptibility to downright hysteria, and from that to overt insanity. In the sexual evolution, in pregnancy, in the parturient period, in lactation, strange thoughts, extraordinary feelings, unseasonable appetites, criminal impulses, may haunt a mind at other times innocent and pure." It was woman's sexuality that made her mad. I suggested that because man's mad-

dening pressure was a given of civilization, the experts said or assumed that man's insanity was harder to cure, and, conversely, that
woman's was easier. And, until mid-century, the experts had concentrated on programs for the support of *man's* physique and
mentality.[8]

After the Civil War men increasingly emphasized woman's contribution to society's sickness and implemented programs to restrain women. Once "the whole movement of modern medicine"
settled on medical materialism (consistent with a generally more
materialistic society, as Tocqueville had anticipated) it was logical that those beings whose insanity had long been held traceable
to material causes—their female organs—should receive the benefits
of the most up-to-date surgery. Obstetricians and gynecologists
(which obstetricians became as they claimed more and more territory and social importance) shared the anxieties of other doctors.
They devalued women as most men did. The gynecological crescendo
was part of the tendency Donald Meyer has called a "special pathology." "The repression being imposed in the 50's and nailed down
in the 70's was a special pathology, not the disciplined, long-prac-
tised style, but a defensive, emergency ideology. . . . Men had
their own passion, and at the prospect of emancipated women re-
coiled with that fright special to those addicted to an obsession."[9]

The men pursuing somaticism, that is, focusing on the physicality
of the body, were disenchanted and pessimistic, moods which seem
to have run through American society generally in the late 1860s
and 1870s. The social breakdown following the Civil War can be
taken as a frame of reference for the rise of gynecology. Among the
identifiable symptoms were the failures and corruption of Recon-
struction, the longest depression in American history, insatiable
trusts, swarms of what were held to be sexually potent and racially
inferior immigrants, and a government discredited at all levels. According to Robert Wiebe, people responded to these changes with
a reassertion of the "old bedrock values." They were laced with the
paranoia endemic to American history. The Civil War had perhaps
dramatized the crudest source of identity, the sexual distinction
between fighting men and nonfighting women, a line that had already been sharpened as a reaction to the women's rights movement.
In 1852 Dr. Gardner, the obstetrician, gynecologist, and general
practitioner, had lashed out at disorderly women, lumping together
feminists, Bloomer wearers, and midwives. "At the present time
there is a proposition mooted—springing from the same high source

which advocates womans rights, the Bloomer costume, and other similar nonsensical theories—to give again the portion of the healing art, if not the whole domain of medicine, to the females," that is, to midwives. His remarks followed chronologically James Platt White's successful opening up of woman's genitals to ocular observation.[10]

Doctors were in no wise apart from the postwar apprehensions Wiebe identifies. One change which seemed to them to affect the constitution and health of the social body was the nature of mass immigration. In 1872 there was, according to Gardner, "more necessity to direct our attention to cleanliness, because this country is being filled up with various nations of foreigners, some whole classes among them are essentially and entirely dirty." Another and, perhaps, more profoundly felt apprehension was what doctors perceived as the increasing disorderliness of women. Body business may have made doctors even more sensitive to the sexual line than other democrats. But women challenged doctors professionally too. By the mid-1870s women had arrived in medicine: the first woman member of the American Medical Association sat silently through attempts to oust her at the annual meeting of 1876.[11]

Doctors at the pinnacle of their profession revealed an abysmal sense of vulnerability to changing sex roles. The president of the AMA in 1871, Dr. Alfred Stillé, warned that certain women "seek to rival men in manly sports and occupations, and the 'strong-minded' ape them assiduously in all things, even in dress. In doing so, they may command a sort of admiration such as all monstrous productions acquire, especially when they tend toward a higher type than their own." Like Marvel's bachelor, Stillé assumed only two characterological slots: if woman was changing roles, she could only be becoming a man. Moreover, he construed this disorderliness on a vertical scale. Woman moved up from under, from a position beneath man, naturally closer to the animal. The relations of men and women on such a scale exposed the pedestal rhetoric for what it was, although characteristically (as we shall see in relation to Todd and Gardner) Stillé reiterated that form of the scale later in the same speech: "If, then, woman is unfitted by nature to become a physician, we should, when we oppose her pretensions, be acquitted of any malicious or even unkindly spirit. We may admit that she is in some sense a perfected man, and was created a little less lower than the angels. . . ."[12] Seen at that elevation, the difference between man and woman was woman's greater perfectedness; and, conversely,

man's distinction from woman (defined by sex organs), his penis and
testicles, was a degrading imperfection. One must allow here the
possibility of an element of admiration or envy, even a desire to
emulate woman—after all, such angels were spared the ordeal of
perplexing and sordid traffic with the world.

On the other hand, Stillé shuddered at the idea of man perfecting
himself according to such a standard. Following a sentence referring
to man-rivaling women as "monstrous productions," Stillé said "a
man with feminine traits of character, or with the frame and carriage of a female, is despised by both the sex he ostensibly belongs
to, and that of which he is at once a caricature and a libel." Emulation or horror, either sentiment implied castration, even at a level
that was not "ostensible."

While Stillé compared each sex to the other, he asserted an in-
transigent distance between them. The ambiguity represented his
fear that the gap was closing, and democracy was heading toward
that "preposterous medley of the works of nature" against which
Tocqueville had warned. In Stillé's view, women were characteristically uncertain in rational judgment, capricious of sentiment,
fickle of purpose, and indecisive of action. Men excelled women even
in activities "essentially feminine," including cookery, hairdressing,
and dressmaking: if the line was to be maintained, women must be
confined to a diminishing compass. Yet such an assertion of the expansion of male competence clearly had a dangerous aspect for
Stillé, given his horror of feminine men. To have it that men were
already like women revealed a combination of defense and the danger against which the defense was erected: men did not have to
castrate themselves after all; but that could also mean that they
were already castrated. The attempt to pull men out of the frightening cracking open and jumbling together of the old sexual molds
restated the conditions that made such an attempt necessary.
Woman was responsible for those conditions. She "breaks" man's
particular strength (moral sense, mental perception, the capacity to
contract an "engagement"), as if it were "a rope of sand." She destroyed this "binding force . . . with a serene unconsciousness that
anything was broken, or that there was anything to break." Stillé's
blaming woman in this way for the erosion of male power seems to
have compressed together both a wish for castration (in order to
become perfect) and a fear of it, and, of course, a deflection of the
origins of such feelings in himself. At that point Dr. Stillé's presidential rhetoric seems to have embodied the assertive, even phallic,

heroine fantasy of the contemporary dime novels.[13] And the somatic reemphasis in medical theory (applied by men to the bodies of women) was coordinate with the male view of woman's upward thrust.

The next (1872) president of the AMA was prepared to give "the people" women doctors "if they wanted them." Medical schools would have to be sexually segregated and unequal in what could be taught, and he hoped such women doctors "would never embarrass us by a personal application for seats in this Association."[14]

Dr. Gardner's rhetoric against the entrance of women into medicine (in 1870) indicates the reinforcement war had given to the notion of the separation of the sexes. In this case he was attacking the New York Medical College for Women. He began an argument, which he saw himself taking to "the people," in the pages of *Frank Leslie's Illustrated Newspaper,* by associating women doctors with the whole subversive range of feminism, the "efforts made to equalize the social and political position of the sexes." Woman's separation from the horrors of medicine was both a privilege and (rather awkwardly) the inevitable result of her psychology.

> More especially is medicine disgusting to women, accustomed to softnesses and the downy side of life. They are sedulously screened from the observation of the horrors and disgusts of life. Fightings, and tumults, the blood and mire, bad smells and bad words, and foul men and more intolerable women she but rarely encounters, and then, as a part of the privileges of womanhood, is permitted, and till now, compelled, to avoid them by a not, to her, disgraceful flight.

The rest of this article was irony founded on the assumption of woman's innate shrinking delicacy. Furthermore, Gardner implied, white women who chose to enter body business would have to consort with black women. Gardner concluded with the suggestion that women would finally encroach on the most exclusively male bastion, taken by Melville as microcosmic of nineteenth-century American enterprise. "The day will come when . . . you will find women on the high seas." This of course was the other side of Stillé's version of role diffusion, men taking over hairdressing and dressmaking. The assertion of male supremacy seems to have been a response to fears of female encroachment.[15]

The Reverend John Todd turned his most passionate guns against women at the same time, having concentrated during his earlier career on the behavior of young men. He addressed *The Daughter at School* in 1853. Two years after the Civil War (and the Emancipation Proclamation) he attacked the emancipation of women directly, linking it with the heinous sins of contraception and abortion (for which Todd, like Gardner, made woman almost entirely responsible). Gardner's tract against women's masturbation, contraception, and abortion, *Conjugal Sins* (1870), was written, he said, to "Arrest the Rapid Extinction of the American People." Rebellious women threatened the United States with disintegration on the scale of the fall of the Roman Empire. Moreover, since women were held to be creatures at the mercy of their physiology, the problem required body experts to deal with them.[16]

The emergence of modern gynecology must be seen in this context (even if, in some senses, it may be construed to have advanced medicine). In 1853, Dr. L. P. Burnham of Lowell, Massachusetts, performed the first successful hysterectomy in America. In 1857 the American Medical Association formed a "Special Committee on the Present State of Science as regards the Pathology and Therapeutics of the Reproductive Organs of the Female," chaired by Dr. Fordyce Barker, a collaborator of Gardner's. In 1868, Dr. T. Gaillard Thomas observed "the specialty of Gynecology is being rapidly separated from its sister branch, Obstetrics," and two years later, Gardner said that the "numerous new class of specialists," gynecologists, had arisen in the period 1845–1870, precisely as they discovered women generally were "deteriorating" to that condition where they needed them.[17] The absence of an equivalent medical specialty for men should be placed in the same context as the emergence of gynecology—and compared with the argument that man's anxiety about woman's potential anarchy, disorder, was a deflection of his own. The editor of the *Journal of American Medicine* correctly predicted the abortive future of those urologists who, in 1891, attempted to constitute an "andrology" specialty, in contrast to gynecology.[18]

The "deterioration" of women which Gardner said called gynecology into existence was moral in both senses, woman's nervous complaints regarded as the result of her sexual transgressions. In any case, all of woman's troubles stemmed from her physiology. Her insanity and her nervous disorders could be treated as physiologically as her physical disorders. In the early 1870s, gynecologists, following this Meigs-style logic, began to practice surgical treatment of the psychological disorders of women. Dr. Horatio Storer, advocate of such treatment, said in 1871 that woman "was what she is in health, in character, in her charms, alike of body, mind and soul

because of her womb alone." The most spectacularly revealing of
these surgical techniques were excision of the clitoris (clitoridectomy) and female castration (removal of the ovaries to cure
insanity) also called oophorectomy and normal ovariotomy. They
should be seen as two among an array of new gynecological operations, for cancer as well as for sexual disorders. Gynecologists' case
histories are suffused with male anxieties over, and attempts to deal
with, women out of their place.[19]

Operations provided the material for the inauguration of specialized publications and institutions. Sims had published his successful treatment for vesico-vaginal fistula, the "stumbling-block of
gynecology," in 1852, and he established the first hospital for a
specific physiological group, women, in New York in 1855. In 1866
he published his *Clinical Notes on Uterine Surgery*. Sims's achievements are generally credited with "raising gynecology . . . to a
respected medical specialty." *The American Journal of Obstetrics
and Diseases of Women and Children* was founded in 1869. The
AMA constituted an authoritative "Section" on obstetrics and the
diseases of women and children in 1873, the year of the publication
of Battey's invention of female castration. The American Gynecological Society was founded in 1876, while Sims was president of
the AMA.[20]

Dr. James Chadwick, the first secretary of the American Gynecological Society, suggested that the new obstetrical and gynecological periodicals and societies were gauges of "the degree of
interest taken in this branch of medicine," and tabulated both.
Between 1876 and 1881 American periodicals increased 100 percent;
in the years 1876–1880 the number of American gynecological
societies increased from six to eleven, more than those of Britain,
Germany, Spain, France, and Russia put together. Chadwick
described a particular psychological style behind these figures. Inevitable vicissitudes in the popularity of certain topics did not
"dampen the ardor" of gynecologists seeking "immortality by pro-
pounding new theories, devising new operations, and above all, by
inventing new instruments." Dr. Chadwick gave an account of the
typical "life history" of a new operation after its first publication.
"Immediately it is tried by many practitioners, who hasten to pub-
lish their results, particularly if favorable, when they expect to
derive renown or practice from being early identified with the
operation." After this novelty wore off, the published life of the operation continued by way of its unfavorable results, until the opera-

tion was adopted, or forgotten. Typical of American operative procedures in Sims's view was the "éclat of sudden success," which he admitted was more dangerous than the more cautious British surgery. The spate of gynecological activity in America and America's international prominence in gynecology were characterized by flamboyant, drastic, risky, and instant use of the knife.[21]

10   Architect of the Vagina

Thomas Addis Emmett, Sims's disciple, rival, and colleague, and his successor as chief surgeon at the Woman's Hospital in New York City, called Sims the "father" of American gynecology, and Sims's only medical book, *Clinical Notes,* "the turning point of modern gynecology." T. Gaillard Thomas, like Emmett a world-renowned gynecological surgeon, said at Sims's death: "If all that Sims has done for gynecology were suppressed we should find that we had retrograded at least a quarter of a century. . . . If I were called upon to name the three men who in the history of all times had done most for their fellow men, I would say George Washington, William Jenner, and Marion Sims." One twentieth-century historian calls Sims the "Architect of the Vagina." Sims experimented with artificial insemination and performed numerous operations to cure sterility in women.[1]

His first and most indisputable claim to fame was his surgical cure of the vesico-vaginal fistula—a tear or tears in the walls of the vagina during parturition—causing continual and hitherto irremediable leakage from the bladder. Thousands of women suffered from this "loathsome" condition. His greatest general influence was to encourage an extremely active, adventurous policy of surgical interference with woman's sexual organs. He was a pioneer in several operative techniques, including pre-Lister cleanliness; the speeding up of healing of the vagina by covering the cut surface with mucous membrane; and the surgical treatment of cancer in women. He was a prolific inventor of surgical instruments, the moving spirit behind the founding of the Woman's Hospital (in 1855), and according to one source was, at one time, the only man in the world with a practice devoted (like the hospital) exclusively to the diseases of women. Sims's contemporaries in the medical profession and Dr. Seale Harris, his modern biographer, insisted on presenting Sims's achievement with parturient metaphors. "The Woman's Hospital was Dr. Sims' bantling. The creation of its germ and the conception of its possibilities were the outgrowth of those discoveries which emanated from his brain alone." Dr. W. O. Baldwin's obituary continued in reproductive vein, linking technological mastery with the fantasy of autonomous birth. It took Galileo, Herschel, Gregory, and Sir Isaac Newton to invent "successive parts of the telescope. Sims alone discovered his speculum, and like Minerva from the brain of Jupiter, it sprang from his hands alone, full fledged and perfect when he gave it to the world." This conception advanced the encroachment that had so angered Nihell: "The day which made [Sims] great was the day when the idea of his speculum first dawned upon him—that day when he first conceived the thought of throwing an abundance of light into the vagina and around the womb, and at the same time obtaining ample space to work and apply his instruments."[2]

Sims's fathering of himself in the conventional terms of self-making was integral to his fathering of modern gynecology.

Originally a country practitioner in Alabama, he succeeded by sheer force of unaided genius, and by the characteristics of thoroughness, simplicity and ingenuity of character and methods in introducing such improvements in the surgery of some of the most obscure and previously irremedial diseases of women, to have brought about something like a revolution in the methods and results of practice.[3]

Sims raised himself from obscurity to the dazzle of success by the elevation of woman's organs from darkness into the light.

In many respects Sims was like the typical American man Tocqueville and Jarvis described: ambitious for immediate returns, dreading the choosing of a career, dreading the moment when he had to face the world's "terrific competition" alone, because he doubted his ability to amount to anything. The doubt remained, not only after he had completed his medical training, but throughout his ostentatiously successful life. His father's financial troubles increased J. Marion's anxiety because of the disparity between his ability and the looming responsibility to his mother and siblings. Both he and his father were prepared at any time to drop what they were doing and try other paths to success. During his boyhood and adolescence, Sims seemed bent on becoming a merchant, but his father sent him to college to be a lawyer. Sims soon changed his mind and went into medicine instead, a decision with which his "poor" father readily concurred, in spite of his "disappointment." In 1835, when Sims was twenty-two, he and his father set out together for the Alabama frontier. They reached Mount Meigs and were persuaded to try their luck there rather than in Marengo County where they had planned; Sims set up practice, and his father returned to South Carolina after a few days. The elder Sims continued to take chances and look "longingly towards the unknown," and soon moved West again, this time to Mississippi.[4]

Sims described himself as "an example of a man who has never achieved the ambitions of his early life. My successes have been in a direction that I never dreamed of when I started." A year after his marriage in 1836, and having become "quite a respectable physician . . . a tolerably successful one . . . I was really ready, at any time and at any moment, to take up anything that held out an inducement of fortune, because I knew that I could never make a fortune out of medicine." In 1838 he gave up medicine entirely for a chance to make some quick money as a clothing merchant in Vicksburg; but the chance vanished as quickly as it had come, and unlike many men in that year he lost nothing. (Dewees had resigned his medical profession in 1812 to follow a "tempting pecuniary investment" but saw his speculation destroyed by the crash of 1817 and returned to obstetrics.)[5] Sims's practice of medicine remained leisurely for six or seven years after his graduation. He combined his visits to great Alabama planters and their slaves with the bagging of game en route. In 1841 he moved to Montgomery, and there took the decisive step of committing himself to surgery performed on women's sexual organs.[6]

While Sims said he "had ambition for surgery . . . and performed all sorts of beautiful and brilliant operations," it was an ambition that had never taken off, least of all in a gynecological direction. At the end of his life, viewing the attitudes of his youth across an intervening span concerned with vaginas daily, Sims admitted that before the mid-1840s "if there was anything I hated, it was investigating the organs of the female pelvis." So profound was Sims's abhorrence that he sent his gynecological patients to other doctors. The case that seems to have mediated between Sims's aversion for woman's sexual organs and his career as a surgical gynecologist was that of twenty-one-year-old Miss Margaret C.'s

"Double Congenital Hare-lip," which he treated in 1842. It prefigures his later career in several respects; it launched him into publication, an essential condition for establishing his name; and it was the first instance in which Sims used the knife (he had previously confined himself to scissors and perhaps a saw). He admitted some dissatisfaction with the knife in this first case, and that it would have been, perhaps, "less painful in the hands of a more dexterous operator." In contrast to his contemporaries Sims very soon came to "look upon the knife not as the last weapon, but as the first." He became famous for his surgical appetite, and it was largely Sims's successful career that served as a catalyst in speeding up the tendency toward general, frequent, and drastic use of the knife in American gynecology.[7]

Sims's own language makes the connection between his treatment of this earlier female deformity and that nether orifice of which he was to become the "architect": he shared the contemporary convention of labeling a woman's generative tract with names from a higher part of her body. Throughout *Clinical Notes,* the vagina has a "mouth," the womb a "neck" and a "throat," and the cervix is compared to the "tonsils." Occasionally Sims made a full-face comparison. "I have seen the inside of an immense number of vaginas, and I never saw two that were in all particulars exactly alike. They are as different from each other as our faces and noses."[8]

In the case of the harelip, "two depressions or holes in the prolabrim of the lower lip" were "perpetually secreting and pouring out a thin, glairy, viscid, translucent mucus." In the case of the vesicovaginal fistula, tears in the walls between vagina and bladder caused a continuous seepage of urine through vaginal and urethral openings. The correspondence was still closer, since this mucus was augmented by fluids that Miss C. ingested. "She swallows fluids with great difficulty, as they regurgitate by the fissures in the lip and superior maxillare." Sims found her condition "horrible." It had made Miss C. socially unacceptable. "This mortifying deformity has excluded her altogether from society. Modest, diffident and sensitive, she avoids the presence of every one, except her own brothers and sisters. Life has no charms for her; and her only solace here is her hope of a blessed immortality hereafter." Sufferers from vesicovaginal fistula were ostracized in the way that Miss C. had been; but their physical deformity could not be veiled from the perception of others as hers was before she was treated by Sims, since it constantly gave off an unmistakable smell. Sims overcame his horror for

Miss C.'s condition: indeed, he was inspired to ingenious feats of gratifying effect. He performed two operations and was eager to perfect his handiwork with a third, but Miss C. declared herself "perfectly satisfied with her present condition, and altogether unwilling to undergo any more cutting." His first vesico-vaginal fistula patients would not be able to balk him that way.[9]

Sims's admittedly hostile (even aggressive) feelings toward woman's pelvic organs were probably linked to a remarkable recollection in 1845 which would form the basis for another of Sims's claims to immortality, in addition to making possible his vesico-vaginal fistula cure. Confronted at that time with a gynecological emergency, he discovered that the appropriate remedy had stuck in his mind from the remark of a Dr. Prioleau at medical school eleven years earlier. A Mrs. Merrill was in agony from the displacement of her uterus, caused by a fall from her horse. By placing her on all fours, inserting two fingers in her vagina (Sims could not bear to place one in her rectum as Dr. Prioleau had recommended in such cases), and then moving them up and down, thereby allowing the air to rush in and equalize the atmospheric pressure between inside and outside, he forced the uterus into position. He adapted a spoon handle for the holding open of the vaginal opening, calling it a "speculum" and attaching his name to it. He named the patient's posture on hands and knees, ready for the application of "Sims' speculum," "Sims' position." Its immortalization of its discoverer's name was of particular significance. Sims had immediately perceived the possibilities of the new instrument and the new position for the cases of vesico-vaginal fistula that recently had been brought to him. "Introducing the bent handle of a spoon, I saw everything as no man had ever seen before. . . . The Speculum made it perfectly clear from the beginning. . . . I felt like an explorer in medicine who first views a new and important territory." Baldwin caught up the metaphor: "Sims' speculum has been to diseases of the womb . . . what the compass is to the mariner. . . ." Sims could see himself as a Columbus, his New World the vagina. He called in the leaders of the Montgomery medical profession to witness his first triumph in curing the vesico-vaginal fistula. His unique and triumphant individuation among men ("as no man had ever seen") was to be registered most tangibly by having other doctors witness their defeat as well as his success. Such individual success was a stronger motive than his hatred for woman's distinctive organs; indeed, the former was a way of overcoming the latter. Cutting into the organs, using

them as material for his personal standing among men, was Sims's
way of dealing with the horror they aroused. Hostility toward
women and competition among men were the conditions for the
rise of modern gynecology.[10]

Once Sims sensed his pioneer track and his opportunity to make
a name for himself, he pursued it relentlessly. He gathered up all
of the vesico-vaginal fistulae he could, embodied in black female
slaves (the first three named Anarcha, Lucy, and Betsy), and housed
them "in a little building in his yard." For four years he operated
and failed, thirty times on Anarcha alone. The stitches always became infected, and the fistulae remained open. Sims became an
Ahab, his pursuit a "monomania," a "consuming interest," an
"obsession." And all of the time the ultimate measure of success
was the acceptance of Sims's surgery by other men, who, even
though Sims invited them, avoided witnessing his operation because
of what was construed to be Sims's humiliation. His stable of female
slaves "clamored" for operations. When no one else would, they
assisted Sims in his surgery on themselves. "But my operations all
failed, so far as a positive cure was concerned. This went on, not
for one year, but for two and three, and even four years. I kept all
these negroes at my own expense all the time. As a matter of course
this was an enormous tax for a young doctor." The tax paid off: it
led to his greatest claim to immortality—the use of sutures that did
not become infected. Sims called his silver sutures "the greatest
surgical achievement of the nineteenth century." Even after curing
all the patients he had in his experiment center he sought more,
operating again and again, so that when his success was consum-
mated by its publication among his medical brethren, he would be
invulnerable to the assault he knew would be mounted against him.[11]

In 1853 Sims entered the ferociously competitive world of New
York medicine. His "principal card of introduction" was his particular cutting of a woman's body, his treatment of the vesico-vaginal
fistula. He had in some sense found himself that way, and women's
generative tracts would be the arena where he and his surgical rivals
would cross swords for decades.[12]

At the same time, Sims's achievement was early recognized by a
number of eminent doctors. One of them was Charles Meigs (a
member of the faculty of Sims's alma mater in Philadelphia). Meigs
wrote in 1851 that Sims's success "entitles him to the praise and
gratitude of our whole profession." Sims shared with Meigs the
contemporary belief that woman's entire psychology was governed

by her sex organs, and Sims would go on in the 1870s to perform both clitoridectomy and female castration.

Other surgeons' appropriation of his operation without acknowledgment drove Sims "to a frenzy of self-pity and despair" when he first arrived in New York. Yet one could not own an operation, even if one's name was attached to it. Other doctors were just as obsessed with making a name for themselves as Sims. One way of feeling oneself at least equal was in negative terms; so the discovery of a new operation automatically entailed denial by other doctors, on grounds either that it did not work or that someone else had already made such a discovery. Sims was subject to such rivalry, and to what might be called priority-anxiety, all of his life. Among those who claimed to improve his operation were Isaac Baker Brown and Robert Battey, the inventors respectively of clitoridectomy and female castration. Nathan Bozeman claimed that his methods alone, not Sims's at all, had cured the vesico-vaginal fistula. He was an erstwhile pupil of Sims, who had cared for Sims's vesico-vaginal patients in Montgomery while Sims was away recuperating from the malaria and diarrhea he had picked up on the frontier. Eventually Bozeman took over Sims's whole practice when Sims moved to New York. At first Bozeman claimed only to have modified Sims's suture technique. As their rivalry dragged on and became more embittered, Bozeman's claim expanded. Sims said "he appropriates to himself every step of the operation that resulted from my own individual and unaided efforts." So each man claimed entire independence, originality, and priority in curing the vesico-vaginal fistula, and each took his claim to the great European medical centers for ultimate judgment. When Sims founded his hospital for women in New York, Bozeman founded one there too. The struggle went on even after death: an article by Bozeman impugned Sims's methods, results, and integrity in the same *Transactions of the American Gynecological Society* that carried Sims's obituary.[13]

Incessant competition among doctors kept them in a continuous state of anxiety, drove them to bitterness, paranoia (intensifying the very conditions that made them paranoid), and even death. Emmett and Sims both thought they were targets of persecution campaigns. Defending himself in his 1875 presidential address to the AMA against his recent reprimand for "self-advertizement" by the New York Academy of Medicine, Sims implied he had been framed. In context of the vicious competition in evidence everywhere, he may well have been right. "Did it ever occur to any of you," Sims asked his audience, that the AMA's Code of Ethics "is capable of being used as an engine of torture and oppression?—that men jealously, maliciously intent upon persecuting a fellow member may distort the meaning of the Code to suit their malign purposes, thus entering into a regular conspiracy to blacken character, and that under the sanctity of the Code's provisions?"[14]

Yet by his own vast claims ("no man had seen," "the greatest achievement in the nineteenth century") and his vituperative attacks on Bozeman and others, Sims contributed to the very circumstances by which he felt threatened. His article on "The Discovery of Anaesthesia" (1877) illustrates his own priority-anxiety, even as he gave the sad story of priority-anxiety in the lives of other men. The point of the article was to establish a fellow southerner's claim to have been the first to have used anesthesia in surgery. Sims was the loyal southerner—the more vehemently so, perhaps, because he took off for Europe during the Civil War. In Sims's account of Crawford Long's claim, the other three discoverers, Horace Wells of Hartford, Connecticut, and W. T. G. Morton and Charles T. Jackson, both of Boston, appealed for recognition to the old European authority, feeling perhaps that there was no final arbitration in America. A man there looked to be confirmed in his self-making by his democratic rivals. This was a paradoxical and therefore doubly self-defeating hope: such confirmation was doomed, of course, in its own terms—rivals would refuse to provide it. But if they had been able to provide it, it would cease to be self-making.[15]

Perhaps the next best thing to owning an operative procedure was getting a patent for it. A patent on anesthesia would make a fortune, since it could be used in all operations, provided the subject did not like pain and could afford to pay for its elimination. Jackson and Morton tried to conceal their anesthetic—sulfuric ether—by deodorizing it and calling it "letheon." But their attempt to obtain a patent succumbed to their own rivalry and their rivalry with others. Sims described the competition among Wells, Jackson, and Morton as "a tripartite war . . . waged with great fury, Morton and Jackson denying everything to Wells, and denying everything to each other." At first Crawford Long was apart from the struggle (largely because he did not know about it), but he was drawn in when the stakes developed from money into priority-immortality. Jackson, Morton, and Wells came to ends the nature of which illustrated further Esquirol's analysis of the risks of modern civilization's progress, and Jarvis's application of it to America. Each of them had been driven to distraction by his disappointment at not having his discovery acknowledged officially as the first: Jackson was in an insane asylum, "hopelessly incurable"; Morton, fretting himself into the "wildest state of excitement," had "exhausted his vital powers," and after a brief outburst of insanity, died; Wells became insane and committed suicide in 1848.[16]

Contemporaries accepted it as a fact that their own behavior could lead to the results Sims described in the cases of Wells, Morton, and Jackson: disappointment, fretfulness, anxiety, wild excitement, fury, and exhaustion were precisely the effects upon men of the democratic struggle that Jarvis observed in 1851. The insanity and death of Jackson, Morton, and Wells were symptoms of American democracy in the same way that Melville's father's were. After repeated business failure Allan Melville "lost his bearings in the commercial world." His contemporaries explained his despair as the result of carrying the pursuit of success too far, that is, according to the model accepted and promulgated by the medical and psychological experts described in Part I:

> Persisting in giving attention to his business—He devoted himself so closely and assiduously, as to produce a state of excitement, which in great measure robbed him of his sleep. It is but a few days since he yielded to the wishes of his friends and remained at home. The excitement however could not be allayed and yesterday he occasionally manifested an alienation of mind. Last night he became worse—and today he presents the melancholy spectacle of a deranged man.

His brother, Thomas Melville, said he "found him *very sick* under great mental excitement—at times fierce, even *maniacal*." He died insane. In the same year that Jarvis published his account of the stresses of American life, Herman Melville described Ahab's "special lunacy" as "monomania" and continued his account according to his contemporaries' psychology. Ahab's lunacy "stormed his general sanity, and carried it, and turned all its concentred cannon upon its own mad mark." Monomania was the appropriate form of derangement for a society preoccupied with self-making and individualism, believing that men's brains should be exposed to the same rivalrous stimulants that produced insanity; and appropriate, too, to the essential insatiability of the normal democratic pursuit as Tocqueville described it, all men harassing and wearying one another in a ceaseless and monotonous pursuit and meeting at every step "immense obstacles which they did not at first perceive," among them a refusal to acknowledge any authoritative standard but one's own. Men had to be monomaniac to confront the conditions which made them monomaniac.[17]

Toward the end of his life, Sims fell ill with pneumonia. At that stage he was internationally famous, the second wealthiest of all American doctors by his own estimate, honored professionally, and his name was attached to various instruments and operative procedures. At Harvard Medical School the students recognized "divinity" in Sims and counted him "one of the immortals." Yet "in his delirium he constantly was contriving new instruments, going through the motions of surgical operations, and fretting over the work he had not finished." They were anxieties that continued beyond his delirious state. Sims was no more "curable" than he had described Charles Jackson to have been, nor indeed than any man could afford to be, given the unquestioned allegiance to the notion of how progress was to be achieved.[18]

Perhaps it is too early in the argument to claim this self-destructive aspect of male behavior as the fulfillment of Stillé's subliminal wish to opt out of the role men simultaneously demanded to monopolize. Sims recognized the suicidal element in the careers of Jackson, Morton, and Wells: "martyrs to science and humanity," they "sacrificed their lives for the good of the whole civilized world." Sims's notion of the advance of civilization, humanity, and science by way of these heroes' cutthroat selfishness should be compared with the way in which he undertook his own missions for the "relief of suffering womanhood."[19]

I have described his monomania and his competitiveness. Another characteristic of Sims's medicine was his desire to display his surgical virtuosity to other men. The idea of "performing" an operation is significant in this connection. Sims loved the theater (of the non-surgical kind) and had met and been fascinated by P. T. Barnum. In 1874 Sims refused to abide by a new rule set by the governing board of "his" hospital, that not more than fifteen spectators— medical students and colleagues—could be present at the performance of an operation. Patients said that when Sims operated, the "noise of the tramp up stairs and the loud talking of such a crowd confuses and unnecessarily alarms the patients. . . . Is the Woman's Hospital to be made a public school or is it to be a Private Hospital where our afflicted Sisters can come without fear?" Sims's illustrious colleagues at the hospital were prepared to settle for fewer spectators as one price for getting rid of the painfully successful Sims. He was expelled by the Board of Governors, and lionized by the rest of the medical profession as a martyr to professional independence.[20]

The other reason Sims opposed a limitation on the size of his male audience bears directly on the subject of gynecologists' evaluation of their patients—female by definition. This is what Sims said:

> The Woman's Hospital is today one of the great lights of gynecological science. The profession throughout the country look to it for instruction. . . . Medical men come up to New York every winter to study the clinical advantages to be found in the metropolis. . . . They go home with enlarged views and improved methods of treatment. They thereby become friends and patrons of the hospital; they send . . . cases to the hospital. . . . But by our illiberality in excluding our country friends . . . I find we are making enemies of them.[21]

The operating room was an arena for an exchange between men.

Sims had taught himself gynecological surgery. Although anesthesia had been invented at the time (the 1840s), Sims did not know of it. By definition, novel surgery was liable to mistakes, which Sims construed first and foremost as his failures. Sometimes he had to be dangerously brutal. His first patients endured years of almost unimaginable agonies.[22] Their bodies were the material for Sims's construction of his success. Once he sensed he was on the track— daring to "blaze the trail," as one of his students called it, like Daniel Boone or Natty Bumppo—Sims scoured the countryside for appropriate surgical subjects. Significantly, given the need for their endurance, passivity, and utter helplessness, they were black female slaves, some of whom Sims bought expressly for his experiments— that is, when the owner was skeptical about Sims's methods. He built his own private hospital in his backyard to house them. Rumors circulated in Montgomery that Sims was using human beings as guinea pigs for his surgical ambitions. The rumors were accurate. As long as he was in Montgomery "it was far harder to operate on white women than on Negroes" because white women were more in a position to express their will in the relationship with Sims. "The pain was so terrific that Mrs. H. could not stand it and I was foiled completely." So the black slaves served as "adequate material" in Sims's "storing" of experience, "finding out more about the applicability of . . . silver sutures" until the invention of anesthesia and of Listerism dissolved the resistance of wealthy white women and Sims could apply to their bodies the techniques he had perfected on the bodies of blacks.[23]

His expansion of his backyard hospital into the Woman's Hospital in New York gave him access to a much larger aggregation of surgical material and the means to inflate his reputation to a national medical stage. Sims emphasized a "crying need" for the kind of specialized hospital that did not yet exist. Some doctors objected on the grounds that there was no such need and that GPs could take care of female problems in private practice (much in the way that doctors were to argue successfully against specialization in male disease nearly forty years later). But the objection was overwhelmed in the case of gynecology. When the hospital first opened, only half the beds were occupied. The paucity of specialized, operable sickness coincided with the fact that surgical gynecology was itself, in 1855, "hardly born." The hospital was constituted to demonstrate to doctors the importance and effectiveness of the surgical treatment of female diseases (mental as well as physical), and most of them had not yet been identified. Gynecologists had a garden of Eden wherein they could discover and name diseases and cures under circumstances which made them profoundly anxious to attach their names to such discoveries. So whether or not there were vast numbers of women out there needing special treatment, there was a growing number of special treaters needing diseased women, the nature of their ambition very similar to Sims's. At the time of the hospital's founding, Sims was isolated in New York, cut off from those people for whose treatment he had equipped himself. The Woman's Hospital was founded very largely as a demonstration ground for Sims's surgical skill. He needed food and fame.[24]

The hospital answered those needs by maintaining the supply of human material upon which Sims, his famous colleagues, and their guests could experiment. The patients were poor. Most of the first ones were destitute Irish immigrant women, whose fistulae and general health were so bad that they allowed Sims and his fellows to keep them there indefinitely, even as the black slaves' medical and social condition enabled Sims to make them literally "his patients." They "had to receive surgical treatment over and over again." One of the first of these Irish indigents, Mary Smith, endured thirty operations between 1856 and 1859, the number Anarcha had endured between 1845 and 1849.[25]

With a supply of bodies guaranteed him, Sims constantly devised new operations and instruments, discarding them when they caused too many accidents. The process was exactly as Chadwick described it. Sims's Scots contemporary James Young Simpson said of surgical risk that a "man laid upon the operating table in one of our surgical hospitals is exposed to more chances of death than the English soldier on the field of Waterloo." It was women who were first selected as a group for surgical innovation, their bodies the field and the contending parties the surgeons. The hospital's patients were treated free; Sims and the other gynecological surgeons made their money by applying the hospital discoveries in private practice, where they charged stupendous fees. The conclusion is inescapable that the hospital was instituted for the same reason that Sims garnered diseased black women into his backyard—to provide guinea pigs for his self-education, before he and the others could convincingly offer care to the wives of the wealthy who were Sims's original backers for the hospital.[26]

In addition to supplying Sims with surgical material for the expansion of his armamentarium and his reputation, and helping him to fulfill his lifelong ambition to make money, the Woman's Hospital provided him with an entrance into the circle of those men who had their hands most directly on the levers of power. Within a year of its founding the Woman's Hospital was in the social and political limelight, the issues a charter and funds for expansion. The public committee supporting the project included Benjamin F. Butler, Henry J. Raymond (founder of the New York *Times,* and lieutenant governor of New York 1855–1857), and James Beekman (who was to become an ardent and long-term president of the hospital's Board of Governors). Among the other prominent supporters of the Woman's Hospital was Peter Cooper, inventor, industrialist, one-time presidential candidate, founder of the Cooper Union—an archetypal self-made man.[27]

These men and the New York State Legislature knew and approved the particular sexual and social values the hospital embodied, by its use of poor women as self-educational material for better-off men, for example; and by its advocacy of the surgical treatment of women's mental as well as physical diseases. The professional male supporters of the hospital's expansion presented a "Memorial" to the state legislators, asking them to give "fostering care to this little hospital." The Memorial was signed by the entire medical establishment of New York City and endorsed by the State Medical Association. These were some of the Memorial's assertions:

> *Women* are subject to diseases peculiar to the sex. The *Virgin* may suffer from a large catalogue of the most painful maladies. The *Wife* may be worn down with untold miseries, growing out of the marital relation. The *Mother,* in giving birth to her offspring, often suffers such horrible lacerations and injuries as to render life unbearable.

Old Age as well as Maturity, has its thousand female sufferings calling for sympathy and aid.

The language is a familiar code—common to James Fenimore as
well as Peter Cooper; its central, physically sexual meaning cannot
be overlooked (as perhaps it can in other contexts—the bachelor's
notion of "the sex," for example). The mother's "horrible lacera-
tions" during birth seems to have referred to vesico-vaginal fistula, a
particular acknowledgment of Sims's importance to the establishment of the Woman's Hospital. In the same way, old age's "female
suffering" meant the physical and mental troubles held to be contingent on the cessation of the menstrual flow; and the wife's "untold miseries, growing out of the marital relation" stood for such
copulatory and pre- and post-copulatory difficulties as vaginismus,
to which I shall return in a few pages.[28]
The legislators were also made aware of the logic that led to
clitoridectomy and female castration.

> These diseases when left alone go from bad to worse till they
> completely shatter the nervous system, embitter existence, poison the
> sources of domestic happiness, lay the foundation for the hereditary
> disease, and in many instances upset the intellect, driving their un-
> fortunate victims to the madhouse. . . . Statistics of our insane
> asylums show that twenty-five to forty per cent of all cases of in-
> sanity in women arise directly from organic female disease which, in
> most cases, might be remedied by appropriate and timely treatment

—that is, by surgery. The Memorialists asked for official recognition
of their response to the "moanings of the mothers and daughters
of our land."
Another way in which the legislators were exposed to such phenomena as tears in the vaginal wall was through the testimony of
one of Sims's respectable "lady" patients. She appeared before the
legislature's Ways and Means Committee, explained the vesico-
vaginal fistula, and described her own sufferings from the condition,
Sims's operation, and her cure. She told them that if the hospital
was granted additional funds "you will build for yourselves a monu-
ment in the hearts of women more durable than granite." To procure the tribute of more women's bodies to gynecologists' feet, she
proposed to lay "the womanly hearts of my sex" at "the feet of your
manly nature." Every member of the legislature was provided with
a copy of the lady's evidence. The officially representative group of
men sanctioned the Woman's Hospital, symbol of the gynecologists'

progress, granting it a charter and $10,000. The 1857 Act of Incorporation took control of the hospital away from the original Board of Lady Managers and gave it to a male Board of Governors including John Jacob Astor, Theodore Sedgwick, E. D. Morgan, Robert Minturn, John David Wolfe, and John C. Green, in addition to Ben Butler, Cooper, Raymond, E. C. Benedict, and a Dr. John C. Francis. The Lady Managers remained in a separate and subordinate position, handling the Woman's Hospital's "moral and domestic management." So this Incorporation embodied the familiar and general terms of the relations between men and women. In this form the Woman's Hospital became a model for the women's hospitals that proliferated in the surgical-gynecological crescendo of the 1870s.[29]

Sims moved to Europe during the Civil War, demonstrated his surgical facility to the great English, Scots, and French surgeons, and developed a clientele in aristocratic circles. After 1869 he spent six months on each side of the Atlantic alternately, skimming the cream of lucrative gynecological cases by so commuting. Both he and his contemporaries were impressed by the social and financial heights his surgery enabled him to scale. He ran a hospital for Napoleon III during the Franco-Prussian War and attended the Empress Eugénie, the Crown Princess of Saxony, and the Duchess of Hamilton. Sims's stature was immeasurably greater in American doctors' eyes because of his success in the lands of authoritative fathers. In America after the Civil War he came as close to the style of the monied "robber baronry" as a gynecologist could get, and opened an additional office in Newport, Rhode Island. The Newport *Daily News* called the wedding there of Sims's fourth daughter "the great social event of the season." He threw a lavish supper and reception for four hundred guests in the Hotel Brunswick's ballroom in New York in honor of Dr. Samuel Gross. He pressed poor female bodies into service for such baronial display in 1879, performing "a series of varied operations for four successive days" to demonstrate his talents to the veteran ovariotomist John Atlee, the entertainment culminating in a dinner at Sims's house for Atlee and fifty or sixty other distinguished doctors.[30]

The nature of Sims's ambition and success corresponds to the generalizations made about male careers. His *Clinical Notes* illustrates the fact that gynecological work was loaded with the other sexual values discussed earlier. After some consideration of Sims's

relation with his wife and of Sims's view of the gynecologists' masculinity, this chapter will conclude with an analysis of *Clinical
Notes.*

Sims's wife Theresa conformed exactly to Tocqueville's account
of the typical American wife. According to Sims's friend Baldwin,
she "was a loving and cheerful companion, a wise counselor, a true
helpmeet; and throughout his brilliant but checkered and eventful
life she shared his prosperity with joy and gladness, and bore his
adversities with becoming patience and resignation. . . ." Thomas
Addis Emmett, who knew Sims and his wife intimately, said that
for Sims's "impulsive nature her placid disposition was as essential
as the flywheel in an engine." She was a source of assurance, steadiness, restraint, buoyancy, and stability. During the years of Sims's
groping toward the establishment of his professional identity, he
went through cycle after cycle of recurrent diarrhea (probably bacil-
lary dysentery), its phases intimately bound up with the vicissitudes
in his career. He was freed of this sickness immediately after the
Woman's Hospital was opened. He had said three years earlier, and
at a point close to death:

> "If I had the physical strength and the moral courage to do what
> I ought to do, I could get well.
> "But, of course, that is impossible."
> "No," answered Theresa, "I don't think it *is* impossible."

And she went on to organize the family's move to New York "em-
ploying the same quiet competence that she had used for the last
sixteen years in running smoothly a complicated and frequently
peripatetic household."[31]

Such a role, perhaps, explains Sims's reservation in his account of
his ideal woman, Queen Victoria. "Taking her in all the relations of
life, as wife, mother, Christian, and queen, no such woman ever
graced the throne or so honored her sex; but, poor thing, she is
queen and therefore not free to do as she chooses about anything.
She has, nominally, great power, but is really powerless." It also
throws further light on Tocqueville's typical American wife, extraordinarily important to democratic society, her power narrowly confined within her separate sphere. So Sims told Theresa early in their
relationship: "I fear you'll set me down as an egotist. . . . We must
always have some one to confer with, some friend into whose atten-
tive ear we can pour our secret thoughts and speculations." When
he had an inspired solution to the problem of suture tying, "I was

so elated with the idea that I could not help waking up my kind and sympathetic wife and telling her of the simple and beautiful method I had discovered. . . . I lay there till morning, tying the suture and performing all sorts of beautiful operations." She may have been the constantly available and open ear into which Sims poured himself at will, but Theresa knew she might never intrude on his sphere out of her own need or willfulness. She observed a rigid line between "wifely watchfulness" and her husband's "professional duties."[32]

It is also in accordance with Tocqueville's model that Sims should have placed on his wife the responsibility for "the moral elevation and religious culture of the rest of us." A letter to Theresa, after his profession of faith in 1854, began by blaming both of them for backsliding, but went on to shift the burden to her alone.

> Have we done our duty to our children, to ourselves, to our God? We have not. . . . What, then is to be done? Repent and give our hearts to God. Let us try to do this and we shall feel that we are in the line of duty. Why hesitate? . . . A public profession of the religion that I know glows in your heart is all that is needed. The power of your example will do more for the moral elevation and religious culture of the rest of us than whole volumes of sermons. Your whole life is a sermon. . . . If you do not take the first step toward, then we shall remain in darkness and doubt.

This letter amplifies one's understanding of Sims's idea of where woman's "power" lay. This woman's power to keep this man in darkness was linked to his hatred for woman's sexual organs. In this moral role, Theresa was, like Queen Victoria, representative of that group identity, "the sex," a physiological definition. Sims's career was devoted to countering the dark power of woman, of overcoming his hatred by his use of the knife.[33]

The terms of a previous letter reinforce the idea that Sims viewed his gynecological relations with a patient in the same way that he viewed his relations with his wife, and vice versa. God's finger threw light on Sims's and Mrs. Sims's troubles in the way that Sims's speculum opened up a patient's afflicted reproductive tract. "Am I not peculiarly blessed? Does not the light shine upon our darkened path as we never dreamed of seeing it? Is not the finger of God visible in all our afflictions?" He then referred to his gynecological role as "a blessed instrument in the hands of God for the accomplishment of good," and such a context suggests that he associated the next sentence's daunting dangers with his resistance to investigating woman's pelvic organs.

> When I look back and remember how my heart quailed before the dangers that surrounded us, how I was just on the eve of surrendering all as lost, how despair almost drove me to madness, and when I call to mind your gentle tones of encouragement, your blind and implicit reliance upon Divine Providence, your high moral fortitude and self-sacrificing efforts, dare I say I would have had it otherwise. . . . Was ever man's wife more literally his ministering angel? . . . All that I am and hope to be I owe to you.[34]

This was written on December 25, 1854. Sims, of course, was "Divine Providence" in his own view of his mission to suffering woman. He was credited by contemporaries and eulogists with "self-sacrifice," and he could see himself as a ministering angel. But here he appeared to reverse that relationship in fairly typical pedestal rhetoric. His wife got the credit. The reversal might have stood for several things: the ambiguous role of a gynecologist in a sexually dichotomized world; Sims's being able to praise his better half only in a way appropriate to himself; and an underlying sense of a gynecologist's dependence on women.

Sims's profession of faith to his wife was the occasion for an attempt to convert his father as well, in terms asserting his moral superiority to his father. One can associate both this overcoming of his father, and his assertion of a "similarity" between his own life and his father's, with his enduring "regret" that he failed "to inherit his father's majestic proportions." He was so small and so long beardless that one of his earliest patients (before Sims became exclusively a woman's doctor) roared out to the man who brought young Dr. Sims: "My God, Evans, do you call that thing a doctor? Take him away; take him away! I am too sick to be fooled with." Women did not react to him in that way. But anxiety over his proportions may have infused his lifetime devotion of his knife to women's genitals. Sims's godlike digital activities suggest that his sonhood's aggression became a general cannonade into the circumambient powers of woman's mons. *Harper's Weekly* picked out this sexual element in Sims's work. "There was a rapture in his work like that of a lover's pursuit or a great artist's creation." Women seem to have reciprocated in kind; they responded to his "handsome face, magnetic personality and professional manner" with "worship." "It is said of [Sims] that no woman ever distrusted him, while his exceptional purity of speech and life, together with the personal magnetism of his smile, his manners, attracted so many to him, and held them chained with the silken cord of love, gratitude and esteem."[35]

Sims felt that entrepreneurial gynecology was as heroic an activity as other male careers, in spite of the intimacy with women which ideology recommended autonomous manhood deny. When Sims returned to Montgomery after twenty-four years' absence he was given a civic welcome, organized by the local medical society. The reception which followed included doctors, lawyers, merchants, governors, ex-governors, judges, and soldiers. Sims replied to the address: "If I were a conquering hero, or a great statesman, you could not vie stronger with each other in trying to do me honor. But when such an ovation is given to a mere doctor, even if he is deemed a philanthropist, and at heart a patriot, it seems paradoxical." Sims characterized himself as a benefactor of the human race, who had made "one of the most important discoveries of the age. . . ." His power was divine. "I feel a power within me that is irresistible. I feel that I am in the hands of God, that I have a high and holy mission to perform." So the paradox of his speech to the awed Montgomery assembly in 1877 is the patent falsity of his humility. He was regarded as a conquering hero by his audience and by himself.[36]

Sims usually referred to his sense of mission in terms involving God's hands. He could emulate "the finger of God" by digital examination and repair of reproductive organs. He could restore woman from the exaggerated separation to which the fistula condemned her, to her regular sphere. To deal with hateful genitalia and return them to childbearing by male skill stood as a kind of archetype of the kind of circumscription and control all gynecologists could claim to work. Not only could they sympathetically restore woman's reproductive powers; they could appear to create them. Sims had a "magic wand."[37]

Sims believed that women should bear babies, and the proportion of his operations to cure sterility and his pioneering in artificial insemination demonstrate his preoccupation with fertility. (That such a concern was ancillary to his fundamental desire to shape women, control them, and thereby to foster his own immortality can be suggested by repeating simply that Sims also castrated women deemed mentally disordered.) Sims's only book-length scientific work was subtitled "with special reference to the management of sterility": uterine surgery was to induce pregnancy as well as to cure disease. His concern was part of the same vision of the body politic ex-

pressed by Gardner in 1872. Childbearing was the foundation of
legal male identities—"perpetuation of names," "descent of property," "welfare of the State," and "permanence of government."
That was how Sims answered his question: "Why take so much
trouble with a fibroid?" The gynecologist's power was anterior to
the heroes' and statesmen's, from which Sims only apparently had
excluded himself on his return to Alabama.[38]

Like Gardner, and in accordance with these values, Sims saw infinitely more social worth in male children. Sims "was devoted to all
his little girls, but for his boys he had a special feeling which his
girls, much as he loved them, could not share. He and his contemporaries might place woman on a pedestal, but a pedestal offered
little scope for ambition or distinction, and for his sons Sims was
filled with vast ambition." They had their names changed from
Sims to Marion-Sims, when, of course, they lived under a father
they knew would be "touched and pleased by his sons' attempts to
identify themselves with him [and] comforted by the thought that
whatever happened to him, the name he had made famous would be
carried on." Sims set his two eldest sons at medicine (the next carried out another project of the father, "working as a clerk in a dry
goods store in the hope of getting a start in the mercantile field").
While both Granville and Harry became doctors specializing in surgical gynecology, they found it impossible to repeat their father's
success. Granville died en route to fight for the South in the Civil
War, and Harry was nothing like the skilled or famous surgeon his
father was.[39]

According to Sims's analysis, gynecologists' role as the perpetua-
tors of society's future should not be limited to the higher stratum
of society. He believed "about every eighth marriage is sterile."
Fortunately, of all organs "the uterus is the most subservient to the
laws of physical exploration." The uterus should be as pliant as its
bearer was to the male will. While "there is menstruation, there is
ovulation, and any woman that ovulates can be impregnated. . . ."
The gynecologist could supply the favorable circumstances, clear
any obstacles, replace what has been destroyed, straighten tubes,
and open the way. This was the central thrust of *Clinical Notes*, surgically to shape and control the uterine cavity, the "nidus of a new
being."[40]

One of the techniques Sims wanted to encourage was "splitting
up the neck of the womb," the incision of os and/or cervix to facili-
tate the egress of the menses and the ingress of sperm. He performed

it in Paris on European cervical canals "with the same fearlessness that [he] did on Americans." And Sims was, perhaps, the foremost practitioner of what he says was typical of American operative procedure—"the éclat of sudden success," which, in the hands of James Platt White, was "brilliant but more dangerous" than the gradual methods of the British gynecologist W. Tyler Smith. Sims performed incision of the cervix and os in spite of those doctors who regarded the operation as "butcherous." There was a sharp differ-ence between American and English gynecologists over its effective-ness and therefore over its morality. In the case of incision of the cervix and os the influential Edinburgh school agreed with the Americans, while in London it was "condemned by the great body of the profession" and on "the Continent . . . this operation is al-most completely ostracized."[41]

Sims admitted the operation was of limited success; sometimes he tried it three times on the same set of organs, and even then it was not satisfactory. A characteristic of this automatic surgery was its repetition, its obsessive quality. Incision of the os put gynecolo-gists "on the highway of improvement; and it seems to me that further advances must be made as heretofore, by means almost purely surgical." But this particular highway was as doomed to supersession as the plank roads. Chadwick took incision of the cer-vix uteri to cure dysmenorrhea as an example of the "life histories" of gynecological operations. By 1881, he said, that operation was "rapidly passing into oblivion. It is still performed in cases of ex-treme stenosis, but is recognized as inadequate to afford relief in the vast majority of cases for which it was formerly recommended."[42]

Gynecological surgery expressed an unyielding aspiration for con-trol of birth. Sims could not construe therapeutic action apart from preparing woman for pregnancy. So he demanded a thirty-five-year-old woman become pregnant in exchange for a cure of general pain and trouble in her reproductive tract. "I asked my patient . . . if she would like to have more offspring. She promptly replied 'No.' 'Well,' said I, 'it's difficult for me to determine what else to do, if you will not consent for me to rectify the condition of the mouth of the womb, so conception can take place.' " Sims cut through her cervix in order to remove the barrier to the inward flow of sperm. He was triumphant. "Notwithstanding her feeble state of health, and the length of time since the birth of her last child, conception occurred a month after the operation. . . . But I am constrained to say that the pregnancy produced no good effect either constitu-

tionally or locally." Nineteenth-century medical literature is rich
in such verbatim evidence, and it marked the triumph of male sexual authority (and the psychology it reflected) over the delicacy of
feminine psychology:

> all false delicacy must be laid aside; it is a matter of the gravest im-
> portance, and must be treated as such.
>
>   I told her and her husband that I must see her just after sexual
> intercourse. The time was appointed; I was at the house, and in four
> or five minutes after the act I saw my patient; and the vagina did
> not contain a drop of semen, but it was on her person and her nap-
> kin in the greatest quantity.

In this particular case Sims diagnosed a kind of spermatic rebound
from a recalcitrant canal wall; he performed his incision of the os
only to realize it had been "not at all necessary."[43]

Sims accepted the charge that his view of copulation was "mechanical." "It is only necessary to get the semen into the proper place
in the proper time. It makes no difference whether the copulative
act be performed with great vigour and intense erethism, or whether
it be done feebly, quickly, and unsatisfactorily. . . ." Under the
conditions man would always experience orgasm, whereas whether
a woman did or did not was entirely irrelevant. This was medicine's
version of the Victorian idea that women simply did not experience
sexual desire—which we shall see conformed to men's wishes.[44]

The "mechanical view" took woman's sexual organs for her whole
identity. Brigham, Ray, and Meigs all believed and taught that
woman's distinction, that is, her sexual organs, commanded her psychology beyond her will. In fact, a gynecologist could get information from a womb as if it were its owner's very self. "If the nose
bleeds we try to stop it by the most direct means in our power. . . .
Why, then, should we permit the womb to lose an unnatural quantity of blood without at once interrogating it on the subject." The
idiom carried over into Sims's invention when he called an instrument for the amputation of the cervix the "uterine guillotine," a
name which suggests the extent to which Sims felt women to be at
his mercy.[45]

Sims said that vaginas were as variegated as faces, but he advocated the imposition of a standard on the rest of the generative
tract (much as Ray had done for the hygiene of the mind three
years before the publication of *Clinical Notes*). Sims frankly "laid
down the ideal of what a womb should be" and described the "perfect form" of the cervix. The standard was the same as that by

which he judged copulation: "we shall proceed to the sterile unim-
pregnated uterus to see how it may differ from a normal conceptive
state." When a womb was open to impregnation it had a "gaping,
graceful form."[46]

His habit of seeing a face in a woman's reproductive organs led
Sims to coin the term "vaginismus," that state of tender frigidity
forbidding all entry by the male; Sims labeled it "by analogy with
the spasmodic contraction of the vocal apparatus" which was called
"laringismus." His elaboration of the image suggests both the fantasy of a toothed vagina and at the same time the gynecologist's
instrumental (and sadistic) way of dealing with such apprehensions: to "examine a case of suspected vaginismus, place the patient
on the back, with the legs flexed; separate gently the labia. The
patient will exhibit signs of alarm and agitation,—not that we hurt
her, but she feels an indescribable dread of being hurt. She is like a
timid, nervous person who has once had a pointed instrument thrust
into the exposed pulp of an inflamed tooth."[47]

Sims saw several cases of vaginismus in which "the virile power
of the husband was unusually strong, but yet powerless to overcome the obstruction." He found the precedent for treatment was
to anesthetize the woman: "a physician etherized his patient, and
then left her to her husband, who cohabited with her with the greatest ease; but he could not repeat the act when she was not etherized.
Fortunately, the period was well chosen, for this single act of copulation was followed by conception." In another case "it became the
business of the physician to repair regularly to the residence of this
couple two or three times a week to etherize the poor wife for the
purpose above alluded to."[48] This physician provided another year
of "ethereal copulation," Sims's pun perhaps revealing a heavenli-
ness for both sides, the man with a totally subordinated wife, and
the wife oblivious to an act which conventionally she was supposed
to find at best a distasteful duty and, at worst, disgusting. "It is a
mistake to suppose that the kindness, the kiss and the loving embrace
of a wife are, in general, the expression of sexual desire."[49] That
belief provides an explanation for the phenomenon of vaginismus;
one of Sims's patients had tolerated for a year her husband's attempts to break through her resistance. "She innocently supposed
that all women had to suffer as she did, and tried to bear it; but her
sufferings were so severe that at last she looked with the greatest
terror upon the approaches of her husband. At her earnest en-
treaties, he ceased all efforts at sexual intercourse and they lived

together like brother and sister." Vaginismus was simply a more
thoroughgoing form of general expectations of woman's character,
a version of Cooper's "shrinking delicacy" and Tocqueville's account
of "natural barriers" that made the "solicitations" of husband less
"frequent and less ardent" and the "resistance" of wife more easy.
"One of Sims' contemporaries asserted that in woman, as in almost
all females, passivity generally marks the sexual act." Dr. Gardner
said that "sensuality" was "unusual in the sex." "I am convinced
that but one question only is to be asked, viz., if healthy spermatozoa are brought into contact with healthy ova, to decide this question. Frigidity may or may not accompany the act; the result is as
independent of sensation, as if there was a chemical transformation
that is going on." The Memorial presented by the Woman's Hospital supporters to the New York State Legislature in 1856 assumed
that one inevitable phase of woman's life was her exposure to the
untold miseries which "the marital relation" might be expected to
cause. One can see how the adherence of doctors to such beliefs
reinforced them.[50]

By the same token the issue of "cure" is historically relative.
Sims's first vaginismus patient's whole "nervous system was in a
deplorable condition." The source of such a state had to lie in her
generative organs. There was no question what Sims's treatment
would be. "When asked if it were possible to cure it, I said—'I do
not know for the books throw no light on the subject; but it appears
to me that the only rational treatment would be surgical.'" He cut
and cut and cut, without effect, although he believed that if he had
not stopped he would have solved the problem. The patient's
mother concluded Sims was experimenting on her daughter, and
Sims admitted as much. Clearly he was in a position to experiment
on rich women now, in addition to blacks and the poor. Sims said
he was justified, since the patient's husband was threatening her
with a lawsuit and divorce. This justification assumed the force of
male prerogative, and of woman's existence's submission to such
prerogatives, not of any intrinsically valued cure. In spite of the
"inexorable" mother, who "unfortunately," in Sims's view, removed
her daughter from Sims's care, "the experience gained by this was
of great value" to Sims. He continued to treat vaginismus surgically,
removing the hymen where necessary, incising the vaginal orifice,
and subsequently dilating it with the appropriate wedges. This
treatment worked successfully in thirty-nine cases out of thirty-
nine, if one can believe him. It is clear from Chadwick's account of

bandwagonry operative procedures that many claims for cure were fabricated. In the first place surgeons were pointed toward claiming success by their separation of a successful operation from the cure of the patient on whom it was performed. And second, there appears to have been virtually no firsthand follow-up of the patient's postoperative life.[51]

But it is reasonable to suppose that Sims did cure his cases of vaginismus because the terms of this sickness and its treatment were so close to each other and to the wider sociology of heterosexual relations. Vaginismus won woman the heightened attention of an authoritative male. Sims's gynecological examination duplicated the terms of the patient's heterosexual relations, to the patient's as well as his own mind. Perhaps Sims's surgery finally confronted his patient with the lesson that better-disciplined women learned earlier, that man's authority was irresistible. They could relax in light of having carried their resistance as far as possible. In any case doctor and patient played out a symbiotic relation in the historically common terms.

Certainly Sims saw himself stamping out disorder in the way that he once pressed a feminist back to pregnancy. Because of the sexually charged relationship of gynecologist and patient, Sims had to cope with the characteristic "delicacy" that sexual separation demanded. Sims made a virtue of necessity in advocating the use of his speculum, which required a third person. Apart from this "real value" of the presence of a third person, "delicacy and propriety" required it. But that, too, could violate delicacy. Like his contemporaries, Sims fell into paradoxical coils. First he took Ray's position in suggesting that the well-educated woman was submissive. "I have never had a patient to object who was educated or sensible; but the silliest person would see the necessity of it when told that propriety required it, even if an assistant were not necessary." He went on to link that education to submission to the "innate feeling of delicacy," and claimed he would adjust his scientific sights to respect such a value. The patient had to be covered with a sheet. "When the speculum is used we should see only the neck of the womb and the canal of the vagina." The logic was that only "silly" women had to be persuaded of their innate delicacy. Their silliness was in refusing to accept the male definition of them. A woman who agreed to submit herself to a second incision of the os after the first failed to work acted "like a true woman." Propriety, sense, and courage on woman's part consisted in her submission to Sims's phallic science. One patient assented to Sims's trying to cure her protruding uterus: "Her pluck challenged my inventive faculties." It was only another expression of the character democratic men sought in their vicissitude-bearing wives: "it is possible even in very difficult cases, to understand the obstacles to conception, and to remove them by persistent continued effort, if our patient has sufficient fortitude and endurance." Of course, Sims's field for his impatience to remove obstacles was woman's body, whereas other men pursued elusive success in the body of the continent.[52]

On one hand Sims would join the husband on his side of the barrier of delicacy, to enforce submission of the sex. He split the necks of the wombs of "delicate, timid women, who were conscious that something was being done, but had no idea that it was a surgical operation . . . the operations were performed at the suggestion and earnest wish of the husbands, who feared that they might not be fully submitted to if fully explained." On the other hand he acted in concert with the wife to protect male apprehensions. For "our sex," i.e., men, the "knowledge of the presence of a vaginal support might be an unpoetical association. . . . Sometimes the wife has insisted that it was not necessary for the husband to know that the uterus was thus artificially braced up." On another occasion a young, childless widow felt she would not be able to get married unless she could produce children. Sims provided her with a uterine support beforehand, she married, neither Sims nor the bride told the groom, and she had a baby within a reasonable time. In short, his relations with his patients and their husbands were shot through with the social assumptions that charged gynecological disease.[53]

Sims, then, succeeded in inducing pregnancy where the husband had failed. His terms recalled his hostility toward woman's reproductive organs, and perhaps his own. To enjoy sex was "mere animal sensuality"; what rendered copulation blessed was the production of children, "it matter not how perfectly and satisfactorily it be done." Science was more virile than nature, and the absence of a need for pleasure in sexual intercourse reinforced the doctor's authority. "Let us turn to pages 331 and 332 and read over the cases in which conception took place while the wives were etherized and ask ourselves what agency mere sensual enjoyment could have had in bringing about the result." This was consistent with the assertion of woman's essential lack of desire (by gynecologists as well as other kinds of experts), which, I suggest, lay behind vaginismus.[54]

Sims literalized his scientific mastery of copulation (or, conversely, his devaluation of its human quality) by inventing what he called "mechanical fertilization" by a mechanical penis: "almost four drops of semen were taken up; the instrument was cautiously carried into the canal of the cervix, till the point was in close contact with the os tincae; then the piston rod was slowly turned half a revolution, which as slowly forced out half a drop of semen; the instrument was held *in situ* for ten or fifteen seconds, and then withdrawn." It was a particularly appropriate activity for one whose relationship to his sexual partner was, in the view of a colleague, that of engine to flywheel.[55]

While the bulk of Sims's prescription for the management of sterility was devoted to the surgical treatment of women, he also turned to the implications of a recent discovery. "A short time ago it was generally supposed that sterility was a thing that belonged almost wholly to the opposite sex." But in 1864 the British Dr. Curling "established very conclusively that sterility in the male does positively exist." The only complete monograph in English on sterility at the time of Sims's *Clinical Notes* (as Sims acknowledged) was Gardner's *The Causes and Curative Treatment of Sterility* (1856), which barely mentioned the possibility that a man could be sterile, only to dismiss it.[56] And *Clinical Notes* was still not concerned in the least to treat men. Curling's discovery was surprising and distressing news to gynecologists who found that numbers of their operations had been as impotent as their customers' husbands. The issue was a mark of the distance that had opened up between the sexes (and, perhaps, of the intensification of the pressure on male identity) since the Puritans: they had been perfectly well aware of man's responsibility for impotence, and Jefferson had been aware of the Puritans' awareness.[57]

The same invidiousness characterized Sims's fruit and vegetable imagery in *Clinical Notes*. Sims compared the woman's reproductive tract's polyps, fibroids, cysts, and excrescences to partridge and pullets' eggs, Sicily oranges, English walnuts, grains of wheat, garden peas, and a cauliflower. In aiming to cure menorrhagia, he says he will have to "strike at the root of the evil." To a gynecologist a woman was judged "fruitful" in her production of diseases, and, again, Sims's terms catch up the symbiotic nature of his relationship to his patients. The creative gynecologist's gardening bore fruit in parturition, and in his own "bantlings," his invention of new diseases for new cures.[58]

Men had not considered that they could be responsible for steril-

ity. The scientific assessment of the relative values of a man and
woman's procreative capacities reflected the social relationship of
the sexes. It was the man's energies which were responsible for the
great work of society (including the perpetuation of dynasties and
governments), and woman's life was devoted to supporting and
husbanding her husband's power. Just as men invaded the home to
tell women how to raise children, so gynecologists reached into the
heterosexual relation to tell husband and wife that their joint concern therein was to keep sperm souped up to a particular level of
richness. "I am satisfied too that too frequent sexual indulgence is
fraught with mischief to both parties. It weakens the semen. In
other words, this is not so rich in spermatozoa after too great indulgence; and when carried to the extent of a debauch, the fluid
ejected may be wholly destitute of spermatozoa. Thus it is much
better to husband the resources of both man and wife."[59]

The idea was to use neither more nor less sperm than was thought
necessary for the production of a baby, thus ensuring the "richness"
of the sperm at next copulation. So Sims was led to another activity
in pursuit of mechanical, economic production. "I do not know that
any one has ever thought of measuring the quantity of semen
ejected in the act of copulation. . . . I was induced on several occasions to remove [semen] with a syringe, and to measure it subsequently, and I found that ordinarily there was about a drachm
and ten minims."[60]

With sperm so valued, and presented as the joint sexual property
of man and wife, it seems reasonable to suggest that Sims's account
of the female organ's postcopulative inactivity was as invidious as
his surprise that a male might be responsible for infertility. After
coition the uterus presented "signs of exhaustion, if I may be allowed such an expression. . . ." The vagina was "relaxed, and pas-
sively holding a large quantity of semen." The uterus seemed "fa-
tigued, and drops by its own gravity down towards the rectum
where it lazily sinks to the bottom of a little pool of semen." Nothing surprised Sims more, he said, than this difference in the condition of the uterus before and after "sexual congress." Perhaps it
seemed unfair that these organs, characteristically passive and re-
ceptive, should somehow act as if they had been as productive as
a penis. Sims's explanation conjured up the ingestive fantasy about
the "mouth of the vagina" which sometimes "grasped" his fingers.
Sims believed that this grasping facility came into play during
copulation. "I have spoken of a superior constrictor vaginae, and

attribute to it a certain office, that of pressing the glans forcibly against the os tincae at a certain moment. . . ." It was, he thought, only a matter of time before someone proved it: Sims had already seen such muscular contractions in the vaginas of women in that state of "general nervous agitation" that Brigham found so threatening to the American state.[61]

Sims's career represents the triumph and consolidation of surgical gynecology. At the time of his death in 1883, gynecologists could apply their knives at will to the whole range of woman's being, reduced as it was to sex.

11   Sexual Surgery

Gynecologists exhibited mad impatience, addiction to chance, ferocious competitiveness with other men—and a paradoxical dependence upon them for judgment of success in self-making. Their anxiety over identity, their measurement of themselves in terms of what I describe in Chapter 15 as "the spermatic economy" and "proto-sublimation," and the consequent and interactive responses to women were typical of democratic American men as Tocqueville had described them in the first half of the century, and as they were of their contemporaries in other fields. They thought of themselves and the world as John Todd and the other popular, Franklinesque stylists of male behavior had assumed and advised. Self-making was a particularly clear (and self-defeating) reproductive goal in the hands of gynecologists.[1]

Clitoridectomy was the first operation performed to check woman's mental disorder. Invented by an English gynecologist in 1858, it began in America in the late 1860s and was performed at least until 1904 and perhaps until 1925. After publishing his results in 1866, the English inventor, Isaac Baker Brown, was severely censured by his profession; he died two years later, and the performance of clitoridectomy in England died with him.[2] In the U.S. it coexisted with, and then was superseded by, the circumcision of females of all ages up to menopause; circumcision continued to be performed here until 1937 at least. Both clitoridectomy and circumcision aimed to check what was thought to be a growing incidence of female masturbation, an activity which men feared inevitably aroused women's naturally boundless but usually repressed sexual appetite for men. As we shall see, men believed they needed to deploy their sperm elsewhere for success—in the gynecological curbing of female sexual appetite for example.

"Female castration," or "oophorectomy," or "normal ovariotomy," was a much more widespread and frequently performed operation than clitoridectomy. It was first performed in 1872, flourished between 1880 and 1900, and slackened pace only in the first decade of the twentieth century. Women were still being castrated for psychological disorders as late as 1946. During the operation's heyday doctors boasted that they had removed from 1,500 to 2,000 ovaries apiece. Female castration was largely superseded by other similar operations, including hysterectomy, which had coexisted as an alternative and auxiliary to castration since about 1895. And of course there is evidence today of "excessive," "promiscuous," and "careless" surgical treatment in America, particularly that accorded women and children. The examples frequently cited include hysterectomy, mastectomy, tonsillectomy, infant circumcision, hemorrhoidectomy—and oophorectomy, the latter indicated by apparently physical conditions. Such a continuation perhaps sustains the argument that the operations reflect beliefs especially true of American psychology: the operations (performed overwhelmingly by men) are distinct from other countries in frequency and in concentration. For example, in the U.S.A. in 1965, 516 hysterectomies and 278 breast operations were performed for each 100,000 of the female population. The respective figures in England and Wales in 1966 were 213.2 and 171.7, two and a half times less. The contrast should be compared to the relative positions of midwives in each country.[3]

From one perspective, the castration of women starting in the 1870s (performed overwhelmingly on noninstitutionalized outpatients, and only later—in the 1890s—on inmates of mental institutions) was part of the general anxiety about the racial future of white America. From the post–Civil War period until World War II there was an accelerating eugenic program in the U.S., carried out on the bodies of the insane and epileptic. In the period I have been studying, such sterilization was actually implemented on the bodies of women, not men. Ruth Caplan has described how late nineteenth-century treatment of the insane combined sterilization, isolation, and dehumanization. Perhaps the same can be said for Americans' experience of each other generally. The purging of criminals, paupers, deaf mutes, retarded, and so on (the period is remarkable for its bizarre and vast compendia of physiological curiosities and abnormalcies) was a major contribution to the process.[4]

Many social leaders and molders—doctors, clergymen, popular novelists, and politicians—saw America as a beleaguered island of WASP righteousness, surrounded by an encroaching flood of dirty, prolific immigrants, and sapped from within by the subversive practices of women. Their masturbation, contraception, and abortion were exhausting society's procreative power. These males saw society as a body invaded by foreign germs, its native blood corrupted and used up from outside and within. Whatever its metaphor, this vision was shared by gynecologists attempting to purge midwives away from the perverted sources of new life, snipping off addicting clitorises and removing the ovaries of women deemed unfit to breed, or too rebellious in themselves to be tolerated. The anxieties intensified toward the end of the century, the critical zenith of the "search for order." The separation and subordination of blacks was formalized at a national level in 1896, and their segregation, castration, and lynching coincided with the growing nativism, the lynching of immigrants, the extirpation of resistant Filipinos and Indians, and the peak of the castration of women.

Advocates and modifiers of wholesale female castration saw themselves reimposing order of the kind conventionally expected of female behavior. As we have seen, a woman was supposed to be dependent, submissive, unquenchably supportive, smiling, imparting an irrelevant morality, regarding sex as something to be endured, and her own organs as somehow a dirty if necessary disease. Above all she was supposed to be entirely predictable. It was a role geared to man's behavior in, and apprehensions of, the ceaseless strife of the world outside home. The overriding importance attached to physiological identity entailed a rigid asseveration of the sexual distinction. Hence any attempt by women to break out of their circumscription signified to men that such disorderly women wanted to become men. Female castration was designed to take care of such a threat. Accordingly, cure was pronounced if a woman was successfully stuffed back into her appropriate slot. An 1893 proponent of female castration claimed that "patients are improved, some of them cured; . . . the moral sense of the patient is elevated . . . she becomes tractable, orderly, industrious, and cleanly." Doctors claimed success for castration when it returned woman to her normal role, subservient to her husband, her family, and household duties. Her disorder lay in her deviation from that role, a broad enough characterization to explain the bewildering and suspicious variety of indications. Opponents of wholesale castration applied the same yardstick—they criticized the operation because it failed to restore woman to her standard role.[5]

Membership of the body politic had always been limited by sex organs. The assumption of woman's special liability to mental sickness by way of her characteristic menstrual and reproductive functions pushed all women close to the criminal category: "an insane woman," in the words of Dr. William Goodell, professor of clinical gynecology at the University of Pennsylvania, "is no more a member of the body politic than a criminal." If women were only sex organs, and female sex organs were by nature a menace to health unless run to earth by pregnancy, then women were by nature sick; and if woman's sickness was construed as intolerable social disorder, then to be a woman was a crime. For Gardner, menstruation was an "infirmity." He held that "it was a crime to be sick." Women, then, were criminals by nature.[6]

Men's growing sense of vulnerability after the Civil War—their notion of social crisis and the concomitant gynecological crescendo —cannot be disassociated from the increasing vociferousness of women at the same time, most noticeably on the suffrage front. Doctors, like other men, also displayed persistent anxiety over the growing numbers of the new, conspicuously consuming, fashionable life style of city women, their style dangerously attractive to all women.

Between 1870 and 1910, women ran 480 campaigns in 33 states, trying to put women's suffrage before the male voters. Women most active in the suffrage movement and related consumer organizations came from the same social background from which gynecologists drew their patients—those new women left workless by the Industrial Revolution's change in work patterns and reenslaved as possessions for display in the way described by Donald Meyer. In the light of evidence supplied by men in gynecology, it does not seem entirely accurate to suggest, as Eleanor Flexner does, that women's suffrage was felt as less of a threat in the 1890s than it had been before. Women's organizations may have become more conventional and conservative in their views toward immigration and race. Moreover, they confined their base to richer women, drawing back from the poor and alien. In this women shared the beleaguered antipathy of their male peers. Nonetheless, WASP women supplied the largest proportion by far of the bodies that were sterilized. In

1906 a leading gynecological surgeon estimated that there were 150,000 women in the U.S. without ovaries, the number, he said, reflecting the profound influence of Robert Battey's invention. It signified the involvement with the operation of many thousands more people as surgeons, husbands, fathers, or other custodial relatives, in consultation with wives, mothers, friends, and GPs.[7]

From the beginning, woman's "right to motherhood" had given the castrators pause in "unsexing" her. The inventor of female castration for nonovarian conditions, Robert Battey, listed "loss of procreative power" as one of the chief objections to the operation. Men assumed women shared this view of their own significance. Battey finessed the issue by asking rhetorically of what value was reproduction to a thirty-year-old woman (the average age of Battey's reported castratees), all her life an invalid, and "hopelessly incurable excepting by the change of life which itself implies the loss of this function." In any case, a candidate for castration was, he said, "in all probability sterile." Battey's followers extended the rationale by arguing that even if she did give birth, a woman disordered enough to warrant castration would bear defective children anyway.[8] Castration, like controlled pregnancy in the right kind of women, helped implement the vision of a healthy body politic for which women simply supplied the material.

A second definition of "unsexing" was the obliteration of woman's sexual desire. If castrators found it impossible to argue that castration did not destroy a woman's reproductive power, they could and did contend that it left her her sexual feelings. But desire was regarded as a symptom indicating castration; so men redefined her "aphrodisiacal power," her "sexual feeling," to be the signals of her attraction which men wanted to receive. One of them was her absence of desire. In taking up this prickly issue, the castrators were as elusive in their evidence as they were over the success of the operation. Dr. E. W. Cushing of Boston declared: "As to the loss of sexual desire, I have heard my patients frankly answer that they have not suffered in that direction." In one of his earlier cases of castration, Cushing had demonstrated his belief that orgasm was disease, and cure was orgasm's destruction. In 1897, Cushing said that gynecological anxieties over "unsexing" represented the projection of male feelings: "we must not impute to a woman feelings in regard to the loss of her organs which are derived from what we, as men, would think of a similar operation on a man. A woman does not feel she is unsexed, and she is not unsexed." Cushing's assumption was that "the sex's" sexuality did not lie in its sex organs as man's did. It was irrelevant to woman's feelings whether she had sex organs or not. Cushing went on, "I have questioned more than 200 of them on that point." Another doctor, Henry Carstens, questioned 400 castratees on the score. Such questions about woman's desire were put by medical authority, male and castrating, to the nonmedical, powerless, female and castrated, both sides sharing precepts of what constituted being male and being female. One woman who had been castrated for the "sexual perversion" of masturbation wrote back to her castrator to report, "My condition is all I could desire. I know and feel that I am well; I never think of self-abuse; it is foreign and distasteful to me."[9]

In effect, male gynecologists without exception revealed a profound anxiety about female sexual appetite. Opponents of wholesale castration agreed with proponents on the need to castrate women manifesting uncontrollable desire. Dr. Archibald Church attacked castration where there were no "underlying pathological changes clinically discoverable." But he fell back on just such questionable ground when he came across willful sexual promiscuity in woman. "Certain women especially at the menstrual epoch are so overcome by the intensity of sexual desires and excitement that they practically lose self-control and all modesty. Here social relations enter into the argument." In Church's view the implicit inner struggle must be weighted by the intervention of the surgeon's knife on the side of the woman's modest self. Consideration of woman's right to sexual appetite is entirely absent from the medical record.[10]

The case histories of the 1890s and the years following paid lip service to other kinds of rights—the patient's right to express a preference for "conservative" or extirpative surgery, for example—provided the surgeon judged such a preference to be consistent with his notion "of domestic happiness." Female circumcision was advocated on the grounds that depriving infant females of it was denying their equality with boys. In the final analysis, the physician was supposed to know what was best for the patient. If "rights" rhetoric reflected awareness of feminist demands, or of contradictions in democratic practice, it was usually pressed into the service of the reimposition of the male order. So it was with Dr. Cushing's allowing woman's "being ready" to have some opinion: he interpreted the readiness and the opinion as symptoms for which he castrated her. Similarly, Dr. W. P. Manton found it appropriate to describe his advocacy of the castration of "demented" women in terms of their "right to relief from bodily suffering." If women were claiming a voice, doctors attempted to control it, scaring patients into choosing what the doctor chose, just as obstetricians persuaded women after 1910 that naturally safe childbearing was unnatural, that parturient women would need expert, male, therapeutic attendance; and just as Tocqueville's typical American male provided his young women with the illusion of freely choosing the course (marriage) he presented to her as the one on which her social existence depended.[11]

There was another way in which woman's participation in the therapeutic relation seemed to expand late in the century. The gynecologists' awareness of woman's voice (only to adjust their techniques in quelling it) coincided with a resuscitation of "suggestive therapeutics" in the 1880s and 1890s and the years following, a precursor of psychosomatic medicine.[12] Suggestive therapeutics was one aspect of the renewed interest on the part of a few gynecologists in their patients' wholeness. They acknowledged that their patients had an entire nervous system, a background, an environment, and a mind.

Gynecological materialism was symbolized by the removal or modification of woman's sexual organs on account of her mental disorder. Yet castrators and clitoridectomists persistently presented their work as an attempt to get woman to control herself. They demanded woman's collusion. As we saw in the case of Church, gynecologists assumed the existence of a will, a "modest" self, which their treatment seemed to deny, even as men separated themselves from women on whom they depended—for order, for reproduction, and to know who they were.

In America, the acknowledgment of the part played by the patient's mind in therapy derived largely from gynecologists' difficulties with the iatrogenic effects of female castration—it drove women insane.[13] Postoperative insanity manifested mind to all but the most dedicated of castrators: the latter argued removal of the ovaries was not enough, and moved on to extirpate uterus and Fallopian tubes. But a Dr. Warner had disputed Cushing's claim in 1887 to have cured a woman by means of castration. Warner believed that the favorable result of Cushing's operation, performed on a woman driven by masturbation to melancholia, came from the psychological impact. Dr. Symington-Brown agreed with Warner on the same occasion, saying that any shock would have had a comparable effect, since the brain was involved in nymphomania, not the ovaries.[14]

Some of these critics were led to a view of disease, treatment, and cure as an interactive process between doctor and patient. But these same critics shared many assumptions with the castrators they opposed. Moreover, awareness of castration's effectiveness as "shock" treatment could and did lead all the way back to Battey's original (1873) advocacy of castration for nonovarian conditions. The suggestive rationale was adopted by the wholesale castrators— they performed the operation precisely on the grounds for which Warner and Symington-Brown had attacked it.[15]

Emphases on mind and wholeness led in several other directions: to the advocacy of a general examination of the patient by the gynecologist, starting with her mouth or eyes; and to consultation with the proliferating neurological and psychological experts (coexisting with the accelerating experiments with the therapeutic transplanting of ovaries).[16] Acknowledging the significant existence of the patient's mind, doctors found they had to diversify to compete with nonmedical experts. Dr. Robert Edes said in 1898 that castration stood "on the same basis as regards its immediate effect on the patient as any of the popular forms of faith cure." Some gynecologists realized that their patients and the devotees of the new mind cures were in the same category as disordered women. Imparting confidence and providing "suggestion" were among the brands of orthodox medicine having to compete with Christian Science. Donald Meyer points out that among the reasons doctors had to compete with mind cure was that their intrusive "gross masculinity" embodied the world that female patients yearned to escape. In a sense, such women were overavid believers in the separated world of Victorian delicacy, the ones whom gynecologists were not able to persuade that their new kind of encroachment was necessary. As we saw, there had been, at mid-century, some considerable dispute in gynecological ranks between the pedestal subordinators of women and the more intrusive ones. Meyer's magnificently subtle *The Positive Thinkers* presents the predominantly female-supported Christian Science and other mind-cure sects as reactions to the aggressive, masterful, self-sufficient, and obsessively masculine life style. Yet the alternative feminine style's sick helplessness was dependent on the achievement and character of such a "tunnel vision of the straining world of male ego," in the same way that women generally were dependent on men. (Ironically, that male vision was dependent on the distinct dependence of women.) Meyer points out the spiraling metapsychology of mind cure, its dependency projecting "upon that on which it was dependent, the same closed self-sufficiency it dared not claim for itself." More than that, the "deliberate drill" Christian Science imposed during its class instruction was for the "maintenance of order," specifically over body. Mind cure shared the ambition of the nineteenth-century crypto-Franklins for the young men they claimed to teach; and mind cure shared the gynecological ambition to reimpose order on the same sort of women flocking to doctors' offices, women whose novel lives were created by the sort of men whom women wished to escape.[17]

If the sick condition of women whom gynecologists demanded collaborate with them derived in part from postindustrial worklessness, it also depended on it for treatment. According to Dr. Palmer Dudley in 1900, "the hardworking, daily-toiling woman is not as fit a subject for [gynecological surgery] as the woman so situated in life as to be able to conserve her strength and if necessary, to take a prolonged rest, in order to secure the best results." In some respects, the workless woman was tailor-made for the therapy dealing with the disorder caused by her tailor-making for therapy.[18]

The voluminous and extraordinarily explicit evidence supplied by medical journals, together with Meyer's account of mind cure, suggest that the variety of symptoms focused on woman's sex organs can be explained as an expression of female anxiety shaped by conventional role expectations. The sound of mass complaint which rises from these case histories may be added to the other kind of female voice protesting political discrimination. Both kinds harmonized with a large part of the register sounded by male voices. In Dr. Manton's phrase of 1909, castratable women were mentally alienated.[19] But all women were supposed to be alien from the democratic norm. It was male. Men wanted women to be shrinking, withdrawn and separate from the sordid traffic of the world. But if the ebullient, masterful male was the standard of social health, then anyone different from it ran the danger of being labeled sick. Such associations were a long-standing tradition within and without medicine, from 1820 to 1920, and later. J. Marion Sims's newly discovered and labeled cases of "vaginismus" reported in 1866 and Battey's candidates for castration between 1872 and 1891 exhibited "exquisite tenderness" in organs shrinking from the male touch— precisely the response women were supposed to make, in bed and in general.

Women were being orderly in asking the appropriate social authorities to help. After Cushing's castration of her, that woman "previously sunk into a state of profound melancholia on account of her belief that her masturbation eternally damned her, told him that 'a window has been opened in heaven.' "[20] Gynecologists were answering women's prayers. But their sexual values condemned gynecologists to sustain the belief that being female was a disease. Doctors' attempts to restore to women a measure of will power was a Sisyphean rock of their own making. As men generally (including doctors) confined women to the butterfly existence that made them sick, more demanding, in need of more confinement (to bed, asylum, or both), and so on, so doctors created symptoms they attempted to cure, their therapy expressing the same assumptions of the male identity which found it necessary to exclude and subordinate women (as they excluded the "feminine" in themselves). Doctors and gynecologists prescribed addictive drugs for displaced and disordered women; if drugs did not work, the same doctor, or another one, castrated the patient, deeming her drug addiction a symptom of her sick condition; if that operation did not work, she was put back on drugs. If only one ovary was extirpated at first, or both ovaries but not the tubes, or ovaries and tubes but not the uterus, the cycle of drugs and operations could drag on and on. It was extended when surgeons began to cure castrated women by transplanting into their bodies ovarian tissue from another woman. This kind of circle permitted men to ignore the commitment to male insanity they believed their competitive and obsessive life style entailed. Castration destroyed woman's one remaining thread of identity, her hope for motherhood, in the way critics of the operation described. Many castrated women were left hopeless, sunk into despair on a scale almost beyond imagination.

But by the same standard of social beliefs generating disease, castration could and did work. If the nature of the doctor's authority, and its expression in his treatment, and the nature of the patient's belief, and its expression in her disorder, were all pitched just right, then she might be restored to an "order" she would be willing to accept. Clearly the missing factors in all of these cases could have been crucial. As I suggested in the case of Sims, one reason for the success of a few cases may have been the gynecological surgeon's necessary decisiveness, which made him more likely to conform to the putatively authoritative role of the male than the dreadfully pressured democrat, unsupported by such expertise. Disorderly women were handed over to the gynecologists for castration and others kinds of radical treatment by husbands or fathers unable to enforce their minimum identity guarantee—the submission of woman. The handed-over woman then underwent a period of intense discipline by anesthesia and knife, or the S. Weir Mitchell kind, developed concurrently with castration (which Mitchell also performed). Mitchell's "rest-cure" consisted of the patient's descent to womblike dependence, then rebirth, liquid food, weaning, upbringing, and reeducation by a model parental organization—a trained female nurse entirely and unquestioningly the agent firmly implementing the orders of the more distant and totally authoritative male, i.e., the doctor in charge. The patient was returned to her menfolk's management, recycled and taught to make the will of the male her own.[21]

Some women refused castration, standing on their right to motherhood and the value of maternal identity which they shared with men, whatever the difference in their reasons. On the other hand, many women went much further than simply allowing their men to submit them to the knife. By and large, women shared beliefs about roles and social order: if such beliefs drove them inevitably to disorder, they went to the proper authorities. One "maiden lady" in 1877 demanded of William Goodell and Weir Mitchell that they remove her womb and ovaries, once they had told her of such operations.[22]

The sequence of such a gynecologist-patient dialectic is clear: men invented or heard of the new operations and decided to try them; they informed women, or women's menfolk. The news got abroad. So some proponents of castration could declare innocently that the patient came in to beg to be castrated. Edes said in 1898 that such pleas reflected the "professional medical errors of a previous medical generation." In 1897 B. Sherwood Dunn considered the doctor's responsibility in such cases. "The fact . . . that women came to us pleading to have their ovaries removed, a thing which happens to every man in practice, is all the more reason why we should stand between them" and the deleterious results. On the same occasion, Dr. Henry Carstens admitted that "a woman does not always come to us to have [her ovaries] removed, but because she has some morbid condition which causes her to apply to the physician, and the doctor, thinking it is the tubes and ovaries that are at fault, removes them. In many cases a wrong diagnosis is made." Gynecologists remained convinced that they knew best, and they either tortured the notion of the participation of the patient's will or simply reneged on a preoperation agreement if a woman managed to extract one—not to remove both ovaries, for example—once the patient was unconscious under the knife.[23]

The conflict in a woman confronted with the Hobson's choice of castration must have been a terrible one, torn as she was by the differing male demands on her. She was troublesome enough to her husband or father (with his persistent apprehensions of her sperm-sucking propensities[24] and the menace of her menstruation) to have him present her for castration. At the same time, she would have been aware of the male demand for race preservation, his woman's ovaries man's route to the future of the WASP nation. Gynecologists accused WASP women of undermining that future by aborting and contracepting. And as a corollary, woman would have been aware of the social calumny that followed her castration; castrated women were commonly known as "its." To paraphrase Freud, what did men want? And woman would have been torn, too, by her own lifetime's interiorization of such feelings. They were hers, together with her feelings about her body's submission to the doctor's surgical appetite.[25]

In 1904 one doctor noted the power of social beliefs in spreading these operations. Female patients were "fully convinced that directly or indirectly, all their grief emanates from the pelvis, and oftentimes this idea is fostered and materially augmented by their friends." Women were "the sex." The gynecological phenomena herein described were symbiotic between patient and doctor, reflecting and refracting the underlying contours of social beliefs and expectations. Another doctor, this time in 1906, reported a case in which a patient had repeatedly requested that the right ovary and uterus be removed. She was refused because no conditions existed warranting such a procedure. But usually friends, relatives, and doctors would confirm a woman's tracing her trouble to her sex organs. In the words of this 1906 doctor, Ely Van de Warker, "the sociological relations of the mistakes about the ovaries have been brought into the daily life of the woman. So constantly have they been held up before her as the one evil spot on her anatomy, that she has grown to look with suspicion on her own organs." "The sex" naturally associated identity problems with that part of themselves deemed by men, and women, to be their raison d'être. According to Robert Edes, "tradition, popular prejudice and accident play no inconsiderable parts in giving that bad eminence to the pelvic organs." While he condemned the carelessness and ignorance of doctors, Van de Warker included women in his account of the "sociological reflex" of pelvic surgery. Another doctor had laid part of the responsibility for the almost automatic mutilation of woman's sexual organs to women's own appropriation of such operations as a "fashionable fad" and as a "mark of favor," an image suggesting that some women understood and responded to the surgeon's invasion of their bodies as a form of courtship and copulation. It may be noted that clitoridectomists and castrators tested woman for indications of the disease of desire by inducing orgasm, manipulating clitoris or breasts. Some women considered their scars "as pretty as the dimple in the cheek of sweet sixteen," and so adopted the views of Goodell and other gynecologists that castration made women more attractive sexually. Van de Warker placed the major portion of responsibility for the operations on the medical profession, but he also described the collaboration of passive, careless, and wealthy women. A man of his times, he bewailed the destruction of what he regarded as nationally owned ovaries.[26]

Nonetheless, one cannot help being moved by the critically distinct perspectives supplied by the handful of thoughtful doctors like Van de Warker. Historical change seems to come about, as William James remarked somewhere, by adding as little as possible of the new onto as much as possible of the old. Van de Warker was ashamed that medical reform had always come from outside medical ranks. But given the symbiotic nature of the relation he described, given gynecological persistence in castration in the face of massive evidence against the operation, and given its significance as the prominent tip of an iceberg of social beliefs, it was reasonable to assume that the iron circuit could be broken only from outside. The final two parts of the book use the "organizing perspective"[27] of two men's lives in an attempt to describe that iceberg.

Part III

The Lightning-Rod Man

12   The Reverend John Todd

The Reverend John Todd (1800–1873) was, perhaps, preeminent among the nineteenth-century experts who addressed themselves to the problems of being a successful male in America. Paradoxically, they told young men how to be self-made.

Todd was recognized as "a kind of bishop" in western Massachusetts. His son, John E. Todd, compiled and edited Todd's autobiography, *John Todd, The Story of His Life, Told Mainly by Himself* (1876). He explained his father's prominence "most of all on account of his strong common sense and practical wisdom, and his unconscious tendency to push to the front . . . from sheer weight and energy of character. There was scarcely a convention or anniversary, a dedication or an installation, or a meeting or gathering of any kind, secular or religious, which did not demand his presence." Ministers, difficult tasks, people in trouble, all called on Todd as the county's best-known troubleshooter. He was the presiding chaplain at the junction of the eastern and western portions of the first transcontinental railroad in 1869, at Promontory Point, Utah. His continental and international fame grew from the popularity of his books. He published at least fifteen of them, together with a number of pamphlets and sermons, and introductions to other writers' work. Todd's books included biblical exegesis, Christian theology simplified for young children, *The Sabbath School Teacher,* didactic tales, personal recollections, and, most popular of all, books to equip young American men with systems of self-discipline. George Bancroft recommended Todd's *Index Rerum or Index of Subjects:* "Intended as a Manual, to Aid the Student and the Professional

Man, in Preparing himself for Usefulness, With an Introduction, Illustrating its Utility and Method of Use" (1834). The fine English novelist George Gissing said the self-educated Edward Widdowston, a main protagonist of *The Odd Women* (1893), "deemed it his duty to make acquaintance with the great, the solid authors. . . . A little work once well-known, Todd's 'Student's Manual,' had formed his method and inspired him with zeal."[1]

Todd was one of those writers immensely popular in one age and forgotten in the next, although their message and the assumptions it represents pass into the fabric of both. "He wrote simply and entertainingly for the masses, not because he could not write technically, but because he wished to do the most good. . . . The results, however, for which he chiefly wrote, have been immense." Todd himself came to see *The Student's Manual* as his most significant book: "I am receiving much attention as the author of the 'Student's manual.' I begin to think that that was the great work of my life; it seems to loom up above all the rest that I have done." Indeed, he said it was "the only good thing that I seem ever to have done." Within two years after its publication in 1835, *The Student's Manual* had run into seven editions, and in the twenty-fourth edition in 1854, Todd pointed out that "there has never been less than one edition yearly published in this country . . . and not less than one hundred thousand copies have been sold across the water." Young men came to Todd to acknowledge: "Sir, I owe most or all of what I am to your pen."[2]

Dr. Gardner was one such beneficiary. He was "emboldened" to address himself in 1870 to the problem of "personal pollution" by the example of

the immense good that has been done to the male youth of this country by the kind and forcible statements of Rev. Dr. Todd in his *Student's Manual*. This work has done an incalculable good in moulding the minds of America's youth; and more especially by his warning chapter on *Onanism*. As a boy, I knew it, for it was the frequent subject of discussion among my academic and collegiate associates. Although the propriety of its publication was doubted by many, the result has proven that the earnestly sought decision was eminently sound, and thousands now live to thank this conscientious teacher for the first information they received of the ills arising from a habit more pernicious to the intellectual man (setting aside the physical disabilities resulting therefrom), than any other habit to which he is usually addicted. Tobacco and alcohol are not so potent to rob man of all the high prerogatives of manhood, as this humiliating, self-abasing vice.

Gardner, then, saw the chief importance of *The Student's Manual* in the book's focus on masturbation.[3]

Analysis of Todd's work supplies further connections between the topics set out in Part I and reflected in the medical and gynecological history described in Part II. It endorses the hypothesis that democratic pressures on men were registered in their conceptions of their own sexual identity and, consequently, on their ideas of the nature and position of women; and it confirms that these pressures were maddeningly circular, and central to the history of American "progress" and expansion in the nineteenth century. *The Student's Manual* and the first volume of *Democracy in America* were published in the same year, and Todd assumes precisely the democratic world view of which Tocqueville was so profoundly apprehensive.

Todd, the last of seven children, was born just after his parents had moved from Arlington to Rutland, Vermont. His father was a frontier doctor, iron smelter, writer of popular medical articles, orator, freemason, captain in the military, state assemblyman, and member of the governor's council, "with a thirst for promotion in civil office," and, in retrospect, was seen to have just missed being elected governor of Vermont. In the end he failed; beaten by the hardships of frontier life and financial failure, like Melville's father he gradually sank under "clouds of poverty, sickness and distress" and died when Todd was six. The feeling Todd remembered most strongly as his response to his father's death was guilt: "I dared not look at him, I felt too guilty"—perhaps over a child's resentment of his father's now permanent absence. After his father's death, Todd's family scattered and Todd himself was traded from relative to relative.[4]

From her first childbirth the mental and physical health of Todd's mother had been undermined. Just before John's entrance into the world his father suffered a nearly fatal accident which was first mistakenly reported as fatal. The news "destroyed [his mother's] reason; and though she lived many years, she never recovered it."

"It was in such circumstances as these, the father lying a helpless cripple, and the mother a hopeless lunatic," that John was born on October 9, 1800. He said he was "born an orphan," a remarkable paradox which eliminated his mother and set Todd up for almost complete self-making. The self-made Todd's feelings toward his mother, usually the magnet for pious, filial rhetoric in the nineteenth century, were those of resentment, hostility, blame, and guilt. He was, he said, "a scrawny puny babe, weighing five or six pounds . . . —that baby! Everyone said, 'What a mercy if that child should die! What can she do with it? What a blessing if it should die! The poor mother almost thought so too. But the unwelcome babe would not die.' " Todd's sense of being an unwanted child never left him and repeatedly cropped up in his sermons and writings. "I can truly say I have never met with any loss so great as that of losing the care and instruction of my mother during my childhood, in consequence of her having lost her reason." He chose to record for posterity that his mother had almost had the unnatural thought that it would have been a blessing had he died at birth. He also chose to record his mother's deranged (and self-checked) attempt to kill him as a child. "At one time my poor mother obtained a naked sword, and ran toward me to give the fatal thrust, when an unseen hand seemed to seize her arm, and the point of the sword stopped within a few inches of my breast." The parent/child, female/male relation here is first presented as total aggression versus total vulnerability, the terms reversed only by the supernatural power of a gripping hand, able to deal with the unnatural power of a progenitrix. Another way was to describe himself as an orphan, despite the fact that his mother was still alive, so one can assume that he wished her dead, whether or not she had first started the murderous circle. In fact his mother does not seem so insane at all. She retained a rational and witty view of her son, even as she was supposed to be his "poor mother" and "a hopeless lunatic." Her penetrating remarks could only have intensified his guilty hostility toward her. Once Todd "called on his mother with his brother-in-law, Rev. Mr. Shephard . . . and . . . told an amusing but somewhat extravagant story. As they were all laughing, Mr. Shephard slyly remarked to the company, 'You know the Todds always did tell lies.' 'Yes,' spoke up the old lady, who hitherto had remained a silent and solemn listener, 'yes, but none of them but John ever printed them.' " She did not die until 1843. Todd's feelings at her death may be gauged by his totaling up what her care had cost him: "I have expended two thousand dollars for her, but it is nothing . . . in comparison with the satisfaction I have in view of the past."[5]

The circumstances of his birth and childhood, saturated in experiences of unwantedness, guilt, transience, and dependence upon powers beyond his control, were compounded throughout his life by his experiencing the world as full of ceaseless anxiety and universal competition among men. Todd frequently idealized a man's return, not to his sexual equal, as it were, but to his mother, and suggested it was woman in that guise whom the man had fled in the first place. In *The Student's Manual*, Todd presented what he imagined to be the thoughts of a young man atop the mast of a "large whale-ship." The "only child of his mother and she a widow," he had run away to sea:

> his mother—would she receive him to her heart, or would she be sleeping in death? Would she recognize her long-absent boy, and forgive all his past ingratitude, and still love him with the unquenchable love of a mother? And may he again have a home, and no more wander among strangers? The pressure of these thoughts was too much. He wept at the remembrance of his undutifulness. Troubles and hardships did not break his spirit, did not subdue his proud heart; but the thoughts of home, or rest, or going out no more, suffering no more, engrossing the love of a kind parent, melted him.

In place of having to generate unquenchable energy to deal with the stormy course among men, a man could rest in the unquenchable love of a mother's bosom. At the same time, the doubts that the wish might be fulfilled, the doubt even that the mother would recognize her son, registered the young man's ambivalence about returning. The doubts expressed in another form those negative, guilty, and hostile feelings toward his mother (represented by "disobedience" and "past ingratitude") for which Todd made clear the young man had left her in the first place. The passage suggests the continuation of an intense struggle in the young man, not to reach a balanced sexual identity in relation to others, but between maintaining a self-made, self-sufficient mask among men (the mark somehow of manhood), and, on the other hand, an opposite tendency, to fall back totally into the arms of mother, to become an infantile, dependent part of a woman.[6]

In Todd's aggrandizement of the role of mother one can detect an implicit assault on his own mother's failure. At the same time, such aggrandizement was a typical one when Todd was writing, and his attitude seems to have coincided with that of men generally, even as it reinforced it. There was a crucial change in the ideology of motherhood during the years following the American industrial and Jacksonian revolutions, and preceding the Civil War. Donald Meyer suggests that this change in the meaning of "mother" occurred as a result of the disintegrating conditions to which Tocqueville was witness. Feminism, gynecology, and the reaction Todd represented (including the new ideology of mother) signaled the vitally important change in the "ancient, irreversible and ascribed" role of women and of their potential inclusion in the "spreading ideology of individualism," trends which are not at all complete.[7]

Todd was dependent on the charity of friends from childhood to early manhood. Those on whom he depended most were women: his aunts brought him up. But he claimed the laurels of self-making in the classic mold.

> I was born an orphan, shelterless, penniless. I was but six years old when I knelt over my father's grave, and vowed even then to rise above my circumstances. I soon determined to have a liberal education. My friends opposed. I rose above all; I went to college half-fitted; I was sick much of the time, owing to too severe application and anxiety; I pressed on, rose above all, and now stand where I can see my way clear.[8]

Of course, he was not born an orphan, nor shelterless. The vow at six years old makes it clear that this was useful fiction. The thrust of the passage is motion upwards, from kneeling to standing. It required opposing force to suggest momentum, hence the exaggeration in the first sentence, the opposition of friends, and his own sickness. The latter, he admitted, was his own creation, suggesting the relation between the need to show a rise in the world and self-destruction. The notion of "too severe application and anxiety" reminds one of the generally held dictum that a certain amount of anxiety was necessary for success. When it suited him, Todd showed how useful pressure was: "I know of no young man who has such a numerous circle of friends and acquaintances, all looking at him and expecting much. Pushed on thus, I must rise and be very respectable in my day." A circle of expectant eyes was a conception of friendship that suggests men saw one another as stimulants (and, paradoxically, that they depended on others in the process of self-making). Moreover, such an attitude placed a man in a position of constant vulnerability, calling down onto his own head the condemnation of precisely those who, it might be thought, would support him in adversity.[9]

Todd, and the son who edited and compiled his autobiography, described his ambition, determination, energy, and self-discipline. He walked barefoot to Yale, where he had to make strenuous "efforts of self-preservation," thrust as he saw himself in a crowd of better-supported young men from 1818 to 1822. Todd earned part of his way through college by teaching school (where he was a savage master to his pupils). His lonely poverty made him vulnerable to destruction at the hands of his all-male classmates, whose condition, in turn, excited Todd's hostility.[10]

Guilt at the age of sixteen had directed Todd toward the ministry. A "Mr. S——" asked the adolescent if he feared death, and if he thought he would go to heaven. Todd replied that he had never done anything against God and therefore considered his "claim upon heaven to be as good as that of any one." Mr. S—— told Todd he was building on a "sandy foundation" and, after giving him a few

> hints of advice, dropped the conversation. I felt a pang after this, such as I had never before felt. I thought much that night upon what I had said in regard to death, and considered it an awful challenge to the Almighty. The next morning was still worse. I felt such . . . a load of guilt lying upon me as seemed nearly to crush me to the ground. I was with Mr. Evarts alone in the forenoon; and although I had to withdraw to another part of the room and wipe my eyes, yet I dared not open my mind to him. . . . Oh the anguish that then surrounded my soul! It seemed as if hell itself had risen up to swallow me. My distress was so great that I expected every moment to drop into hell.

Such an expectation shaped the precipitous road Todd adjured young men to follow. The imminence of personal defeat and oblivion was one prospect ahead of the sickening roller coaster ridden by Tocqueville's American man, the mundane experience which, projected onto a wider scale, became the continual flux of relentless ambition and commercial panic.

Henry Ward Beecher, lecturing on moral dangers to a young man's character, argued that "once the first step was taken, the youth would be committed to a life of degeneracy and sin." Such an attitude repeated the Calvinist style Max Weber described as "systematic self-control which at every moment stands before the inexorable alternatives, chosen or damned." After Yale, Todd entered Andover Theological Seminary and was granted the opportunity to give a Fourth of July Oration. "If I succeed, it will be a great advantage to me. . . . If I fail, it will kill me as to all my prospects." When consulted, his professors said they thought "it was a case of life and death—that I must put forth my mightiest exertion, or it would ruin me."[11]

Early nailing his colors to the orthodoxy of Andover Congregationalism, Todd's reaction to the troubles it faced was to become increasingly rigid. Unable to beat the popular appeal of revivalism, the orthodox sects were forced to adopt it—indeed the seminarians of Todd's day "thought only in terms of producing revivals" and the tangible results which could be more easily compared with results men could gain in other fields. Like doctors, ministers suffered from the anxieties peculiar to their profession—lack of central institutional authority and fratricidal competition among sects. Todd recorded the existence of strife within his sect and did a great deal to intensify it. "It is the vice of Congregationalism that in it every man's hand is turned against his brother."[12]

After Andover, Todd drove himself like a wedge into three communities, Groton, Massachusetts (1826–1833), Northampton (1833–1836), and Philadelphia (1836–1842). An orthodox rump in Groton invited Todd to become an assistant pastor for what amounted to an eight-week trial. His success, Todd said, depended on his resisting the Unitarians, whom he called "unclean fowl," their "snare" both "bewitching" and a "delusion." Like other male competitors, from railroaders to doctors, Todd saw himself at war. "The result of my labors here, should my health continue, will probably be a most severe struggle between orthodoxy and Unitarianism. That the latter will obtain the conquest I doubt not." His relentlessly orthodox efforts during this probationary period "left the scene of his brief ministry in uproar," a result of which he seemed proud as he prepared to assume the permanent position his hard line nevertheless had won him. "I have no expectation of bringing this great town over to orthodoxy, but I intend to split it, so that an orthodox society can grow out of it." He did split it, and became full minister of the orthodox part. He remained in a state of "warfare," "a fight to the death," with the Unitarians. He swung from confidence to despair, feeling like Daniel thrown to the lions—whom he himself had aroused—his "every movement . . . watched," a sense, it should be noted, that he said he experienced in his relations with his friends. At the same time he regarded himself as a prophet spearheading a revival in Groton, giving eight churches in the surrounding area the courage to raise their heads. "In all this region, they consider me a fearful foe . . . a most perfect general." He wanted to believe his enemies admired him.[13]

He was partly dependent on the Unitarians for the drumming up of the energies of his troops, leading his constant revival meetings in opposition to them. "The explanation which Dr. Todd used to give of the restlessness and tendency to extremes which were developed in his Groton church was, that the excitement of the struggle with Unitarianism, without which the separation from the old church could never have been accomplished, caused a high-pressure condition of mind in the people which could not at once subside." The group had been overenergized in the way Todd had driven himself to sickness during his rise under the pressure of his friends, exaggerating the normative course of behavior in the competition for success. Revivalism was a similar process on a larger scale, with the preacher acting as the energizing agent. Todd's son pointed out in the autobiography that the

> reader may have noticed that after every season of great effort, and especially after every revival in his church, Mr. Todd suffered in health, and resorted to powerful medicine and violent exercise . . . thinking himself the victim of dyspepsia caused by bodily inactivity. It is a very common mistake among ministers. There can be little doubt that he injured himself by maltreatment of what was in reality nervous exhaustion.

Todd was preoccupied with this kind of exhaustion throughout his life, feeling his essential energy was susceptible to "running out" through his fingers. This preoccupation reflected Todd's sharing in the common belief in the fundamental law of animal economy. Todd called energy "that moving, active spirit." The belief in the need to arouse and discipline it was the common denominator between orthodox and revivalist groups, between ministers and doctors, professionals and businessmen.[14]

There was a close connection between the disciplining of energies at home and the sending of them abroad. Revivalism and missionarism had "reciprocal action to invigorate each other." Todd was deeply concerned with missionary activity. His first ambition had been to "bury [himself] in heathenism," although he decided to devote himself to energizing men at home. His vision of the West played a vital part in that task, and he made the very significant trip to Promontory Point and on to California. In 1871 he urged the construction of three more transcontinental railroads. He regarded the Indians as so much "filth" to be swept aside. In Todd's view the God of the WASP males recognized that their energy qualified them to brush aside the unenergized Mexicans, and to bring home Chinese as imperial booty to build railroads and educate blacks. The latter were too inferior a group to qualify for direct contact with the white, abolitionist Todd. The expansionism Todd developed between 1835 and 1871 was nearly identical to the Reverend Josiah Strong's mixture of "race, religion, and geopolitical mysticism" in the last two decades of the century. Todd intended that his transmission of unabashedly imperialist visions would encourage young men to go West.[15]

In short, Todd identified with that exhilarating combination of sexual and geographical freedom comprising one part of the arena of American history. His imagination soared with relief from the other part, settlement and heterosexual obligation. Alarmed by the sexual imbalance in the East ("over seventy thousand more females in Massachusetts than there are males"), Todd blamed women. Feminists were responsible for driving men away, thereby depriving their own sex of what Todd believed it automatically wanted, that is, marriage. Yet Todd himself idealized the sexually imbalanced West. He described the California gold rush like this: "In a time incredibly short, there was at least a quarter of a million of the wildest, bravest, most daring, and most intelligent young men digging gold. There was no female society, there were no homes to soften and restrain, no laws, and no magistrates." Moreover, Todd recommended flight as the ultimate solution to masturbation, and to sin generally. Careful analysis suggests that Todd believed men to be more capable of admirable and valuable achievement to the extent that they withdrew their energies from women.[16]

It is probable that Todd attended every annual meeting of the American Board of Foreign Missions, and he was the chief organizer of two annual general meetings which he persuaded to come to Pittsfield, in 1849 and 1866. In 1869 he delivered the sermon before the board's commissioner in Pittsburgh, its inspiration the joining of the transcontinental railroad. The sermon was a history of Christianity, culminating in America's manifest destiny. The prophets "saw the hills brought low, and the valleys exalted, and a highway made for our God, though railroad cars, crossing a continent, are not named. They saw simple dromedaries, not then known as cars and steamboats." Todd's view of the history of Christianity was shaped by the belief that the fullest expression of male power, of male identity, required the separation of the sexes and the subordination of women.[17]

According to Todd's sexually loaded iconography, when the church sank low it became female, passive, and suffering, and relieved only by the rise of a great man—Abraham, Moses, Christ, Luther, and Todd's own contemporary "prophets" each disseminating truth from a scroll in his hand. At such peaks the church became male. He extended this sexual iconography in the metaphor of "propagation." David's "eye was dim, but he could see the King's son coming down upon the poor and needy like rain upon the mown grass . . . a handful of corn scattered upon the mountains, whose fruit would shake like Lebanon." During the low and female points of church history, "she" became entirely meretricious, a bejeweled whore sharing an "unholy alliance" with the state. What was necessary at such moments was a hygienic separation: male inventiveness had to "cut free," "undo itself" from the "drying flesh" of the Daughter of Zion, and sort out pure church body from historical dross. "Among the rubbish which the world has heaped upon the church [by the time of the Reformation] Luther's great hand is feeling till it lays naked upon the Rock of Ages." Todd saw ministers, and the gold miners and railroaders he idolized, as the contemporary proponents of male power, groping among the rubbish in themselves and their surroundings to render it into pure and eternal self-propagating energy.[18]

The pressure at Groton finally became too much for Todd, and in 1833 he accepted a call to Northampton, where the Congregationalists had grown too large for a single church. Todd had the new church named for Jonathan Edwards (the name he also gave to one of his sons), and he set to as he had in Groton, drumming up tensions to produce conversions and professions. Todd adopted corresponding behavior. His wife said she had "never known him so absolutely driven as at the present time." Todd complained incessantly of tiredness, sickness, and indolence. He wrote *The Student's Manual* in Northampton, beset with doubts that he would ever succeed in nourishing in himself the kind of life force the *Manual* insisted its audience foster. "I begin to feel that I shall never acquire or create that unconquerable, unquenchable fire which is so necessary to prevent life from running through the fingers, leaving not a distinct mark of remembrance behind." This anxiety recalls Morton, Jackson, and Wells's pursuit of immortal distinction.[19]

By 1836 Todd's revivalism had greatly agitated Northampton, and he had the chance to go to the Clinton Street Church in Philadelphia. The circle of expectant eyes around him was divided between the opposition and those he had helped save: "the old society here long to have me go," but Todd was loath to "lose in the opinion of [regenerate] men in this region." His departure, Todd said, would be "death to them." He looked at the move as Tocqueville's typical American democrat looked at chance. His standard in deciding was success and other people's recognition of it. "Success, decided and splendid, and nothing else, would lead people to say and feel that I

had done right in going." The opinion of men in Philadelphia was
not reassuring: "the hazard seems very great," because of the extraordinary "obstacles in the way," that is, the strength of Presby-
terianism. But Todd accepted the risk, went to Philadelphia, and
picked up those baubles of success that he claimed to discount—
twice his former salary and "a most beautiful church, the largest in
the city."[20]

Once more Todd had plunged into a lions' den; his son described
him as "sacrificing himself" by going to Philadelphia. Again Todd's
calling was the result of the disintegration of an old church and consequent attempts to bring back orthodoxy and purity. Todd was
chosen as the obvious man to preside over such a process. He sailed
in with his combination of rigid orthodoxy and revivalism, con-
sciously creating that anarchic tension of disintegrative energies:
"but a spark was needed to produce a general explosion. The opening of this splendid house wrought these feelings to the highest
pitch, and the dedication-sermon [which Todd proudly gave] was
the spark. Upon its production one universal howl of rage went up
from Presbyterians, Episcopalians, and Unitarians alike." Like
Lyman Beecher, Todd managed his revival effects to produce "electricity." He lashed himself to the same pitch as he lashed his church.
"I never lie down without having conscience reproach me for not
having done at least four times what I have done; and I never rise
in the morning without feeling that I *cannot* do what I must during
the day." Todd sought out his sectarian enemies and engaged them
in bitter infighting. Confronting these, racked within by agonies of
guilt, Todd and his son depicted Todd's Clinton Street position as
"severe trial," an "ordeal," "in a furnace," and "being eaten." He
failed to realize (or misrepresented) the contribution of his explosive ministry to the disintegrative process he described. "The fact
is, that some of my church have been at swords' points for the last
year and a half; and I have been barring up between them. . . . I
shall leave, and my poor church will quarrel and tear each other a
while, and then fall into the hands of the Presbyterians." Todd
looked back on his Philadelphia attempt as a pointless kind of enterprise, like the construction of a superfluous railroad.[21]

Todd's last and longest ministry was at Pittsfield (1842–1873),
where, as his son pointed out, he assumed the duty "not to revolu-
tionize, but to conserve; not to draw upon the strength of other
churches, but to maintain strength upon which others were constantly drawing." The metaphor here is one of physiological econ-

omy, a limited amount of strength either conserved or drawn upon, and it suggests that Todd's son adhered to that law of animal economy with which his father was preoccupied. Melville lived in Pittsfield from 1850 to 1863, and different kinds of evidence suggest very strongly that his story "The Lightning-Rod Man" is based on Todd's character and teachings. After the trip to California in the spring and summer of 1869, Todd offered his resignation to his flock, together with a self-righteous request for the continuation of his salary, but they demanded he stay on until 1873. He had a minor attack of "numbness" in New York in the spring of 1872 and took the opportunity again to ask to be released. He recovered his health for a while but died the next year amid scenes of fundamentalist delusion.[22]

I shall follow the example of the form of *The Story of His Life,* by next describing briefly something of Todd's home life and his hobbies. Todd married Mary Brace, daughter of the Reverend Joab Brace of Newington, Massachusetts, in 1827, and reveled in being able to address filial sentiments to his mother-in-law. In the compilation of his father's letters that he included in *The Story of His Life,* John E. Todd admitted a distinction between the way Todd addressed his family and his public language: "he seldom allowed these turns of depression or their effects to be seen in his writings or public life; but his family were familiar with them, and their letters from him were almost uniformly sad." John E. Todd perceived that his father had a "secret inner life," and although Todd "had a multitude of friends everywhere, there were very few indeed, almost none, with whom he was so intimate as to open them his heart, and real character, and inward life." His life was the paradigm of the style advocated by his works. He warned young men never to show feelings outside, lest such showing be taken advantage of by enemies. The fruits of his oft-claimed success, his pastorates, writings, sermons, and harvests of souls, were won at the cost of unremitting self-discipline. Like Sims, Todd was spurred on from the cradle to the grave by anxiety and guilt. While he perceived that this "inner life" was one of "melancholy pathos," Todd's son was duped into representing his father's humor as "so spontaneous as it overflowed on the slightest occasion." Duped because it is apparent from the whole style of Todd's life in *The Story* and from the style he advocated in his behavioral tracts that Todd believed that one could sustain a successful defensive outer shell only by dint of the severest control of any spontaneity; and he specifically warned against misuse of humor, adjuring young men to calculate and control its use.[23]

It also seems possible that Todd saw the psyches of the members of his family to be divided like his own—good, acceptable outside, sustained by a distinct and effortful inside. He taught them to be affectionate, that is, to exhibit behavior that others would perceive as such. "If there is any one thing which I especially mourn over, in the education of my family, it is that I have not taught them to be more affectionate." It is doubtful that Todd would have taught his wife more affection in spite of his son's account of his parents' relationship. "Of demonstrations of affection between the parents there were very few. The titles by which they addressed one another were always the formal and distant ones, 'Mr. and Mrs. Todd'; nor did their many and different duties permit them to enjoy much of each other's society." Mrs. Todd's behavior was perfectly consistent with Tocqueville's generalizations about American marriage. Todd was

> very dependent for his success upon his wife. His obligations to this "wonderful woman," as she was considered by all who knew her, who cheerfully sacrificed great beauty, brilliant powers of mind, and unusual social gifts, to the servitude of the care of a great family of a poor minister, and the work of helping forward her husband's success, keeping herself in the background, and toiling day and night the servant of all, he recognized and acknowledged as fully as any one. He was always joking and laughing about his obligations to his wife, and his obedience to her; but at suitable times he spoke of what she had done for him in more serious language. . . . "In my house has been a life swallowed up in my success, willing to be unknown and out of sight; unwearied in giving encouragement and arousing to effect; prompt and cheerful in concealing and in covering my defects and deficiencies; kind to apologize for what could not be approved; uncomplaining when worn down by heavy burden such as few are called to bear; more than ready to be unselfish and to wear out that others might profit by my labors."

Todd's obedience to his wife and even his obligations to her were insignificant compared to the magnitude of her sacrifice. This all may be seen, of course, as an escalation of pedestal rhetoric, but it does record very exactly the pattern of nineteenth-century wifehood, and that it was shaped entirely by the needs of success-hungry, deficient men. The most striking metaphor is, I think, the ingestive one, "a life swallowed up in my success." Apart from the

swallowing up by success rather than failure, such a pattern repeated Todd's parents' relation in significant ways, which clearly
had a direct bearing on the way he perceived his mother to have
treated him, which in turn led him to repeat the pattern.[24]

Todd's son's account of his father's hobbies is revealing. He saw
them as characteristic of his father's whole life style. Every year
Todd took a long hunting trip into the wilderness, which he saw as
a place for the replenishment of the "fountains of life." He "heard
nothing from his family to worry him, and so could throw off all
care." Todd's lone hunting trips for the purpose, in part, of throwing off the debilities of family obligations demonstrate the active
operation of the alternatives represented by Marvel's bachelor (and
Lantern-Jawed Bob), which should be related to the general form of
American expansion.[25]

Wilderness hunter-guides, according to Todd's son, were annoyed
at Todd's refusal to use them, and so "gave him the reputation of
being simply murderous and wasteful, killing for the mere fun of
killing, and leaving his victims to taint the river-banks." His son's
account of his father's behavior contradicted the hunters but seems
more in character, even though there is an integral connection between that behavior and the ruthless, wanton destruction of the
hunters' version.

> He had a mania for shooting-irons and ammunition of every kind.
> Every new gun or rifle had to be tried as fast as it appeared, and he
> always kept three or four on hand. Every one of them had a name,
> and was a kind of pet—till the next style came out. Not that he did
> much shooting: more than once he has been known to lug two or
> three guns through the wilderness for weeks without firing a shot. It
> was the fun of getting the best guns and adjusting sights to them,
> and preparing ammunition for them, and contriving all kinds of belts
> and boxes and cases for them.[26]

He showed the same character in his other hobbies.

> He would walk a dozen blocks in New York City to get a hook of
> a particular twist, or a line of a special make. And when he had se-
> cured them, he would make all sorts of wooden and leather cases to
> keep them in. He has been known to lug patiently for weeks, in the
> woods, a heavy case, containing tackle enough to furnish a small
> store ingeniously packed and arranged. But he could hardly ever be
> persuaded to fish except when absolutely starving.

His equipment was obsessively complete and well ordered—but not to be used. The point of his hobbies seems to have been to experience perfect equipment, perfect preparation. "Keep all your tools bright and *very* sharp, and have the handles all alike, and every tool in its place when not using it."[27] The hobby could have been anything, provided it had enough moving parts to require organization, or enough pieces to make a set, and that it allowed him to conduct it alone. Another determining factor was that the equipment was phallic[28]—guns, fishing rods, tools. He had an extensive collection in his workshop.

> A room in the house adjoining his study was appropriated . . . where he could guard his implements from the meddling of others, especially servants, and could have his recreation near his desk, so that he could turn to it at any moment. . . . it was his boast that he knew the use of every instrument, and knew the place of each so well that he could lay his hand on it in the dark. That he made no use of all these tools will readily be understood . . . after all it was the collecting and arranging of his implements which he enjoyed, rather than in the use of them in hard labor, for which, in fact, his infirmities unfitted him. He took the greatest care of his tools, keeping every one of them well-oiled and in its place, wiping off all particles of dust or rust from their shining surfaces as softly as tears from the faces of children. They were too precious to be put to ignoble uses. He did indeed condescend to do a little tinkering that is called for in a household.[29]

Todd was perpetually hounded by the thought that his life force would run through his fingers. Great mental efforts—revivals, writing books—exhausted him physically. He felt he was under constant attack from enemies, both outside (other sectarians) and within (personified as, for example, "Procrastination," "Indolence").[30] Yet he drove himself into these inevitably debilitating circumstances because he believed they were essential to success. They were a kind of inner, self-made counterpart to that stimulating circle of expectant eyes. It seems, then, that these hobbies permitted him to experience perfect potentiality, adequate to any challenge, and entirely free of the danger of failure. He used them as preparations for preparations: of his lathe he said, "I have mine in a recess in my study; and when the mind sags, five minutes at work will send you back to your study wide awake." Yet the lathe was kept "neat and . . . in such order, that it is perpetually a matter of joy and pride."[31] Obviously his arrangement of his tools was the objective correlative of an inner organization he craved but found impossible. His enjoyment was appropriate to the bounds of a body he did not want to extend because of his infirmities. Perhaps the hunters' idea of Todd's prowess was based on what Todd told them he had done or would do.

There is a hint of something else in the accounts of his guns and tools: Todd named his guns. The conferring of a name on a pet also confers an element of humanity on it, and I think it is a truism that people treat pets as children (and both as extensions of themselves). Todd treated his tools like children. Now his son said Todd derived much of his power from the "enthusiasm and earnestness and eagerness of interest and purpose" with which he pursued his goals, including his hobbies.[32] As we have seen, Todd was anxious that he be able to "acquire or create" the same kind of power, which otherwise would slip through his fingers. "Acquire" and "create" were cognate in Todd's imagination. Perhaps his fingers could retrieve or generate such power by acquiring and handling phallic implements. In short, his hobbies gave him a life of self-made, autonomous control, together with some sense of reproduction, indestructible generative power, and iron children, all entirely and invulnerably his. The fantasy would be consistent with that desire for immortality at which he said his acquired or created "unquenchable fire" was aimed. His lathe stiffened his sagging mind; it was "easily kept in order, and the results are so quick, so varied, and so beautiful that you never get tired of it." Todd found he "could hardly speak of it too warmly." If you take care of your lathe "you will soon love it as the sailor does his ship." Such a relationship resulted in offspring: "the productions of the Lathe, for beauty and variety, surpass everything I ever saw or conceived."[33]

Todd's other hobbies showed related characteristics. He had successive manias, as his son called them, for raising chickens, bee keeping, dairy farming, flower gardening, compost heaps, and the fire department. The word "mania" recalls the contemporary transportation revolution. We call children's successive and short-lived obsessions "crazes." Todd's son also called these bursts of enthusiasm "fever" and "being seized with a passion." Keeping bees and chickens allowed Todd the fantasy of creating worlds totally under his control, treating chickens and bees like people: "the wretched fowls were compelled to walk up curious gangways, and roost on ingenious perches, and eat and drink out of patent machines." For the bees Todd made "hives of all possible and impossible shapes . . . making a perfect miniature model of the Parthenon, large enough to contain two or three hives, which stood for years . . . and [the bees] died as fast as they were put into its dampness." There are some people with whose chemistry bees disagree, and who, as a result, are inevitably and repeatedly stung if ever they come into the vicinity of a bee hive. Todd was one of these. His son described Todd's bees' "peculiar aversion to him. He could scarcely go near them without getting stung . . . he would presently turn deathly pale, lose consciousness . . . [and suffer] terrible nausea, vomiting and half a day's sickness." His son makes it clear that anyone else could go near the bees with impunity. "But all this did not in the least damp his enthusiasm." The remarkable questions are why Todd kept bees at all and why he kept killing them. His placing them in a Parthenon suggests that he humanized them. It seems plausible that the bees' manifest aggression toward him represented Todd's sense of the hostility he aroused in the course of his life, at Groton, Northampton, and Philadelphia, for example. He cultivated it, at least in part, as a stimulus. He both welcomed and feared this experience, his share of the universal competition among men. He kept the bees that stung him. His placing the bees into a hostile environment (mortal dampness) allowed him a commensurate sense of control and revenge.[34]

The *sanctum sanctorum* of Todd's externalized and reified self-sufficiency was his study. His son pointed out that it revealed Todd's inner workings: "in looking at the objects which he gathered around him, and in the midst of which he sat, and thought, and labored, and prayed, we see but the keys which unlocked the world in which he really lived." It was full of guns, spears, revolvers, gunshells, tools, traps, fishing gear, and a collection of canes and clubs, each of the latter a memento of a male friend. But these symbols of other men could not compete with the object standing in the center of the study. Todd himself supplied a lavish description. "I have many memorials of kind friends in my study which are beautiful; but the stranger hardly notices them, he is so much delighted with my tiny fountain."[35] Todd's repeated use of the possessive pronoun suggests the extent to which he identified with his fountain, not at all tiny, unless of course in that sentence he was letting his mind wander to an even tinier and more personal fountain. You

see an eight-sided pillar-shaped thing with a marble-colored basin, and a pure marble top, the top being several inches larger than the pillar, which also is eight-sided. The whole height is two feet and nine inches. Then, on the top of all this is a glass cover about two and a half feet high, and large enough round to more than cover the basin. In the centre of the basin, is a little brass jet, containing nearly forty little holes in a circle, each hole just large enough to admit a very fine needle.

Three marble figures "white as the driven snow" were poised on the marble top, "intently looking at the little jet," overwhelmed with "astonishment," "satisfaction" and, above all, "admiration of what they see."

> I have only to touch a little brass cock, and up leaps the water through those little holes, nearly forty little streams, and each spring-ing two feet into the air, and then turned into a myriad of silver drops, bright as diamonds, leaping, and laughing as they rise and fall, and dropping into the basin with the sweetest, ringing, singing sound ever heard. It seems as if the fairy daughters of music had got under my glass cover, and were each playing on her own harp. I can think of nothing but pearls dropping into a well, or golden balls fall-ing into cups of silver. With what profusion the jewels are tossed out!

Todd's relation with the fountain was an intimate one; it is doubt-ful that he allowed anyone else to touch the sensitive controls. The idea of the fairy daughters getting under his glass cover suggests that Todd in some sense saw the fountain as himself or part of him-self. (The reader should note the diamonds, pearls, and jewels for future reference.)[36]

His lathe was a perpetual source of joy, directly assisting his mind never to tire. The "beautiful instrument" was a "blessing," on "whose creations skill can produce variety inexhaustible."[37] His feelings for his anthropomorphized fountain were identical: "I never tire of this beautiful thing. . . . There it stands a living foun-tain. Nobody can see how the waters get there, or how they are car-ried away. There it leaps and rings day and night, never weary, never pausing, never other than beautiful." With his fountain Todd had succeeded in acquiring, even creating, that unquenchable force for which he yearned, and in guaranteeing it could not run out be-tween his fingers. His fingers raised that danger (by touching the little cock), only to allay it, since one of the fountain's most striking attributes was its inexhaustibility—"forty little streams," "a myriad of silver drops," "profusion."

> I almost imagine it the fountain of life, and my little marble men [around the top] to be angels "desiring to look into" it. But, ah me! that fountain was opened thousands of years ago, and has been gush-

ing up ever since; and it will still gush up when I and my dear little fountain shall be forgotten. But a few can ever see mine; thousands will see that, and rejoice in it forever. O fountain of life! opened by the Lord Jesus Christ, not to bless one solitary study merely, but to well up in every sanctuary, and in ten thousand human habitations.

The fountain stood in the center of Todd's study—at the heart of his mental equipment. In his own imagination it became his idea of himself, generating a stream of life-giving power, that is, his words, his lies. "O my little fountain, speak to my reader, and whisper in his ear, 'The waters of life, the waters of life! Whoso drinketh of them shall never thirst.' "

13   Primers for Anxiety

In Todd's view, men were forced to enter the world outside home by virtue of having their particular set of reproductive organs: "the whirl and contact with the world . . . is the inheritance of our sex." Conversely, women's sexual organs precluded such contact. Todd pointed out the majesty resting on the ownership of male organs but believed men had to be reminded of the fact; or, perhaps, he felt men might not realize to what their effortless possession of male organs entitled them. "Do not forget the majesty of the destiny of Manhood, and though you will pass through foes as numerous as the leaves of autumn, yet you are not to forget that you are in the midst of a boundless magazine, filled with every kind of armor and weapons." It was the manhood that gave men access to this arsenal, the metaphor suggesting how closely Todd associated penis and testicles with explosive, deadly weapons (to be discharged against other men). His private study was the objectification of such a metaphor, his hunting, fishing, and handicraft collections extensions of that reified, personal arsenal.[1]

Todd addressed "the most important class of [his] fellow men now on the face of the earth," that is, young, WASP males. Their necessary "whirl and contact" turned out to be precisely the ordeal Tocqueville and Jarvis described, Todd's childhood attuning him to the continuous sense of vulnerability that was the normal condition of American democratic men. Todd's young man had to plunge into a "tide," his "whole journey of life [was] a continued series of checks, disappointment, and sorrows." Exposure to this daunting prospect dated from the period of democratic sonhood, in which, in Todd's view, the young American had no opportunity to establish a mature sexual identity in relation to the other members of his family:

> The whole body of the young men in our country are fearfully exposed. The reason is, that our circumstances are such, that our very boys have to buffet those waves of temptations which men can hardly resist. Long before they are grown up, they leave the homes of their childhood—they must go abroad and play the part of men, and long before experience has had time to teach them they must tread over quicksands that are to be found in the country, and the breathing holes of hell which fill the city.[2]

According to Todd's most popular works the most perpetual and ubiquitous dangers young men faced were not the hell holes, by which, in this context, he meant bars and whorehouses, but the hostile competition from other men. "You are . . . a football among men, thrown wherever they please, and in the power of every man; for every man can take away your peace, and every man is more tempted to bestow censures than applause." Todd presented a picture of universal competition similar to Tocqueville's, if less dispassionate.

> You look at men as individuals, and their object seems to be to gratify a contemptible vanity, to pervert and follow their low appetites and passions, and the dictates of selfishness, wherever they may lead. You look at men *in the aggregate* and this pride and these passions terminate in wide plans of ambition, in wars and bloodshed, in strifes and the destruction of all that is virtuous or lovely.

According to Tocqueville, social leveling "led men to imagine that their whole destiny is in their own hands." But it was illusory to believe, as the American man did, that an "easy and unbounded career [was] open to his ambition." The individual's daily experience was frustration.

> When men are nearly alike and all follow the same track, it is very difficult for any one individual to walk quickly and cleave a way through the dense throng that surrounds and presses on him. This constant strife between the inclination springing from the equality of condition and the means it supplies to satisfy them harasses and wearies the mind.

In Todd's words, the "pursuits of ambition are a succession of jealous disquietudes of corroding fears, of high hopes, of restless desires, and of bitter disappointments."[3]

Yet Todd welcomed the pressure of competition; rivalry was "a mark of health." The more one responded, the more others responded, the higher the rate of stimulus to mental excitement. "Who can see the field of knowledge continually and boundlessly opening before him, with multitudes who, like himself, have staked their character and happiness upon success, ready to compete with him, without having the excitement continually increasing and growing in him?" Todd assumed that he and his class of WASP males desired to be footballs kicked and thrown by other men. Such "shock" produced "electricity," which gave "all the powers of your mind a new energy." The alternative relationships at home with family and women did not contribute to the accumulation of energy: "we need stimulus and pressure to call out mental labor,—the hardest labor in the world,—and we cannot get this at home." Mental labor mobilized energies otherwise wasted. Todd advocated the same discipline as his contemporary, Dr. Ray.[4]

So Todd both feared and needed the circle of hostile eyes. "Beset with enemies" or surrounded by "thousands" of harshly expectant friends, the young man faced a buzzing swarm. The prospect may well explain the violent effect of this passage on Todd. "I have often been struck with a passage in the travels of the celebrated Mungo Park, describing his situation and feeling when alone in the very heart of Africa. 'Whichever way I turned, nothing appeared but danger and difficulty. I saw myself in the midst of a vast wilderness, in the depth of a rainy season, naked and alone, surrounded by savages.'" Todd seems to have identified with Mungo Park and his sense of isolation and exposure. The paradox of being alone yet among savages suggests first the implicit and conventional racism of the attitude that discounted savages as human beings; and second, it was directly analogous to Todd's experience of universal competition. It was the isolation-among-others for which Todd prepared his young men, who were supposed to treat other men as if they were intrinsically hostile, and as if they were commodities. To prepare for such a world was a self-fulfilling prophecy of one's experience of it. Todd himself had aroused the lions to whom he complained he had been thrown at Groton.[5]

Like other clergymen attempting to foster self-help, Todd effectively subordinated religious imperatives to those of worldly success. Todd's young man pursued the mirage Tocqueville described, unattainable yet engaging the insatiable passion of democratic man. Todd asserted in 1844: "That upon which the young man fixes his eye . . . is SUCCESS." He assumed religion was as much a psychic utility in the pursuit of success as Tocqueville said it was. Todd advised a young man to fix his religious principles early in life in order to avoid the distraction of religious doubt during the more important and lifelong pursuit of success. Tocqueville pointed out that the practice of men's lives in democracies prevented them from ever acquiring "fixed ideas about God and human nature." That practice was the compulsive, obsessive, and exclusive pursuit of success by way of physical gratifications—money. It is not surprising that Tocqueville described American ministers' adapting their teachings to a life style they could not control. The religious side of Todd's books was overwhelmed by the earthly struggle for success. The usefulness of religion was its capacity to stimulate, to "call forth the highest efforts." It could be added to rivalry as a stimulant to the production of energy. Todd's appeal for some conscience was finally on that basis. "Were you seeking only for a powerful motive to impel you onward in your studies, and were you regardless of your moral culture, still would I urge you, on this ground alone, to cultivate conscience most assiduously."[6]

Religion could aid the pursuit of success in another way. It could check the tendency to take the recommended male concentration of energies too far, to become an Ahab. Todd said that to succeed in business "a man must give his time, and thoughts, and life to it, with an intensity that knows no diversion, and a concentration of thought that excludes everything else." He "cannot compete with those around him" unless he follows such a track. Todd confessed his admiration for it. His acquaintance with "men of business has given me a very high idea of the strength of intellect of the disciplined and concentrated mind, essential to their success." They showed a quality Todd desired and advocated, "an energy that can surmount any obstacles, and overcome any difficulties." The danger was that "this very concentration of strength and energy" would distort a man's mind and prevent him from understanding that occasional religion augmented and rejuvenated a man's other qualities and made it more likely that he would succeed. Religion, Todd argued, "bathed, cooled and refreshed" a man's weary spirit by "turning off" his otherwise monomaniac thoughts. Second, it was good public relations. "The community will have confidence in a conscientious, holy man, and will do much to aid, to sustain, and to encourage him," that is, by doing business with him. So it was not true that a religious man was "less successful in business. I have no doubt that, if you make the calculation, you will find the reverse to be true." To alter the pace of the pursuit would, in Todd's own terms, only extend and amplify a man's commitment to it.[7]

If man's religious activity on earth conformed to the same ceaseless and monotonous passion, the pursuit of material success, so, too, did God. He had written the most valuable success manual; it was a fund, according to a fiscal metaphor, that reduced all reading to the same utilitarian purpose, the incorporation of resources. Todd said, "I have a great many books. . . . There are silver books and a few golden books, but I have one book worth more than all, called the Bible; and that is a book of bank-notes." That standard came close to suggesting that money was as unarguably authoritative as revelation, that God was simply the greatest of financiers. Henry Ward Beecher, the son of Todd's mentor, told men in 1844 that adversity "is the mint in which God stamps upon us his image and superscription." God could play with man as if he were made of money, and man could play with the expression of God's power, God's identity, in the same way.[8]

The young man following Todd's prescription for success would evince those qualities Dewees demonstrated in 1826 in his recommendations for childrearing—pertinacity, aggression, indomitable willfulness, righteousness, and an obsessive desire to control the body's eruptibility. He should be obsessed with the profitable use of himself and of everybody and everything around him. Abstractions like order and time should be reified as money in a drum-tight economic system. A man should handle time as a miser handled money.

> A miser will frequently become wealthy—not because he has a great income, but because he saves with the utmost care, and spends with the greatest caution. . . . It is a prodigious thing to consider that, although, amongst all the talents which are committed to our stewardship, time, upon several accounts, is the most precious; yet there is not any one of which the generality of men are more profuse and regardless. Nay, it is obvious to observe, that even those persons who are frugal and thrifty in everything else, are yet extremely prodigal of their best revenue, time. . . . It is amazing to think how much time may be gained by proper economy.

Time-money was a quantifiable resource, equally disbursed among everyone (much more so than money-money). To fall back on time as a resource illustrates, perhaps, the same desperation of conditions that drove men to glean their being born white and male. But the generous bestowal of time had the corollary of inescapable guilt if anyone failed in the "proper improvement of [his] time." It should be noted that it was this second characteristic, the ubiquity of abuse of time, and of consequent failure, that Todd emphasized. "Alas, how many have squandered this precious gift, and then, when they came to be on the bed of death, have reproached themselves with a keenness of rebuke, which language was too poor to convey!" The poverty of the squanderer's language demonstrates that Todd measured words, too, as if they were money, and suggests that a man's use or abuse of his resources in one area was in keeping with that in another.[9]

Todd prepared his young men for a world of limited resources fought over by other young men similarly prepared. There was no room for useless friends. "Choose your company for profit, just as you do your books." Todd described books as money and, like Henry Beecher, saw men to be made of money and relations between them simply ferocious profiteering. "In conversation all are free-booters and may carry away and appropriate to themselves as much as they can." Every gain was at the expense of someone else, and every loss someone else's gain. This seems to have been the external counterpart of the fundamental law of animal economy. Indeed, the operation of that law, which assumed the world had a direct effect on the mind, the brain, and thereby the body, makes plain the fact that both outside and inside economies were parts of the same system.[10]

The young man's mind was a vulnerable mechanism, its operation and protection requiring the reduction of human exchanges to information gathering. Todd's young man should waylay the man whose knowledge could be useful. "Seek him out; ply him with interrogations, and be in earnest to obtain information you need." His son said Todd pumped everyone he met, and "had an exhaustless store" of anecdotes, which gave him "immense power." A lifetime's practice of this use of others underpinned Todd's skillful and competitive conviviality.

> When in the right humor [Todd] was the life of any company; but when he found himself with a few kindred spirits of similar culture and taste and humor, then there was a perfect storm of stories, and hits, and repartees, and outbursts of droll remark, which kept the company in a roar; and in which, whoever came off second-best, it was not Doctor Todd.

Todd, it seems, was a past master in the technique he advocated, the creation of a mask and its interposition in the hostile relations among men. Todd's young man should attempt to make himself number one by besting others. He should loot a supply of word-money without exposing himself to the adverse opinion of the man or men thus looted. He should then invest the supply for a profitable return in other people's opinion of himself, taking precautions against the dangers that invariably accompanied Todd's notions of resources. But beneath the fragile mask, Todd's man was as vulnerable as a hermit crab inside its borrowed shell. The hearty, episcopal Todd was a fraud, or at least deeply divided, in private bewailing his lack of "fire," castigating himself for failure, retreating to the woods to recoup lost energies, and, as I have suggested, retiring to his hobbies, his study, and his fountain to console himself with fantasies of inexhaustible power.[11]

But the young man was also beset with enemies from within. Ideally, he should manage to "confine the attention" and call forth the highest efforts of body and soul. "The two difficulties which will meet you constantly, are to keep the thoughts from wandering, and from wandering in forbidden paths." Just as one's relation to others was always precarious, the individual teetering on a precipice of unmaking, waste, loss, disappointment, contempt, and disgust, so his own mind could somehow expose him to self-destruction. "At some particular time of day, or in some particular situation, you may find yourself exposed to debasing thoughts. They fill the mind and crowd out everything that is good." Again one can see the intimate connections between the outside world (the debasing thoughts to which you were exposed) and the health of the mind. The situation here anticipated was one slip followed by catastrophe. It was a typical apprehension. Most significantly, it suggests that just below the surface of a rigorously, ruthlessly, willed style of life lay surrender to total will-lessness, the mind a helpless container.[12]

A single self-indulgence, warned Todd, placed you "in the hands of your enemy." One chapter in *The Student's Manual* is arranged according to the metaphor of "thieves" who steal time—sleep, indolence, and sloth. The personification of such failings suggests that Todd internalized universal competition and that its effects were to split and diminish the self, and, perhaps, to confuse it with the generalized other.

> Do you know two bitter enemies of mine, who follow me, and haunt me, and almost ruin all my peace? The wretches! I can hardly contain myself when I think of the mischief they have done me! Their names are Procrastination and Indolence; and they look so much alike that I hardly know which is which. Alas! were it not that these fellows had got hold of me, and borne me down like the

nightmare (they *are* a kind of day-mare), I should long since have
written you.

These psychic enemies made one's mind as much a jungle as the
one Mungo Park faced. "He who tampers with a temptation is already under its power. The lion will frequently let his victim move,
and will play with it before he crushes it. What is necessary, is the
constant supervision and cultivation of temper." Todd was suggesting that a piece of the young man could break out and break
off, to join the ring of savage beasts already attacking him. But
Todd and the young man desired such enmity. Again, he seems to
have implied an incipient passivity and self-destructiveness. The
second sentence is a kind of reversal; instead of a bad part of the
mind attacking and controlling the good, a good part supervises and
cultivates the bad.[13]

Todd's young man had to immerse himself in the whirl of all-
male rivalry to stimulate the mental energy that would enable him
to follow a program that fueled him enough to risk immersing himself in the whirl of all-male rivalry, and so on. His psychological
technique was vulnerable from without and from within. He had to
pursue success when his chances, in Todd's calculation, amounted
to one in five hundred. Todd's young man's entirely selfish and
essentially vulnerable monomania perpetuated the fearfulness of
the world which Todd regarded as the special burden of his sex. The
ubiquity of hostility and fearfulness will be plain if one imagines a
world of men all following the Toddian style—the only road to
success. The very definitions of success and independence made them
impossible of achievement. Todd himself described the pursuit as
a long prospect of bitter disappointment. Why, such disappointment
would serve to stimulate the young man to continue the pursuit.
It was a disease of temperament.

Donald Meyer has pointed out the "pathos" of the Protestant
ethic. "In the mid- and late nineteenth-century ideology of success
we have the purest testimony to the psychology of self-entrapment."
Tocqueville agreed that the effects of the fantasy of autonomy
(which he called the "habit of always considering themselves as
standing alone") were tantamount to imprisonment: "not only does
democracy make every man forget his ancestors, but it hides his
descendants and separates his contemporaries from him; it throws
him back forever upon himself alone, and threatens in the end to
confine him entirely within the solitude of his own heart." American
men could not bear freedom. They imprisoned themselves.[14]

14   Todd's Masturbation Phobia

In his relations with the outer world of people and things—the external sector of the fundamental law of animal economy—the young man either consumed or was consumed. His best course was to be a parasite or a pirate, freeloading resources from other-than-self. On the other hand, what if "you were driven into a corner, and compelled to produce something as your own thoughts and opinions on an important point, at once you would wish to stimulate your mind, and key it up to the highest point." The young American might finally have to face the lonely vulnerability of independence, and John Todd assumed the inadequacy of his normal state of mind. At the same time he believed that stimulating either body or mind could foster the development of the other. This was how Todd answered the question of how to key up the mind.

> You might reach it through the body, and, by stimulating that with wines or opium might stimulate the mind. But, then, the results thus produced would be uncertain. They might be correct, and they might be like the ravings of the mind excited by disease. But, at any rate, the body and mind would both suffer by this unnatural excitement. The reaction is awfully great; and therefore, you may not do it.

The mind must be excited, but too much excitement, or the wrong kind, could lead to insanity. It was a familiar and nearly inescapable bind for men pursuing success. "What can you do? I reply, that you can stimulate your mind at any time, when the body is healthful, by reading." The qualification reflected his belief that in the case of an imbalance between mind and body, a supercharged mind could burn

out the body. Todd's book was written just three years after Brigham's, and they betrayed a common world view.[1]

René Spitz, E. H. Hare, and Robert H. MacDonald all locate the
beginnings of modern European masturbation phobia in the very
early eighteenth century. They support their findings largely by way
of the dates of publication of antimasturbation works. The first
publication devoted exclusively to masturbation was *Onania: or, the
Heinous Sin of Self-Pollution and All Its Frightful Consequences,
in both sexes, considered with Spiritual and Physical Advice to
Those who have already Injur'd themselves by this Abominable
Practice, to which is Subjoined A Letter from a Lady to the Author,
concerning the Use and Abuse of the Marriage Bed, with the
Author's Answer.*[2] It was published in 1700, and must be seen as
part of a general concern over sexual identity and marriage. In 1727,
Daniel Defoe published *Conjugal Lewdness or, Matrimonial Whore-
dom: A Treatise concerning the Use and Abuse of the Marriage Bed.*
He said he had begun the book thirty years earlier and had developed
its ideas during the 1690s. Both Watt and Schücking associated
Defoe with the English Puritan tradition, and Watt explains the rise
of the eighteenth-century novel—the work of Defoe, Richardson,
and Fielding—largely in terms of the social history of the English,
Protestant middle class. The context for *Onania* and *Conjugal Lewdness* was the same as that for *Robinson Crusoe, Clarissa,* and *Tom
Jones. Onania* inspired a spate of readers' letters, which were printed
in later editions together with the author's replies. In fact the
sixteenth edition comprised 194 pages of text and 142 pages of
letters and replies, so *Onania* took on the epistolary form of
Richardson's novels.[3]

Onania also fell into the category of hugely popular didactic
works of the eighteenth century offering a great deal of practical
advice on individual conduct and domestic life, and reflecting the
changes in sex roles and relations with which Watt has associated
the novel. Changes in the England of that period were similar in
certain respects to the changes in American society in the first half
of the nineteenth century; they included the Industrial Revolution,
the growth of towns, challenges to the old patriarchalism within and
without the family, the pressure of individualistic male ambition,
marriage at a later age, the separation of the sexes, the growth of a
class of nonworking women, and male anxieties over the latter. The
issue raised in the first line of the English poem of 1744 "The
Bachelor's Soliloquy": "To wed or not to wed, that is the question"

may be compared to the choice represented in the American *Reveries of a Bachelor* of 1850. One cause of masturbation considered in *Onania* was postponed marriage.[4]

Spitz's explanation for masturbation phobia coincides with Watt's account of the more general questions of sexual identity. The Reformation led to the destruction of the patriarchal schema in heaven and in society at large, which had interlocked with the father's authority within the family. In Spitz's opinion, the crucial point in that process lay between the Reformation and the French Revolution, that is, around 1700, when *Onania* was first published.

> Each father began to realize that he had to regulate the conduct of his family on his own responsibility. His bewilderment about the distinction between venial and mortal sin became more and more intolerable. In a manner reminiscent of phobic and compulsive processes, the feeling of guilt soon extended from the mortal to the venial sins. Unavoidably defenses were erected against sexuality in general, and particularly against those of its forms which were most difficult to check and control. As in the compulsive ritual, it was against the least controllable, least harmful, furthest removed derivatives that the battle raged strongest.

This description of post-1700 fatherhood's preoccupation with masturbation suggests the connection between Puritan self-inspection and masturbation phobia. In the terms of Watt's analysis, masturbation phobia might be seen to correspond to the priesthood of all believers, the "egalitarian tendency of Puritanism [which made] the way the individual faced every problem of everyday life a matter of deep and continuing spiritual concern." Masturbation was equally accessible to all.[5]

Spitz suggests that masturbation phobia (represented by *Onania*) started in England and spread to the continent only later in the eighteenth century. He dates the "wildfire spread" of masturbation phobia from about 1750, betokened by the publication in 1758 of a Latin work by Samuel Tissot, rapidly translated into French as *L'Onanisme, ou Dissertation physique sur les maladies produites par la masturbation,* and then into English, German, and Italian. It was reprinted as late as 1905. Benjamin Rush incorporated some of Tissot's views in *Medical Inquiries,* and the influential Esquirol lent his weight to masturbation phobia in works published in 1816, 1822, and 1838.[6]

According to Spitz's argument, masturbation phobia would be increased in proportion to social leveling and the antiauthoritarianism so characteristic of nineteenth-century America. Pervasive Puritan values, the democratization of father's role, the accretion of sexual guilt under the conditions of democratic sonhood, and the ordeal of perpetual self-doubt under the glare of the unappeasable hostility of public opinion—these conditions made American democracy fertile ground for masturbation phobia. Earthly fathers could no longer supply satisfactory definitions of identity.

The beginning of this modern efflorescence of masturbation phobia coincided with the expansion of democracy between the publication of *Medical Inquiries* and *The Student's Manual*. In 1835, Todd cited Rush's chapter "Of the Morbid State of the Sexual Appetite" (which gives two cases of "onanism") and at the same time claimed that he, Todd, was the first to attack onanism directly. "I cannot satisfy my conscience without . . . saying what others have, to my certain knowledge, wished to say and ought to say, but which no one has had the courage to say, in tones loud and distinct." Yet Todd was constrained to say it in Latin (consistent with the novelty of his publishing the subject). In the same place where he mentioned Rush, Todd supported his own warning about masturbation by reference to the "very intelligent and respectable Superintendents of the Insane Hospitals at Worcester and Hartford. [They] will say, not only that this is the cause of bringing many of their patients there, but an almost insuperable obstacle in the way of their recovery." The superintendent of the Retreat for the Insane at Hartford, and one of its founders, was Dr. Eli Todd, a relative of John Todd, as his son records in an appendix to Todd's autobiography. The superintendent of the Worcester Insane Asylum was Samuel B. Woodward (1787–1850). On Christmas Eve 1838, three years after Todd referred to his views on masturbation, Woodward wrote to the *Boston Medical and Surgical Journal* that masturbation was "doubtless very much more common in this country than is generally supposed, or than most medical men are ready to believe." In 1835 the same journal had published some "cases" of masturbation by "W," which may well have been Woodward's initial, given his Christmas Eve letter. This kind of anonymity may be compared to Todd's use of Latin in his account of the effects of the "secret" vice.[7]

It is obvious that Todd was not the first to speak out on masturbation, even if he was drawing a distinction between a medical forum and a popular one: one of the articles in the *Boston Medical and Surgical Journal* described how the doctor's masturbation patient had been "first arrested in his career by reading the chapters on the subject in the *Young Man's Guide*," one of Todd's self-help competitors. Richard Shryock links anxiety about masturbation to the popular literature "on the exalted theme, of 'What a Young Man Should Know,'" and placed its emergence in the 1830s and early 1840s. America was in no sense immune from eighteenth-century masturbation phobia, either at Rush's level or at that of the popular imagination: *Onania* and a similar work, *The Pure Nazarite*, appeared there during the century. But pervasive and obsessive masturbation phobia in America took hold during the early nineteenth century, possibly in the early 1830s, and was extraordinarily intense through the first third of the twentieth century.[8]

What Gardner remembered as Todd's "warning chapter upon *Onanism*" in *The Student's Manual* was in fact a chapter on "Reading." Reading was seen as a trebly useful exercise: it was an independent act of concentration, it stimulated the powers of the mind, and it stored up potentially invaluable material. It could also be viewed as a dangerously solitary and secret act, the stimulus overcharging the mind which would, in turn, ruin the body. In Ray's words, the "mischievous effects" of nonpurposive reading were obvious. "By a law of our constitution, violent mental emotions thrill through the bodily frame, and this participates in the vital life movement. Here, body and mind act and react on each other and . . . it seems to be immaterial whether the first impression be made on one or the other." He went on to describe the next step—masturbation—to which reading drove the young man. The notion that wrong reading led to masturbation was coexistensive with masturbation phobia. And as we have seen, Jarvis implied what Ray made explicit, the close connection between masturbation and the male need to prepare himself for his competitive course under American democratic conditions. Until the Civil War, reported *cases* of masturbation seem to have been confined to men and masturbation phobia directed almost exclusively against them. This is consistent with my argument at the end of Chapter 6.[9]

On one hand, reading was essential to the young man's successful launching and his voyage; on the other, it could lead him to self-destruction. The solution to this dilemma was strict control. It should be obvious how central reading was to the relationship between self-help authors and their putative audience of millions of young men. The relationship consisted entirely of the young man's reading the self-help author and then, hopefully, of introjecting him, seeing him as part of himself. Writing, printing, and reading allowed the men writing these manuals to reach into the young man's family (or whatever social group he inhabited), to touch him intimately in his most private self. The writer aimed to persuade the reader to do things, even to become someone, that, previously, surrounding authorities had personally persuaded young men to do and become. Self-help manuals fell into that vacuum of relationships Tocqueville described and Todd encouraged. Reading, then, could be seen as the basis for the success of both author and reader. And in describing the most fruitful ways of pursuing the goals of reading (independence, stimulus, and acquisition of information), the author was describing the reader's relation to himself. Todd's fame and fortune depended on a particularly large circle of male eyes, his enormous readership.

According to Todd, reading had a direct bearing on mental powers.

This effect of books will last through a life; and he who knows how to read with advantage, will ever have something as applicable to his mental powers, as electricity is to move the animal system. The man who has sat over the workings of a powerful mind, as exhibited on the written page, without being excited, moved, and made to feel that *he* can do something, and *will* do something, has yet to learn one of the highest pleasures of the student's life, and is yet ignorant of what rivers of delight are flowing around him through all the journey of life.

If the reader were to follow Todd's rules, he could tap these rivers.

You must not only read, and make books the fountain from which you draw your knowledge, but you must expect to draw from this fountain through life. What you read to-day, will soon be gone—expended, or forgotten; and the mind must be continually filled up with new streams of knowledge. Even the ocean would be dried up, were the streams to be cut off, which are constantly flowing into it. How few read enough to stock their minds! And the mind is no widow's cruse, which fills with knowledge as fast as we empty it. It is the hand of the diligent which maketh rich.

The hand might well be seen to be somehow generating the stream. The most obvious quality of this flow is its limited nature and thence the necessity to economize, to match income with expenditure. Todd here compared the reader's supply of knowledge with the oil in the widow's little vessel that, in I Kings 17:12–14, God's word made as everlasting as the "waters of life" of Todd's fountain, which this passage also evoked. The purest, longest-lasting oil in antebellum America was sperm. Such an association may seem tenuous, until one recalls that self-help authors addressed themselves to the common assumption that reading ran the inevitable risk of encouraging masturbation; and that Todd was, in this self-same chapter, about to plunge into a diatribe against masturbation. The sinful counterpart to the independent, stimulating, and acquisitive act of reading was the solitary and debilitating act of masturbation. In the final sentence of the last passage quoted, "eye" or "mind" would have been the more appropriate instrument for engendering the wealth of reading, unless, of course, Todd has masturbation on his mind. The reader's conversion of words into the liquid currency of expenditure also betrayed the masturbatory danger, since sex no less than any other function conformed to an economy of body.[10]

Todd devoted more space to the dangers of reading books conducive to masturbation than to the dangers of masturbation itself. The subtitle of the section describing both was "Beware of bad books." Similarly, he dwelt at greater length on the corruption of the writers of "bad" books than he did on the masturbator's corruption. It was as if Todd reserved his greatest hostility for those who exercised power over the student for whom the *Manual* was written. But his attack on the writers of masturbatory books may have been simply an oblique way of approaching masturbators themselves. Todd's words on masturbation were also oblique in that they were in Latin. This may have represented the secrecy of the sin they embodied. Todd was aware his reader might have been tempted to skip the passage. He risked such a response, he said, because in spite of his pioneering courage, he could not bring himself—or believed his readers could not bring themselves—to unmask the secret vice. "I have chosen to risk the charge of pedantry rather than not say what I could not say in English." The entire context was riddled with the danger of reading's becoming masturbation, and it is most plausible to argue that Todd felt that either he or his readers could not get past the address to masturbators without masturbating unless they were shielded from its direct glare. The passage[11] is physically distinct from the rest of the book, separated by a gap from the preceding and following text, in very obviously smaller type. It is the longest piece of Latin, and the only part of the text distinguished in both these ways. (There is a model letter in smaller type to the model student's mother, not, of course, in Latin.) This is my translation:

No light, except that of the ultimate Gods, can uncover the practice of pouring out by the hand (the vicious act of Onan), in spite of its frequency and constancy. No light can reveal as many modern adolescents as one can imagine, debasing themselves day by day in that way, and doing so over many years. The incitement to this crime, within the power of all, is very great. I have lamented the case of many which, solely from that execrable cause, I have seen come to premature death, some in academic halls, some very quickly after leaving college, and some having graduated with honors. Many are known to defend this practice as if it were some sort of instinct and imperative impulse, and so would have God himself to be the instigator of this debauchery. "This conceals guilt as excuse." Most foul hypocrisy! Those people taught by the light of nature have reproved that crime with many words. "Hand—stay your lasciviousness! Do you think this nothing? It is a vicious act, believe me! an enormity, how great can scarcely be conceived by your soul; restrain your importunate hand. More than perpetrating an enormity in young boys—it SINS."

God shows his mind most clearly concerning this crime. The practitioners will be hunted down by the resentment and wrath of God. "Indeed, we know the verdict of God, in accordance with right, to be against those who behave in such a way. Moreover, do you believe, you who do this thing, that you can flee the judgment of God?"

Remember the result of this practice to be:—

1. Memory is very much debilitated;

2. The mind is greatly deteriorated, and foolishly weakened;

3. It bears deadly seeds of sickness, and death itself to a debilitated body;

4. Everything which pertains to the soul crumbles closer to ruin;

5. Punishment by God, who examines you in secret, will certainly come to pass. His eye, always vigilant, observes you. "For assuredly, God himself brings to judgment every deed, including every hidden thing." "And assuredly, to speak truth, they become foul by these deeds." Flee, flee for the sake of life, of soul. "Stand on principles." This is a vice you cannot conquer except by fleeing. Whoever lives in fear of God will teach you, "this is the way to the grave," this way leads to the hinterland of death.

Translation is not susceptible to the kind of analysis one can make of generally existential language. It may be said, however, that Todd associated the addressable problem of masturbation only with males, and that he was disturbed by the secrecy of masturbation; its ease of repetition, deception, and self-deception; and, most

of all, perhaps, by its devastating effects on mind and body and its
sheer power to override a young man's will. "Hoc scelus vincere non
poteris." Todd's evident alarm that masturbation was in the power
of everybody ("cum pene omnibus") suggests an association between masturbation phobia and that equalization of men which
seriously eroded the traditional source of male identity, and is consistent with Spitz's explanation for the intensification of modern
masturbation phobia.

Todd's hostility to the writers of masturbatory books straddled
the Latin passage directed at masturbation per se. Todd began the
bad-book section with this:

> Some men have been permitted to live and employ their powers in
> writing what will continue to pollute and destroy for generations
> after they are gone. The world is flooded with such books. They are
> permitted to lie in our pathway as a part of our moral discipline.
> Under the moral government of God, while in this state of probation,
> we are to be surrounded by temptations of every kind. And never does
> the spirit of darkness rejoice more, than when a gifted mind can
> prostitute itself, but to adorn and conceal a path which is full of
> holes, through which you may drop into the chambers of death.

By pollution and destruction Todd meant masturbation and its
effects, in this case induced by bad books, in turn the products of the
perverse use of creative male "powers." The last sentence of the
passage suggests that writers of books conducive to masturbation
are themselves masturbators, and compares their persuasion of their
readers to masturbate to prostitutes' perverse selling of themselves
in sexual intercourse. I have already quoted Todd's characterization
of brothels as "breathing holes of hell." In *The Young Man*, Todd
warned against those men who led an unwary youth to a brothel,
"entering the door of women whose house is the gate-way of hell."
It would not be unreasonable to suggest that entering "the door of
women" in that context particularly given the absence of a qualify-
ing "those" before "women," was identical in Todd's imagination
to entering the vagina. Then Todd, perhaps, used a common image—
hot, deadly, and ubiquitous holes—for both masturbation and illicit
sexual intercourse. What they had in common is their diversion and,
eventually, removal of a man from the majesty and destiny of manhood—not sex, but the single-minded pursuit of the fixed path
to success.[12]

The striking metaphor, a path full of holes through which one
would drop into the chambers of death, is almost the same as the

one whereby Todd described his own guilt and distress on the occasion of his deciding to become a minister. "It seemed as if hell itself had risen up to swallow me. My distress was so great that I expected every moment to drop into hell." The adolescent who later saw himself pioneering an antimasturbation "path" in America may well have been suffering at his moment of dedication from an acute attack of guilt over his own masturbation.

Even in approaching the subject of masturbation thus far Todd ran the risk of exposing his readers to its dangers. Reading about manhood and womanhood could trigger the very degeneracy it was meant to prevent. "Books could be named, were it not that there is a possibility that even the information conveyed in naming them might be perverted and used to obtain them, which, seemingly, could not be excelled by all the talents in hell, if the object were to pollute and to ruin. These are to be found everywhere. I do entreat my young readers never to look at one—never to open one." Todd could see himself creating the danger which he aimed to obviate: Gardner witnessed the stimulating effects of Todd's book upon the minds of his fellow students; they frequently discussed masturbation because of Todd. Todd said he wanted to arouse his readers' feelings "to fear and to beware." He admitted his remarks about masturbation "may be condemned by some," presumably because they held Todd's words would encourage the activity they purported to condemn. In short, Todd knew he could be interpreted as one of those perverse writers leading young men to masturbation.[13]

Todd acknowledged the question springing naturally to the reader's mind. How did Todd know which books were dangerous and what their effects were?

> "But," say you, "has my author [i.e., Todd] ever read Byron, and Moore, Hume, and Paine, Scott, Bulwer and Cooper?" Yes, he has read them all, and with too much care. He knows every rock and every quicksand; . . . those who wrote to show how they could revel in passion, and pour out their living scorn upon their species— and those who wasted life and gigantic powers merely to amuse men—have come far short of answering the great end of existence on earth.

How could Todd know masturbation without experiencing it? What did he mean exactly by "too much care"? Did Todd, according to the logic of the inevitability of the effects of reading bad books, continue to revel in masturbation? He said he found Rush's chapter on masturbation "thrilling and harrowing." It was logically im-

possible to support the terms of his warning: either reading masturbatory books led inevitably to masturbation and therefore Todd
had read them and masturbated; or else Todd had read them and
remained immune, in which case they did not inevitably lead to
masturbation. His readers could follow Todd's example—and he
might have led them to masturbate.[14]

Bad books did not only tell the reader directly what a later
masturbation phobe called "sensational love stories." In Todd's
view, books were bad if they inspired the reader to dream up his
own masturbatory fantasies.

> In connection with these books, allow me to lift up a loud voice
> against those rovings of the imagination, by which the mind is at
> once enfeebled, and the heart and feelings debased and polluted. It
> is almost inseparable from the habit of revery: but, in this life, a
> heavier curse can hardly hang upon a young man than that of pos-
> sessing a polluted imagination. The leprosy fills the whole soul.

A roving imagination led to reverie and habitual masturbation.
Marvel's bachelor's "reveries" were about women—and the attraction of doing without them altogether. Perhaps the popularity of
that book reflected a need to give vent to the dangerous habit Todd
said men should repress. Tocqueville found that no "men are less
addicted to reverie than the citizens of a democracy, and few of
them are ever known to give way to those idle and solitary medita-
tions which commonly precede and produce the great emotions of
the heart."[15]

Since Todd was describing the effect of imagination and reverie to
be the "disease" of addiction to masturbation, manipulating the
penis to erection—and, as the fancied effects demonstrate, to ejaculation of semen—it seems likely that the "curse" of the habit of
reverie has been assimilated in Todd's own imagination to that part
of the body it stimulates, which can be said to "hang upon a young
man." Perhaps the masturbator's penis hangs rather than stands
because it was by virtue of its owner's addiction always in a state
of just having ejaculated.

In a similar way and in the same context, Todd transferred the
actions of the masturbated penes to the books he described as inducing such actions. The masturbatory books were "secreted in the
rooms of students," and they "leave a stain" which can never be
removed. The latter was an effect that appealed to Todd, since he
repeated it: "some books will positively injure if they do not destroy
you. Others will have no positive good effect; and from all, a tinc-

ture, like that left upon the mind by the company you keep, will be left." One can see here how the kind of economic absorption and expulsion of other men slides into the terms of masturbation phobia.[16]

If, as seems apparent, masturbatory books became the penes they so easily stimulated, then what is one to make of a passage such as the following (again in the masturbation section in *The Student's Manual*)?

> I have known these books secreted in the rooms of students, and lent from one to another. They are to be found too frequently. And if you have an enemy, whose soul you would visit with a heavy vengeance, and into whose heart you would place vipers which will live, and crawl, and torment him through life, and whose damnation you would seal up for the eternal world, you have only to place one of these destroyers in his hand. You have certainly paved the way to the abodes of death; and if he does not travel it with hasty strides, you have, at least laid up food for many days of remorse.

The passing of book/penis to one's enemy was both aggressive (to condemn one's enemy to hell) and a homosexual act betokening some form of passivity (like depending on rivalry for stimulus of energy). It placed him in your power (you could play God to him), or it placed you—your penis—in his power. By casting a book onto his path you were opening a hot hole before him, into which he would drop himself. The metaphor repeated the masturbation-prostitution identification in the road full of holes and expanded the passivity of placing one's penis into enemy hands into the more thoroughgoing fantasy of playing a female role to one's male enemy. At the same time, the aggressive, godlike placing of one's viper into the feminine-associated "heart" of your enemy reversed the roles. So perhaps the "whirl and contact" inheritance was not unequivocally attractive to men after all. Todd betrayed the same confusion of sex roles that Dr. Alfred Stillé exhibited.[17]

Masturbation was vitally important to Todd. Reading was the foundation of a young man's self-making. It comprised his relationship with his guide. The inevitable accompaniment of reading was the risk of masturbation. According to these terms it was his most dangerous and persistent adversary. Todd made these connections explicitly. Masturbatory books were "the most awful scourge with which a righteous God ever visited our world." In a sense masturbation was the chief rival to Todd's system of male behavior.

There was an intimate relationship between masturbation and the recommended concentration of energies, as the young man attempted to succeed in that arena polarized between settlement and expansion, marriage and bachelorhood. The hoarding of energy by way of self-induced habit into a system obsessed with masturbation (that is, avoiding it) was very much like the contemporary definition of the autonomous, secretive, addictive habit it was designed to avoid. Todd's, Ray's, and Brigham's books would, as Todd claimed for his most popular book, "aid in forming and strengthening the intellectual and moral character and habits of the student." Masturbation would "enervate the physical and mental powers of man." *The Student's Manual* warned against masturbation, and Todd admitted that the *Manual* could be accused of causing it.[1]

The treatment of masturbation, the absorption of a young man's energies in the enterprise described in Chapter 2, was identical to the course a *normal,* non- (or undiscovered) masturbator would take. Doctors recommended tonics, stimulants, cold showers, gentle exercise, and invigorating diet. They recomended that the masturbator confine his imagination and that he "abstain from the indulgence."

> The great remedies for the onanism of boys are instructions as to their nature by some other means than the reading of vile books, and the experience of vile companions; instruction from parents or teacher: occupation for the mind, and bodily exercise; simple food and personal cleanliness; last, proper control of the imagination, scrupulously avoiding all impure literature, plays or pictures, and associates who suggest erotic thoughts.

This was a typical collection of remedies—and all of them were, as we have seen, part of the *normal* programs for male success advocated by Todd, Ray, and Brigham. An article in the *New Orleans Medical and Surgical Journal* of 1855 described a "young man of fine physical development who wrote good verses and practiced masturbation to excess. [He] asked for medical advice . . . [and] was persuaded to try severe manual labor, he cleared six acres of heavily timbered beech and sugar tree bottoms—was cured and rose to distinction in civil life."[2]

Todd's young man was supposed to fix his eye on success, clearly an act of imagination. Yet such an act entailed the risk of masturbation, just as reading did.

> I have spoken of the practice of building castles in the air,—a practice which will be very apt to steal in upon you till it becomes a regular habit, unless you are very careful. You can hardly be too solicitous to keep clear of this habit. I have spoken of worse results of permitting the thoughts to wander when alone,—evils which want a name, to convey any conception of their enormity.

The context makes clear that by worse results he meant masturbation and its effects. This imagination was not distinct from the kind the businessman exercised. And, according to Todd, the overimaginative businessman ran the risk of masturbating his life away.[3]

Clearly the program Todd advocated placed a man in a potentially self-destructive bind identical to the general terms following Esquirol's dicta. Like the general, insanity-producing male energization of which it was a specific form, masturbation was "the accompaniment of civilization and refinement." The frequency and nature of the "cases" demonstrate that men generally shared Todd's anxiety. As early as 1835, one "fickle and capricious" twenty-year-old man "in a fit of desperation . . . attempted to emasculate himself, but succeeded in removing one testicle only." His act suggests that he was resisting the inheritance of his sex in a very direct way. Another symptom, this time typical of the masturbator, also expressed resistance to the expected male role, and in a way that reflected it. The young masturbator displayed an "inability to fix his mind upon any subject, or give his attention to business." Instead he devoted himself singlemindedly to masturbation. "W" reported a patient trying desperately to follow the *Young Man's Guide,* but still suffering the effects of masturbation: he was "feeble" and "irresolute," "unable to fix his attention to any subject, or to pursue any active employment." We can add such evidence to the undercurrent in Sims and Stillé (and, as we shall see, in Todd and Gardner), away from the pressures of the particular kind of malehood offered by nineteenth-century America.[4]

The close relation between masturbation and normal, masturbation-phobic male behavior can be explained to a certain extent by the idea that each society evokes, by means of particular sanctions and a particular commitment to their enforcement, its own most appropriate form of deviant behavior. "The deviant and the conformist . . . are creations of the same culture, inventions of the same imagination." I have suggested at several points already that it was democracy's reduction of sources of identity (together with the effects of industrialization on sex roles) that placed a new and unrelenting pressure on manhood. It is in this change that one can look, I think, for the beginnings of the masturbator/antimasturbator cycle. There were other such obsessions and counterobsessions in the nineteenth century. Tobacco and drink are the most familiar examples. But in all cases they were believed to threaten manhood (and womanhood to a lesser extent) very specifically, that is, the sexual identity that democracy had left so exposed. Like masturbation, tobacco and liquor were addictive stimulants, leading to reverie and distraction, debilitating the will and the body, rendering it sterile or productive of stunted offspring, the source of innumerable diseases, and destroying a man's chances for success. (Yet men believed some kind of stimulation was essential to success.) The proliferation of dietary cults should be viewed in the same context: in 1872 John Todd had an account of his workshop published in *The Herald of Health and Journal of Physical Culture—Advocates a Higher Type of Manhood—Physical, Intellectual, and Moral.* (The article consists overwhelmingly of twelve "hints to young, professional men . . . tools make you independent.") Nothing illustrates better the belief in the interdependence of mind and body, and the connection between Todd's hobbies and his programing of young men's energies. Pressures on residual physiological identity were the context for the rise of patent medicines (very largely aimed at the restoration of lost manhood and womanhood) and the sectarian communities focusing on sexual identity—the Shakers, Noyes's Oneida, and even the Mormons.[5]

But masturbation phobia may have been more widespread a mode of anxiety over physiological identity than the others (and, conversely, more widespread a factor in the formulation of male identity) for very obvious reasons. First, those Spitz has given; second, masturbation may be one of the few universal human habits, its general practice a preexisting crop for antimasturbators to harvest. One did not have to identify oneself as a masturbator, as one did as a smoker, a drinker, or a Mormon. Both habit and guilt were open to imagination, and profoundly vulnerable to the tide of antimasturbation sentiment. Above all, masturbation mirrored the normal male obsession with a selfhood defined as the autonomous accumulation of energy; a central part of that selfhood was masturbation phobia, drawing a "boundary" between it and the behavior the term evoked, that is, masturbation.

The system of male behavior so bounded operated according to the law of animal economy, which Brigham also called the law of the distribution of vital powers. If the body's powers were concentrated on or expended by one organ, it was inevitable that they be withdrawn from the rest of the body. The world consumed a man's energy; he had to be on perpetual watch to restore it. Todd believed that if "the powers of the body be palsied or prostrated, or in any way abused, his mind must so far sympathize as to be unfitted at making progress in study." On the other hand, he believed that "the Creator has not so formed the body, that it can endure to be confined, without exercise, while the mind burns and wears upon its energies and powers every moment." At the same time, Todd did not regard these two interdependent entities as at all equal in value. "We consist of two parts; the one [the body] inert, passive, utterly incapable of directing itself, barely ministerial to the other [the mind], moved, animated by it." His final concern was the health of the mind: if the mind wore out the "energies" of the body, then its own further activities, the pursuit of success—and to "persist therein with greater resolution and steadiness"—would be undercut. A prodigy who neglected his health would fall by the wayside, simply burned out: such a concern was identical to Brigham's and Ray's. I have emphasized the direct and ongoing relationship between the unrelenting stress of American life and the exactly corresponding stress felt by men inside themselves. The chapter in *The Student's Manual* from which these remarks are taken is entitled "Exercise-Diet Economy." The way in which a man handled the intimately economic relation between mind and body was seen to be continuous with the way in which he handled money, specifically debt and expenditure.[6]

That the young man should engage the world at all (and thus expose his interior economy to its dangerous vicissitudes) was due to his possession of penis and testicles. Appropriately, the easiest and most dangerous "abuse" threatening a young man's energies was his ejaculation of sperm. Describing the catastrophic effects of masturbation on the "physical and mental stamina of a man," in the first of a two-part article in 1835, "W" widened his focus to the ejaculation of sperm under any circumstances. "Nature designs that this drain upon the system should be reserved to mature age, and even then that it be made but sparingly. Sturdy manhood, in all vigor, loses its energy and bends under the too frequent expenditure of this important secretion; and no age or condition will protect a man from the danger of unlimited indulgence, [even] legally and naturally exercised." Loss of sperm in marital copulation, though preferable to masturbation, was dangerous and had to be performed according to strict rule (which is described in Part IV). What should be noticed here is that "W" regarded the body as a system of energy or vigor, represented by a metaphor of liquidity (the ejaculation of sperm was a "drain"), which pervaded Todd's account of a young man's behavior, and his own and his son's view of himself. His notion of his writings as a fountain of the waters of life for young men was literalized in his study. Todd and "W" used the term "energy" in the same sense. Todd's "unquenchable fire" and "everlasting go forward" were synonymous for manly vigor and energy. "I have no *time* in which to do anything; and secondly I have no courage to do it, had I time . . . alas for me! I have not so much wide-awake about me, and what little of the 'everlasting go forward' I once had is about all run out." "Run out" recalls Ray's record of the popular phrase "used up," and both may be compared to "W's" use of "expenditure." If the system was economic, then the ejaculation of sperm was equivalent in some sense to the expenditure of money. "W" repeats the metaphor in the conclusion of this first article. The effects of masturbation are cumulative: the more the will is weakened, the stronger the genitals' tendency to ejaculate. After a while only "slight irritation will produce an expenditure of the secretion quite involuntarily."[7]

Accounts of masturbation always assumed such a system. "W" said that weaknesses in adolescence usually attributed to the growth rate in fact were due to masturbation. The change from "adolescence to manhood" "requires all the energy of the system." His second article, about the effects of masturbation on the mind, described how the waste of sperm "prostrated" *all* of the "energies of the system." The "victim of masturbation passes from one degree of imbecility to another, till all the powers of the system, mental, physical and moral, are blotted out forever." The discharge of sperm obliterated, prostrated, and blotted out the energies of the system altogether. Instead of concentrating those energies onto the nonsexual end of success, the masturbator concentrated what was left of them onto his penis and testicles. "All the remaining energies of animal life seem to be concentrated in these organs, and all the remaining power of gratification left is in the exercise of this . . . loathsome and beastly habit." That the ejaculation of sperm then diminished and exhausted all of the rest of the body's energy suggests that, somehow, in its focusing on the genital organs the previously undefined energy was transformed into sperm.[8]

During Todd's lifetime men were preoccupied with the fear of a loss of sperm, connected as it was to the whole question of manhood and to a man's hopes for some kind of immortality. The ancient connotations of sperm took on a particular significance in the nineteenth century; the context was the pressure on man's sexual identity. People believed in "pangenesis": each part of the body was believed to contribute a fraction of itself to the sperm by way of the blood. Buffon had been its most famous exponent in the eighteenth century, in spite of the contemporary discovery of spermatozoa and competition from consequent theories of generation. The belief that sperm represented its bearer was probably intensified by Lamarck (1744–1829) at the turn of the eighteenth century and was widely held both popularly and by such scientific luminaries as Charles Lyell, Herbert Spencer, and Charles Darwin.[9] Lamarck's belief in the inheritance of acquired characteristics pulled even closer together the moral and physiological parts of the anti-masturbators' attacks, since they believed that the masturbator's debilitation would be passed on to his children, in exactly the way that drunkards were believed to bequeath their weaknesses. Gardner defined sperm as "the concentrated powers of [man's] perfected being." According to him, "Sperm is the purest extract of the blood, and according to the expression of Feruel, *totus homo semen est.*" It was this spermatic summary of man that Todd had in mind when he described the effects of ejaculation as debilitation of body and memory and the deterioration and weakening of the mind. Men believed their expenditure of sperm had to be governed according to an economic principle. I have called this principle the "spermatic economy."[10]

It was part of a broader attitude toward the utilization of the self. The notion of concentrating the body's energies, whether on the genitals (as "W" described masturbation's doing) or on success (as Todd advocated), suggests how energies were something a man deployed from a preexisting form. In 1870 Dr. J. H. Walters used the word "organization" for such deployment. His statement is a reference point for the rest of this book.

> In 1850, while yet an under-graduate student of medicine, I could not accept the doctrines of life, at that time generally received and taught. Those doctrines uniformly started with the assumption of some peculiar vital force or forces, either as existing independently of the matter of the organism, or as properties originally "stamped" upon matters capable of assimilation, and which become phenomenal by the act of organization. How different soever might be the fancies as to the nature and origin of this peculiar force, it was assumed to account for those phenomena which are peculiar to living organisms, such as the development of special forms, nutrition, reproduction, etc.; and also to account for phenomena, it was assumed allowable to endow it with any imaginable property to meet every emergency, such as the capacity of being dormant or depressed on the one hand, or of being excited or stimulated on the other.

"Vitalism" as Walters here defined it dated from Aristotle at least. Among the medical students vulnerable to such generally taught doctrine were Brigham (whose book appeared in Boston just three years before Todd's *Student's Manual* in Northampton), Eli Todd and Samuel Woodward (both acknowledged by Todd to have influenced his views on masturbation), and Isaac Ray, whom I have quoted to have demanded the "quickening of torpid energies." The belief was in no way limited to doctors, as Todd's own bewailing of the "prostration of vital powers" illustrates.[11]

We have seen how Ray criticized American men generally for failing to "concentrate their energies on any particular point."

Everyone had "a given amount of original endowment," but he needed a "course of suitable discipline" to bring it to focus. Such "discipline" was synonymous with Walters's notion of "organization." While Walters's account of vitalism suggests the variability of energy organization, existentially and popularly men seem to have aligned the organizations of their energy with the most commonplace and traditional split, between higher and lower, mind and body, intellect and passion, work and sex, knit together, of course, by the fundamental law of animal economy. Todd intended his work to supply a model for the disciplining of energy in terms of the internal and economic organization of the self.

In short, "sublimation" was a general belief long before Freud formulated and refined it as "a process of deflecting libido or sexual motive activity from human objects to new objects of a non-sexual socially valuable nature." I have found the notion, usually in terms of the organization of vital energies, to have been basic to the writings of all nineteenth-century people, male and female, black and white. It should be noted that Freud's 1905 description of "the libido theory" was nearly identical to the belief Walters was describing as outmoded in 1870.

> We have laid down the concept of the libido as a force of variable quantity by which processes and transformations in the spheres of sexual excitement can be measured. This libido we distinguished from the energy which is at the basis of the psychic processes in general as far as their special origin is concerned, and we thus attribute to it also a qualitative character. In separating libidinal from other psychic energy, we give expression to the assumption that the sexual processes of the organism are differentiated from the nutritional processes through a special chemism . . . this sexual excitement is furnished not only from the so-called sexual parts alone, but from all organs of the body.[12]

Todd's "we consist of two parts" passage is one version of the pre-Freudian form of sublimation; I shall call it "proto-sublimation." Another, and even more precise, expression was Thoreau's in *Walden* (1854): the "generative energy, which when we are loose, dissipates and makes us unclean, when we are continent invigorates and inspires us." This was Gardner's version in 1872: the sexual "passion may be restrained within proper limitations. He who indulges in lascivious thoughts may stimulate himself to frenzy; but if his mind were under proper control he would find other employment for it, and his body, obedient to its potent sway, would not become master of the man." Gardner restated such proto-sublimation in the special context of the democratic anxiety described by Tocqueville, Todd, and Jarvis.

> In American life . . . [there] are few whose minds are sufficiently freed from the cares and anxieties of life, from the necessity of earning a livelihood, with the consequent employment of time and the fatigues of body and brain. The physical energies are too completely used up by these necessities to allow for much excess in [sexual] pleasure, save at such infrequent intervals as to be comparatively harmless.

Theophilus Parvin implied the same connection in his 1884 article "The Hygiene of the Sexual Function." Newton, Kant, Pascal, Beethoven, and Fontenelle lived, he said, "without sexual intercourse, and some of them had their years wonderfully prolonged, and though they left no children to perpetuate their names, they were prolific in great works. . . ." That conception of a man's work, equivalent to sexual reproduction, is identical to Sims's.[13]

Todd's adherence to this general belief in the need to divert energy away from the inevitably tempting sexual expression and to concentrate it on higher goals shaped his view of all of the young man's transactions with people and things. Of course, those transactions (above all, democratic competition among men) shaped the belief—the shapings interactive and ongoing, a perverse but general version of the process described by Erik Erikson as "the metabolism of generations." Erikson uses the same neo-Freudian metaphor as Todd, that is, energy and capital.

> Each human life begins at a given evolutionary stage and level of tradition, bringing to its environment a capital of patterns and energies; these are used to grow on, and to grow into the social process with, and also as contributions to this process. Each new being is received into a style of life prepared by tradition and held together by tradition, and at the same time disintegrating because of the very nature of that tradition . . . the social process does not mold a new being merely to housebreak him; it molds generations in order to be remolded, to be reinvigorated by them.[14]

In one sense it is pointless to argue that Todd and his young man's social beliefs can be explained by more fundamental exigencies— i.e., their attitudes toward sex. Where did *they* come from? In fact, the young man's relations with books, Todd, other men, success, were all of a piece with his attitude toward his body.

Words, books, sperm, money—all were construed as resources, hoarded or expended, vital to the young man's perpetually challenged energy system, and in that system's terms, exchangeable with one another. His belief in the spermatic economy throws further light on the meaning of reading to Todd, and on the apparently homosexual undertones of his relations with his reader. Todd's metaphor for reading is insistently physiological. Reading was eating: "We want to have the mind continually expanding, and creating new thoughts, or at least feeding itself on manly thoughts. The food is to the blood, which circulates through your veins, what reading is to the mind." To feed on other men's thoughts was easier than being original. One became a more successful man by consuming another man's manliness. It is clear from the context of this passage (the "bad books" section of his "Reading" chapter in *The Student's Manual*) that the unmanly thoughts generated by masturbatory writers were those that led to masturbation, its debilitating effects tantamount to unmanning. The comparison of reading to food and of mind to blood was particularly important because of the inherent danger that reading would lead to a loss of sperm and because sperm was construed to be the quintessence of the blood. Perhaps the "manly thoughts" were gathered from the mind's blood as Todd believed sperm was gathered.[15]

According to Todd, the food supplied by masturbatory books was "tainted meat." The reader had to have the strength of mind to resist the "fine-looking joint," and not "eat through it." If he should "stoop" to pick up a beautiful thought that, say, Byron had thrown out, he would find Byron

> chain[ed] upon [him], a putrid carcass which [he could] never throw off. . . . But [Byron] will quickly pass from notice, and is doomed to be exiled from the libraries of all virtuous men. It is a blessing to the world, that what is putrid must soon pass away. The carcass hung in chains will be gazed at for a short time in horror; but men will soon turn their eyes away, and remove even the gallows on which they swing.[16]

This is an extraordinarily elaborate image for Byron and the masturbatory writers of which he was the archetype. The carcass in this passage is at first chained to the young masturbator, hanging on him as, Todd said, the "curse" of masturbation hung. So overwhelming is the weight and size of this version of the masturbatory vehicle that the young man might be said to be hanging from it. It dominates its owner. That and its putridity (according to Webster, putridity's connotations are both moral—depraved—and powerfully physical—decomposed, rotten, and foul-smelling) suggest that Todd felt both awe and disgust for the tumescent, masturbated penis. In the next sentence in which the carcass appears, the owner has vanished, or rather he has turned into the gallows on which the carcass is hung. But Todd has made himself responsible for holding up Byron, masturbatory books, and masturbation to other men's eyes. So once again Todd the antimasturbator was also Todd the masturbator. The same confusion of opposites is true of the young man he addressed. The young man turns cannibal as his mouthful from the fine-looking joint evolves into the corpse of an executed criminal. There is an apparent difficulty in the passage in that the logical antecedent of the "they" swinging from the gallows is the singular carcass. Perhaps Todd betrayed the cannibalism of his good young men rejecting Byron's exemplary carcass, since they were supposed to feed perpetually on other men's manliness. They were to choose Todd, not Byron.

Todd quantified outer and inner resources as money as well as food. Selfhood was something to be measured. Time, language, and thoughts were money. Not to "dig for gold" in books was "to spend one's self in beating about to discover a path." Books were halfpence, silver, gold, and bank notes. The stream of knowledge was a cash flow, to be diverted to the mind, and converted to the bodily economy of energies, then hoarded, judiciously "expended," and constantly replaced. The Bachelor compared his mind to a "purse." Good books induced investment toward the goal of success; bad ones, or reverie, induced the "waste" of expenditure as sperm. The system assumed the interdependence of mind and body, and Todd, throughout, assumed the exchangeability of their currency. Todd admitted that once he read 124 volumes in six months. "I might as well have poured gold-dust through a coarse sieve, thinking that by pouring it by the bushel my sieve must certainly retain much." California gold captured Todd's imagination long before he went to California and described gold mining with especially loving care in *The Sunset Land* (1871). Todd's comparison of reading to searching for gold either by panning or by digging was a frequent one, demonstrating his identification of studious eastern activities with extractive outdoors out West. In this case, the waste of bookish fluid through a mass of holes (the sieve) recalls Todd's picture of spermatic waste in the masturbator's road full of holes, an association reinforced by Todd's own ineluctable connection between bad reading and masturbation. In Todd's words, masturbation was "effundendi manu"—pouring out by the hand, most frequently induced by writers of bad books, appropriately said by Todd "to pour more than seven vials of woe upon the family whose affections are bound up in the son who is thus destroyed." Their action anticipated precisely the one they stimulated: they "revel in passion, and pour out their living scorn upon their species—and wasted life and gigantic powers merely to amuse men—[they] have come far short of answering the great end of existence on earth." The masturbator poured out his "living" sperm, whose properties embodied and should have contributed to "the species"; the masturbator's "end" was not extended to the greatness of existence—the immortality of proto-sublimation and siring of sons—connecting the young man with religious heroes past and future, but instead his "end" was "short," wasting its life, its sperm, in amusement. It may be, then, that Todd's description of his wasteful reading as pouring through coarse holes implies that he felt it was tantamount to masturbation, or even that it led him to masturbate. That feeling would be consistent with his warnings about wrong reading, and the strong possibility that he experienced its effects firsthand. If so, the "gold-dust" lost through holes was in a sense equivalent to sperm. In Todd's view golden books were part of a hierarchy culminating in bank notes. So the passage suggests that Todd shared with "W" and the popular imagination the connection between sperm and money illustrated by the terms "expenditure" and "spend." There is an obvious connection between the imaginary water, bearing gold and directed by Todd through a myriad of holes in his mental sieve, and his favorite metaphor for selfhood in a universe of liquidity— streams, rivers, and oceans of knowledge, unquenchable fire, waters of life—that is a fountain. The one in his study squirted water through forty little holes: Todd compared the drops of water to golden balls falling into cups of silver.[17]

We have seen that Ray measured the popular mind according to the fundamental law of animal economy, complaining about the appalling amount of mental power that America had wasted, compared to the tiny portion it had "suffered to work out its destined purpose" in measured American male accomplishment. Todd, too, projected spermatic economy and proto-sublimation—the arousal of energies and their channeling away from sex into self-education, business, "success," in short, into "the majesty and destiny of Manhood"—onto a social scale. In his 1841 book, *Great Cities*, he said that cities were like stagnant lakes, with "no circulation of waters" and "darkness almost Egyptian." He contrasted these dark, poor, stagnant depths with "the enlightened and the rich," and said what was wanted was social movement up, from darkness into light.

> Now what we want, is something that will put these waters in motion, and thus purify them, and that something is education; and never can you hope to raise, and enlighten, and save our great cities, till you have got the mind of all this darkened mass in motion, and in a state of being educated. You want to take it out of the influence of ignorance and depravity; you want to form new, and permanent habits; you want to create mind, and call out thought, and show the poor man that his child can rise to any station for which he is prepared. You want to call children from the cellar, and the shop, and educate them, and show that enlightened virtue will be rewarded.

Todd had taken this route, from kneeling destitution at his father's grave, via liberal education at Yale, to the big, beautiful houses and churches in Philadelphia and Pittsfield. Todd's desire to impart permanent motion to the waters, and to purify them, links the vision to the intimate meanings of Todd's fountain, while the more specific methods—removal from bad influences, formation of new and fixed habits leading to reward—were those embodied in his manuals.[18]

Of course, the overall vision of the energizing of still waters—from immobility and darkness into movement and light, the evocation of thought from the stuff of ignorance and depravity—was the social version of proto-sublimation. Habit, virtue, thought, and mind emerged from the darkened mass, from stagnation and depravity, by way of arousal, evocation, purification, preparation, and education. The upward direction of this willed movement makes it plain that these states bore a vertical relation to each other. Todd here saw this hierarchy in three forms: an inner, psychological, and physiological one, mind culled from the depraved inertia of individual being; an outer form, which also matured in time, from the "child in a cellar" to the "higher station" in life, presumably that occupied by the concentratedly energetic businessman; and third, the vague, abstract view of a state of being in darkness transmogrified into a state of being in the upper reaches of light.

One can also see Todd's projection of proto-sublimation in his apocalyptic social vision. He warned the readers of *The Student's Manual* to "look at the great amount of abuse and perversion of

mind, of which mankind is constantly guilty." At the time of
Christianity's beginnings

> the world had exhausted its strength in trying to embrace paganism;
> and yet not so low, as not to try to exist in the shape of nations. The
> experiment had been repeated, times we know not how many. Egypt,
> Babylonia, Persia, polished Greece, iron-footed Rome, mystical Hin-
> dooism, had all tried it. They spent, each, mind enough to regenerate
> a nation, in trying to build up a system of corrupt paganism; and
> when that system was built up—let the shape and form be what it
> might—the nation had exhausted its energies, and sunk and fell
> under the effects of misapplied and perverted mind. No nation existed
> on the face of the earth which was not crumbling under the use of
> its perverted energies, when the Gospel reached it.[19]

Todd anthropomorphized society on the scale of nations, empires,
the whole world, all abusing their bodily economies by perverting
their expenditures. Nations spending mind for the regeneration of
themselves: the language suggests that Todd viewed such a process
as a sublimated act of self-reproduction. But their particular form
of discharged mind—corrupt paganism—was the wrong one. So
there was no feedback, the discharge simply drained, and the bodies
politic sank and fell.

Todd wanted to prevent America from going the same way as
earlier civilizations. He saw his work summoning young men to the
"high destiny" of the nation—the sublimation into WASP civilization of the resources conquered by westward expansion and absorbed by immigration—but he felt these new energies could under-
mine American destiny, or pervert it as their equivalents had the
Roman Empire, the comparison a profound and insistent apprehension in nineteenth-century history, and one shared by Brigham and
Gardner. Americans permitted Byronic prostitution of mind and
subordinated religion to business. They hungered desperately for
the applause of their fellow men: "there is no stream so sweet as
that which flows from this fountain." Todd's work contributed to all
of these tendencies.[20]

16   Men Earn—Women Spend

Todd's sense of male vulnerability shaped his attitudes toward women. Such a statement does not preclude the reverse, that his attitudes toward women shaped his sense of male vulnerability. Obviously the notion that male behavior depended on the control of eruptive sexuality, most specifically the prevention of the waste of sperm, encouraged men to draw apart from women just as Tocqueville said they did. "W's" warning against the too frequent expenditure of sperm in legal copulation was typical nineteenth-century advice.[1]

After devoting twenty years to addressing young men on self-discipline, Todd turned in 1853 (with the publication of *The Daughter at School*)[2] to the discipline of women. The date, five years after the first Woman's Rights Convention at Seneca Falls, was the starting point of the gynecological crescendo. The attitudes toward women to be found in Gardner, Sims, and the other gynecologists were, *by and large,* the same as those held during the thirty years prior to mid-century—or 1848: Tocqueville's analysis of American attitudes toward women helps to explain the rise of gynecology thirty to forty years later. What was new about them after mid-century was their intensity, and the growing intensification was interactive with other radically changing circumstances—abolitionism, the Civil War, more and more rapid industrialization and urbanization, the flood tide of immigration, the possibility of women's rights—all were felt to contribute to the further erosion of male identity, which led to Todd's new focus. Todd's work is a very useful bridge because he both reflected and endorsed the conditions

Tocqueville described, and he had a direct influence on the sexual attitudes (toward themselves, masturbation, and women) of the men who followed him. The views about women that Todd addressed *to them* in 1853 and 1867 he had assumed in his books of 1835, 1841, and 1844 "Addressed to the Young Men of the United States."[3] In 1867 he addressed women because he had by then identified the "root of the great error of our day [to be] that woman is to be made independent and self-supporting." In the same year that he published a short tract attacking *Woman's Rights,* 1867 ("Tracts for the People No. 4"), Todd published a pamphlet, *Serpents in the Dove's Nest,* attacking abortion and contraception, for both of which he held women responsible.[4] These dates (1853–1867) coincided with the publication of the bulk of Gardner's work warning Americans of the dangers women and sex posed to male identity.

Todd's modification of direction was one expression of what Donald Meyer calls a "special pathology . . . a defensive, emergency, improvised ideology." This is in no wise to say that the concern to shore up male identity by way of self-help techniques and other methods (some of them new, patent medicines and electric belts, for example) did not continue: Todd's *Student's Manual* was published throughout the century. On the contrary, I am suggesting that attitudes toward women were contingent on the anxieties such self-help techniques betrayed. As success became more remote and more threatened, male identity became more vulnerable, and the concern to discipline women increased.[5]

The title of that half of *Serpents in the Dove's Nest* devoted to abortion was "Fashionable Murder," and "fashionable" was Todd's most frequent characterization of women who had abortions. Addicted to winter "gayeties," and "summer trips and amusements," they were that class of women enabled by their husbands to lead indolent lives, the "women of the future." They were the trend setters, which may partly explain Todd's simultaneous widening of his focus on the guilty to "women in all classes of society, married and unmarried, rich and poor, otherwise good, bad, or indifferent," just as Gardner widened his in bemoaning "The Physical Decline of American Women" in 1860. The same kind of fashionable women, said Todd, practiced contraception for the same reasons, namely that they would not forgo pleasure. They had the best education, and their husbands provided them with "worldly comforts." They were the women Ray had identified four years earlier leading "butterfly existences," the wealthy, urban, newly workless women of

Brigham's account thirty-five years earlier, but only increasing in number, enervated by leisure to the extent that they were prone to insanity and, according to Todd, that they feared childbed. Yet Todd confessed it was "we, cruel men" who for the last half century (1817–1867) "have invented, manufactured, and bought, and brought home, the piano." It was men who had given women leisure by supplying them with "knitting machines; washing, ironing, churning machines," and "sewing machines almost numberless." Some men concluded that sewing machines drove women to masturbation and insanity, and operated on them to cure both. I have already pointed out the circularity of men's driving women into a role men then held led women to social subversion, political and physiological disorder, and suggested that such circularity was the displacement of men's need for order onto women, given men's commitment to the anarchy of their own individualistic malehood. It was also a circuitous attack on themselves.[6]

Todd's messages assumed that the modern, nonworking and predominantly urban woman stood for woman-in-general, and that sex roles should be rigidly distinct. When Todd spoke to a rural audience, he was concerned with those women who had broken from the traditional patterns of work, wherein men and women had "hung on the same co-ordinates." "Lady" finally had become democratized. "If a man has a field of grass to mow, or a wheel to build,—or if a lady has an article to sew, or a nice cake to make, each one can see, at every step there is progress made." Men and women expressed common qualities in entirely separate spheres. "In all the departments of life we need a balanced judgement. . . . No lady can make a custard pie or a cooky, a jelly or a garment, spread a table or a cradle, without it, nor can a man well provide for his family, accomplish much in business, or gain in property or influence."[7]

Woman should see man's heroic offices as the "hard drudgery of earth" from which she was exempt. Such offices were the prerogative and burden of the possessors of penes. Woman

ought not to be made a sailor, to hang on the yardarms,—to chase and kill and try up whales,—to be a surgeon, to pull teeth, cut off legs, or cut out tumors,—to go into the mines, and dig ore and coal,—to burn over the smelting-furnace. She ought not to be compelled to be a barber, a boot-black, to carry hods of brick and mortar up the ladder,—to be a soap boiler, to groom horses, dig canals, dig out peat, tan leather, and stir the tan vats,—to go to the Arctic Ocean for seals, or to spend the long winter in the forest cutting down timber, and in the snow-water of spring to drive logs for hundreds of miles to get these logs out of their native forests. She ought not to be made to butcher, bleed calves, knock down oxen, stick swine, and slaughter cattle.[8]

Now this was part of Todd's challenge to women's rights, and he dwelt here on those activities he believed woman would find most distasteful: he carefully excluded the other activities he had mentioned elsewhere as particularly male, such as mowing grass, tailoring and making hats, the calculations of his ubiquitous businessmen, the soft professional activities of doctors, lawyers, and of his own profession, the ministry. Self-evidently the tough drudgery of earth here was Todd's own selection, and one can suggest the various forms touched a particular chord of distaste in his own breast, not woman's. Many of the forms were violent bloodletting. He took such drudgery to be the most remote from the sewing, cakemaking, table and cradle spreading he took to be the most essentially feminine of activities; in short, he was enumerating the most "masculine" of activities. But Todd the minister was in a soft job himself, remote from the miners, explorers, and railroad builders he so admired: he held up the sailor and Mungo Park as models for his young men to emulate, yet he had given up the project of becoming a missionary. He found the circumstances of American democracy jungle and ocean enough. Todd was one of those easterners in whose imagination the West so luxuriantly grew. It is possible that his desire to prevent women from entering not just the male sphere but its roughest, hairiest sector was to prevent himself from being left even further behind that sector himself, and even behind the point where the social spheres just touched. Already behind what he regarded as the toughest tide of masculinity, he would then find no fixed line of "the feminine" behind him, or rather, beneath him.

Donald Meyer has described the "frustrating simplicity" of the situation faced by women whose husbands succeeded. "The more their husbands worked, the less they had to work." One result was make-work, dusting the famous massed clutter of Victorian rooms, clutter accumulated as part of the new workless role, the "democratic phase" of conspicuous consumption. Women immersed themselves in choosing and buying possessions. For men, "work . . . had become an obsession. As for women, conspicuous consumption, whether on the level of the most marginal or on that of Fifth Avenue, occupied them closer to the heart. If it in one way signaled a woman's freedom from one sort of labor, it also gave her another job. The career of the woman whose busyness is shopping had begun. Man earns, woman spends." The "ambiguous uselessness" of women's new role presented the danger that they themselves would "be turned into possessions, hence enslaved and possessed." Women tried a variety of escapes. Increasingly large numbers of them provided the material for the rise of gynecologists.[9]

A few women reacted to the dangers in the new role by way of the women's rights movement. Todd seems to have made the connection at some level, since his 1867 assaults on fashionable aborters, fashionable contraceptors, Bloomer wearers, and political and economic feminists included the observation that "the wealth of the age is expended by woman—earned by man—for the most part." It was an arrangement he appeared to applaud, enjoining woman to stay in "her sphere," married, bearing and raising children, exempt from "drudgery," enjoying herself and the worldly comforts her husband supplied, playing the piano her husband hauled home, taking care to wear clothes that aroused men's admiration, respect, and reverence, and educated up to a point. "Queen of the home," she should let her delicacy rule her activities. The arrangement was one basis for the male monopoly of power in a nominal democracy.

> The property of the world, for the most part, is, and ever has been, and must be, earned by men. . . . It would seem best, then, for those who, at any hazard or labor, earn the property, to select the rulers, and have this responsibility. . . . [The man] wants rulers in reference to the industry and business of his age. Let him select them.[10]

But Todd's feelings on the "men earn—women spend" division of labor had another side. It was, he said, necessary that such a division be made, but inevitably it ran a terrible danger: women could spend their husbands into bankruptcy. Depriving women of one kind of power gave them another. More specifically, woman's very disqualification from exercising political and economic power—at the behest of men—made her an unwitting but extreme danger to male achievements in that outside sphere.

> It is impossible for any one to know the worth and value of money, unless he has earned it by honest, every-day hard labor. In large cities, it is not to be supposed that women who are peculiarly exposed to the sin in question [extravagant expenditure], can know the worth of money by earning it themselves. Here, then, at the outset, is a strong temptation to spend money, and one of which they are not apt to be conscious.

Todd placed the primary responsibility for extravagance on the woman. As

> long as Christians are so extravagant [that] they fail in business . . .
> there *must* be something wrong in their slavery to fashion. And here
> I hope I shall be pardoned by those whom I wish particularly to
> address, if I say a word to Christian females; and I hope they will
> brace up, and bear it, while I tell them my fears that they have much
> for which to answer to God.

He carefully described the new urban style (1841) of female consumerism, spending much time in examination, comparison, and deliberation, rivaling other women in the exhibition of taste, and in the demonstration of most patience and skill in finding "what is beautiful of its kind." Such a process, he said, grew by what it fed on.[11]

In the "men earn—women spend" relation, the sexes were at one-sided war: the "Christian female besieges her father, or her husband, for this or that beautiful thing, which he is unwilling to purchase." Todd's imagery became bloodier as he described a Christian female behaving like Eve and putting a man at war with himself.

> She is not merely trying to be extravagant, but she is wounding the
> feelings of her father, or husband, and that, too, severely, and is
> tempting him to do what his conscience tells him he ought not to do.
> There are very few men who do not desire to see a lady handsomely
> dressed; and there are very few fathers, or husbands, who do not love
> to see their daughters and wives adorned by what is beautiful, and
> who will not go to the utmost extent of their means to procure such
> articles for them; and when they are pressed and urged by those they
> love, to go beyond this, there is injustice, and, I may say, cruelty in
> it. And we have no doubt that many a man had his heart wrung by
> the increasing tendency to extravagance in his wife or daughters, who
> profess to be Christians; and we have quite as little doubt that the
> wounds were unconsciously given.[12]

Nor were these wounds simply let bleed: the spending female "wrung his heart." Her squeezing out of his blood was perhaps the most overdetermined part of this sequence, and Todd suggested her spending action was insatiable, and that she absorbed man's earnings, man's heart's blood, into her own absorbing system. "We have watched the progress of things with an anxious eye, and we are satisfied, that the vast amount of extravagant expenditure is the horse-leech which continually cries, Give, give, and which never says enough; that this is a crying sin, and one upon which heaven frowns." His own contrasting, finite feeling of satisfaction lay in knowing about woman's insatiability and identifying with God in putting it down, checking it in woman: she would have to answer to God for her appetite for man.[13]

Now Todd construed a man's whole being as an economic system, whose fundamental orientation was the accumulation of resources he depicted both as liquid energy and as gold. A woman's spending of what an American democrat had gleaned from other men in the marketplace was a fundamental assault on all he was. But this direct and intimate physical image, a woman reaching into the very center of a man, like an Aztec priest, had narrower connotations too, given Todd's assertion that a man entered the economic struggle of the age as a function of his ownership of penis and testicles, and given the contemporary belief (Todd's too) in the sexual dimension of heart's blood and expenditure. The metaphor makes clear that Todd saw the "man earns—woman spends" role division as a potential sexual assault on men by women. The spending female could cut her way into the male's desperately willed control of his expenditure, and either get him to ruin himself by spending or else spend him out herself. This assault, Todd suggested, was the natural expression of woman's heart, her equivalent to the vulnerable pump of his being. From a free and economical kind of behavior, adding up to the successful exercise of the male role, a man was tempted by a naturally bloodsucking and irresponsible woman, extravagant of time, money, and his blood, into failure, slavery, and self-betrayal, the process epitomized as a sexual struggle resulting in the loss of that substance from which a man was held to make blood.

Furthermore, men participated in the process of being "wrung" in this way: Todd said most men "desire" to dress ladies handsomely; husbands and fathers "love" to see wives and daughters adorned, and "go to the utmost extent of the means to procure" beautiful dresses and adornments. In return they were "pressed and urged" by those they had loved, finding their core squeezed by insatiable women. The dyads here were expressly heterosexual, the interaction physical, and the sexual feelings "desire" and "love" realized perhaps as erection—"going to the utmost length," finite on the male side, the female response of appetitive pressing and urging suggesting that the female had been aroused to what the whole context depicts as insatiable absorptiveness. Such circumstances reinforce the spermatic connotations to suggest very strongly that the relationship Todd described came close to a copulative one, epitomizing that typical nineteenth-century sexualizing of economic matters and economizing of sexual ones. I have quoted Ray's use of "consume" for the loss of energies, the word echoing that felt omnivorousness of world view to be found so readily in Todd and Ray, as well as Emerson and Thoreau. It anticipated the economic denotation of "consumer" later in the century, first applied to woman's economic role, then to both women and men, once rugged individualism had been preempted and men had to live with being "feminized." If this analysis is correct, then Todd held there to be a direct relation between man's primary economic activity and copulation; the latter was demanded of men by women and demanded always potentially excessively; if a man gave in to such demands he would be drained of his life's blood and enslaved by woman's appetite, and he would fail in business. Conversely, success in business required sexual abstemiousness. The view accorded with "W's" 1835 advice that a man avoid excessive copulation in marriage as well as masturbation, and it accorded with the apprehensions of doctors and advice given by marriage manuals in the second half of the century.[14]

Todd's attributing woman's adoption of the new fashionable life style to the wishes of husbands and fathers suggests that men laid themselves open to the business failure to which such consumption could lead. In *The Student's Manual,* Todd personified a young man's own urge to spend as a greedy, spending woman, acquiring irresistible power over a young man's economy.

> But your soul spreads in her desires; she thirsts, she rises: and do you suppose that any amount of wealth which you *can* obtain will satisfy her? Will the little time which is yours, cheer the soul in her everlasting progress? No; the bag in which you drop your gains will have holes in it. Every river which flows over golden sands like the river of Egypt, will turn to blood.

The image recognized the psychological connection between a man's own urges and those he attributed to woman. Her insatiable appetite had the effect of converting whatever earnings a man had incorporated into himself into blood, which the heterosexual context permits one to suggest was life blood, sperm. Instead of a profitable sieve, the young man found himself holding a leaking bag full of holes, that image connecting the interiorized draining power of a woman on a man to his own draining of himself along the masturbator's road full of holes.[15]

17   Woman's Refinement

We have seen the power Todd attributed to mother. In 1853 he said
that women were incompetent mothers. (He also said that men were
either incompetent fathers or else preoccupied with business, a preoccupation Todd's books encouraged.) But it was women's bad
mothering that was responsible for the low level of wisdom, discretion, amiability, and ambition among men. Todd's *The Daughter at
School* was intended to restore the traditional moral role of mother,
for which Todd believed a woman should be trained from a very
early age.[1]

At home the daughter was to be screened from "the cold world
and its vices . . . under the eye of love." Her purity could be en-
sured only if she were "shut away from contamination, and from
evil associates." In school she was to learn how to interiorize her
subordination still further. "You cannot become a scholar, nor can
you discipline your mind in a day; but every day you can take a
step forward, and if faithful to yourself, you can learn, while at
school, how to make your mind an obedient and willing servant to
the will, how to quarry out beautiful and polished stones from the
deep earth, and how to create, for the soul a palace of truth, of
light, and of joy." As an adolescent the American woman should perfect "self-denial" in its most literal sense. Between school and marriage, her family should force her to substitute for any intellectual
direction she might have a systematic subjection of herself—by way
of "frequent interruption," doing "little favors," and make-work. A
woman's education should be cut short in the interest of her hus-

band: the marketplace, not home, was where man wanted to be exposed to competition.[2]

A wife was to remain a dependent, undeveloped daughter to her husband. Unable to joke about her mistakes, indeed, not permitted to make them, woman would lead a life as unrelentingly demanding as the one man faced. Men wanted women to become workless, desireless, smiling, delicate, and undemanding panders to men, with an inner structure of undeviating repression, the whole amounting to an antenna sensitive to every male need. (In some respects the design resembled Todd's personality, a confident, jocular bishop to others, yet inside, an essentially vulnerable, depression-prone, defensive, parasitical being, eternally on watch.) The demand for a wife's daughterhood shaded into the demand that she play mother to her husband. She was to be as tolerant and constant as Sims's "ministering angel," or Marvel's bachelor's ideal of a wife, or Todd's fantasy of the forgiving mother taking back her prodigal from the harsh, unloving world of men. "Be cheerful when everything is discouraging, be patient when everybody else is fretful, be hopeful when the night is the darkest." Todd poured out his depressions to his family while he repressed them outside. He wrote to his wife before their marriage, anticipating that he would bring the effects of the outside world—sorrows, trials, discouragement, despondency—to her, and suggesting she model herself on a mother-figure to deal with the demands he intended to make.

> You need not that I tell you that a minister's wife is often as useful as a man himself. Your own good mother has taught you this by her example. She [the minister's wife] can be active herself, and by example and precept she can do immense good among the people of his charge. Add to this she is to be the adviser of her husband, is to sympathize with him in his sorrows and trials, to cheer him under discouragement and despondency, to check all his improprieties, to mend his weaknesses, to soften all his asperities, to help him grow in piety and holiness. You will doubtless find many frailties in me. My pride you must curb and restrain.

This letter spelled out exactly how it was a man saw himself owing his wife the debt a son felt he owed his mother. Like a baby at the breast, Todd "swallowed" his wife's life to "help him grow." And like the errant sons pursuing democratic and anarchic malehood in the real West and the mythic one, he made this maternal wife responsible for checking him.[3]

Describing the reluctant copulation of rising husband and fash-

ionable wife, Todd made a connection between the sex act and male
nervousness. He asked, "What makes the husbands go into temptation and sin, or else become dyspeptic and nervous? What takes
away the glorious sanctity of the married relation, and makes the
institution distrusted, and honors the man who lives in violation of
the most solemn vows?" He answered, "It is woman who, in our
day, for the most part, shrinks from meeting her appointment." The
context makes it clear that it was copulation from which women
shrank. It seems to have been a fact that many women did shrink
from sex, and I have suggested they did so as a response to another
male signal: men did not want to copulate because of their apprehensions about the spermatic economy, their need to save the energy
wasted in spermatic ejaculation for deployment in the marketplace.[4]

Man's division of sex roles according to head and heart by definition corresponded to a division within himself. Todd told his young
man to "break off from all associates whose influence is against the
great object of disciplining the heart." It was a great object because
it was basic to the attainment of success. Of course, Todd used the
terms "head" and "heart" symbolically, to represent the same sorts
of qualities Jarvis described in comparing the liability of each sex to
insanity. "Head" connoted self-control, will, intellect, undeviating
persistence in the pursuit of success, hardness, educability, political,
scientific, artistic, inventive, and mercantile activity; the capacity
to master the sordid traffic beyond home, and the progressive conquest of the West and the world in the interests of Christianity and
civilization. "Heart" connoted feelings and their expression, morality, sensibility, softness, gentleness, spontaneity, lack of staying
power, intuition, eruptibility, nervousness; it was very easily influenced (as Ray pointed out in his account of "sympathy"). In
Todd's world, woman's lack of the power of persistence, "cool
energy," put her in the same category as Indians and Mexicans. By
definition, head was higher, further away from physical sensation
and sexuality, and capable of increasing the distance, whereas heart
was lower, closer to latent energies, directly and nearly ungovern-
ably susceptible to sexual urgings. Above all, head was masculine
and heart was feminine, which explained why men were better able
to discipline their own hearts, and why women needed the support
of men to supplement their own meager capacity to govern their
larger hearts.[5]

The respective imbalance in each sex permitted the convention
Todd expressed in calling men the "head" of the body politic and

women its "heart." Reality would not conform to such simple categorization. It seems to have been the projection of man's division of himself ("discipline the heart") onto sex roles. In a way Todd was extending the man's discipline of his own eruptive, even feminine part to those beings naturally weaker of will, reversing his dependence in the way described, and assimilating the female area of reproductive power to those other physical and psychological regions beneath the sway of the male will. Man's disciplining of woman (society's heart) represented sexual and social order, and avoided the curtailment of man's own anarchic tendencies. The discipline of women ("the sex") *represented* man's subordination of himself. Conversely, ungoverned woman represented man's loss of control over himself and his society. To see man as head and woman as heart also entailed man's extrusion of his own heart and his decapitation of woman, the former to defeminize man and the latter to demasculinize women.

Men did not find the view of men as head and woman as heart incompatible with their application to women of the nineteenth-century, vitalist, proto-sublimatory theory of psychology defined by J. H. Walters and applied by men to themselves. Repeatedly Todd described woman's "organization" as tender, refined, and delicate. "Organization," it was believed, mediated between the pressure exerted by one's own will and the world on one hand and the vital powers, the latent energy, on the other. Woman was inferior to man, Todd explained, not "because her immortal mind is inferior,—far from it,—but because her bodily organization cannot endure the pressure of continued and long labor as we can." Todd had researched the point: "in medical colleges, in medical books, in medical practice, woman is recognized as having a peculiar organization, requiring the most careful and gentle treatment, and the consent of the world, all go to show that her bodily powers are not able to endure like those of the other sex." Todd suggested that this psychological model was a mechanical one by comparing it to the workings of a clock, or rather, two clocks, female and male respectively: "The wheels and workmanship are too delicate to be driven with the mainspring of the old-fashioned bull's-eye."[6]

Todd's urging woman to quarry out from her lower depths material which she should polish and elevate as a palace for her disembodied and pure self was a metaphor for proto-sublimation. Man's will controlled woman's will, which disciplined her mind to

discipline her body. Todd here was speaking for "we educators,"
"we men."

> We must not forget to say, or to impress it upon you, that we edu-
> cate the soul for eternity; that we feel that we are far out of the way,
> and have too narrow views, when we think of you as creatures of
> earth. We wish your manners to be polished, your conversation pure
> and instructive, your countenance lighted up with intelligence, and
> your mind bright and away; but we desire more. We want the heart
> trained to commune with God, and the soul to rise up into his light
> and plume her wings for the flight of eternal ages. A right education
> embraces that humility which a conscious sinner ought to feel, that
> self-denial, which the Christian spirit ever carries with it, that cheer-
> fulness which Christian hope creates and cherishes, and that adoration
> and love of God which the opening prospects of eternity inspire. The
> great question which the parent and the teacher who feels rightly
> will be. . . . Will the daughter understand that the mind is as much
> loftier than the body, that knowledge is as much better than wealth,
> as the heavens are superior to earth?

Somehow men had to tear themselves away from the most salient
characteristic of women, that they were "creatures of earth," remote
from eternity. Instead, men must look at the goal of refined woman,
polished and transformed like the raw marble or jewel originally
buried in the earth. It was because of the strength of male vision
and wish that woman must sublimate herself, move away from the
dirt, darkness, impurity, and lower depths of earth, to the polish,
light, brightness, and purity of the height of heaven. She was to rise
up to submission and self-denial and cheerfulness in accordance with
men's desire. Of course, her delicacy of "workmanship," "organization," and lack of immodest, copulative desire were fruits of the
same process. It corresponded to the mind's transcendence of body.[7]
Todd thought it particularly difficult to persuade the daughter
that "the mind is much loftier than the body." The reason was his
initial premise, that women were creatures of earth. That was why
they needed men's more capable mental "organizations" to supplement their own efforts at disciplining the heart. But willy-nilly Todd
depended on woman's earthy part, her body, for the production of
men who were loftier and could tell women how to transcend their
bodies. While urging her to strive to elevate herself above body, he
argued against the overdevelopment of her mind on the grounds of
her essentially physiological function, motherhood. Women were

the source for the future vital forces of the nation, including its
politicians, soldiers, judges, doctors, and ministers. And the heart,
identified with the feminine as I have pointed out, was also identified
with vitality. In Todd's own theological province, it was acknowledged that "a production which originates in the head is, as such,
artificial and arbitrary; while one which originates in the heart is
vital." Calvin Pease went on (in 1853) to argue that the glory of
American Protestantism was that, in its preaching, "the brain . . .
is held in 'solution' by the heart, and thus made strictly subordinate
and tributary to the end of influencing the conduct and controlling
the will." Todd might urge men to discipline the heart, but to be
entirely masculine they would have to become heartless. The splitting and projection of the man = head—woman = heart metaphor
was a solution that tended very much in that direction. In any case,
Todd regarded woman's particular "organization" of the heart's
vitality, that is, love, as "inexhaustible." It was imperative, therefore, that he master woman and persuade her to bend her vital
powers to his vision of the body politic. In short, men should assimilate woman's power to themselves just as they attempted to do
with the rest of the resources of the earth.[8]

18   Sex and Anarchy

Todd's vision of the American body politic was the typical white supremacist one, and the tradition Todd represented held women responsible for racial destiny. The danger of the submersion or extinction of what he called the "Anglo-American" race was a constant theme after the Civil War. Todd's appeal to WASP women to stop aborting and contracepting was in the context of his anxiety over the decline in what he called "our native population." His authorities for this decline, and the men he believed responsible for organizing social energies to resist the process, were doctors and ministers.

> To the watchful eye of the physician, and to that of the far-seeing clergyman, too, it has been apparent that through our country our native population is not on the increase, but diminishing fast,—that our families now in the country will not average over three, or three and a fraction, of children born,—and that while our foreign population have large families, our own native American families are running out, and, at this rate, must and will entirely run out. The statistics presented to our legislatures on this subject are fearful.

The decline was most apparent in the New England population (although he believed the WASP population was declining in America as a whole). Todd did not make a direct connection between the decline in the New England population and men's geographical withdrawal from women. Nor did he connect it to the male apprehensions about copulation expressed by the belief in a "spermatic economy." Todd blamed women for the decline in the WASP birth rate, and in effect excused and justified male withdrawal.[1]

The press reviewers of Dr. Storer's attack on abortion echoed Todd's alarm over women's betrayal of WASP racial destiny, believing with the doctors and ministers that it was women who chose and implemented abortion and contraception. "Already in many parts of our country the number of foreign births is largely in excess of native ones, and the large families of our ancestors find no counterpart in our day . . . we . . . recommend to every woman a perusal of the work." Did the press assume with Todd and Storer that men could not or would not interest themselves in, let alone control, the issues of abortion and contraception? Had wives capitalized on the separation of the sexes to carve out an area of secrecy in their sex lives? Gardner advised women when they were menstruating to conceal the fact from their husbands. Todd assumed that men accepted their wives' refusal to copulate, or their wives' choice to use contraceptives if and when they did agree to copulate. Perhaps the complement of men's fearful reluctance to spend sperm except on infrequent and carefully monitored occasions, together with men's general isolation of themselves from their wives, was women's refusal to bear men children, thus intensifying the fears with which men drove themselves from women in the first place.[2]

Todd said that abortions were "fearfully common." He implied that merely to associate with women who had had abortions was dangerous, and he asserted that "seventy-five per cent of all the abortions produced are caused and effected by females." This last phrase seems to refer to the general and traditional association of midwives with abortion, and clearly *Serpents* would have contributed to the popularization of the antimidwife brief of doctors claiming to supplant them. Todd had a personal and professional kinship with doctors. He was a trustee of the Berkshire Medical Institution, taking "a lively interest in its prosperity and in its students." He was also an honorary member of the Berkshire Medical Society. His son suggested that his interest in doctors "arose partly from the fact that his own father and uncle and many others of his name, had belonged to the profession." One of Todd's last acts "was to make a speech at the annual dinner of the Massachusetts Medical Society," of which Dr. Gardner was a Fellow.[3]

Todd regarded contraception as "an evil, a calamity, and a sin," essentially related to abortion. Again he believed women were managing to override the will of their husbands in the nature of their sexual intercourse, since: "Generally, the husband usually wants children. He is disappointed if he has none. He is willing to toil, to run the risk of poverty and want, to support them. . . ." I suggest that such a man's instinct for fatherhood was the exact counterpart of the motherhood he wished on his wife, that is, desireless, undemanding, unsung, infrequent, modest and delicate copulation, followed by the production of sons. I have quoted Todd's assertion that the wife frustrated the husband's desire (not for *her*, but for sons) by refusing to meet her "marital appointment." Todd believed that, in 1867, the "means to prevent [conception] are well understood, instrumentalities shamelessly sold and bought. . . ." One must remember that his generalizations were based on his experience of middle- and upper-class men and women, that group which first became generally aware of effective, mass-produced contraceptive devices and which would set the trend in that as in the other directions Todd found so appalling. (Such contraception would not become more widely known and accepted in America until the 1890s or even 1900s.)[4]

That the WASP birth rate should be declining, and at the hands of women, Todd believed reflected a collapse of social authority. Women had substituted "the reign of extravagance and fashion" for the rule of man and God. Like the disillusioned democrat Brownson, the Reverend Todd looked admiringly to the traditional authority exercised by Rome. Gardner would do the same. Todd was sorry to learn "from undoubted testimony, that the practice [of abortion] is far more common among Protestants than among Catholics." So strong was the attraction of more authoritarian standards when confronted by the potential freedom of women that Todd was prepared to retract his lusty admiration for the anarchy of the mining camps and to return to the predemocratic political order that had prevailed in America before the movement which the Jacksonian Revolution capped and represented opened up that democratic tide Tocqueville charted. Todd was disgusted by the mobs and rowdies in New York City, draggling and wrangling around the ballot boxes; he went on to admit his feeling: "It may be a misfortune that property does not now vote, but not so great a misfortune to the world as to have the sex go out of their sphere and enter into political life."[5]

Todd's tendency *in extremis* to move away from the dogmatic egalitarianism of both Protestantism and American democracy was an accurate reflection of just where the source of his troubles lay. In questioning Protestantism's institutional weakness in the face of women's claims he was in a sense confronting Winthrop's problem with Anne Hutchinson. The women at Seneca Falls took the Declaration of Independence for their model in writing the Declaration of Sentiments, and Todd found himself arguing: "As to 'women's rights,' I hold that they have great, inalienable, and precious rights," even if he said they were the rights to be queen of the home. In short, the reaction to women's rights was linked to the erosion of male identity. As far as Toddian psychology was concerned, Darwin's *Origin of Species* (1859) hastened that sense of erosion. This is how Todd began his attack in *Woman's Rights:*

> The tendency of our generation to break up old associations, and to be emancipated from the beliefs of our fathers, is so strong that many would rather feel relieved to have you convince them that they spring from a race of apes and gorillas. This is among the male sex. Among the other sex, there is a wide-spread uneasiness,—a discontentment with woman's lot, impatient of its burdens, rebellious against its sufferings, an undefined hope of emancipation from the ordinary lot of humanity by some great revolution so that her condition will be entirely changed! This feeling crops out in publicly ridiculing marriage, dwelling on its evils, raving about the tyranny of men, crying for the "emancipation of woman," getting up Women's Conventions, and propagating theories, weak, foolish and criminal. The demand is that we shall acknowledge our abominable cruelty exercised towards woman since her first creation;—that she shall be allowed hereafter to be in all respects equal to man. . . . This undefined feeling is not confined to the strong minded women, who clamor and disgust their sex and ours in demanding "women's rights." It is felt more or less by those who shrink from these moral Camillas. It is to this class of the sisterhood I am wishing to address myself at this time.[6]

Against Darwin Todd ranged the biblical version of creation, which incorporated the myth that women originated in the bodies of men (a solution to the anxiety aroused by the reality), together with the authority for male "tyranny." His use of that term, his reference to longtime "abominable cruelty," and his repetition of the word "emancipation" suggest another context, that of the Emancipation Proclamation of four years earlier. In Todd's view, woman hoped for an act "so that her condition will be entirely changed." Todd's acknowledging the "wide-spread uneasiness" and "discontentment" among "the other sex" registered women's reaction to that enormous social change in her role that Meyer points out raised the specter of women's enslavement. "Behind the manifold indictments of the slave system, there flickered, dim, fascinating and horrifying, the fact of the slavery of women. Black women, but white women too." Increasingly after the Civil War, with the intensification of American industrialization, women nationally faced the role pioneered by America's answer to the European "lady," "pure Southern womanhood, sexually helpless, the most purely a possession, the most purely passive of all." Todd may have been an abolitionist, but he was adamantly against the emancipation of woman. His racism and his sexism shared a common denominator in their assumption of a social and individual order repressing the darkness of passion or the passion of darkness.[7]

Toward the end of *Woman's Rights,* Todd reasserted that woman's whole valuable being lay in her subordination to man. "Any other theory is rebellion against God's law of the sexes, against marriage, which it assails in its fundamental principles, and against the family organization, the holiest thing that is left from Eden." Abortion, according to Todd, was "a direct war against human society, the best good of the country, [and] against the family order." Contraception, like the claims for political, economic, and educational independence, was "rebellion." Again the context for this language—civil war, rebellion, revolution—was the recently ended American Civil War. It is possible to suggest that the Civil War, taken historically to be the great outpouring of heroic male qualities, was in part a reaction against the threatened eruption of women as well as the threatened freedom for black slaves. Physiologically based identity was at stake, and war can be a final refuge of uncertain male identity.[8]

Todd put his apprehensions about female rebellion into another historical context. The French Revolution had unleashed, he said, an infidel, fiendish, "voluptuous," and dreadful experiment. French revolutionaries turned an ancient civilization into a "nation of fiends and furies." For the traditional patriarchal authority they substituted a goddess: they "ordained the worship of a vile woman. But the consequences were too terrible to be endured. And now their heirs threatened to dissolve ordered, God-fearing American society. American "infidels" (feminists) would "abolish" the "entire corroborating action of the government of God" and "let in upon society, in wrath without mixture and without measure, the impatient depravity of man." They would bring about that raging, anarchic, competitive social condition that Todd in his advice manuals assumed already existed, to which they contributed, and for which he, and other men, made woman-as-mother responsible. These particular quotations warning against a future social collapse are from *The Young Man* (1844). They illustrate the new significance Americans attached to the last bulwark, the family, even as it was being torn apart by the same democratic phenomena (including Todd's own work, his own psychology) that led men to attach so much significance to it.[9]

In Todd's imagination individual, psychological order was the microcosm of social, political order. The one was the extension of the other, and each depended on the other for support. The neatest representation of the idea was the analogy between individual and social head and heart. In Todd's view the psychological equivalents of social radicalism were nature unregulated—vagrancy of desire, rage of lust, sensuality, beastliness, intoxication, inflamed and maddened passions, disease—and the eruption of "the sex" in every sense. His equivalents of the necessary and ordered social hierarchy were mind, subordination of sex and "the sex," and regularity of habit.

The metaphor of the body politic linked man's view of the state to his most personal source of identity, his body. Western man's apprehensions of a conflict between order and enthusiasm, reason and passion, head and heart, had been increasing in the period between the Reformation and the eighteenth-century Enlightenment. The Revolutions cut off the head, or at least seemed to bring it closer to the passions, to the genitals. And revolutionary rhetoric promised further leveling. Freud neatly represented what I would regard as a characteristically post-Revolutionary apprehension of the association between head and heart, and order and anarchy: "Civilization behaves towards sexuality as a stratum of its population does which has subjected another one to its exploitation. Fear of a revolt by the suppressed elements drives it to stricter precautionary measures." Freud's previous definition of civilization as male activity clearly put women into the subordinated stratum, just as Marx did. Marx's consideration of the bourgeois's exploitation of "his" wife makes that clear. The bourgeoisie was male.[10]

In Todd's imagination the final effect of social leveling in the presence of women was a crumbling of his definition of male identity, a breaching of that demarcation line between the sexes that Tocqueville found so remarkable a trait of democracy, and which tells us of the danger it was intended to avert, the equalization of women as well as men. Men's continued insistence on inexorable difference and separation seems to have indicated an anxiety that the sexual distinction would not be sustained. The social gap was identified with the distinction between sex organs. Close the gap and the organs would be lost, or jumbled up, or distorted. The obliteration of the external (and externalized) separation of the sexes would be coordinate with the obliteration of its internal, interiorized form, that is, man's separation of his masculine part, his will, his mind, from his feminine part, his heart and his passions. His malehood depended on this division.[11]

A woman who did not play a narrow and predictable role converted a man's sanctuary into a bottomless pit of uncertainty, the more threatening in proportion to his previous certainty of predictability.

> We have had the misfortune to know a very few ladies who wore pantaloons on occasions, and who could climb trees for crows' nests before breakfast, and leap fences and shoot with a double-barrelled shotgun; but we never found it in us to respect them. You always draw yourself up when you see such a young lady, not knowing what may come next.

So Todd's *The Daughter at School* shared the apprehensions the dime novelists betrayed with their aggressive, shooting, betrousered heroines, just as Stillé's speech did. A cognate passage is one in *Woman's Rights* to which I have already referred, where Todd attacked Bloomer wearers.

> Some have tried to become semi-men by putting on the Bloomer dress. Let me tell you in a word why it can never be done. It is this: woman, robed and folded in her long dress, is beautiful. She walks gracefully. The waving of her robes makes the walk graceful. If she attempts to run, the charm is gone. . . . So long as she is thus clothed, there is just enough of mystery about woman to challenge admiration, and almost reverence. Take off the robes, and put on pants, and show the limbs, and grace and mystery are all gone. And yet to be like man, you must doff your own dress and put on ours.

Todd believed it was because a woman wanted to be like a man that she wore pants: men have limbs; therefore she would show she had limbs. But women were supposed to pretend that they did not have limbs. In fact Todd wanted to see them as made of cloth below necks and short sleeves, that is, without lower bodies at all. Todd was quite frank in telling the reader that the explanation for this was male feelings and male needs, and his belief that women would allow their beliefs and feelings to be determined by male requirements. Women's wearing dresses signified to men that women would defer to male definitions of women. If women wore Bloomers and men perceived that the Bloomer wearers were still women, men would be forced to recall that women had bodies without the prophylactic cipher, as it were, of the dress. Men wanted women to be distinguished in a way that hid from men the physical reality on which men based their need to have women distinguished. Women served the function of placing male identity in high relief.[12]

Nineteenth-century writers acknowledged that their readership was hungry to be told of what true manhood or true womanhood consisted, and flew to the simplest, most extreme kind of definitions; hence the common use of the phrases "the sex" and "the other sex" and the common assumption that everyone knew what they meant. Thus, Todd held up womanless miners as exemplars of the "noblest passions" of men, and flaunted sailors and whalers, canal diggers and loggers, butchers and surgeons, before women who aimed to escape the waving-dress role, an aim which Todd interpreted to mean that women wanted to become men. His metaphor was a pair of mutually exclusive spheres, one male and one female.

> She will not be allowed to be a man and to be treated with the tenderness due to woman [then the list of supermasculine activities quoted in Chapter 16, above]. . . . she must go in for all this if she leaves her sphere and tries to be a man. . . . Suppose we allow it, and admit that she has a *natural* right to wear jack-boots and spurs, horse-pistols and a sword, and be a complete soldier, and a "natural" right to sing bass and beat a bass-drum, and that *men* have a natural right to wear petticoats, dress with low necks, short sleeves, wear pink slippers with paper soles,—but, would it be wise to do so?

The male sphere was war, requiring people to behave like soldiers. Todd here elaborated his fantasy of the aggressive, gun-toting woman, taking on the supermasculine role that Todd himself was able only to admire. He may have tantalized women with such fantasies, implying that he partook of that fantastic male world, but he also yearned to escape the violent conflict men inherited in the way that women escaped it.[13]

The sexual fantasy of the role reversal—women booted and spurred and armed with sword and pistols, men dressed in soft, vulnerable, and feminine clothes, adds another touch to the glimmering of a picture of relations between husbands and wives. It was consistent with Todd's picture of women taking charge of contraception, of wife-mothers becoming murderesses, "devastating with poison or with steel their wombs" and killing incipient—or surrogate—male rivals or oppressors. It was psychologically consistent, too, with the fantasy of a husband's playing passive, dependent infant to his wife's playing mother.

Those three fantasies—aggressive, sword-bearing women confronting men dressed in the soft clothes of women or children, the irresponsible, callous, and unnatural mother killing her own fetus (which Todd said was the same as killing her own child) with a steel point, and the omnipotent, godlike mother enfolding her guilty son in death—combined like a little stack of coinciding transparencies to form the single ambivalent image of Todd's mother both as he recorded her, running at him with a sword to kill him and checking herself, and as he wanted her to be, the whole charged with the accumulated resentment of his childhood and youth, and the social-sexual apprehensions with which that particular history combined. Todd shaped his response to rebellious women in accordance with his childhood. That he expressed it with a rationale and metaphors common to a large number of men suggests that if his childhood experience of a threatening mother was keener than theirs, the difference was in intensity, not in kind.

In *Serpents,* Todd addressed himself directly to the effects of role changes on sexual behavior.

> What if you do pass through life, seeking your ease and comfort, leaving the world no larger or better, and no influences to be handed down to the future? What then?
>
> The sin of Sodom! What was it? What led to it? Very likely the very fashion of our day was the stepping stone to the fashionable sin of Sodom! We are drifting fast that way. O Christian husband and wife, do you know you are pitching your tent towards Sodom? "How is it that ye have agreed together to tempt the Spirit of the Lord?" You sometimes hear people laugh at the large families of clergymen. You see the reason why they are large. They have too much conscience to violate the known laws of God. The great object of the marriage institution—the rich blessing left from Eden—is not that the husband may live in legal fornication, and the wife in legal prostitution, but fulfil the first great command in the Bible.

That command was "Be fruitful and multiply" (Gen. 1:28).[14]

Todd's definition of an unnatural relationship between husband and wife—copulation for pleasure and payment respectively—provides us with one idea of what he meant by sodomy. But he recognized the question that the term would raise. "The sin of Sodom! What was it?" Genesis makes it clear that the sin of the men of Sodom was homosexual acts between men. Todd's use of the term cannot be dismissed as promiscuous vagueness: the connection in his mind between homosexual acts between men on one hand and intercourse between men and women that contravened the "first great command" on the other was probably infertile sexual intercourse. In Todd's view that aspect of homosexual behavior was equally true of contracepted (or eventually aborted) heterosexual copulation.

There are other connections to be made between sodomy and Todd's sexual attitudes. In his Sodom passage, Todd moved from indolent woman's responsibility for sodomitical intercourse to a joint husband-wife responsibility; earlier in the pamphlet he blamed women for frustrating nature by killing their fetuses or insisting on abstinence or the use of contraceptives: men wanted children, so Todd said. But women's actions drove men to "temptation and sin"; so to the hell holes of masturbation and prostitutes, one may add what Todd himself saw as a resultant vice—sodomy. Such a motif (sexually damaged men leaving women for a homosexual world) can be discerned in the novels of Cooper, Melville, Twain, and less celebrated authors, Horatio Alger, for example. But that mythologizing reflected the kind of psychological and ideological structures I have been at pains to describe in Todd's world, the configuration of the democratic family and sexual relations, the course of an American male's childhood, adolescence, and assimilation into a world exclusively of men, anxious to enforce their own masculinity and the separation of the sexes, identifying with male progress, and with the prophets, with Columbus, Washington, Benton, Boone, Bachelorhood, the self-made man, and the place of those things in the particular arena of American history.

It was men who required women to be workless and fashionable; so if fashionable women demanded contraception and abortion in the interest of sustaining their butterfly existences, then men were responsible. Todd said men, not women, drew women from marriage into independence for their own perverse purposes. And finally Todd's language betrayed his own homosexual tendencies, expressed, for example, in the intimacies of his relations with his male readers. Todd could describe a married couple's heterosexual copulation as a homosexual one, the wife playing a man to her husband; but given the preoccupation with balanced role reversal, *that* fantasy opened up the possibility that the husband was playing a woman to his masculinized wife, as indeed Todd envisaged in his role-reversal picture. So Todd's sodomy fantasy matched and extended his fantasy of the jack-booted, pistol-packing, sword-girt woman's relation with a man in drag.

The most striking expressions of Todd's ambivalence about his sexual role were his envy of woman and his identification with her. I describe the latter in the next chapter. Todd devoted his life and his priorities to the defense of young males (and in doing so increased the dangers they defended themselves against). Women were not so exposed, in contrast to the vivid vulnerability of man's course.

> We know God has ordained that if woman be weak, she shall be protected, and not exposed to the rude, rough and violent storms of the world:—but the young man, we know, has them all to buffet— all to meet, and all to break over him, while with the spirit of man he neither flinches nor bends. We know his bark must be tossed on the ocean of life, and that the waves must swell and the winds must roar, and the storms must break, and he must stand unmoved at the helm. . . .

He had to both experience such tremendous pressure and refuse to show it. Woman was "exempted" and "privileged," whereas man "must endure." His lot was the "hard drudgery of earth" and "wading in the dirty waters of politics." The "rougher, coarser nature of man" required him to "bear the strain," and Jarvis recorded its terrible effects.[15]

That was the reason Todd argued that "men *must* be educated for their sphere" and educated "long and severely." "Mortality awaits so many of them after they are educated." One thinks of Todd's father and Melville's, of Jackson, Wells, and Morton. Todd's insistence on the burdensomeness of a man's whirl and contact with the world may be compared to what he asked the young man to see as the majesty and destiny of manhood; indeed his more frequent resentment at the role perhaps explains why Todd had to aggrandize the inescapable "inheritance of our sex" as majestic destiny. Tocqueville said: "Nothing conceivable is so petty, so insipid, so crowded with paltry interests—in one word, so anti-poetic—as the life of a man in the United States." Yet that man was persuaded (by Todd among others, and by the pressure of democratic equality) to the exclusive and bootless pursuit of the mirage of success, which brought ceaseless dread, fever, anxiety, fear, regret, trepidation, despair, and mental disease. Here are very easily understood grounds for Todd's envy of workless, shielded women and his hostility to those women he saw capriciously adding to the competition men had to endure.[16]

19   From Mother to Mother Earth

Todd was, in part, terrified of being dependent on a woman who might repudiate him or absorb him as a horse leech absorbed blood. But at the beginning of *Woman's Rights* Todd partly agreed with his hypothetical, feminist adversary. She wanted woman to be "far more independent of him [man] than he ever was *or can be* of woman." Man always would be more dependent on woman, and the explanation lay in woman's "own deep instincts," by which Todd meant her reproductive and nurturing power. "Our mothers train us and we owe everything to them." He went on to say that wives assume similar comprehensive power so that men are equally "indebted" to them (demonstrating that he saw wives as mothers): "no man is ashamed to say he is indebted to his wife for his happiness, his influence, and his character, if there is anything noble in him." This is a remarkable if familiar rhetoric, given that the great mass of Todd's work was devoted to the principle of independent male autonomy, avoiding debts and overexpenditures of every kind. The fact that women were felt to be a persistently explosive threat to the survival and prosperity of men explains the well-known and otherwise perplexing coexistence of an ideology of male self-sufficiency with that of woman's power over men's lives. The insistent assertion of the need for total autonomy was an impassioned reaction to that fear of total dependence that broke through in Todd's confession that he owed everything to his mother. Todd felt he could be swallowed up by woman, and it was perhaps as a defensive reversal of that fantasy that according to his own admission, he "swallowed up" the life of his wife.[1]

All men shared Todd's scale of indebtedness. Every one of their lives was inescapable proof of woman's immeasurable productive power. "If she must go down almost to the grave during the pilgrimage [of gestation], she brings up priceless jewels in which the heart may rejoice to all eternity." Moreover, behind man's success or failure was his mother's unlimited control over him during the first crucial years, whatever the relevance of his later education at her hands.

The professions of men are many; we are lawyers, physicians, clergymen, mechanics, manufacturers, politicians: the profession of woman is that of being the educator of the human race. By the very arrangements of his providence God has made it so, and to refuse to believe it, or to throw off this responsibility, is as unwise as it is wicked. If now, any one should say that this is a small profession or a low duty, I reply, that it is more lofty and more responsible than if it were assigned to you to lay the foundations of many suns to shine in the heavens for a few ages; it is taking what is immortal at its setting hour, and deciding what path it shall tread, what character it shall bear, and what destiny it shall obtain. You are deciding, during the first years of its training, whether the new star shall travel and shine through the bright heavens, mingling its light with that of glorious constellations, or whether it shall be quenched shortly and be lost in darkness and forgetfulness.

The very immensity of woman's maternal power conjured up the danger of its abuse; woman's reproductive power and her motherhood could be used to prevent men from blazing like Todd's exemplary stars, Napoleon and Washington. Such an apprehension explains Todd's horror at contraception and abortion. In the case of contraception, women may literally have "quenched" the origin of a great man by douching. Appropriately, Todd expected that he could be quenched even at this late date in his life, since he said that as a result of his address on *Woman's Rights,* "Very likely I may have a torrent of abuse poured upon me for it; but it is time your real friends should no longer have utterance choked." And he pictured man "pumping" others from the frail craft of his being in a world of hostile liquidity, ready to mop him up like a sponge unless he did it to the world first. Todd's longing to "acquire or create that unconquerable unquenchable fire which is so necessary to prevent life from running through the fingers, leaving not a distinct mark of remembrance behind," represented perhaps his sense of near-helpless resistance against what he felt as the obliterative power of woman.[2]

The two passages are remarkably similar. The "life running out" one suggests that Todd's capacity to guarantee himself unconquerable force was identical to his capacity to exercise his will in preventing himself from masturbating. His allowing his life to run out through his fingers, his giving in to the self-destructive waste of energies in the form of spermatic ejaculation, was identical to a man's succumbing to the obliterative capacity of "the sex" as mother. Self-destruction by way of masturbation would be the fulfillment of the male fantasy that wife-mother would use her special sexual power to extinguish him. It is easy to imagine the effects of such a belief on sexual intercourse.

It was democratic, male society that threatened a man with extinction of selfhood. The attribution of quenching to mother (and the demands that all wives be mothers and all women be wives) might have been the kind of projection—from male reality onto women—I have mentioned. Or vice versa, men might have created an all-consuming society as the realization of men's deepest fears, as the emanation of their "disease of temperament." An interactive, mutually reinforcing process was most likely, a circle of projection and self-fulfilling prophecy, of sexual ideology, democratic parenthood, childhood, and parenthood again.

There is clear evidence that Todd himself saw male activities of all kinds, from his own to those of the California gold miners, as the emulation of woman's powers of gestation and parturition, which he depicted as the bringing up of jewels (babies) from the grave, the abode of death (woman's reproductive tract). The grave, like woman's undisciplined psychology, was part of the natural earth. The frequency of Todd's use of the jewel-digging metaphor, and the variety of contexts in which he used it, reflects the emotional force which he attached to that unique and undeniable quality of woman, which, *ipso facto*, men could not reproduce.

But Todd assumed that men were capable of educating children while women were not, an idea, in light of his statement of a mother's power over her child's life, that can be seen as a defense against that power, as an attempt to rival it, and as an interposition of male authority between mother and child. In the case of male children the purpose was protection, and equipment for a male work-world; in the case of female children it was to subdue them and prepare them for the fulfilling of individual and social male needs. "We" male educators provided a true and proper education to a child: "when that child is truly and properly educated, you have a jewel polished which will outlive and outshine the sun. We are training up an angel for eternity." So men either assumed completely woman's bringing up of jewels, in which the heart could "rejoice to all eternity," or else took over the process at an early stage of development and perfected it as only heady, high-minded men could. Todd believed that his ability to make a jewel of a daughter's soul was superior to the process that it imitated, that is, woman's making of a daughter's body.[3]

Todd compared woman's education to teaching her how to mine her own resources, "to quarry out beautiful and polished stones from the deep earth, and how to create for the soul a palace of truth, of light and of joy." As her educator, Todd took over woman's jewel-producing function, then imparted it to woman, as he said God did His creative power. That process was an expression of proto-sublimation. The renewed popularity of the ancient notion of proto-sublimation was itself an expression of democratic psychology, the desire for self-making and the cognate subordination of woman a male reaction against the almost overpowering sense of engulfment at the hands of a mother left cloistered by a husband himself trying to avoid engulfment. But the very depths of the obsession to escape drove men to reiterate their sense of woman's power by emulating it.

> We may have beautiful stones to sparkle and flash before the eye, but they must first be dug from the earth then polished with immense care, and finally set with skill. Even then they are hideous unless they adorn the person of the virtuous. We may take a pound of steel, which is worth but a few cents, and bestow labor and skill upon it, till it is made into tiny springs for ladies watches, and that *one pound of steel is worth forty thousand dollars!* We may throw out the stones of a quarry, and they are almost worthless; but labor and skill lay them up into the walls of a palace, and ages hence they are admired and in use; and in the hands of the wonder-working artist, the rough block of marble becomes the beautiful statue.

Men should first emulate a woman and then surpass her by following Todd-style self-discipline. The metaphor here extends proto-sublimation to man's working with natural resources external to himself. Todd believed that man's refinement of nature was the objective correlative of his "organization" of his own latent energies.[4]

The desperate obsessiveness of that process (charged by the emotional and ideological configuration I have described) was applied to the world, and explains the kind of exploitation and devastation wrought by the expansion I sketched in the first two chapters. For Todd, mining was the epitome of the exteriorized version of proto-sublimation. It was the vehicle for the expression of the "noblest emotions" of men. It bore a direct and continuous relationship to the most crucial area of concern to Todd and the men he was helping to become self-made, that is, to reading. It provided the model whereby a man could identify his Toddian discipline as peculiarly manly. Todd compared his own reading to panning for gold, and he asked his readers to do the same with their reading, including, presumably their reading of his work. Parallel to the heroic and womanless passion of the gold miner was the young man's extraction of gold and its assimilation to the fountain of his energies thus made more autonomous. The reader's avoidance of the accompanying tempta-tion to masturbate was equivalent to the miner's going womanless. The gold miner should choose the opportunity to achieve a higher, nobler purpose than husbandhood (and all the absorbent dangers such a state entailed). The young man shored up his manliness by striking at a mass that yielded "copiousness and wealth." But con-sistent with the psychological project that these activities mani-fested (the establishment of autonomous, inexhaustible malehood, or "unquenchable fire"), the mass which both reader and miner were up against was maternal. "I hope no one, who intends to strike for a character for language or thoughts, strength or beauty, will ever be trying to clothe himself with the puissance of a novel, when he can boast the language of Burke as being his mother tongue." The miner saw the earth as fecund and nurturant: "from the bosom of mother earth, all draw their nourishment . . . all must come out of the earth. . . . Nature finds materials, and it is for man to take and improve them." California was the place "where enterprise will find a thousand sources of wealth; where wealth may sleep in the lap of beauty." Lap denotes and denoted a part of the body, as well as the clothing that covers it. The lap is a hollow resting place connoting safety and comfort, especially that supplied by a mother to a child. Given the lap's location in "mother earth," it is clear that Todd saw the miners and other men extracting her wealth, first as her children suckling at her bosom, and second as men returning to her womb to master and exploit it as a displaced act of incest. Bring-ing gold up from the earth, the irrepressible miners had provided a "foundation" for the United States, together with its psychological dimension, a "Confidence-Bank." They had repeated the feat of "laying of foundations" denied woman, even if she could quench sons.[5]

The view of nature as a potential and bosomy mother ("virgin land" before its conquest by men) has long been a cliché, never more so than in nineteenth-century America. The very familiarity of the image is evidence of its significance. Emerson, for example, assumed that nature was his "beautiful mother," whose mass men penetrated to assimilate her powers to his in pursuit of sublimation, immortality, and self-reproduction. Emerson's assertion that men should transform her into measurable bourgeois achievement went hand in hand with his apprehension that they bore to her the dependent relationship of a child to its mother. And both attitudes were integral to a world view resting on the spermatic economy and proto-sublimation.[6]

It is in the context of the belief that nature was the maternal source of new life that one should see another familiar belief, that a return to nature could restore lost energies. Todd used to take trips to the West to recover from the mental exhaustion of a revival. Men left wife-mother to plunge into symbolic mother, over whom they could see themselves having complete control. They could draw on her apparently inexhaustible generative powers (like those of Todd's fantasy mother) without fear of rebuke or psychological extinction. The womanless miners were in constant touch with those powers, and that may have been part of the explanation for their capacity to exemplify men's "noblest emotions."[7]

Railroad visionaries held the same view of nature as democratic minister and democratic philosopher. In Chapter 2, I quoted William Hall's description of the railroad as a bridegroom making his way into "the body of the continent." Smith catches the displaced eroticism in the relationship between Benton and the Far West: Benton was "in love" with it. "One feels a kind of awe in the presence of a faith so triumphantly able to remove mountains; but a more appropriate attitude would be that which greets the ecstatic lover praising his mistress. . . ." Benton's relationship with his mistress was regularized, and the "holy question of our Union" which in 1860 William Gilpin would have preferred to see "in the bosom of nature" rather than in the internecine horrors of conflict between people in settlement was resolved in marriage. Gilpin's statement of these alternatives—displaced and all-male sexual expression out West or Civil War—was the intensified form of the historical dialogue Cooper, Marvel, and Lantern-Jawed Bob represented. This particular form throws into sharp relief the psychological meaning of American expansion, its relation to the past, to mother, to women, and to children.[8]

Todd officiated at the 1869 "Wedding": he can be seen at the center of the famous pictures of the driving of the golden spikes uniting east and west sections of the Union Pacific at Promontory Point. To Todd the

> whole thing seemed like a wild dream. The telegraphing seemed to be magic, and we could hardly realize that creatures so small and feeble as man, had accomplished a work so great it made all other works of this kind seem small and insignificant. This was May 10, 1869. The little ring on my finger, bearing the significant words, "The Mountain Wedding, May 10, 1869," and presented me in commemoration of the occasion, was made, as I know certainly, from a piece of one of the golden spikes. And thus the marriage was consummated, under the bright sun, in the desert place, and under the eye of Promontory Point—hereafter to become historical.

The inscription on the rings is evidence of the general assumption of the sexual meaning of an ostensibly nonsexual event. Emerson believed that "all the facts in natural history taken by themselves, have no value, but are barren, like a single sex. But marry it to human history, and it is full of life." And to Emerson, nature was female and men were the bearers of human history. Substituting nature, or iron mined from it, for woman, men could act out their sexual feelings toward her. Since it was obvious that such actions were only symbolic, their sexuality could be admitted.[9]

Moreover, such a "consummation" was representative (albeit the outstanding example) of all male achievement. "All the discoveries which men make, all the inventions which they bring out, all the facilities for intercourse which they create . . . is taking the materialism of earth, and sanctifying it and making it not merely harmonize with, but be a carrier of spiritual things." Todd's reiteration of proto-sublimation, by way of a metaphor which he used to characterize gestation and parturition, suggests that proto-sublimation was a way in which men could believe themselves rivaling and outstripping woman's reproductive power, and being that much more independent of her. But to remind himself of these processes by sexualizing nonsexual actions was to remain dependent on that being, and on that mode of being which she represented and he wished to escape.[10]

The railroad was "evidence of new life,—this mingling of new blood." Its generative, sublimating power should be extended to the dormant masses across the Pacific. The imperialist energies of womanless men could refertilize the globe and make vital the disappointing reproductions of women; to use William Gilpin's 1874 metaphor, they could "cause a stagnant people to be reborn." The energization afforded by successful competition with other races, the conquest of the West, and men's assimilation of mother nature's power would give them a boosted reproductive power beyond anything of which women had been capable. "I feel assured that here [in the West] will be developed a physical manhood, such as has nowhere yet been found. . . . And this standard of *doing* something and much, with the climate and the thousand incentives will, in the future, I have no doubt, produce, not giants, but a noble race of men, if, not superior to any now in existence" (1871). Such reproductive power was the result of the will, a male prerogative.[11]

Gardner also felt that the same kind of American intercourse would breed uniquely powerful people. He said in 1872:

> There never has been a people with larger opportunities for building up a fine national physique, than we Americans enjoy. . . . The enervating heats of the south do not stop our vigor. . . . The mountains and the forests, vast reservoirs of health and strength are behind us. From them we may annually recruit our exhausted energies. and like Antaeus, redouble our strength, at every fresh contact with our mother earth.

Men could incorporate maternal, reproductive power into their proto-sublimatory systems, the terms and mythic reference suggesting very strongly that the "contact" was incestuous intercourse. In this displaced form men could fantasize the reversal of woman's absorption of their energies. Furthermore, it was males who would show the benefit. "We have the blood of strong races in our veins, and the traditions of a simple life, from our Puritan Fathers. Already our superior height of frame, our independent carriage, and the nervous vitality, that looks through the eyes and breathes in the nostrils, show the improvements of the American male." Such development was a male project requiring women be as passive as earth. Since it was the expression of male sexual anxiety, it went hand in hand with alarm over woman's threatened sexual independence.[12]

It was also contingent on racial anxieties, for the reasons I have given. It showed the power of the will and the head, and their purest embodiments in the white male; it asserted their independence of passion and body—and betrayed the fear that men were fundamentally vulnerable to those beings whose subordination represented white men's control over their own passions, their success in sublimating themselves into will and ideal. Opposing Lincoln's

Emancipation Proclamation in 1862, Ohio Congressman Samuel
Sullivan Cox demonstrated the vision's vulnerability.

> Our statistician boasts that Ohio has men of greater height, by
> actual measurement, than England, Belgium, or Scotland, and in
> breadth of chest nearly equal to that of Scotland, and above all
> others. I do not offer myself as a specimen [laughter]. But how
> long before the manly, warlike people of Ohio of fair hair and blue
> eyes, in a large preponderance, would become, in spite of Bibles and
> morals, degenerate under the wholesale emancipation and immigra-
> tion [of blacks]? . . . Equality is a condition which is self-protective,
> wanting nothing, asking nothing, able to take care of itself. It is an
> absurdity to say that two races as dissimilar as black and white, of
> different origin, of unequal capacity, can succeed in the same society
> when placed in competition.

The assertion of extraordinary male physical development was an
expression of anxiety over sexual identity (being "manly"). Men
feared the competition that included women and blacks: conversely
they wanted a source of identity immune from competition (the
fruit of equality). The project of male aggrandizement, even to the
extent of reproductive autonomy, was part of the same democratic
configuration I have described.[13]

What was the relationship between the manner of sexual intercourse men projected onto their relation with virgin land and mother
nature and the manner of its performance with their wives-cum-
mothers? If men could not face the reality of a woman's body,
perhaps they could treat it as part of the landscape. When their
spermatic calculations did allow them to copulate, they may have
done so with all the obliterative hostility that they projected onto
woman's feelings toward men. But it is far more likely that most
men symbolically did to mother nature and virgin land what they
could not bring themselves to do to women except in fantasy. The
same apprehensions that might have led to rape resulted in severe
sexual inhibitions and the deflection of rape into fantasy. Both the
spermatic economy and the rape of the land were sanctioned by
democratic ideology.

The most powerful sexual themes in Todd's work, manifesting
extreme sexual anxiety and role confusion, were masturbation
phobia, homosexuality, and the emulation of woman's reproductive
power. All three expressed the apprehension that heterosexual intercourse was dangerous to men, and masturbation and the emulation
of woman seem to have expressed the desire for total sexual auton-

omy. I pointed out that the masturbatory exchange of books and the masturbatory relations between reader and writer were in one sense surrogates for homosexual intercourse, while in the preceding chapter I suggested that homosexual and role-reversal fantasies had a great deal in common.

An image in Todd's discussion of the temptation to masturbate while reading sheds more light on the relation between masturbation and the emulation of woman. One could not find the valuable bits in Byron, Todd wrote, without being seduced into masturbation. "There are beautiful pearls in the slimy bottom of the ocean, but they are found only here and there, and would you dive after them if there were many probabilities that you would stick and die in the mud in which they were imbedded, or if not, that you certainly shorten and embitter life in the process of diving and obtaining them?" Being lured into masturbation was like being trapped and drowned in the slimy, muddy, and dangerous bottom. Yet such a plunge into the depths was a necessary part of proto-sublimation, that is, the discovery, awakening, and "organization" of latent energies. The danger in this passage was identical to the one a son ran of not emerging as a jewel or a star from the maternal depths, but instead being "quenched shortly and . . . lost in darkness and forgetfulness." The similarity of dangers suggests a connection between the loss of selfhood by way of masturbation and the obliteration of self by mother and by her surrogate, the wife (to whom also the man was totally indebted for his being). The sexual relation then aroused all the confused, obliterative fantasies I have described. Masturbation and copulation threatened man's "unquenchable fire"; the physiology of stimulus and the ejaculation are common to both; men feared excessive copulation for the same reason that they feared masturbation. Think of the connotations of Todd's wife-leech metaphor. Masturbation and masturbation phobia reminded men of sexuality and the waste of energies. They were also reminders of the same dangers woman represented to man. She shared with his baser nature a susceptibility to passion and a lack of control. I have argued that man's control of woman symbolized his control over himself. Masturbation unmanned a man, took away his distinction from woman, left him unorganized, irresponsible, irregular, made him a "she." No longer would he be capable of self-making, that is a rebirth beyond the power of woman.[14]

But in the case of the masturbatory threat of absorption, the man had some choice (that was the point of Todd's pearl-diving rhetoric) and could call on men like Todd for a leg up. In the case of the maternal threat of engulfment there was no appeal: the generative power was hers. Presumably intercourse with wife-mother aroused similar fears of getting lost, of not being able to pull oneself out of the darkness, of never being able to distinguish oneself from woman and from the mass. Perhaps one can reverse that notion that the subordination of woman reminded men of the subordination of their own passions. Perhaps their suppression of masturbation also stood for men's capacity to subordinate "the sex" as easily (and as easily as they could subjugate virgin land). His several uses of "holes" metaphors shows the connection Todd made between the draining of a man's energies by a woman and his draining of them by his own hand. That a young man's exploitation of his own buried resources should be modeled on a miner's bringing up refinable gold from mother earth reflected an identical connection. It is reasonable to suggest that the relation between head and heart was an internalized model of the heterosexual relationship, and that masturbation—or the refusal to masturbate—was as close as men could come to total sexual autonomy. Indulging one's appetite or refusing it became an act of narcissism which incorporated the fantasy of identifying with woman even as one protected oneself against her. Todd's own fountain could discharge a profusion of "pearls" simply at the touch of his cock. The fountain's sexual character was ambiguous. Remarkably, the statuettes around its marble top, representing the fertile sequence of the seasons, were male, frozen in admiration for Todd's "little jet." Inside its glass cover were the "fairy daughters of music." Todd could represent the phallic whole as a female figure, in spite of its cock, jet, and balls. When a stranger entered Todd's study, the walls hung with swords and sticks, he hardly noticed the beautiful memorials of Todd's friends,

> he is so much delighted with my tiny fountain—the wood-nymph whom I have coaxed to come in here in the second story, and to pause long enough to sing her wild song in her robes of light. There it stands a living fountain. Nobody can see how the waters get there, or how they are carried away. There it leaps and rings day and night, never weary, never pausing, never other than beautiful. . . . I almost imagine it the fountain of life.

The nymph was like Todd's ideal of a woman, robed in mystery, and susceptible to male coaxing. Her robe appeared to conceal the mysterious and incessant flow of life, but Todd could reveal its reality. The fountain represented Todd, as his son perceived, so the nymph was also Todd dressed as a woman, and secure in the knowledge that her apparent power was really his, dependent on his little brass cock. Todd periodically had to return to what he regarded as mother nature to replenish his "fountains of life." His heaven was the return to the unquenchable love of a mother. He held that "Woman is to hold the wires that are to make the world advance or move backward. She is to stand at the head-waters and send out the streams that are to make glad the cities of our God." In short, this molder and reflector of so many familiar attitudes could escape woman's terrible power only by the fantasy of becoming female.[15]

Part IV

Augustus Kinsley Gardner

20   **Dr. Gardner's Education**

Dr. Augustus Kinsley Gardner (1821–1876) admired both Todd and Sims. While, like Sims, he was anxious to establish a professional, gynecological identity by invention, experiment, and operation, he also addressed himself to a popular audience. Gardner's newspaper and magazine articles and two of his books warned people of the dangers of unguided sexual intercourse and of the serious social effects of woman's attempts to control her own childbearing. He claimed for these writings the authority of his professional expertise, and because of his assumption of the physiological basis of identity and social function, he shared the claim of democratic doctors to possess fundamental social authority. His more strictly medical works betray the same sexual values. He was a bridge between medical discovery and Toddian psychology, and he helped to pave the way for public acceptance of the drastic and widespread gynecological surgery described in Chapter 11.

Gardner was born in Roxbury, Massachusetts. He was, like his father, Samuel Jackson Gardner, "an only son but had two sisters." The "but" reflected the value placed on a male child, and it is very likely that the evaluation was Gardner's own. This and other evidence about Gardner's early life is from the brief account by Dr. S. W. Francis in his series of "Biographical Sketches of Distinguished Living New York Physicians" (1866). Francis was in the same New York literary circle as Gardner.[1] His account of Gardner's life was based on an interview with Gardner. His father, Dr. John W. Francis, an "elder statesman" of New York City medicine and a

founder of the New York Academy of Medicine, had been one of
Gardner's teachers, an early leader in the development of obstetrics
in New York and, complementarily, in the attack on midwives. He
was a principal sponsor of Sims's Woman's Hospital, of his *Clinical
Notes,* and of Sims's whole career, so influential in the direction
taken by American gynecology. Gardner delivered a eulogy on the
elder Francis's death in 1861.[2]

S. W. Francis made the same sort of claim for Gardner's ancestry
as Todd's son did for John Todd. Francis wrote that on

> his father's side the family can trace as far back as to within twenty
> years of the landing of the "Mayflower"; and on looking over the list
> of passengers we find that a Gardner was on board. His grandfather
> Kinsley was the first representative to Congress from Maine, and at
> one time, Judge of the Court of Common Pleas. His grandmother
> Kinsley was a daughter of Bellows, the first settler of Bellow's Falls,
> N.H.

Such typical claims ran counter to the other and concurrent claim
to self-making. Franklin had recorded his ancestry at the outset of
his autobiography, but had emphasized its lack of distinction in
order to enhance his own. By Todd's and Gardner's time men felt
they needed all the inherited identity they could get, even if it was
contradictory and antidemocratic. The context for the rise of the
various patriotic hereditary societies like the Daughters of the
American Revolution was the fear aroused by what were perceived
to be teeming immigrants. Daughters and Dames took on the racial-
and social-preserving responsibilities assigned them by such kinds
of opinion leaders as Todd, Gardner, and Theodore Roosevelt, in a
national version of the southern "great pattern of pride in superiority of race" centering on woman "as the perpetuator of that superiority in legitimate line, and attach[ing] itself . . . before everything
else, to her enormous remoteness from the males of the inferior
group. . . ."[3]

Dr. Gardner based his hopes for an improved male physique in
America on the maintenance of the traditions of his "Puritan
Fathers" and on his idea of the racial inheritance that specially
qualified doctors to control reproduction. "We have the blood of
strong races in our veins." There was, he said, no reason why "a
physical culture, and consequent perfection similar to that of the
Greeks should not take root in America." But the proper precautions should be taken. "In a new region, where multitudes of institutions are yet to be erected. . . . the well-being of society de-

mands, that means shall be adopted to separate its good elements from the bad." If, indeed, there was "gradually developing in this country, a national type of form and feature, essentially different [as opposed to simply bigger] from that of our Saxon fathers" (and Gardner implied he did not believe that was so), it behooved Americans to make sure that "the coming man" measure himself according to the kind of masculinity demonstrated by the Puritans, whom he called that "stalwart ancestry, who felled the forest, fought the red savages, and made the ways smooth before the feet of politic, but let us hope, not less manly generations."[4]

The project of ensuring social perfection was physiological. Asserting: "We have . . . a public mind, singularly active and enquiring, interested in the subject of health, and capable of national investigation for itself," Gardner then pointed out that it was "for the public to cooperate with the doctors in adapting their habits to national standards." These habits included mating: Gardner said that "we" experts

> find some individuals, few indeed, we fear, using good judgement in entering upon marital relations. They select their wives from a healthy stock, from families of high mental endowments, or more frequently of superior physical excellence. They calculate in advance upon the probabilities of the character and appearance of the offspring to issue from such a combination of stocks.

Men should consult doctors before turning to the available pool of women. Gardner had been preceded by Dewees and Jefferson in this view of marriage. And John Winthrop's description of his goal in settling in America would serve to describe Gardner's goal in writing *Our Children:* "to preserve our posterity from the corruptions of this evil world, so that they in turn shall work out their salvation under the purity and power of Biblical ordinances."[5]

Gardner passed through what he later defended as the "Puritan," American Common Schools System, and the Walpole Academy, New Hampshire, under the presidency of Benjamin Abbott. Francis says that the pupils of the academy under Abbott received "careful training of the first principles of moral and physical education," which was "appreciated" by these "ambitious" pupils. It was at this stage of his life, Gardner records, that he and his fellow students came to know Todd's *Student's Manual* and were, presumably, among the "male youth" of America who learned from Todd's work that they should not masturbate.[6]

Gardner was sent to Harvard, "alma mater of his father and grandfather," "contrary to his desire." He left in 1842, at the end of his junior year. His father, a newspaper editor and a poet, had run out of money in 1841, the year of the final financial collapse of Todd's Clinton Street Church in Philadelphia in the aftermath of the 1837 panic. Francis's account also implied that the death of Augustus's mother (in 1841 or 1842) may have facilitated his withdrawal, since he had been kept at Harvard "in accordance with the expressed desire of his mother." A third element in Francis's ambiguous explanation for Gardner's dropping out of Harvard was the censure of his professors, who notified his father that Augustus "was not making sufficient use of his time to render his further stay desirable." He had, in Francis's words, "followed a desultory system of reading and general observation that did much towards enlarging his mind and training his faculties for other pursuits." A failure to "use time," coupled with desultory reading, with perhaps a hint of a straying imagination, were precisely the sins Todd warned against. Gardner was careful to record that Todd's words about masturbation specifically were frequent subjects of discussion among both his "academic and collegiate associates," that is, at Walpole Academy and at Harvard. In acknowledging the validity of Todd's ideas and the power of his influence, Gardner also acknowledged his subscription to masturbation phobia and the possibility of his own masturbation. These may have been the precipitating causes for Gardner's masturbatory guilt and his contribution to the published reinforcements of masturbation phobia.[7]

Gardner's book *Our Children* (1872) included his most extensive consideration of male masturbation. That part of the book began with infancy, then moved on through the age when "children are fond of sleeping in one another's company, and spending the night together, even when they live next door to one another. It is a habit frought with evil. . . ." But the most dangerous age was adolescence, which Gardner regarded as a phase of childhood. He warned of the "enervating heat" of feather beds, which acted as a kind of sympathetic magic on the dangerous fecundity of the heated brain. "The very softness is not desirable, while the very excess of heat, conduces to a frame of mind not desirable, engenders and ferments lascivious thoughts in the adolescent, and is otherwise very objectionable."[8]

At the same time Gardner maintained that actual masturbation was initiated at the suggestion of somebody else. Like Todd, he denied that masturbation was natural (perhaps supplying some evidence that some people, at least, held such a view).

> The secret vice which saps the manners, mind and morals of so many of our youth, is not in truth a secret one, in the full sense of the expression. It is not a habit self-induced, the result of nature, as many would have us believe, and to which one is led by a power superior to his judgment and his reason, viz: an uncontrollable natural want, whereby one is compelled to get rid of certain irritating secretions appertaining to the nature of man.

Even if that were so, in the first place a young man should be able to control himself whether he was fourteen or twenty-eight, and, in the second, masturbation took hold before a young male's passion was ignited. Gardner was, like Todd, full of awkward contradictions, particularly over masturbation.

> There is a natural prurience in the human mind, that loves to contemplate wickedness, and demons, and enormities. This [masturbation] is one of them. The habit once formed, it is kept up in after life, as a sensuality—and then comes its dangers and physical disabilities. As suggested already, the animus is not from within. When the vice is commenced, nature is yet tranquil, no internal fires are raging, no imaginations stir the brain, no stimulus comes from the well-turned ankle, or the graceful form of one of the opposite gender. The youth is simply led into this wrong-doing as he would be seduced into robbing a watermelon patch or a peach orchard.

He was so led by a youth of his own gender. Gardner here drew a distinction between the original "prurience" and the sensuality into which it later grew. He distinguished the motive for masturbation from the heterosexual provocation of the sight of a woman's ankle or form, suggesting that an adolescent male began to masturbate in the same way that he might steal a little fruit. The metaphor "seduced into robbing" revealed the sexual reality; after all, Gardner was saying that one young male explained and/or showed another how to manipulate the penis for sexual arousal: he assumed in all-American fashion that homosexual relations were somehow innocent of sexuality. Conversely, it was not the sex of sex that was bad, but the contact with women.[9]

Gardner repeated the seduction metaphor, explaining that the motive for masturbation was in part a result of the need to confirm adolescent manhood. "The imagination of the boy, is seduced by the excitement of doing something wrong; by the mystery attached to the secrecy of the matter; by the idea of being engaged in something manly, something which works an era between the past boyhood and a coming manhood." And while his description of one of the effects of the secret vice coincided with that of his transatlantic contemporaries, it must have taken on a keener significance in American democracy, where social authority was further diffused, individual guilt perhaps intensified, and each man saw himself surrounded by enemies looking for a chink in his armor.[10]

The masturbator robbed his testicles of the sperm as peach orchards and melon patches were robbed of their juicy, round fruit. Gardner said that masturbation had the same effects as castration. "As in the East, the Eunuchs seem ever ready, as fit persons, to perform any act of cruelty or oppression, from a seeming unnatural absence of all moral principle, the victim of self-abuse is also apparently open to any project of wrong-doing, and is a fitting instrument in the hands of the plotter and designer." Believing that spermatic expenditure drained the physical vigor otherwise available to the will, Gardner here described the masturbator as not much more than a penis in other men's hands. Shorn of testicles and will, his punishment fit the crime.[11]

Treatment assumed the energy model Walters defined. Self-control required will, and will required vigor, which the masturbator had spent; so at first his energy had to be recouped by external means—chloral, for example. Treatment also required the boy's mind to be pulled away from its obsession:

> In such cases, severe exercise is especially beneficial, such as will produce physical fatigue to overcome, and thus neutralize the nervous disability, such as a prolonged fishing excursion in a regular cod fisherman to the Banks of Newfoundland, or out stock raising in Colorado, which means a constant life in the saddle, amid stimulating air, new and exciting scenes and constant occupation. Improvement is very slow, but an entire arrest of the sin and perseverance in the path laid out only will eventuate in a final cure.

Again the cure for masturbation was identical to the course taken by the normal nonmasturbator, who was supposed to separate himself from sexual temptation and, in a real sense, from women—and one is reminded of the intimate relation that existed between normal and deviant behavior. Perhaps American men depended on masturbation guilt (and therefore on masturbation) to launch themselves on their careers. In any case, men believed that male success depended on the channeling and elevation—proto-sublimation—of the same passions and impulses otherwise fueling masturbation. "All the feelings, and passions, and impulses of the now pubescent being, should be developed, restrained, governed, not abrogated, destroyed, unrecognized. His enthusiasm should be directed to noble ends; his thoughtful seriousness not permitted to brood itself into melancholy, but directed to elevated sources of inspiration."[12]

After dropping out of Harvard, Gardner nearly adopted a course similar to Todd's, that of "keeping school for the instruction of young men as a means of livelihood." What gave Gardner pause was "ambition" and his desire to make money, for which, at this stage of his life, he viewed medicine as a vehicle. "But the career promised so little in a financial point of view, and opened so small a path to ambition, that he decided in favor of Aesculapius." Nonetheless, his gynecology and his conjugal advice were complementary to the psychology of Toddian education. Moreover, the classroom teaching Gardner forsook was the one job outside home that men willingly left to women.[13]

Having made his choice, Gardner plunged into medicine, applying self-disciplined energies unremittingly in the way that Todd recommended. He had found his calling. "He had failed in college, where he had been sent contrary to his desire; but in his medical capacity succeeded, for he was doing that which pleased his taste, and afforded him more real pleasure than the exercise of any recreation: and even at the present time he enters into the science of treatment with gusto." Part of that pleasure he derived from a special concern with sexual organs, since his thesis was on syphilis. Gardner received his medical degree from Harvard in 1844, thus returning to his paternal tradition and conforming to his mother's "desire." He then apprenticed himself according to nineteenth-century custom.[14]

Gardner's first book, *Old Wine in New Bottles: Spare Hours of a Student in Paris,* provides considerable evidence about his choice of career. In the fall of 1844 Gardner went to Paris for postgraduate "study of obstetrics and lunacy" (*Old Wine* was a collection of letters he sent back and published in his father's paper, the Newark *Daily Advertizer*). In Paris, Gardner was fascinated, even obsessed, by women. He sent back to the Newark *Daily Advertizer* reports of grisettes, courtesans, and prostitutes, how they became prostitutes, how much they charged, their relations with their lovers, and their behavior at masked balls. He gave detailed accounts of vivisection, flower girls, crime, theaters, guillotining, French mothers and chil-

dren, sewers, and the morgue. These and stories about them were
interspersed among the dominant themes of the book—the vast,
gloomy, and frightening interiors of hospitals, prisons, and asylums.
(He was acquainted with the same sorts of institutions in America.)
He was obsessed by these buildings, to which the inhabitants were
fastened physically or by the bonds of illness. In contrast Gardner
could escape to his independent roles of student, traveler, bachelor,
doctor, and finally American, able to look away from the cities' "cess
pools" as he called them, to the healthy freedom of the New World.
Yet he set out from the first to "lose himself" in the city, noting his
passage through its walls. "You may not be surprised . . . if I am
sometimes lost in exploring the recesses of these labyrinths." And
he plunged with gusto into the city's "generally dirty and narrow
streets." In Gardner's view his explorations were sexual, since he
personified the city as a woman's open and demanding lap. "The
wants of a voluptuous city have caused the globe to be ransacked for
the choicest productions of every country; the most cherished gems
of nature and art are poured into her lap with luxurious profusion."[15]

Gardner also associated prisons with female power. Prison nurtured the life it enclosed: a delinquent in prison could "taste the
comforts" which "surrounded" him. It was where "charity has mistaken her vocation, and left her proper sphere to feed the criminal
with luxuries beyond the power of the honest laborer." The dungeon
fostered growth in the inmate: "Submission to wholesome authority is almost the only growth, to which the dark, damp atmosphere
of a dungeon is favorable." Prison was the bed where seeds were
deposited (and of course the offspring was human): "the seeds of
vice, instead of dying, were only planted in a hot-bed, to germinate
and bear a fearfully increased harvest of crime." Much to Gardner's
disgust, prisons in France provided beds for the deposit of human
seed and added perhaps to the generative power of the nurturant,
growth-fostering, criminal-breeding cell: "the wives of the prisoners
are indulged with visits to their husbands in their cells twice a week
for several hours." Note Gardner's belief that such copulation was
to serve the interest of the wife, consistent with his overall view that
the prisoner was at the command of a female power. Prisons and
prison cells reminded the budding obstetrician of the womb.[16]

Anthropomorphized prison had other connotations. "Within its
frowning walls have been enacted many of the bloodiest and most
horrible tragedies of tyrannical power." Prisoners were at its mercy
and could be tortured and/or executed. In their evocation of horror,

too, the prisons were like Gardner's experience of woman's generative function. In 1855 Gardner wrote that because of the streams of
blood and clotted gore he found no "scenes more appalling than
[those] in the obstetrical chamber." It was the bloody action of
woman's own reproductive chamber that imparted the pall to the
room. Yet it was Gardner's special "taste," his persistent fascina-
tion as well as his horror, that drove him to a profession of regularly
facing such bloody danger. His gynecological surgery was Gardner's
way of mastering his horror for that which he was compelled to face,
exactly as it was in the case of Sims. Gardner's obstetrics and his
gynecological surgery were his obsessive, reiterated enactments of
his power to escape from the imprisonment with which he felt the
womb threatened him. He made this clear with a pun: "if you ever
have the misfortune to be imprisoned in a crowd, I advise you to
summon one of these 'ole saws' to your aid; for you will find, as you
shall see I did on a recent occasion, that they are eminently useful
instruments to cut a passage through."[17]

This preoccupation was identical to Todd's need constantly to
create his own unquenchable fire, to prevent being quenched by
woman's maternal power. Todd's doing so revealed its origins by his
emulation of woman. An obstetrician was closer than Todd to such
a process. Gardner viewed wombs as prisons, and his method of
escape trapped him into incessant readmission. In Paris he had to
make "great exertions" to gain entrance to the prisons, and had
"much difficulty" in contending with the authorities. His own sense
of the process linked his obstetrics and gynecology to his relation to
a woman in copulation (again something he had in common with
Sims). His exertions to overcome these difficulties represented a
number of things, including his apprehensiveness in the face of
woman's power to trap and kill a man who entered her.[18]

A remarkable aspect of Gardner's descriptions in *Old Wine* is his
consciousness of the young ladies who, he assumed, were reading
them. Having described the "beautiful shoulders and naked breasts"
of a "more than uncommonly handsome" corpse in the morgue, he
put himself in these readers' shoes. " 'What!'—I think I hear the
ladies say—'so many wearisome long letters, and not a line about
the idol of our hearts,' " by which he meant Paris fashions. He saw
these readers as his potential customers. So after a passage evoking
the possibility that tailors and dressmakers might take over "the
propagation of men and women," Gardner prayed that such a revolution would be "postponed beyond my day; else my long laborious

attendances of hospitals of maternity and kindred institutions will avail me nothing in my anticipated practice among the fair portion of New York." The bodies of handsome American women would be as accessible to a well-trained gynecologist as the Parisian corpse. His telling young ladies about shocking and sexually charged relationships anticipated his gynecological approach to their bodies. He said the shocking accounts were justified because they were true and serious in intent. Justifying his detailed description of the vivisection of a horse, he said, "Let the authors of fictitious cruelties answer for their loathesome delineations, whose immediate tendency is to harrow up the sensibilities of the soul, make the reader wretched for the time, and afterwards callous to real suffering, and for what? Would you believe it?—for amusement!" Of course Gardner's "truth" would have had the same effects. He said he "trusted" his studies in Paris were not without some success, and he joked about the possibility of his irrelevance. Perhaps those doubts contributed to the hostility of his approach to his potential customers.[19]

His verbal assault on young ladies was one expression of the deep social and sexual resentment which his professional career embodied. He saw himself as a poor outsider, whatever his claims to Puritan ancestry. Looking at some rare old coins in a Paris window, he was reminded of an American experience. "Having little money in my pocket, I gazed upon these rich and glittering commodities with the same pleasurable emotions as one may be supposed to feel on looking into the kitchen of the Astor House just before the dinner hour." (J. Marion Sims's surgical éclat would allow him access to Mrs. Astor's most intimate parts, as well as her money.) Once a lady in Paris showed Gardner a "voluptuous" article of "luxury." "I could scarce refrain from telling her that my thrice great grandfather made his own table of pine boards with hemlock legs, and on that he ate his frugal meal one hundred and fifty years ago in the wilderness of America, with keener relish, than I fear the buyer of this gew-gaw will know." But his father was vulnerable to financial failure, and Gardner had gained his medical education at the cost of hardship and privation. His sense of a status revolution, like Todd's, was endemic to the vicissitudinous democracy Tocqueville described.[20]

Anxious about his reception by the fair portion of New York, Gardner pandered to what he regarded as young ladies' fashionable interests in his articles from France. And once established in America, he made no bones about his target. Indeed, it was the very fact that they were fashionable that made modern women sick and therefore in need of the special services of the self-made outsider, Dr. Gardner. "The fashionist of the day forgets the laws of love, religion, and the joys of maternity, and by every hellish art seeks to prevent and subvert the laws of nature, of life, and of love." He was specific about the activities that made his work necessary: "silver fork and spoon, six napkins and ring—all the dancing master's and elocution-ist's teachings, with the use of globes added will not make a girl fit for a wife, and the duties of a mother."[21] His customers could afford luxurious food and send their daughters away to school: "Julia and Clementina Angelica go to a fashionable boarding school, where they learn to play a polka, crochet," and to masturbate. "This is one of the greatest evils of our boarding-school educational system, where the advent of one girl thus corrupted will introduce a moral epidemic into this large family of pubescent, hot-bed brought-up girls." They rode in coaches, went to the theater, parties, and balls almost nightly. The last activity was a particular *bête noire* for Gardner, and he condemned it repeatedly, remembering perhaps his own experience of masked balls in Paris. The modern woman could also afford contraception and abortion; "they are not the sins of the ignorant, the poor and the starving; but the sins of the rich and the lofty and the educated."[22]

The gynecologist depended on the new, workless women, the women of the future whom Meyer has identified and whom Todd attacked on the same grounds as Gardner. It was, Gardner said, modern woman's freedom from the necessity of work and her assumption of the new role of display and consumption as the mark of her husband's success that caused her peculiar ills. It should be obvious that in the terms of his own analysis Gardner depended on the life style of modern woman for his professional identity and he yearned to be accepted by her. Toward the end of his life his attacks on fashionable women became more vehement and desperate, yet he still accepted and encouraged their life style. When telling women what to do besides bear children he said, "Find out how your coral ear-rings are made, how obtained; learn what is the composition of the bronze statuette which your uncle gave you, read about their antiquity, endurance, and why they are esteemed valuable."[23]

Gardner realized that fashionists could become the models for all women (the term "fashion model" denotes its ideological function). His customers shopped at Lord and Taylor's, and Stewart's, visited Broadway twice a week, and set a style working girls followed. "What Fifth Avenue does, the girls who can earn their living by

dress-making, book-folding, shop-keeping and the like . . . do."
The trend was not limited to urban women, and it was facilitated
uniquely in America by young women's freedom: "all New York,
and all America (the only place in the world where young girls of
sixteen are allowed to do so), are doing the same foolish thing." The
logical result of following fashionists would be female diseases and
the diminution of childbearing on a national scale, and the consequent debilitation and extinction of the race. Gardner's concern with
the generating of models for women to copy (like Todd's for men)
represented the same democratic phenomenon to which his friends
the Duyckincks said their *Cyclopoedia*'s writers addressed themselves as apostles of true manhood and true womanhood: the "fashionable woman whom we once met dancing wantonly at a city ball
when her only child lay at home sickening with scarlet fever, is not
the type we urge you to copy."[24]

Gardner's apprehension that the new fashionable women could
well set the pattern for the future lives of all women is one explanation for his persistent fluctuation in target, from the very specific
account of rich, urban, workless, upper-class, female wrongdoers to
his assertion that such wrongdoing was characteristic of American
women in general. "The deterioration of the health of females is not
general, it is local, and it is not only local, it is confined in a great
degree to classes even in that locality." This locality was the city.
"It is the females of the cities and large towns, imbued with city
manners and customs, where those maladies are most rife, and found
only in exceptional cases among our poorer classes who are not
exposed to fashionable follies."[25] Yet he could also say it was "the
women of my own country," without qualification, who refused to
work. Gardner said that the female diseases attendant on masturbation were rampant throughout "the entire community," and such
generalizations combined easily with the significantly common abstraction of "woman." The "ills of maternity are great . . . personal abuse lies at the root of much of the feebleness, nervousness,
pale waxen-facedness and general good-for-nothingness of the entire community." The psychological meaning of the abstraction (its
synonym "the sex") is a second explanation for Gardner's fluctuation of target. In the final analysis the characteristic that men held
determined every woman's fate and definition also made her susceptible to sickness. Gardner defined her normal function of menstruation as a sickness. To be female was to be sick. The common
denominator uniting rich and poor women was their genital organs.

A man could marry any woman and be equally happy, according to Gardner. Conversely, any woman's organs could appall Gardner and trigger his fantasies of imprisonment and bloody extinction.[26]

The final explanation for his fluctuation was simply that he looked at all women from the narrow perspective of his emotional and professional involvement with women whose husbands were wealthy and successful. In short, Gardner's analysis of the prevalence of female diseases was determined by his social and sexual preconceptions. He found female disease where he looked for it, and he looked for it in that group whose characteristics he said caused the disease. One of the characteristics was being able to afford a male obstetrician and, later, a gynecologist, and, of course, the diseases they diagnosed. Gardner virtually ignored the poor[27] and said that the quality of their lives made the incidence of his female diseases infrequent. They were closer to his ideal of female existence. Dr. W. R. D. Blackwood of Philadelphia pointed out in 1888 that "the land is full of wretched, broken-down women today whose lives have been wrecked because they have become mere machines for the reproduction of the race," and he went on to advocate contraception. His view was expressed in the first professional medical symposium on contraception in America; such views had to deal with an attitude fostered by such men as Todd and Gardner.[28]

Gardner's attacks on American medical education in *Old Wine* manifested the same social animus: most of them were directed at those students who come through on the inside track because of money, prestige, or influence. He discussed the advantages of medical education in America and France, saying that one should experience both and thus justifying his own course. He pointed out what an American student had to sacrifice to have the best training. Even after completing his medical training Gardner had to face those frighteningly competitive circumstances that I described in Chapter 8, in addition to his doubts about his reception by American women.

Would that the American physician were adequately encouraged in his toil: Some few are, it is true, but ah! how many, after years consumed at college in laying a basis for years more in building the superstructure live but to see some ignorant blacksmith rolling in wealth, derived from the sale of a nostrum! Yes, so long as the world seized with such eagerness every new pill, which professes to raise the dead; as long as homeopathy, magnetism, hydropathy, "laces" are in vogue; so long as the laws of the country suffer quacks and charlatans of every description to live in a state of piracy against the world, robbing and killing all who come in their way, or are allured by a false flag. . . .

Gardner's view of the world was identical to Todd's (which saw it infested with freebooters). Competition was tantamount to warfare or anarchy, even if it was sanctioned by American law, and in Gardner's view it hindered medical progress, or rather prevented genuine American doctors from elevating their competitive urges to an international arena:

> so long as the ignoramuses, or something worse, are sustained and allowed to collect their exorbitant exactions for poisons sold under the protection and by the help of the law's strong arm—while these exist, it cannot be expected that American physicians will devote their energies to such an extent, as to rival the French in their attainments, who are not protected merely but spurred on and animated by "the powers that be."

Like his male compatriots, Gardner asserted that society was a "market-place." But faced with open competition, Gardner looked wistfully to a more authoritarian society. The disheartening effects of the democratic prospect were precisely those Jarvis described, and Gardner's terms, like Jarvis's, assumed the energy model J. H. Walters defined.[29]

By the end of his career Gardner felt he had failed in his attempt to use gynecological medicine to break into the circle from which he felt excluded. He said in his last book: "I came to the conclusion that so far from esteeming health more than mortality, both seemed matters of comparative inconsequence with the more glittering virtues of wealth and ambition." At the outset of his career he had adopted medicine as a road to both of those things.[30]

Gardner's hostility to the new women remained yoked to his fear that they found his profession and his sexual identity irrelevant:

> Although I am fully convinced that few of you have ever arrived at a realization of perfect health, and that most of you are too lazy or too indifferent to attain unto it—yet I cannot pay you the poor compliment of presuming that your whole nature has become so impregnated with foul humors, as that the desire after health should seem injurious, or its attainment, bodily translation, or rather disembodiment, a process which ignorance has led you to contemplate with terror.

This sour statement is thoroughly ambivalent: he says women's new laziness makes them unreceptive to the treatment of the diseases such laziness causes. He grudgingly allows that they are not totally indifferent (otherwise he would exclude himself completely), but implies he has to compete for access to woman's generative tract with foul humors that impregnate her. Of course, his entrance did accompany disease—and vice versa. He equated health with disembodiment, an equation assuming the same values as those of Todd. If woman remained locked in her body, unsublimated, inevitably she would be sick. He imputed woman's resistance to gynecological recommendations to terror, a projection of his own terror for the bloody and appalling meaning that the womb held for him. But gynecologists fulfilled women's expectations by terrorizing women as they had done from the earliest history of instrumental man-midwives. Women in late nineteenth-century America had special reason to feel terror for gynecologists like Gardner, terrorizing their fancied terrorizers.[31]

21   Gardner's Career

In the fall of 1845 Gardner returned to New York City from Paris and spent the rest of his life there, having "rapidly acquired an extensive practice." At first he lived at 151 Wooster Street in lower Manhattan, a neighborhood he found especially rich in evidence for someone so deeply interested in the diseases of the sexual organs in women. In his article "Gonorrhoea: A Non-Specific Disease," he referred to his "personal observations" of "the harems of pleasure in Church and Mercer Streets where once I had an extended practice."[1]

Gardner's first piece of writing after his return suggests the pressure he felt he was under, as well as his determination to face it and rise in the world; and it demonstrates the connection between a doctor's identity and more general masculine identity. It was a eulogy on John Snowden, M.D., that Gardner contributed to the handwritten "Obituaries of the New York Academy of Medicine" in 1848, probably just after his admission as a Fellow.

> The lives of few young men in any sphere contain much that is worthy of remembrance out of their own immediate circle. Dr. Snowden's was, however, an exception to this rule, not from any one peculiar excellence, though he might contest the laurelled wreath bestowed upon the brave, with the dead upon the battlefield. The world however rarely consider [sic] the vocation of a physician one demanding courage. But it was from the continued aim of his life in the early period when his future path was marked out—the inflexibility with which he pursued it, that our friend was distinguished. One star only directed his steps—*Right!* He saw but one end to his efforts—*Success!*

The life of our friend thus shows but *two characteristics* markedly developed perseverance and reverance [*sic*]. The first was proved in the constant struggle of his life maintained throughout, against numerous obstacles. Poor, friendless, an orphan, without education he acquired all by assiduous effort. . . . The old respect his memory, and the young his mottoes. Success, Right.[2]

Like Sims, Gardner was confronted by what he believed to be the popular notion that a doctor's vocation did not require courage; he compared Dr. Snowden to a victorious hero slain in battle. Sims compared himself to a "conquering hero." Gardner had written from Paris that had "I lived in those tempestuous times, my heart tells me how easily I could have shouldered the musket, and drawn the trigger, under the auspices of that glorious commander," Napoleon. In 1861 Gardner gave a belligerent talk to the New-York Historical Society, connecting his competitive and figuratively warlike, piratical aspirations to their consummation in the Civil War, wherein "bodies of men" were already "possessing strategic points" of their "mother Earth." Gardner saw such violent male action siring fruit even as it kept its purity: "the last traitorous Secessionist shall be crushed out from the land. Peace has planted its roses beneath it, and War, if it must be, shall reap its gory harvest to protect its integrity and purity." The harvest was death, perhaps because even the fantasy of male reproduction evoked the fears of women against which it was a defense. But many men have long preferred violent death to heterosexual relations.[3]

In measuring their professional identities against the most general and conventional standard of successful manhood (victory in battle), Sims and Gardner seem to have shared the popular doubts about sexual identity. It was an issue that concerned Todd at the same time, in his holding up to feminists those supermasculine activities (lumberjacking and whaling, for example) in which he himself could not participate. Todd dealt with the issue by claiming to prepare men for supermasculine roles, by identifying himself with gold miners and railroaders, and by supplying to the not so masculine action of his readers—that is, reading—the technique of identification.

The rest of Gardner's eulogy of Snowden was the typical account of the course and application of the self-made man. He rose like Todd from lonely orphanhood by way of assiduous effort, inflexible pursuit, perseverance, single-mindedness, and constancy in struggle (all synonymous with a denial of what Tocqueville described as the typical course of tergiversation in a sea of baffling mirages). The prize was distinction and success. Such a career duplicated S. W. Francis's account of Gardner's rise to become a distinguished New York physician. But the earlier part of the eulogy—the comparison of a doctor's vocation to battlefield heroics—suggests a profound doubt about the kind of life necessary to self-making. Were reading, studying, and developing the mind truly manly in the way that soldiering and gold mining were? Should not so intense and constant a battle with self and circumstance be externalized and translated into *physical* terms to be really manly? "It is now the problem—how to spare time from our occupations to develope [*sic*] our bodies, or even our souls symmetrically. It takes time to be an athlete, and time is money."[4] It may be suggested that such an anxiety, deriving from the establishment of a modern, urban, industrial civilization (and corresponding to the anxiety over the effects on women of the new workless role), explains the widespread anxiety I described in Chapter 4, that children's brains were being overdeveloped at the expense of their bodies.

This was the context for Gardner's belief that parents "seem to forget that a boy without a true, noble, manly character had far better be dead." Gardner believed that too many American males were becoming unmanly, for which he blamed the parents and offered this advice: "The timidity of parents, should not stand in the way of the physical and moral development of their sons. There are too many like ancient Greeks, that will not permit their sons to go into the water until they have learnt to swim. They are not willing that their sons should have guns, until they have learned to use them. . . ." He may have resented the robbing and killing in American competition, but he recommended a military education for all men.[5]

Gardner married Anna Louisa Hidden on July 27, 1850. All that is recorded of Gardner's wife is that she bore him three children, a boy who died of whooping cough at six weeks old and two daughters, both living when Francis wrote his article in 1866, but only one, Lulu, a "beautiful daughter," at the time of Gardner's death ten years later. The substance of his poem in the Duyckinck Collection addressed to "L——" (Louisa?) suggests that Gardner wrote it to his wife at the time of their marriage. It is undated.

> The word is spoken! Now forever
> Ever to my heart she's bound,
> And naught can come on earth, to sever

> The chain so strongly thrown around.
> For rolling years shall come to test
> The bond now formed on high;
> But *Time* shall only find them blest
> And harmless pass them by.
> From *Friendships* sterling ore
> That precious chain was riven,
> The merit formed the links
> *Love* rivets them in Heaven.

Hidden in chains: Gardner's wife is the subject of the passive form " 's bound." She was chained to that part of Gardner's physiology which generated the blood from which he believed new life originated. So it appeared that Gardner was attempting to reverse the dangerous sexual relation of the prison: but the most salient aspect was his evocation of that situation at all. Clearly the adult heterosexual relation recalled his fears of being fixed to a maternal power (like Todd, he believed marriage was to make women mothers), and he was chained to his wife as surely as she was chained to him. Opposing the "emancipation" of women in 1872, Gardner expressed a variant of the same image for marriage: "The sex, have had the inconsistency, while claiming to emancipate themselves from past slaveries, yet they have endeavored to render themselves physically incapable of any real, laborious undertakings." Like Todd and Tocqueville, Gardner realized the connection between slavery (permanent domination on the basis of physiological difference) and woman's position in marriage. He also implied an understanding of the new role as enslavement based on woman's freedom from work. Gardner accepted the old form of marriage (i.e., "slavery") and wanted to deprive woman of her freedom from work, defining such freedom as sickness. A free woman was trapped by her sickness. He defined health as "disembodiment." Enslavement in marriage was a way of being free of body. The purpose of marriage was to chain woman down, deny her appetite, and free men from the power of woman's body. Yet that picture, idealized in Gardner's poem, still evoked Gardner's deepest fears of woman. It was a circle Gardner reiterated.[6]

Sometime between 1852 and 1855 the Gardners moved uptown, to 141 East 13th Street, closer to the Fifth Avenue fashionists Gardner excoriated, but who supplied what was soon to be the new specialty of gynecology with its clientele. Gardner's first teaching post was "instructor on obstetrics in the New York Preparatory School of

Medicine," which he had given up by 1858, probably when he became professor of the diseases of women and children at New York Medical College, an appointment he held at least until 1861, but not after 1864. For six years Gardner was

> "Attending Physician to the City Dispensary; six to the Northern Dispensary, having charge of the class of diseases of females and children; and was also physician to the lying-in Asylum District many years. He had at one time sole charge of the Private Hospital, Bloomingdale, for three years, attending from two to five hundred patients of all grades, and afflicted with divers diseases.[7]

Between 1866 and 1876 a daughter and perhaps his wife died, and Gardner again moved, this time just a block, to 237 East 13th Street. It may be that the move followed Gardner's suspension from the New York Medical Academy in 1867, which it has been assumed "hampered both his private practice and his clinical work," and he moved only as far away from Fifth Avenue as straitened circumstances demanded.[8] Until the mid-1860s Gardner does not seem to have given up his ambition to become rich by way of medicine. In his eulogies on Drs. John W. Francis and Richard Sharp Kissam in 1861 and 1862 respectively, Gardner admiringly gave their gynecological earnings. In 1861 he had succeeded Kissam as "examining physician" in the Connecticut Mutual Life Insurance Company, and in 1865 he took the same position with the Connecticut General Life Insurance Company.[9]

But this ambition seems to have turned bitter during the same decade. He was making a virtue of necessity when he told Francis in 1866 that the humanity of his profession made it superior to the simple pursuit of money. In *Our Children* (1872) he claimed his views were closer to reality than some other doctors writing about sex because he had heeded "the peremptory call of business." But in the same book he recorded with disgust the extent to which people were attracted by "the glittering virtues of wealth and ambition." The same attraction had dictated his own choice of career.[10]

His feelings about men were significantly ambivalent. He exulted in nineteenth-century technological achievement, identifying with manifest destiny, the acquisition and refinement of resources, James Fenimore Cooper's myth of the West, in short, with the conventionally more heroic male activities than his own amid frivolous urban women. While he attacked rich women's husbands only rarely, Gardner knew whence his customers got their money and their life style. He felt threatened by, aggressive toward, and envious of other men, feelings which increased in proportion to his sense of remoteness from the wealth and success of men on whose wives he was dependent for a living by definition always inferior to theirs. That may help explain why he represented it (and preindustrial, pregynecological American life) as more moral, healthier, and more humane. He could add his hostility toward their husbands to the sexual hostilities he brought to his treatment of rich women. Gardner's experience of his professional world reflected and compounded these feelings. He had known from the start that it was one of ferocious, even deadly, competition, where theory succeeded theory, and what he believed to be quacks multiplied under cover of the law. He had hoped his special training in authoritative Europe would give him decisive advantage in America.

On his return he had signed the roll of the New York Academy of Medicine and was one of the earliest members, if not a founder-member. He plunged into "strenuous" activity, in contrast to the other members, and by his reports of the Academy's proceedings to the New York *Times* demonstrated an appetite and a flair for publicity that may have been connected to his continued association with his father's editorship (until 1862) of the Newark *Daily Advertiser*.[11]

An account of Gardner's activities in the New York Academy of Medicine was included in a long letter to the New York *Times* (November 1, 1867), signed by "Medicus" and defending Gardner on his suspension (on October 18, 1867) from his Fellowship in the Academy for "violation of his pledge." His suspension confirmed his apprehensions about American medicine. The Academy accused Gardner of consulting with a homeopath, one Dr. Bartlett.

In *Old Wine* Gardner had listed homeopathy as one of the current medical vogues allowed to luxuriate under American conditions of laissez-faire, along with quackery and charlatanry. He pointed out in his defense against the Academy's charges that during his twenty-three years of practice he "had striven to uphold the regular practice." Indeed, he had been accused of radical opposition to all "peculiar" systems, especially homeopathy. At the same time, Gardner "admitted that he had held consultations with Dr. Bartlett, and claimed he had a right to." Under the rules, all the Committee of Ethics had to show was that Gardner was an intimate of Dr. Bartlett, and that Dr. Bartlett was a homeopath. Gardner was belligerently unrepentant, and it was only by a vote of 11 to 10 (a considerable number abstaining) that he was suspended. Gardner pointed out that "the names of other members who had done the thing were in the hands of the Committee." In other words, the heresy of homeopathy had riven the New York Academy of Medicine nearly down the middle.[12]

Twice before, the Academy had preferred "unjust charges" against Gardner, and he admitted he had opposed men who had been in the position in which he now found himself. Medicus said that the Academy had been born of a union of "cliques," in order to combat the "new invader," homeopathy. The medical profession had been weakened by division, "cut up by cliques and rampant with feuds." With consistent irony, Medicus described the history of this enforced union of disparate elements which muddled along, infused with any energy only by the efforts of two or three members, most notably, Dr. Gardner. His activity and its successful publicity may well have rankled with other members. But his was not the only case. Medicus described a continuous history of factionalism, coming to a head previously in the cases of Drs. Valentine Mott and Horace Green (and which, he said, "culminated" in the case of Gardner).[13]

Gardner's feelings toward Sims further illustrate the effects of medical competition. He dedicated *Sterility* (1856) to Sims and was lavish in his praise of the great man. He called Sims's operation for the cure of the vesico-vaginal fistula *"the* operation of the century," helped him perform it, and called him "my friend." But in "The Rupture of the Perinaeum" (1874) Gardner revealed some other feelings about Sims:

> The great apostle of vaginal surgery, Dr. J. Marion Sims, told me but a few days ago, that he never operated any other way [i.e., with "interrupted sutures"]; and so likewise Dr. Emmet, I understand. I don't doubt it. Dr. Sims, with a needle and a bit of silver wire, can do anything; but I can't, and I don't believe but what in anybody's patients they will cut out before the parts become united. Perhaps, in his hospitals, with his skilled nurses, and under his God-inspired eye, he may have success such as I never could get with the liberties and exigencies of home, with ordinary monthly nurses and my bungling ways! All I say here is "God bless Dr. Sims for all he has done in these localities!"—but my legs are not long enough to step in his every track.

On one hand Sims, a missionary spreading light and truth about the need to treat women's genital organs with knives and scissors, was godlike; he could do anything, and Gardner was a convert. In contrast, Gardner presented himself as essentially limited in scope, in fact a bungler. On the other hand Gardner said he did not believe Sims's suturing method would work at all. If it did it was due in large part to Sims's privileged access to hospitals and skilled nurses —money—that Gardner did not have, and that contrast touched a raw nerve. The "localities" of the last sentence were women's organs; Gardner's track-making metaphor repeated Sims's own view of his work as the exploration and conquest of new territory. Because this particular manifestation of the male ambition toward virgin land was gynecological, its objective the vagina, the phallic nature of that ambition is fairly naked: so, too, Gardner's measuring his length of insertion into Sims's vaginal tract tracks. Sims was the emotional point of contact, so there are perhaps homosexual connotations to Gardner's measurement. Women supplied the occasion for a male display of feeling about self and other men. Gardner's feelings toward Sims in this passage ran the gamut from awe and basking in his reflected glory, to bitter rivalry and denigration.[14]

Gardner published regularly throughout his life after 1851, with rarely more than a year between articles. The exception was the period 1865–1870, which was another sign of the stress accompanying his probable financial troubles, possibly the deaths of his wife and one of his daughters, and his suspension from the New York Academy of Medicine. Thereafter, for the remaining six years of his life, his assault on women and his sense of gloom about America's future intensified. He produced two books in that period, whereas he had published only two during all the years previously. Nearly all of his publications concerned woman's sexuality, and most of that concern focused on gestation and parturition. They give a sense of the danger emanating from women, danger to men, to children, and to society. They advocate the discipline and control of women by men at the direction of experts like himself, in association with the clergy. Doctors and clergymen had professional knowledge of the intimate darkness of human nature (which is why Hawthorne gave them such prominence in his novels and short stories). Gardner said, "There are two persons in every town, who know as much of the secret history of that town, as all the rest together. These two people [are] the clergyman and physician." Just as Todd associated his efforts with doctors, so Gardner associated his with ministers, believing that many of them were shirking their duties. Gardner exempted Todd from this charge, quoting and citing his work on masturbation and abortion. He dedicated *Conjugal Sins* to "the Reverend Clergy of the United States," hoping to convince them of their duty in light of the evidence the book presented. He explained: "I have dedicated this volume to the clergy of America, because they are the great moral lever-power of the country. They can make this vice disgraceful; they can compel it to be kept dark; they can prevent its being the common boast of women, 'that they know too much to have babies.'" The book's title suggests that Gardner himself took on the role of preacher and minister.[15]

Only one of his four books, *Sterility,* was, strictly speaking, a medical text, although it, too, was shot through with his sexual values. Its whole thrust was to put women back into production. For Gardner, the chief sign of a female disease was its effect on woman's childbearing capacity. So he modified Drs. Tyler's and Meigs's analyses of "ulcerative degeneration": while Gardner acknowledged that they recognized the condition's appearance, he pointed out that the former did so "without connecting with it its most invariable concomitant of barrenness and the latter passing it by so casually as to deprive his observations and remarks of their proper force." In *Our Children* and *Conjugal Sins* he argued that the more babies there were, the better social health would be. That belief was based on his need to restrain women by keeping them pregnant, and so sexual anxieties prepared the way for the American reception of Social Darwinism.[16]

Sims thought very little of *Sterility*'s medical innovativeness. Introducing his account of his own work on the subject ten years later, Sims surveyed the literature and implied Gardner had added nothing. "Indeed, little or nothing has been added to the labours of McIntosh and of Simpson; and the English language presents us with but one complete monograph on the subject,—that by Dr. A. K. Gardner, of New York." Of his other references to Gardner's work in *Clinical Notes,* one refers to the practice of dilating the cervix by sponge tents, which Gardner used "most extensively and perseveringly, but has now abandoned the practice as unfruitful." The other criticized Gardner's modification of Sims's own invention, the "uterine elevator," by the addition of a screw, which Sims said was "objectionable because it robs us of the faculty of determining the power of resistance by a sense of feeling." So in Sims's view Gardner tried hard and could summarize what his predecessors had done, but he had not demonstrated any originality. Gardner wanted to make a name for himself in the same way Sims had.[17]

Of Gardner's last two books, *Conjugal Sins* was an "amplification" of his article "The Physical Decline of American Women" published ten years earlier in the *Knickerbocker Magazine*. Gardner felt that the increasing gravity of the situation justified both the book and the inclusion of a slightly abbreviated version of the original article as an appendix. A large proportion of the book is quotation of other men's work. Gardner said it was "intended for and served as a warning." It warned against the effects of woman's new role, masturbation, physical excess, contraception, abortion, and assorted conjugal, copulative transgressions, for most of which Gardner held women responsible: hence their "physical decline." It was very similar in its message to Todd's *Serpents in the Dove's Nest*. Gardner sent a copy to Todd, the act acknowledging the lifelong effect Todd had had on him. The publisher of the second edition (1874) included Todd's reply to Gardner, identifying him as "Rev. John Todd, author of the 'Student's Manual,' etc., etc."

My Dear Sir:
   Your letter and book came to me last month, and I have delayed to acknowledge in the hope that I might find time amid my heavy duties pressing on age to read the book a second time and weigh it more accurately. My impressions about it are: 1. That it is ably written; full, clear, explicit, and instructive. I think the poorest parts are your quotations from French authors. 2. That it will do good when put into the right hands. I confess to fears lest some of the information you convey may be abused both by the married and the unmarried. . . . Perhaps these secrets had better be told, but the devil may thrust one's fingers into a flame even though the fire came from God's altars. You have done well, and I hail every attempt to lift up or hold back poor humanity from evil most praiseworthy. Were you to hear all the confessions about "Conjugal Sins" which might be made, your ears would give out under the wail. Be of good courage; do all the good you can; every man in his own way.
                                                  Yours, sir, most truly
Pittsfield, March 31, 1870
                                                  John Todd[18]

Todd's chief qualification here represented the problem that bedeviled his own presentation of masturbation thirty-five years earlier—would it provoke the very activity it was intended to forestall? The difficulty was a sign of the scorching explosiveness of sexuality, and perhaps the tantalizing attraction it held for those who denied it. Todd implied that his own parishioners had been confessing their conjugal sins to him; one recalls his admiration for Catholic views on contraception and abortion and Catholic enforcement of them. Could Todd give Gardner's book to the parishioners who had fallen into conjugal sin? But why would those who had not need such a book?

In his introduction to the first edition, Gardner pointed out that his book supports

> opinions very generally entertained by the community, enunciated by the Rev. Bishop Coxe [included by the Duyckincks in the *Cyclopoedia*], of Western New York, in his pastoral address to his people, and promulgated by the resolutions of the Presbyterian Assembly held in this city last spring [1869]; also by Rev. Mr. Frothingham in a series of articles in the *Tribune*, in the spring of 1868; by Rev. Mr. Higginson, in various pungent magazine articles; by Dr. Allen of Lowell, Mass., in his Report to the Massachusetts State Legislature, on Hygiene; and by many other thinkers of the day.

Gardner also said that the original *Knickerbocker* article "was very generously welcomed and quoted from by numerous writers." The reviewers of *Conjugal Sins* gave it a similar welcome. "There is no class of subjects on which the community at large needs more plain, wise teaching" (New York *Tribune*). The New York *Independent* said it "is written in the best spirit, scientific and moral, and it ought to be read by husbands and wives, and fathers and mothers." *Halls Journal of Health* echoed the book's implication that conjugal sins were a woman's responsibility. "Such important information is given in this book in reference to the more healthful bringing up of our daughters, morally and physically, and the relation of the sexes, that no parent will fail of reading every line of the book with the most absorbing interest. It is a boon to womankind."[19]

Conjugal Sins seems to have reached the large audience for which Gardner intended it. In his preface to the second edition (1874) he said it had received public and private commendations. For the last four years letters had reached him nearly every day "from the married and single, from priests and sisters vowed to celibacy [the book answered the question "Is Continence Physically Injurious?" with a firm no], from the libertine, the depraved, the imprudent, of criticism, praise, thanks, asking for advice, for guidance, for professional treatment." Gardner believed these letters, together with the frequent references to it made by speakers and writers, were evidence that *Conjugal Sins* "filled a want, and effected a real, lasting good to the community." It had sold 20,000 copies in spite of being out of print for two of the four years since its publication, owing to the retirement of its first publisher. Within two years after its republication in 1874 it had sold another 10,000 copies. Together with the fame gained by his frequent publication in mass-circulation newspapers, *Conjugal Sins* may have been a reason for the presence at Gardner's funeral of an "immense concourse" of people. The 30,000 total sales figure of 1876 was included in Gardner's obituary, along with the details of his funeral. The preface to the ninth edition of 1923 still claimed an "increasing demand."[20]

Our Children (1872) was Gardner's longest original work, and his darkest statement of the doom awaiting America unless men and women followed his advice. His anxiety about the sexual transgressions of women was combined with his apprehensions about the effects of immigration on America's radical future. He said he would "attempt in this volume to show the individual man and woman, what is the highest type of physical excellence and how to attain it—although I am fully convinced that few of you have ever arrived at a realization of perfect health, and that most of you are too lazy or too indifferent to attain unto it."[21]

Gardner also published separately as *The History of the Art of Midwifery* (1852) his introductory lecture to his edition of an authoritative work in America, the British W. Tyler Smith's *The Modern Practice of Midwifery* (1852). Gardner's little book advocated a purge of midwives from the American scene, in apocalyptic language. In 1861 Gardner published his translation of the French translation of the German Friedrich Wilhelm Scanzoni von Lichtenfels's *Practical Treatise on the Diseases of the Sexual Organs of Women*. It became a highly respected and widely used authority in America. Sims cited it with respect in *Clinical Notes,* and so did one of his most illustrious successors, T. Gaillard Thomas, in his *A Practical Treatise on the Diseases of Women* (1878), which also quoted Gardner's extensive notes to the tome.[22]

Of Gardner's published articles that I have been able to locate or identify, seven deal with the social aspects of his medicine, and eight are more narrowly medical, although, of course, I am attempting to break down such categories. I have incorporated most of the relevant evidence supplied by these articles in the following account of Gardner's beliefs about women, men, and sexual relations.

Gardner wanted to explain why, in 1860, the American woman was "a haggard creature, dull-eyed and sallow, pinched in form, an unfit mother, not a help-meet, but a drag on the energy, spirits and resolution of her partner." His defenses of American man's "energy" and of America's social future were always prior considerations in his diagnosis and treatment of woman.[1]

Gardner believed that there was a great disparity between men and women in "strength, endurance, and capacity," all qualities, it should be noted, that writers like Brigham, Todd, and Ray were so anxious to develop in males at an early age in order to equip them for the lifelong struggle in American democracy. So one can already hypothesize wish fulfillment in Gardner's assertion that men, in some sense at least, were strong. The disparity, he said, was a recent phenomenon. Woman was not physically "inferior" to man in the Garden of Eden or when considered "as a simple biped." But now "she is carefully guarded and not allowed to do anything, so far as this is possible. The rich being able to effect this end, their women are all sick—the poor, comparatively so. The whole sex are being killed by kindness."[2]

Gardner's explanation first turned to the childrearing practices that initiated this different development of boys and girls. It all began with the outward recognition of the sex difference, when babies left the swaddling clothes for their respective girl and boy clothes. The reader then was led to expect that an account of the boys' freedom of limbs and movement from boyhood to manhood would follow. But this was not the case. "The shape of his garments, does, indeed give liberty and play to the muscles, but the exigencies of rich velvet jackets, silken trowsers and white shirts with their lace 'fretwork' of frills and furbelows, require him to be constantly guarded." So the male was afflicted by the same condition that Gardner had originally set out to show weakened the female. These and other destructive "exigencies" turn out to be a phase of the "drag" women were on the "resolution" of men: they were the "demoralizing influences" which "fed" the "sickly vanity of his enervated mother." It was only to the extent that the boy escaped her attempt to confine and deck him, to treat him as a pet or a doll, indeed, to consume him, that he managed to gain strength, endurance, and capacity. The young American boy had to be wary of the feminizing clutches of his mother.[3]

The mother's "pride" in dressing her young boy in "heavy pantaloons" (and in providing him with "featherbeds and soft furniture") debilitated his manhood in another way, according to Dr. Abraham Jacobi in 1875. Not

> only are the parts kept too hot and are sometimes compressed, but the frequent micturition of the child necessitates the frequent protracted handling of the penis. The young child is but clumsy and the reverse of adroit. It takes him time to disentangle the organ. Frequently in the streets and gardens have I seen sympathizing little friends, mostly of the other sex, and then somewhat older, or servants, busy with rendering the required aid in the emission of the urine.

The result was masturbation and the whole train of diseases leading to debilitation, insanity, and even death, all attributable in the first instance to the mother's treatment of her son.[4]

Even if the little boy escaped enervation at his mother's hands, in Gardner's view he did not embark on a steady course of healthy growth. Parents "stuff" his stomach with improper food. He suffered from the bad effects of tobacco and "alcoholic stimulants"; he breathed the "air of a city thronged by near a million souls" and the air of ill-ventilated schoolrooms, where he neglected "healthy exercise for the ambition of literary superiority; or, in our own city [New York], most frequently bent over a ledger." Gardner noted the unhealthy conditions under which clerks, bankers, and merchants lived, worked, and traveled. Then, as if echoing the title of his article, he asked, "Is it strange that the health of the businessmen of this city is deteriorating?" But he was, we must remind ourselves, describing the physical decline of American women.[5]

Why were men thus exposed to "gout, dyspepsia and all chronic diseases, in addition to consumptions" and "greatly on the increase"? The answer lay in that psychology suggested by Gardner's account of the young man's need for stimulants, of his "ambition for superiority," his neglect of his body in the interest of developing his mental powers, and in his commitment to ambitious work in the city. Gardner himself was committed to it. Because of this kind of life, the American male was only "comparatively vigorous." To look vigorous at all, men needed an even less vigorous yardstick. "But although the physical stamina of the men is not what it might be, it is far superior to that of the women."[6]

As soon as the baby girl was dressed in sex-distinctive clothes as "soon does the bodily degeneracy commence." Expectations of little girls reflected expectations of women: once given female clothes, the child was "then considered as an ornament, in the present or the future." Her mother was "dependent" on the "immaculate purity of its worked pantalettes and under-clothing" for her own "respectability," just as she was in the case of her son. According to Gardner, the responsibility for the ill health of both boy and girl lay with the enervated, vain, sickly, fashionable mother. The boy was healthier to the extent that he escaped her: the girl was sicker to the extent that she did not. She was not allowed to play outside in the sunshine, was sent to a fashionable boarding school where she learned to play the polka, to crochet, to masturbate, and to walk up and down Broadway as an agent for the villainous female proprietor of the boarding school. Then came the "tyranny" of adult fashion: "woman has become a doll, to be decked and draped, and carried out, instead of an active, working helpmeet to man." Made useless herself by her new role, the new mother made her daughter useless and threatened to make her son useless too. By his own efforts the male escaped that fate; little girls did not, and went on to make dolls of themselves, of their daughters, and of their sons if they could.[7]

Who was doing the decking and the draping? Who first made women dolls? According to Gardner, women did it to themselves. The terms of his irony connected the turning of a woman into a doll with slavery. "Look at the dress of woman. Were man to so direct the fashion of woman's dress, in order to enable him, by physical force, to overcome her and tyrannize over her, he could not more completely fetter her than she shackles herself." The sentence reveals what the blaming of woman was meant to deny, that is, that she became what she was—an idle, fashionable doll—because men wanted her to be like that. In doing so he initiated a cycle, since she then attempted to feminize her son and planted doubts in his mind about his masculinity, leading him to require confirmation by demanding and dominating a superfeminine wife-mother. Todd admitted men wanted to dress and adorn their wives and daughters— to treat them as mannequins. A female contemporary described how such husbands wanted to treat their houses as display windows in which to place the mannequins; Donald Meyer has explained the history. And Gardner himself complied. "Against the decrees of fashion there is no appeal." Accepting both that and implicitly male demands that women spend and display what men earned, Gardner then took a familiar tack. "We must, therefore, seek for other evils more curable."[8]

More than concern for proper gestation and lactation, and more than social animus, can be detected in Gardner's obsession with women's clothes. Clothing could make a woman's sexuality visible in a new way, and Gardner found that disturbing. He had located the beginnings of an American woman's physical decline (and of the maternal threat to the male) at the time she assumed sexually distinctive dress. Gardner was remarkably circumspect in expressing that idea, and I think that was because of the sexual meaning dress held for him; he could deal with woman's sexuality only if it was concealed, sublimated, or totally under male control. "We feel that we are treading upon a delicate subject, and we beg our readers to attend to the general idea, rather than to any peculiar form of expression, or to any particular illustration, about which there may be more than one opinion." Gardner identified woman's fashionable appetite with her control and expression of her own sexuality (via masturbation, contraception, and abortion). Fashion outwardly manifested woman's independent sexuality. That led to bodily degeneracy. Victory over "self-degeneracy" required subordination of self in motherhood and envelopment of the female body in loose-fitting, figure-hiding clothing. Motherhood sublimated a woman; it disembodied her. Logically a female child could have avoided degeneracy the same way her brother did, by wearing his kind of clothes. At the time of the sex distinction, he left behind cumbersome garments. Gardner admitted that (in terms of his own analysis) the "right of woman to be free and equal with man will come with a Declaration of Independence which shall strip off the fetters of petticoats and the gilded meshes of lace which have so long bound down the gentler sex." But Gardner balked even at bloomers, a very mild approach to dress hitherto monopolized by males. They would have revealed that woman had legs. Again Gardner's views were identical to Todd's. Instead of the fashionable cinctures, lacings, and low-placed sleeves, women should wear a dress with "a simple waist" and "shoulder-straps upon which the skirts may all button." The effect of these recommendations would have been to tone down the outward manifestations of a woman's sexuality in the interests of more efficient motherhood.[9]

The rest of Gardner's list of the causes of woman's physical decline and the diseases of her sexual organs were all aspects of her new role. Woman was rid of the exercise of cleaning because of "modern conveniences for warming, lighting, [and] watering." She consumed champagne, cream, ices, oysters, and jellies at late hours. Gardner blended these causes of her sickness with the various forms of her self-assertion; going out at "improper times, and seasons, and hours"; spending "hours in the most outrageous muscular exertion, in dances . . . invented by some arch enemy of woman, so effectually do they, aided by a too great weight of clothing, shake up the whole frame and dislocate every internal organ pertaining to womanhood." If there was such an "enemy" around, like the slaver, it was woman herself. He listed the sexual self-assertion of "personal abuse" and "infanticide," which, he said, women had performed "from a devotion to dress and vain pride of outward show," or because "the demands of society, the cost for food, clothing, education is so great that we could not live with such a family." And again Gardner betrayed his underlying apprehension: some women had abortions because "the care of children is such a slavery." An identical set of motives explained contraception.[10]

Gardner understood that some of these motives for the physical decline of American women added up to a kind of independence very close to their husbands' Faustian activities which Gardner so admired. Females who practiced abortion and contraception pretended "to guide the course of events, [and] make the laws of Nature conform to their wishes"; they were "wise in their own conceit" and because of that were "sufferers, invalids, and useless." So Gardner's list expanded to take in women who claimed political freedom. He placed "himself in opposition to this reform movement" not because he thought woman was naturally physically weaker—he had begun by stating that was not the case—but because her freedom made her sick. And again, calling on her to subject herself to his analysis, to her husband, to motherhood, and to the law of nature, he characterized her freedom as slavery. "Any opposition [from Gardner to her emancipation] must therefore arise from her own slavery to forms, and customs and observances, from being tied down by fashion and folly." Fashion and suffragism were equally productive of sickness. Woman's physical freedom caused her disease, which then undermined her aspirations for intellectual freedom. "At the bottom of all superiority is physical vigor. An inferior mind, backed by robust health, can accomplish all that it undertakes, but tortured by disease, and restrained by debility, the proudest intellect is futile to obtain results." Physical freedom led to sexual display, sexual pleasure, and sexual assertiveness, that is, the domination of even the proudest intellect by the lower parts. Women needed to subordinate their bodies to a man, to God, and to the laws of nature, in order to be able to organize their "physical vigor" for intellectual and spiritual purposes. Independent women were sick. It will be seen that his argument included the application of the Walters-defined model of proto-sublimation to female psychology. The model was a constant assumption in Gardner's world view. He said of the woman who gave in to sexuality that the "sensuous intemperance is sufficiently to be reprobated when its aliment is drawn from the vigor of physical energy."[11]

In short, Gardner's analysis of the physical decline of American women represented the same sexual perspective we saw in Jarvis's assessment of the comparative liability of the sexes to insanity. The point of departure for Gardner's diagnosis of woman's decline (for which he blamed her and at which he directed his efforts) was the given-ness of man's running the danger of mental and physical ill health, indeed, the given-ness of his deterioration. Against the categorical and imperative demand that women give up their ambitions because of the effect on their bodies (a demand with which Gardner concluded *Conjugal Sins*) one must set the speculativeness and reluctance of his and other men's dealing with the same problem:

Addressed to women: "The height of earthly desire can only be striven for with earnestness, to say nothing of attainment, with the *mens sana in corpore sano*, a healthy mind in a healthy body."

Addressed to men: "It is now the problem—how to spare time from our occupations to develope bodies, or even our souls symmetrically. It takes time to be an athlete, and time is money."[12]

That last passage illustrates Gardner's concern with masculinity; one way masculinity was constantly shored up was by emphasizing the wide and uncrossable gulf between men and women. However

destructive of themselves men made their own lives, they could still
hold their society more destructive of women: "the female is . . .
far below the male even in his imperfect physical development."
The invidious comparison and consequent targeting was defensive
and self-fulfilling.[13]

Gardner dated the decline of the American woman very specifically. It had happened in the half-century before the publication
of his essay, that is 1810–1860, the period of political democratization, urbanization, and industrial takeoff. In Gardner's view, women
now escaped work because of male achievements. "The necessities
of life are obtained with a far less expenditure of physical energy
than ever before. Steam, in the fields, at the anvil, and the loom, have
materially abridged man's toil." By implication he still had to spend
mental energy. Gardner was most explicitly resentful of woman's
idleness, but, believing doctors had to work harder than "men,
women, and children" because of the advances of American technology, he was envious of them all. "None but the doctors find their
work never done. They are hitched to a bell wire, and like a jumping
jack, must work when the string is pulled." He resented the most
salient aspect of the male role—work—and his image, the "hitched,"
comparing his position to that of a draft horse, also suggests a form
of slavery or imprisonment, and in the case of the doctor specializing
in obstetrics and gynecology, the person pulling the wire (as it was
with an identical image in Todd) was a woman.[14]

Gardner's frame of reference was that "half-remembered, half-
imagined way of life" Marvin Meyers has uncovered in Jacksonian
political rhetoric, the simple, virtuous, agrarian world foreclosed by
the incessant ambition and anxiety Tocqueville found everywhere
in America in 1831, not just among the Jacksonians. Concentration
of outwork in factories, the transportation revolution, and their
revolutionary effects were coming about in Gardner's childhood and
youth, and he was very conscious of the changes. In his view the
urban corruption with which he was preoccupied had not existed
before. "Our grandparents lived on coarsely ground flour, and corn
black with unbolted husks, rich in phosphates, ammoniates, and
never knew what a tooth brush was." Woman's role represented a
"change from the active housekeeper of our forefather's pattern to
the vacuity of mind and flabbiness of muscle of the ornamental
women of the present epoch." In fact the change was as recent as the
difference between his life and that of his parents. "Modern life has
not the labors of our parents, spinning, churning, and the thousand

in-door employments, so full of variety and exercise." This sense of having witnessed such a recent change helps explain Gardner's idea that he could so easily turn back the clock. And in telling women to return to their "noble office" and the standards of the past, all of them to be mothers like his mother, he was expressing perhaps her power over his own life.[15]

After the Civil War, the change from pure, healthy country life to hothouse, sick, city life was compounded by changes in the cities' populations. By 1872 he recognized that "those halcyon days of innocence and purity, will never return again. This country is the refuge of the poor and oppressed, the bold and the daring, the speculative and hopeful of every land. The suffering poor, and the criminal refugee, flock to these shores." It was not a vision of America with which Gardner sympathized. "Locks and bars, and bolts are needed for our dwellings, our families also require watching, and our young sons and delicate daughters must be guarded against the company they keep." He projected his attack on the immigrants' morality onto their attitude toward what Gardner fantasized as the WASP tradition. "The pure and simple manners of our past days, are to them but evidences of depravation. Be the cause as it may, the days of security are past." Foreigners and cities were fine when he was able to dip into them as a traveling bachelor, tasting the vices he associated with the *bal masqué*, prostitutes, and grisettes, and inspecting beautiful, foreign, female breasts in the morgue. Once back home in America, Gardner derived his sense of "security" from racial consolidation of the body politic and from the subordination of its "female portion." In the face of what all of them believed to be social collapse and consequent racial eruption, WASP men clung even more desperately to their women, whom they demanded be utterly subordinate and safe, and on whom they said they were dependent for any future at all.[16]

Gardner felt the looming sexual anarchy now required the authoritarianism of Europe, instead of the democratic forms that had allowed its young girls to model themselves on the corruptions of the rich.

The freedom of intercourse between the sexes—never known out of the United States—is a thing of past days, it is impossible in the future. "Sparking" and all the antecedents, and relationships, are greatly to be modified, and the European methods of marriage are to be adopted, long courtships, and the freedom of indiscriminate visit-

ing, and to stay hours in utter privacy—this is a barbarism of the
past, which the present disowns.

The new conditions already had canceled that American characteristic Tocqueville recorded forty years before.[17]

Like Todd, Gardner demanded to take over the mother's role in
the rearing of daughters on the basis of her incompetence. Mothers
were

> themselves often ignorant and regardless of the actual condition of
> their children, when they send them to dancing school, or permit them
> to an evening party. A great portion of the prevalent female debility
> is owing to the severe exercise of dancing the polka, and like dances;
> and violently shaking down the internal viscera, when excited by the
> ordinary monthly functions, and preventing the natural engorgement.
> Trivial diseases thus commenced, ignorantly neglected, aggravated
> by succeeding imprudence, and thirty years of age finds this girl a
> confirmed invalid.

Her invalidity was her incapacity to bear children. Instead of permitting her to dance in such a way, a mother should lead her
daughter toward "refinement," a very familiar word standing for the
proto-sublimatory belief I have described. The more refined, the
more disembodied, the higher the intellectual elevation. Gardner
went on to reiterate Todd's metaphor for the process. Woman's
reproduction of children "shall gild a virtuous life with brightest
gold and as a true mother raise her to a pinnacle of glory that man
can ever attain, creating herself an object of the sublimest adoration, to be henceforth respected by all mankind, an object of reverence and worship, by her own children, next to her God." Paradoxically, the physical actions of gestation and parturition transmuted
woman's baseness into gold. By giving birth she brought about her
own existence as goddess and doll, a self-entrapping circle that men
demanded women enter before they would accord them respect. At
the same time it was a statement of the psychological power woman's reproductive capacity exercised over the male imagination.[18]

A girl's whole life should be governed by her awareness that reproduction is "the great work for which the division into sexes was
created. . . ." By that Gardner meant for which women were
created, since he pointed out that giving birth was regrettably the
only great work men could not perform. All of Gardner's advice and
criticism was focused on the reduction of woman to the proper
performance of her maternal function. Young girls should engage in

the "manly" sport of rowing, because it developed the bust. When choosing her clothes, the adolescent girl should foresee their bearing on her eventual nursing. It will be seen that the nineteenth-century view of women that Gardner and Todd represented was identical to that expressed in Nazi ideology. Perhaps American men were sexually reactionary earlier than European Fascists in part because they faced the emancipation of women sooner, in turn because of the democratic premise (and the familial, sexual, and ideological changes associated with that).[19]

Gardner's reductive definition of woman's role and his preoccupation with the new rich shaped his response to abortion. Abortion had hardly been an issue in the United States until the democratic intensification of pressure on male identity. Prior to the passage of more stringent antiabortion laws, most of them after mid-century, abortion before "quickening" (when the fetus first kicks in the womb) was not a crime at all in the prevailing common law; and even if it was performed after quickening it was regarded as a minor offense, if not ignored. The transition to the familiar twentieth-century prohibitions was a gradual one, two states (Arkansas, Mississippi) retaining the quickening distinction until the mid-twentieth century. But the rash of thoroughgoing legislative acts against any abortion was in the period beginning 1860, particularly intense in the 1870s, and lasting until the 1920s and beyond. It coincided with the gynecological crescendo. Antiabortion legislation often gave the medical profession control over the abortion decision, and so can be interpreted in the same way that the campaign against midwives has been interpreted—as a professional and humanitarian cleaning up of dirty, amateur, and barbaric practices: it was "to protect the woman from butchery by incompetent, non-medical abortionists. . . ." But analysis of the writings of Todd and Gardner, and the coincidence with the male tensions manifested in the Civil War accompanying the sexual anxieties I have described, suggests that the antiabortion campaign and legislation expressed a darker, more defensive impulse. Lawrence Lader's connecting anti-abortion legislation with the concern "with American expansion and the perpetuation of the race" comes closer to the psychology involved, for I am suggesting that the impulse was part and parcel of the male attempt to discipline women, to take charge of the procreative function in all of its aspects, and in doing so, certainly, to establish or consolidate professional and sexual identity.[20]

As each of woman's sins came under Gardner's purview, he made it out to be the worst. In "Physical Decline" (1860) abortion was "the most horrid social enormity of this age, this city, and this world." In *Conjugal Sins* he made clear the distinction between infanticide and abortion, and condemned both. In his last and most apocalyptic book two years later, he estimated that "the proportion of women at the present day, who in some unnatural violent way, are striving to avoid the necessities of their nature, seems to be at least nine tenths of the entire number."[21]

If Gardner believed abortion was common among all classes, his social predisposition led him to single out the married rich. He could exercise occasional sympathy and forgiveness for poor or unmarried girls when they had abortions, but not at all for the rich and married. Fashionists (who by definition required rich husbands) would set the general trend for abortion as well as for clothes. So Gardner's targets were from the class from which he drew his customers, those women whose ostentatious exterior Gardner believed corresponded to an ostentatious and appetitive sexuality.[22]

Gardner called abortion the mother's "crime," and his prognosis fit the crime. Disease was a punishment.

> The health of the mother suffers materially, from the violence done to her system, and from the shock to her nervous sense. Whether it is effected by powerful drugs, or by mechanical and instrumental interferences, the result is deleterious to the animal economy. . . . a fruitful origin of neuralgias, debilities, and miseries. Be assured this is not exaggerated, for we cannot recall to mind an individual who has been guilty of this crime (for it must be called a crime under every aspect), who has not suffered for many years afterward in consequence. And when health is finally restored, the freshness of life has gone, the vigor of mind and energy of body have forever departed. Languor and listlessness have become a second nature by habit.

Those symptoms that the new gynecologists found so common among women enslaved by their new role—pain, weakness, neuralgias, debilities, miseries, languor, and listlessness—Gardner was able to attribute to what he believed was the undiscoverable ubiquity of the secret crime of abortion.[23]

Most of Gardner's chapter in *Conjugal Sins* setting out the evils of "Methods Used to Prevent Conception, and Their Consequences" consists of quite extensive quotation from the French doctor Alexander Mayer's *Des Rapport Conjugaux* "considerées sous le triple point de vue, de la population, de la santé et de la morale publique" (Paris, 1868) and Mayer's own quotations of other Frenchmen, which Todd had found the "poorest part" of the book. Gardner's endorsement of these French writers and his republication of them illustrate the continuity between American and French views about the sexual area with which they were concerned, and his dependence on them recalls that anaclitic tendency of American medicine. At the same time his translation from the French allowed him to impart a personal flavor, while his own, original introductory and concluding pages provide some idea of what was distinctive about his own, American view of contraception.

The context Gardner supplied for his use of these authorities was the infrequency of "leisure and ease" in American life. He believed that men were not "sufficiently freed" to allow for much "excess in pleasure" (the subject of the preceding chapter was "The Injurious Results of Physical Excess"). Conversely, they were enslaved by the "cares and anxieties" of American life, by "the necessity of earning a livelihood, with the consequent employment of time and the fatigues of body and brain." Such constant demands "used up" the "physical energies" and drastically limited the frequency of sexual intercourse. These sentences illustrate Gardner's belief in the spermatic economy. He went on to suggest that any physical energy left over for sexual expenditure had to be used for the production of a child (and a male if the man played his cards properly) and not wasted by contraception and/or copulation for pleasure. Gardner blamed American women for contraception, as Todd had done. Gardner said unequivocally that "women in every station in life sedulously seek to diminish the number of their offspring" in the interests of fashion seeking, the other aspects of the new role, and the assertion of female independence. This blaming women for contraception was the one clear difference between the American and French accounts.[24]

Gardner described "the injury resulting to both parties from incomplete coitus," and the immediate harm done by douches to a woman's organs when "congested and turgid with blood." "Often too, women add strong medicinal agents, intended to destroy by dissolution the spermatic germs, ere they have time to fulfil their natural destiny." Such astringents eventually result in "debility and exhaustion, signalized by leucorrhoea, prolapsus and other diseases."[25]

In "Physical Decline" Gardner said any difficulties "in prospect" that a woman attempted to avoid by using contraceptives were

"imaginary" compared to the certainty of the effects of contraceptives—"a host of ills that will leave no rest or comfort to be found."
Those certain ills included the inevitably vague but constant refrain
running throughout nineteenth-century American gynecological
case accounts—"local congestions, nervous affections, and debilities," and the pain, weakness, neuralgia miseries, languor, and listlessness Gardner also attributed to abortion. The state new women
were in provided Gardner with an excuse for his analysis of the
sexual condition of the body politic and a justification for gynecological practice. His admission of the failure of doctors to find causes
for effects in the case of the diseases he wanted to believe derived
from contraception included the kind of biased prognosis he made of
the effects of abortions. Again the punishment fit the crime, diagnosis no more than moralism and sexual prejudice, the betrayal of
the effects of American life on male attitudes toward women.

> Inquiry of any gynecologist will convince the most skeptical that
> the general employment of any means for the prevention of concep
> tion is fraught with injury to the female certainly, if not to the other
> sex also. Exactly how these evils are effected is not perhaps of easy
> explanation, for all the physiological laws are not known, but on this
> fact there is no mistake, and reasonably enough, for sexual congress
> is thus rendered by a species of self-abuse.

In spite of his admitted ignorance he could still assert:

> We know the toil and wear connected with the raising of large
> families and we can willingly concede something to the statement;
> but it is far more observable that the efforts at the present day, made
> to avoid propagation, are ten thousand fold more disastrous to the
> health and constitution to say nothing of the demoralization of mind
> and heart which cannot be estimated by red cheeks or physical vigor.

In 1882 Dr. O. E. Herrick, in one of the earliest articles in favor of
contraception published in a medical journal, argued that "since
many of the diseases of women are associated with childbearing, the
incidence of these diseases would be reduced if offspring were
limited. There are large numbers of couples, married for many
years, who have practiced prevention during the whole course of
their married life without injury."[26]
I should point out that it is plausible that some of the contraceptive astringent douches Gardner mentioned could have caused
injury to a woman's organs and opened the way to infection. But my
chief concern is the sexual attitudes of American men, and not the

question of whether or not the contraception they favored or opposed was damaging or effective, unless such a question can tell us something more about male psychology. Gardner's opposition to contraception seems to have been the expression of his sexual anxieties.

Gardner's final contribution to his chapter opposing contraception in *Conjugal Sins* took up the

> use of intermediate tegumentary coverings [that is, condoms] made of thin rubber, or gold-beater's skin, and so often relied upon as absolute preventives. . . . Their employment certainly must produce a feeling of shame and disgust utterly destructive of the true delight of pure hearts and refined sensibilities. They are suggestive of licentiousness and the brothel, and their employment degrades to beastiality the true feelings of manhood and the holy state of matrimony. . . . Furthermore they produce (as alleged by the best modern French writers, who are more familiar with the effects of their use than we are in the United States) certain physical lesions from their irritating presence as foreign bodies, and also from the chemicals employed in their manufacture. . . .

I will take the points of this paragraph in reverse order. If women demanded the use of contraceptives and contraceptives damaged a man's penis (as well as the vagina), then women demanded men damage their penes. Second, Gardner's admission of the greater familiarity of French writers with the effects of condoms (surely an oblique explanation for his extensive quotation of them) reflected a time lag between France and America in the general acceptance of contraception.[27]

Third, Gardner showed he believed that nonproductive sexual intercourse engaged in for licentious reasons, that is, for pleasure, was at variance with sublimated feelings derived by "pure hearts and refined sensibilities," presumably from the knowledge that their intercourse would result in the elevation of woman into the abstraction of holy maternity. The use of contraceptives turned the wife into a prostitute and the husband into her client. In *Sterility*, Gardner had said: "Conception is prevented and pregnancy interrupted by excessive intercourse with the married as with the courtezan, and if not generally, at least with sufficient frequency as to be noted and guarded against." Since he argued that the female complaints described in "Physical Decline" and *Conjugal Sins* were the symptoms of woman's chosen transgressions, then it was wives who made themselves prostitutes, and thereby led their husbands to see themselves as clients, or worse. In sum, men were forced into a degrading version of copulation at the behest of their appetitive wives who wanted bestial, licentious copulation and not the redeeming outcome of child production. Gardner believed with Sims that women should endure copulation, not enjoy it, and thus should echo their husbands' copulative anxieties. Gardner's argument here seems to reflect and attempt to reverse the feminist observation that the completely dependent position of woman in nineteenth-century marriage, spending what her husband earned, made her in effect a prostitute.[28]

These connections explain perhaps why Gardner said the use of a condom degraded the "true feelings of manhood." That particular kind of contraception touched him more immediately, of course, than a douche, and it could damage his mark of distinction, his penis. But Gardner's concluding metaphor for the effects of contraception makes even clearer why it was he felt contraception affected manhood so seriously. "I will not further enlarge upon these instrumentalities. . . . It matters little whether a railroad train is thrown from the track by a frozen drop of rain or a huge boulder lying in the way, the result is the same, the injuries as great." According to Gardner, the railroad train and its track stood for the conjunction of sexual organs in copulation, and the drop of frozen rain (he had twice described the damaging effects of cold water douches two pages earlier) and the huge boulder stood for contraceptive "instrumentalities." In *Old Wine* Gardner had demonstrated his identification with the "iron horse," and for him steam locomotion was the great manifestation of male power. This metaphor therefore suggests that Gardner saw sexual intercourse as an occasion for men to identify with great male technological success, in a fantasy accessible to all men. Men could impose on their wives the role they had nature play as an escape from woman in the first place, and see them not as women, but as virgin land (or tracks thereon). They could substitute the "natural destiny" of their spermatic germs for the manifest destiny of successfully going West. So when copulating, they weren't making love to a woman but were pretending they were like Hall's locomotive pretending it was a bridegroom. But the same fears that drove them to this fantasy of a fantasy (and the next stop on the line, the fantasy of finding and refining the gold of her body) could thwart the whole construction and destroy what Gardner called the "natural destiny" of their "spermatic germs."[29]

In Gardner's view, contracepted intercourse affected the male's physiology through his mind and his work. But the effects on a woman were more serious. According to the French authority Gardner quoted,

the uterine neck, the same as the penis, is congested during copulation. But while with man the congestion is dissipated with the stimulus that has provoked it, in the woman it persists for a greater or less degree, when the genital function is not physiologically completed, and new congestions coming to be successively added to the preceding, under the same circumstances, there results, first a flammatory or atonic engorgement, then ulcerations, and finally—particularly if there be some predisposition [to] encephaloid degenerations, to which so many poor creatures owe a premature death.

Such intercourse provoked in woman

desires which are not gratified . . . a storm which is not appeased. . . . There occurs then what would take place, if, presenting food to a famished man, one should snatch it from his mouth, after having thus violently excited his appetite. The sensibilities of the womb and the entire reproductive system are teased for no purpose. It is to this cause, too often repeated, that we should attribute the multiple neuroses, those strange affections which originate in the genital system of woman.[30]

The view of the vagina as a consuming mouth was common to Sims and Gardner. The food it demanded was sperm. According to *Conjugal Sins,* Mayer asserted a connection existed between the arousal and frustration of a woman's procreative faculties and the frequency of her neuralgias, uterine enervation, and degeneration of the womb. He said it was probable that

the ejaculation and contact of the sperm with the uterine neck, constitutes for the woman, the crisis of the genital function by appeasing the venereal orgasm and calming the voluptuous emotions, under the action of which the entire economy is convulsed. . . . And finally, who can demonstrate that there does not exist in the fecundatory liquid some special property *sui generis* which makes its projection upon the mouth of the womb, and its contact with this part, an indispensable condition to the innocuousness of coitus?

Copulation aroused normally refined woman to a creature of demanding appetite that must be appeased if coitus was to be rendered harmless. In copulation a woman became a hungry mouth to be fed, a crisis-ridden storm, a convulsive, consuming entity to be propitiated, as violent in appetite as an excited man. And only the magic of sperm could fend off this creature and change it back into a woman of "perfect calm . . . gaiety and warmth of heart."[31]

This attitude was common to the American views of sexual intercourse and contraception; the sales of *Conjugal Sins* gave them further currency for more than fifty years, along with Gardner's additions, his blaming of women, and his linking contraception to American male sexual anxieties and the fantasies to which they gave rise. It is male sexual anxieties to which one should look for part of the explanation for the decline in the WASP birth rate in the nineteenth century.

The third of women's sins ("venial" compared to the others) to which Gardner attributed the remarkable array of female diseases was masturbation. Gardner's belief that masturbation was widespread geographically and socially and that America led the world in the incidence of masturbation among its female population must be placed alongside American gynecology's uniquely long-lived and extreme surgical treatment of female masturbators. Gardner's anxiety about masturbating women and his claim that they fell under the new specialty's jurisdiction represented a new stage in the history of masturbation phobia, a stage not relinquishing the male target but adding females to it and concentrating the most radical treatment on them.[32]

So distinctive an American characteristic was the extent of female masturbation that

[f]oreigners are especially struck with this fact as the cause of much of the physical disease of our young women. They recognize it in the physique, in the sodden, colorless countenance, the lack-luster eye, in the dreamy indolence, the general carriage, the constant demeanor indicative of distrust, mingled boldness and timidity, and a series of anomalous combinations which mark this genus of physical and moral decay.

Gardner traced the prevalence of masturbation from these clues, as he had done in the cases of abortion and contraception. What made it particularly difficult to give statistics was that deception was a symptom of masturbation (although it allowed doctors full freedom to fantasize). Masturbation

is not a matter within the scope of general investigation; truth is not to be expected from its *habitués*, parents are deceived respecting it, believing rather what they wish than what they fear. Even the physician can but suspect, till time develops more fully by hysterias, epilepsies, spinal irritations, and a train of symptoms unmistakable even if the finally extorted confession of the poor victim did not render the matter clear.[33]

The apprehension that they were being deceived ran throughout doctors' and gynecologists' accounts of cases of masturbation. Male masturbators were believed to lie about their activity too. But the belief that a woman who should "Be a mother!" and may have been representing herself as one was in reality "degrading the nuptial couch" by indulging in the secret vice coincided with the generally dual vision of women. They were seen as all maternal love and as obliterators, pure and insatiably appetitive, an ambivalence corresponding to the split view of human psychology—physical energy, and willed, sublimated organization—that men held of themselves, and which they saw having a geographical correlative in America. The distrust in the relation between doctors and what they believed to be masturbating females reflected general male feelings about women and sex, although the conditions were set for a spiral of mutual distrust. That doctors were defending sexual orthodoxy (including their dominance) and applying moral and social norms to their cases is made clear by Gardner's typical view of the doctor's role to "extort confessions" from masturbators. The reality of victimization was close to the surface when he described the patient as "the poor victim," especially since he regarded her as the victim of a condition—masturbation—that he defined and detected, and of which her denial was only further evidence for her guilt.

Gardner had two explanations for his belief that the habit of masturbation naturally snowballed. One was that women became jaded by aesthetic stimulation, "dead to all ordinary sensations," and were forced to move on to bigger and better bestialities. Two pages previously he had argued that women who masturbated were the "unfortunate," affected by a

nervous super-excitation, and in whom the least impression is redoubled like that of a "tam-tam," [who seek] for emotions still more violent and more varied. It is this necessity which nothing can appease, which took the Roman women to the spectacles where men were devoured by ferocious beasts, and which now actually attracts them to bull-fights and capital executions. It is the emptiness of an unquiet and sombre soul seeking some activity, which clings to the slightest incident of life, to elicit from it some emotion which forever escapes; in short, it is the deception and disgust of existence.

In the first chapter of the book he had said that women's diseases, caused by their new life style and its sins, rendered "the days and nights of their unhappy possessors, hours of uselessness, and often of actual misery, and making of life itself a burden which is worse than valueless." He was observing not the effects of woman's alienation, but the causes.[34]

According to Gardner, watching ferocious beasts devour men had the same effects on women as meretricious theater performances; the same women who showed the unnatural sexual appetite of masturbation would become mothers who "fed" on their sons. Masturbation was an

> utterly uncontrollable frenzy, [an] unnatural appetite which will not be appeased, which defies bars and bolts, the rigors of a bread and water diet, the constraint of fetters and the straight jacket, the threats of punishment, and its actual severe physical castigation, [an] indulgence [which] of itself will, of necessity, destroy the throne of reason, from the overthrow of all nervous power.

Itself a sin of "the bagnio," its practitioners attracted to "capital executions" (a projected enactment of the severing of reason from passion), the masturbatory appetite could break out from the kind of medical-penological control with which Gardner identified in facing the imprisoning and murderous sexuality of woman.[35]

But Gardner's work also reflected the older form of masturbation phobia, holding that masturbation was a *male* sin. This equivocal paragraph from *Conjugal Sins* represents the conflict. "Far less common, indeed, is [masturbation] among females than among the male youth of this country; perhaps, too, less disastrous in its results to the mental and physical economy; yet much of the worthlessness, lassitude and physical and mental feebleness attributable to the modern woman are to be ascribed to these habits as their initial cause." He vacillated in extreme terms over the incidence of masturbation in woman, in his "Physical Decline of American Woman," and *Our Children,* as well as in *Conjugal Sins.* The equivocation would continue throughout doctors' sexually invidious operative treatment of masturbation. It reflected a fundamentally ambivalent attitude toward woman's sexuality and the transition to a world where men would have to acknowledge woman's desire.[36]

23　　Punishing Women

Gardner attempted to sway his readers by contrasting the new woman's sexual transgressions with the social norm of good female behavior. He said that once women had "recourse" to masturbation, "then farewell to female purity, to virtue, to anything worthy!" Female purity stood for all social worth: the social body's purity was in woman's hands. The complementary rhetoric was that men were acceptably base, appetitive creatures, engrossed in sordid traffic, the whirl and contact with the world. Woman's symbolic aggrandizement as purity and man's self-abasement as sordid and dirty was an exact reversal of another set of deeper and just as commonly expressed feelings, that man was above woman as head was above body.

In her deified form woman did not have feelings of sensuality and appetite, and did not take pleasure in copulation: "sensuality," Gardner said, was "unusual in the sex." Woman's pleasure in copulation, including her orgasms, was dismissed as irrelevant to the scientific perspective Gardner cut out for himself. He warned that an aroused woman could have destructive effects on the man with whom she was copulating. He fenced "the act" around with rules and defined copulation as religious duty and holy work. Women, he believed, should derive their deepest "interior satisfaction" from motherhood, which he sublimated. He cited with approval the case of a fellow doctor's wife who performed her childbearing duty of "one a year" and who "never has experienced any sensual gratification." She illustrated woman's natural "frigidity."[1]

Frigidity may have been natural, but parents could not take

chances. They should not overlook the "moral" (i.e., psychological)
effect dancing would have on their young daughters.

> The animal nature cannot be disregarded, and the appetite, and
> passions of some are excessively strong, and often dominate the whole
> nature. The parent cannot overlook this fact and delicacy shall not be
> allowed to prevent an allusion to it here. The natural instincts can-
> not be supplanted, if restrained and held in check. Especially, at this
> period, are they most ungovernable.
> While I would not consider that there is the least danger to virtue
> from the ordinary comminglings in the measures of the mazy dance,
> there is an unrestrainable excitation of the senses from the sight, tone,
> and contact of the sexes, and the imagination is stimulated and react-
> ing on the body, a warring in the elements commences, which is
> perhaps, borne in quiet, perhaps, is immediately manifested in faint-
> ing, in paroxysms of intense pain, or in the spasms of hysteria. How
> far better, an avoidance at these periods, of any such opportunities
> for the initiation of difficulties, that may be the seeds of life-long
> disease.

The phrase "at these periods" refers to menstruation. While the
danger was not limited to the time of menstruation or to youth, it
was particularly keen then. If sensuality was unusual in the sex it
was only as the result of the constant imposition of strict controls.
Woman could go out of control so easily. Parents, doctors, and
husbands had to shore up woman's own capacity to repress her most
vehement passions and throw a shelter around her, not to protect
her from other people's explosiveness but from her own. At the
same time, outer forces—seen, heard, and touched—could ally themselves with her own "instincts" and operate on her mind and body
in the way that Brigham's and Ray's books illustrated.[2]
Using the same social metaphor that Freud used in a virtually
identical context, Gardner described woman's psychological condition as war, her better elements fighting for domination of the self
with appetite, passions, and natural instincts. The latter part of her
was "almost ungovernable" but had to be restrained and held in
check if the virtuous and delicate mask was to be created and remain
in place. It was a microcosmic struggle between civilization and
"animal nature" and, in Gardner's view, lasted a lifetime. But soon
after the publication of *Our Children,* Robert Battey did find a
method of supplanting woman's "natural instincts," thereby deciding the struggle in favor of virtue, delicacy, and the permanent
government of woman's appetite.
So underlying men's wish that their women be delicate, not sen-

suous, even frigid, was the apprehension that women were by definition always on the verge of being sexually appetitive, in the same
way that they were nervous and liable to insanity. A woman's
physical capacity for sexual intercourse was unlimited, in direct contrast to a man's. The most concise statement of this that Gardner
supplied was by way of his translation and quotation of the French
expert, Claude-François Lallemand, in *Conjugal Sins*. "To the man
there is the limitation of a physical capability which no stimulants
from within or without can goad to further excess. The erethism of
woman has no boundary." The context—a very specific account of
excess in sexual intercourse—strongly suggests that the language
referred to male and female orgasm, the former limited, the latter
potentially multiple. That physiological fact could take on a horrifying meaning to men already obsessed with female power and the
limitations of their own spermatic economy.[3]

Gardner agreed with European authorities that hysteria was not,
as previously believed, caused by continence. "Hysteria . . . is un-
questionably the result, in my opinion, of uterine irritation, be it
produced as it may. More often is it found as the result of excess in
venery than as connected with its entire absence." In *Our Children*
he wrote of hysteria: "It is a very common female trouble, one productive of great annoyance and anxiety. It is a complaint intimately
allied to the sexual organs of females . . . connected with it is invariably a local disease of the sexual organs." This was a typical
assertion, and it would provide a rationale for the surgical treatment
of hysteria.[4]

Woman's greater sexual capacity explained the deadly danger
"exercise of the genital sense" posed to an old man married to a
young girl. "These dangers exist only for the man, as is easy to
imagine; but they are all the more dangerous as the young bride is
more or less capable of over-exciting the sexual appetites. . . .
Unfortunate is the imprudent man who dares to drink without
care from this cup of delight. Nature knows how, in such a case,
to punish cruelly any infraction of her laws." The absorptive, consuming quality is transferred to the male (daring to drink), perhaps
as a defense against the danger the fear represented. The young wife,
"over-exciting the sexual appetite," was the agent of the larger,
unassailable, and punitive female power with which we have seen
Gardner associated motherhood.[5]

There were other ways in which men conceived woman to threaten
them in copulation. In his 1864 article "Gonorrhoea: A Non-Specific Disease," Gardner said: "Women sometimes, and not very in-

frequently, communicate disease to those men who have sexual intercourse with them, in close proximity to the period of their monthly courses. . . . I do not believe that a man often communicates disease to a woman." Men should avoid copulating with a woman at the times immediately proximate to her menstruation: "the human female is nearly the same [as animals], and although she may possess sensual appetites at other periods, they are notoriously heightened, somewhat anteriorly, and very manifestly immediately subsequent to this epoch." Gardner based this generalization on the evidence to which his profession gave him authoritative access. "Of this fact I am fully convinced from the testimony of very many females who have replied to my questions. . . ." This was an unqualified statement about female appetite, that its origin, unlike masturbation or physical excess, did not depend on outside stimulus, but was the regular, inescapable function of all women everywhere. All women were, in a specific sense, "notorious." And Gardner's frequent warnings about contact between the sexes during dances when the woman was having her period were charged with a concern for the danger to the man's sexual organs, as well as to the future operation of the natal mechanism.[6]

Gardner's attitude toward menstruation, like so many of the attitudes I am describing, was common to Europe and America. (I am claiming that these attitudes were more extreme in America because of the effects of more extensive social leveling on traditions otherwise common.) Most of Gardner's chapter in *Conjugal Sins* on "Conjugal Relations during the Period of Menstruation" consists of his translation of quotations from Mayer, including Mayer's quotations from "R. P. Debreyne, the celebrated Catholic casuist," and from Jules Michelet's *L'Amour*). And again, Gardner's original contribution to the chapter emphasized sexual dangers to men.[7]

The French authorities Gardner quoted revealed ignorance and fear in the face of menstruating woman. Her menstrual flow made all undue excitement dangerous to the woman herself; moreover, menstrual blood could, they said, "become corrupt" and "acquire . . . a virulence . . . participate in the other idiosyncrasies and conditions of the woman, the exact amount of which it is impossible to appreciate." The peril was not confined to woman.

> The contact of this vitiated fluid with the gland and urethra of the male organ may, and frequently does cause superficial excoriations which resemble chancres without having their gravity; blenorrhagias

which resemble specific gonorrhoeas and which would deceive us, if they did not speedily yield to appropriate treatment.

To these dangers Gardner himself added that of spermatic depletion, since women, he explained in *Sterility,* became notoriously sensual during their periods, perhaps luring their husbands to do damage to their penes (as women did by initiating contraception), finally breaking them in frame and health.[8]

The doctors projected onto woman the definition of menstruation as a source of disease:

> The woman when she has her periods takes the greatest care to conceal it from all eyes. She is affected instinctively, we will not say willingly, in her dignity. She considers her condition as a blot or infirmity; and although her modesty—the most incendiary of the female virtues—has been spared by the omnipotence of her husband she blushes to herself at the tribute which she is compelled to pay to nature. To constrain her in this condition, is evidently to do violence to what is most respectable in her nature; it is to rob her of the prestige which the graces of her sex assure to her. Do not seek to contradict such legitimate repugnance. The first step in this path infallibly leads to ruptures the most to be regretted.

The implication was that woman would rather not have periods, that is, would share Gardner's definition of female health as disembodiment, his transformation of the reality of gestation, parturition, and lactation into "holy maternity." Woman should regard a normal part of her existence as a sickness, an "infirmity," while the term "blot" connoted a stain or a disgrace. Believing that her sensuality was notoriously aroused during her periods, men attempted to have her stifle them by persuading her that they found such repression most "incendiary" of all (by definition it did not require a sexual response on their part). This could be a paradigm of the male attempt to shape women. The claim was that a man showed his "omnipotence" by sparing his wife copulation, but he was protecting himself against her appetite and its dangerous effects on his penis. Her prestige depended on her hiding her body's functions. Men granted to her the validity of her introjection of male feelings, legitimizing repugnance.[9]

Bertrand Russell said of his first wife, Alys Pearsall Smith, that she

> had been brought up, as American women always were in those days, to think that sex was beastly, that all women hated it, and that men's

brutal lusts were the chief obstacle to happiness in marriage. She therefore thought that intercourse should only take place when children were desired. As we had decided to have no children, she had to modify her position on this point, but she still supposed that she would desire intercourse to be very rare.

As I have suggested in connection with a number of other cases, this well-known female attitude was the interiorization (thence handed on) of male desires, in accordance with men's experience inside and outside the family. This delicacy was shared by figures as apparently disparate as Lantern-Jawed Bob, Marvel's bachelor, Cooper, Todd, Dr. Gardner, and, of course, all of the doctors and clergymen attempting to reimpose the modest and delicate role upon women. While their language—and world view—does reveal these feelings of sexual repugnance, it has been far more usual to encounter its direct expression in women.[10]

Nor were gestation and parturition free of the destructive dangers that women represented to men, as Gardner's prison metaphors have already suggested. Prisons were also like ships. According to Gardner the master of the Boston House of Correction was "at the helm." In fact both prisons and palaces were like ships: "The difference in the architecture, and the whole external appearance render comparison as impossible, as one between a ship of the line and a pleasure yacht." In *Our Children* Gardner made more direct his association of ship and womb.

How sturdy is the duty imposed upon woman: If there is considered to be an idea of awe connected with the ship that bore the ashes of the dead Napoleon from·Saint Helena, to the Paris of his love; if there be sanctity connected with the burial place of kings and common men and paupers—there, where we are all alike—surely there is a holiness connected with maternity. The germs of immortality are struggling beneath that mother's breast, and the whole powers of nature are quickened and developed, and exhausted, to perfect this grandest of works—a labor wherein man and divinity work together—one which oft repeated as it is, is still a constant miracle: one that calls down the constant blessing of heaven. To this work where God does his part, man surely should give his best efforts—no immature, defective offering—but the concentrated powers of perfected nature.[11]

Gardner said that woman's gestating a fetus aroused feelings in him similar to those aroused by a ship bearing a dead man with whom Gardner admitted he identified. He had personified Paris as a "voluptuous" woman before, into whose lap men poured the most valuable things. So the ashes of Napoleon were one more tribute, and his loving relation with her took on the deadly appetitive meaning of a man feeding an insatiable woman with his body. To Gardner, maternal and copulative woman reflected each other's terrors. A mother's womb reminded him, too, of a grave to which all men bore the same relation whether they were rich or poor. Todd had compared gestation to a pilgrimage "almost to the grave." For these men the womb's generative power connoted death to men (and obstetricians soon translated such feelings into the rationale for their control of parturition: birth was deadly dangerous, and parturient woman was a patient). We have seen that Gardner wanted to exclude women from prison visits, and from possible service on board ships; he also wanted to exclude them from midwifery—and even from parturition altogether.

These fears and fantasies about woman's sexuality charged his obstetrical role. "Startling and fearful as may be the sight of streams of blood and clotted gore in various scenes, there are none found more appalling than in the obstetric chamber; none where more instant aid is required, and where the whole energies of the medical attendant are so imperatively demanded, or where presence of mind is more important." Blood in a sexual context had several meanings to Gardner: the blood of executions in a womblike prison, woman's dangerous menstrual blood, and the spermatic distillation of blood, the summary of a man's whole being also evoked in this passage. By "medical attendant" here Gardner meant obstetrician, and, of course, he was expressing his own feelings in the position. He faced the irresistible demands of what he regarded as the culmination of a power he could not duplicate, a natural, bloody power he had to rival and which could destroy him. "Presence of mind" takes on the very specific meaning of overwhelming his own fears, triumphing over matter, representing science's successful control of nature and man's of woman and manifesting the successful translation of his "whole energies" to do so. It was a control man should demonstrate in facing potentially imperious woman in copulation.[12]

Gardner tried or imagined several ways of dealing with explosive women and sexuality. His career, and the rise of gynecology, were yoked to that purpose. He believed that "Science . . . in its future progress may yet refine us and separate the pure from the impure." The branch he chose was obstetrical medicine, and he applied the Manichaean principle to the body politic, agreeing with the proposition that it was "a crime to be sick." Modern women, then, were criminals, their sexual diseases symptoms of social transgressions for which gynecology supplied detection, judgment, and punishment. Nineteenth-century gynecological cases are thick with such legal metaphors. Conversely, "Health was the great prophylactic against sin. . . . The vigor of the body is the basis for a robust morality." Gardner held the effects of disease to be punishment. His own language suggests he wanted to bring women's imprisoning wombs under control by acting as if he were a prison reformer, cleaning up, ventilating, and even sterilizing prison cells. In fact, he said he would have liked to do away with criminals—and prisons—altogether. Gardner also wanted to purge society of the wombs whose owners contravened natural law, flouted male authority, and burdened society with criminal sickness.[13]

Gardner warned the American people that "while we shall seek for physical excellence, it will be found that as a corollary, mental and spiritual perfection follow clearly in its wake." For the benefit of future generations men and women should purify and refine their copulations above what Gardner called the gross, animal realities. But for immediate and ongoing social necessity, men should separate themselves in a general sense from the impurity of women, according to the dictates of scientific medicine, copulating rarely and under strict guidelines. The project was a renewed formulation of the traditional attitudes I have described, a more specific version of the attitude epitomized by Beaumont's observation that "kissing families" in America were considered deviant.[14]

Gardner's fear and hostility toward woman's sexual organs explains why he liked best those women who were cut off from copulative and reproductive functions. In *Old Wine* he described nuns as having transformed appetite into their simply nursing people. "When I see these women thus engaged, I forget that they are attendants and nurses, and regard them with sentiment of veneration. They appear to me to be fulfilling a holy mission upon earth." American men wanted their wives cloistered. The most salient feature of their sanctimonious pedestal rhetoric was its denial of woman's sexuality; men were devoted to an ideal by definition disembodied, and identified it with mother. Gardner dedicated his translation of Scanzoni's *Sexual Organs,* invidiously, to his father "scarce weakened" and "To the Memory of a Sainted Mother, whose Approbation is still the incentive and reward of every worthy act, This Volume is Reverentially Inscribed." Acknowledging the totality of power a mother exercised over her son (such acknowledgment was typical), this rhetoric incorporated a defense against it: the sublimation of parturient, flesh-and-blood maternity into sanctity. Women should be like nuns to preserve their sons from fear of mother's organs.[15]

There were other ways a woman could become nunlike. According to Gardner, female disease was commensurate with her sexuality; the freer, more appetitive a woman in her sex life, the more diseased. For the same reason he believed "these diseases rare in the virgin."[16] Defining the ideal woman as incorporeal, health as disembodiment, the doctor welcomed the disease that destroyed a woman's body:

> the most marked evidence of the benefits to the whole character is seen in those early afflicted by that disease of lingering suffering, commonly known as white swelling, and usually originating from some accident. What angelic serenity! What beautific gentleness and love! What a mild radiance pervading the whole being of one of those afflicted! Those days and nights, those weeks and months of persistent agony have purified the whole nature, have seemingly eliminated every grain of gross alloy, and left the fine gold, purified as by fire. . . . I never enter into the presence of these "deformed transformed," into a vision as of heaven's purity and beauty come down to earth, but what I feel that these compensations are not limited to the mere physical strengthening of other kindred organs and facilities; but that this baptism of pain and privation has regenerated the individual's whole nature, and as the physical creature has been weakened and destroyed, the spiritual being, in humble, submissive resignation to the loss which it has sustained, has been nurtured and strengthened by resignation, and beautified, by the chastening made but a little lower than the angels, and seemingly wanting but their cerulean pinions to wing their joyous way to more congenial spheres, where both sufferings and their scars are forgotten, rendered invisible, and renounced, as the mere scaffoldings by which they have mounted into heaven.[17]

The woman Gardner most admired was the one physically destroyed, the grossness of her body eliminated, the person transformed into an abstraction. The terms reproduced Gardner's sublimation of gestation, parturition, lactation, and all the rest into the abstraction of sainted motherhood, and I will repeat it: he said that by bearing children woman "shall gild a virtuous life with brightest gold and as a true mother raise her to a pinnacle of glory that man can ever attain, creating herself an object of the sublimest adoration to be henceforth respected by all mankind, an object of reverence and worship, by her own children, next to her God." Gardner's desire to transform modern woman into such a being was based perhaps on his transformation of the reality of his own mother into a saint. The fantasy was a defense against the reality, and I have suggested that defense was the reason and the model for the attempts at proto-sublimation, objectified and reinforced in the man's relationship to the wife he wanted to be mother. Much of the language here is identical to nineteenth-century men's descriptions of their wives.

Donald Meyer suggests how the "moral" change in a woman Gardner perceived might look from her own point of view, her own understanding and transmogrification of what men demanded of her.

> Natural, normative respectable female existence decreed the passivity and weakness of woman. In that event, where was salvation but in demanding a world for the weak? . . . What then if passivity could be strength? . . . She could make herself sick. Though she was exalted, something was wrong; but though something was wrong, she was weak. To be sick was a route for the pure but weak, neither the masterful, aggressive reform of reality by the strong nor the anarchic selfish rebellion of the weak and impure to make oneself sick was an escape, for it invited a project which at the same time did not require one to wrestle with the world.

The "aggressive reform of reality" in Gardner's case seems to have included feelings of pleasure in women's "lingering suffering," "week and months of persistent agony," and "baptism of pain and privation," a suggestion borne out by analysis of his surgical orientation.[18]

Gardner's approval of the cloistering and sublimating of women was intimately connected to his feelings toward his mother's bearing him. Lured, perhaps, by his preoccupation with women he deemed out of control, Gardner attended a women's rights convention session.

> There was a most touching pathos, in the words which fell from the lips of a woman-speaker, at a late Woman's Rights Convention. After a plea for the equality for either sex for equal work, in which she said that this would do much to take away the sin, and prevent the shame of 20,000 women of this city, living lives that could not be described, she said, with a tone I shall not forget, "There is something holy in maternity!" . . . I felt then, as her soft sweet voice enunciated this truth—I have felt it often before, without possessing a consciousness of this thrilling truth—however abject may be the

mother, however low and degraded may have been her life, however
ignorant her mind, or low her birth, or despised her race, when I
recall her sufferings, when I think of the sainted mother to whose
agonies I owe my own existence, my heart echoes back to Mrs. Kerr's
thrilling words: "There is something holy in maternity". . . .

Mrs. Kerr says that the ballot for women, i.e. equality with man
will remedy this [being a prostitute]. Pray God it may. Yet the
fashionist of the day forgets the laws of love, religion, and the joys of
matrimony, and may by every hellish art seek to prevent and subvert
the laws of nature, of life, and of love . . . [f]or the sake of dress,
and fashion, and ease. . . . When women do vote, may they vote
their sex a Retreat, with the words engraven over its portals *"There
is something holy in maternity."*[19]

He confessed that the notion of motherhood touched a deep
chord; it "thrilled" him, and at least part of the thrill derived from
the agony the issuance of his own body had caused his mother. As
we saw earlier in this chapter, Gardner connected "the holiness of
maternity" with the death of males, so perhaps he felt woman's
birth pangs were just recompense for such a threat. Or vice versa;
he said he felt his dependence on his mother for existence as a psychic debt, a feeling perhaps synonymous with guilt. Once the spiral
of guilt and hostility had begun, it would be impossible to distinguish one from the other.

Now the general meaning of this passage about Mrs. Kerr is very
close to his account of the effects on women of the white swelling
disease in which suffering and pain purged a woman of body, made
her a saint. In the Kerr passage he implied that feminism, prostitution, abortion, and fashion were all equally bad, they were diseases
even, since they needed a "remedy," and all of them could be cured
if women would reduce themselves to childbearing. They then
would experience purgation by way of birth agonies, and be sublimated as saints, just like Gardner's mother. Women should be
secluded as sexual mechanisms in a place very much like a cloister
or a sanitarium: indeed, Gardner's only other use of the term "retreat" that I recall was the "retreats for the insane" that contained
the human evidence for the frequency of female masturbation.
Woman's sexual organs brought her close to insanity, an association
Gardner made several times. In any case Gardner wanted to place
all women in a position—having babies—over which the obstetrician
would preside. He wanted to cure them by making them dependent
on a doctor, in a retreat behind portals, that is, by making them patients. He could take charge of motherhood, take charge of the pro-

cess his own mother epitomized, and of all woman's maternal functions. He required women to experience maternal suffering. But he would be in a position to inflict agonies on them himself, in part as a way of dealing with his own guilt over the pain he had caused his mother, and of which his obstetrics would remind him continually. He would punish mothers in the way he felt he should be punished for having inflicted such pain on his mother.

In *Old Wine,* Gardner's surgical ambitions had been directed partly toward his control of woman's reproductive power. In the same book he had anthropomorphized trees as women: the "trees and shrubbery in the gardens are evidently thinking of putting on their green dresses, and their swollen buds foretell new charm." Man's cutting and treatment of their bodies perfected them. "By constant pruning and attention their symmetry is rendered perfect. The branches, which when bare and leafless in winter have such an air of prudery, now clothed in gay attire, and adorned with their blossoms. . . ." The metaphor suggests to what extent he believed women's bare and barren bodies depended on men's instrumental science to bear.[20]

The characteristics Gardner admired and emulated in his operations were identical to those Sims said were typical of American surgery and other male achievements:

> My esteemed friend Dr. H. Weeks Brown of this city, during the last year united the labia majora, the only operation possible, to relieve the dire effects of a complete prolapsus uteri. This serious and bold operation was entirely successful. Within a few months, I assisted my friend, Dr. Sims in his operation—*the* operation of the century—for vesico vaginal fistula. The base of the bladder was entirely destroyed, and the only possible operation was to destroy the vagina. This unique and hazardous, yet successful operation, was effected by passing sutures of silver wire, fastened by clamps from the rectum posteriously, through the labia majora anteriorly.

Gardner's satisfaction at the success of these particular operations was not unrelated to his attitude toward woman's sexual organs and his belief that disembodiment was health. He had helped these two patients on their way to a purer, more sublime existence. Both Weeks Brown and Sims would become proponents of female castration, the removal of woman's ovaries largely to rid her of sexual "symptoms." In *Our Children,* Gardner noted how surgery could bring about the same morally beneficial results as the white swelling disease. He said that the loss of a limb could turn "the fiery, impetuous temper of a soldier into gentleness and peace . . . his after life evinces the moral growth after a physical pruning, as we see fruits in our orchard increased and sweetened by the lopping off of a limb." This could stand for the guiding belief of the gynecological treatment of disorderly women for the next half century.[21]

The most radical surgery following such a rationale was only just getting under way at the end of Gardner's life. Nonetheless his last professional article describing the "Causes and Cure" of the ruptured perineum in parturient woman suggests Gardner was moving in a more radical direction. Gardner said the accusations that obstetricians ruptured perinea were "more denunciatory than true." Accusations, denunciations, their repudiation, and, more significantly, the responses of the male experts to gynecological diseases all existed in the context of ferocious male rivalry that Gardner had faced from his return to New York in 1848 to the date of this article, 1874, two years before his death. Such a context explains, in part, why gynecologists saw the woman's condition belonging to themselves.

> We all know the feelings of the accoucheur to whom this grave accident has happened. We all know the envies and jealousies of the profession. We know how the former desires to screen himself, and how easy it is to say "rigid perinaeum," "deviations in the bony structure," "head too unyielding, large, etc.," "too old, or too young a mother;" and better still, how easy to attribute this sad result to unskillfulness of the (former) attending physician—especially if of another "school,"—to "want of care when instruments are used."

But it was in this selfsame article that Gardner expressed his own ambivalent feelings toward Sims, and his operation for the cure of the ruptured perineum was an attempt to rival Sims and to come up with a procedure that would enter medical history as "Gardner's Operation." That such an ambition existed in relation to male heroics out West is brought home to us by the inclusion of a two-line column filler in this professional journal, *The Medical Union,* at the end of Gardner's article, affirming a doctor's successful conquest of a female disorder. "New and very rich gold mines are being discovered in Australia and California."[22]

In spite of Gardner's recognition that the obstetrician, hurt by the ruptured perineum's happening to him, blamed the woman as a "screen" for his own responsibility, Gardner went on to argue that the condition was due to the patient herself, her "excessive vigor and a too great muscular energy." Her generative tract had the power of a gun. "We scientifically know that a candle can be shot through a board; but *momentum* seems to be forgotten in obstetrics. . . . We read of cases where the head has punctured the perinaeum, going through it, avoiding both the vaginal and rectal canals. These are the bullet heads, which have gone through, like the candle through the board, by excess of speed!" These are very suggestive similes. He compared a woman's life-bearing function to a death-dealing one, her womb a gun, her baby a projectile entirely dependent on her for propulsion (Gardner saw his mother as the "incentive" for all of his acts). The mother expelled her baby in an act of aggression against the world. It became a hard, death-dealing missile because of its mother's explosive effects upon it. But it was a Jekyll and Hyde of a baby, a hard, metal bullet that could go soft, turn into a candle that could so easily melt or burn out—or harden again under the impetus imparted by its mother, to fly, bulletlike, through a board. The metaphor might stand as a summary for how men viewed themselves and whence they derived that view.[23]

The most significant part of the article in suggesting Gardner's feelings about gynecological surgery was another metaphor, like the gun explaining the womb's power to expel the baby in the wrong way:

> How many of us have practically felt the strained perinaeum under our hand, and we have urged upon our patient to refrain from all voluntary expulsive efforts. But the jaded uterus, with a sudden burst of energy—like a fagged horse near to home, that takes the bit between its teeth, and spite of all attempts at restraint, rushes impetuously to finish its journey—defies all our efforts and the mother's uncertain will, and we feel the leathery band under our very fingers, despite our most energetic efforts to hold back the head, yield, crack and tear, with a seemingly unending continuation. . . . Had [the *accoucheur*] suspected such an eruption of nervous energy, he might have quieted it by some treatment. . . .[24]

The picture of a woman unsuccessfully applying her unreliable, weak will to the explosively energetic animal in her was a familiar one, and this occasion was an illustration of the general view of woman's psychology. She was supposed to use her will to repress her "voluntary efforts." So powerful was the animal in her that it overcame both woman's will and the obstetrician's energetic efforts, presumably the "whole energies" Gardner believed an obstetric chamber required of the medical attendant. According to the metaphor the rider of the horse was both woman's will and the obstetrician (or rather her attempted introjection of his will, and his whole sublimated force), the typical male view of how the government of a woman worked, her own feeble effort reflecting the authority of a man. He in turn found it necessary to draw support from male ideology (under attack at this time) and from the treatment provided by gynecology and other locations of male power, religion and politics for example.

There is an ambiguity in the woman's animal nature, the horse, strained, jaded, and fagged, yet capable of a sudden, defiant, eruptive, and impetuous burst of energy breaking through all restraint. The former concealed the latter, lulling the obstetrician's suspicions. The eruption was an event he should have suspected all along; it existed beneath the surface as a horse's hard, powerful teeth exist beneath its soft, velvety muzzle. It was the same kind of energy as woman's sexual appetite. Moreover, "jaded" amplified the horsy connotations; the adjective is a derivative of the noun jade, meaning a worn-out, ill-conditioned, worthless horse, made that way by overwork or by being overridden. But it also means (and meant) a loose or disreputable woman, a term of reprobation connecting this woman, whom Gardner said had brought her condition upon herself by her idleness, with the same kind of sinful, physically declined, modern women whom Gardner associated with the brothel. The good, normal behavior of the uterus (in Gardner's world view the woman's raison d'être) was well disciplined, its owner willing herself to the manipulations of a male obstetrician. An eruptive body threw him.

The horse metaphor spanned Gardner's work. One of the two mottoes on the title page of *Old Wine* is a quotation from Disraeli's writings. "The moment that you anticipate your pen in forming a sentence, you get as stiff as a gentleman in stays; I use my pen as my horse; I guide it, and it carries me on." A man should control his horse to avoid getting stiff. A man's bending a horse to his will was a common metaphor in the nineteenth century for self-discipline, most appropriate to the ubiquitous project of proto-sublimation. Todd, for example, in the book Gardner said was so influential, described the Swedish King Charles XII riding a horse to death to illustrate the technique of inflexible self-discipline his reader should use to achieve success.[25]

Nineteenth-century man could also model his inflexibility of purpose on an even more powerful manifestation of power, his driving of a steam engine, as we have seen in the case of Melville's Ahab. It was vastly superior to the horse in power, but also it was entirely man's creation. Like his contemporaries, Gardner called the steam engine an iron horse and presented this "horse" as an expression of American power, bringing progress behind it. He regarded steam, that "great motor principle," as "the great Briareus of the nineteenth century." According to Gardner, mastery of horse and steam demonstrated the male's power specifically. Indeed, we have seen that Gardner compared the penis to an iron horse.[26]

In short, Gardner associated the idea of the horse with his own literary and sexual power (and his penmanship was a sexual assault on his readers). Man's control of the horse and its successor, the iron horse, represented his capacity to discipline his energies to the pursuit of the highest form of manhood, its fruit, progress, the mastery of nature and of the world. The term was linked to his most intimate and ambitious sense of sexual identity. And his discipline of woman, the jaded, uterine horse, was the objectification of this discipline of himself. That this was so was an additional source of anxiety when she bucked or bolted. She represented social order.

Gardner also felt that the lower part of the self that the horse represented required severe punishment, basing that belief on his own childhood experience.

> In the *punishment of misbehavior,* I think the French are not severe enough. One thorough correction, it seems to me, is more effective than many slight ones. My own experience when at school adds force to this opinion. The lower animals afford illustrations of the same principle. A horse soon becomes insensible to perpetual slight cuts of the whip, especially when administered with the characteristic gentleness of lady equestrians, whose most efficient *lashes* are those of their eyes. Thus, according to the old doggerel,
>
> > At first he starts and winces,
> > Then presently he minces,
> > Till fast asleep and dreaming
> > He thinks all drivers women.[27]

Beating with a whip was similar to the application of a knife, since the whip gave "cuts" to the body. Gardner associated the whipping of the horse with a horsewhipping he had received and with what he found sexually provocative in a woman—her ambiguous "lashes"—that "natural coquetry" which he had diagnosed as something to be disciplined, even treated medically. He had compared his professional, gynecological obligations to patients to being "hitched." But here, in this verse, the gentle cuts of a lady's whip first hurt the horse, anthropomorphized as a conscious male, and then gradually that feeling changed, until he was transported into dreams. He enjoyed the pain inflicted by a woman in a fantasy very similar to Todd's vision of woman booted and spurred. He associated the pain she brought with sexual pleasure. No wonder he believed much more violent punishment necessary to discipline a man's horse.

But what further bearing does this imagery have on Gardner's attitude toward gynecological surgery? Part of Gardner's verbal/sexual assault on the fair portion of New York was the following harrowing passage.

> The government provides poor old work horses for the use of the students, to accustom them to operate, and give them facility of execution. The unhappy creature is led in, snorting and trembling at the sight of, and smell of blood around. Before he has time to recover from his amazement, his legs are drawn firmly together, and he is thrown to the ground. A rope is twisted from a stick around his upper lip, so that his head is perfectly commanded. He lies prostrate and helpless. A dozen pupils leap upon him and begin their horrid operatior. With a red hot iron his skin is cauterized in every part of the body where the cautery is applied. One cuts off two inches of the tail, a second two more, another takes out the muscle, and a fourth a bone, till that member is entirely gone. Every variety of shoe is put upon him, his hoofs are cut to the quick, experimental nails are driven in, as if they were accidental, and dug out again. Imaginary wounds are probed. The ears are then cut off, the eyes extracted. Every artery in the body is "taken up," operations for tenotomy performed, besides many other acts of refined scientific torture. In the meantime, the poor helpless animal struggles and flounders, sighs, weeps, groans, *screams*. He cannot move. The blood oozes from a hundred orifices, "those poor dumb mouths," till finally death, the angel of mercy to the miserable among men and beasts, comes to his relief:—
>
> "And the o'erloaded slave flings down his burden."[28]

The most obvious association here is between the budding veterinarian students' patient, the horse, and the young, medical student Gardner's prospective female patient, whom he described on several occasions as a "slave." In the selfsame *Old Wine* he described the social "descent" of the grisettes, which anticipated the physical decline of American woman, and linked it to the surgical destruction of the horse. Young "and innocent now, very soon they become kept mistresses, and their descent is afterwards rapid to the conditions of the common courtezan, the street sweeper, the inmate of the hospital, *the subject of the dissecting room.*" American women were turning themselves into courtesans and, dead or alive, would soon be subjects for Gardner's knife. Gardner also used the cautery for some diseases of the female sexual organs.[29]

For Gardner the cutting up of a horse also connoted the punishment of masculinity in its genital and sublimated form, and perhaps of the son guilty of being born, and embarked on the spiral of hostility, more guilt for it, more hostility, and so on. Gardner had identified himself with the horse receiving cuts from the lady rider's whip (which suggests another reason why he may have accepted being the hireling of rich women; his position combined business with pleasure, as well as with hostility). So this vivisection of a horse also seems to have represented a male desire for radical punishment, the destruction of the genital horse and the extinction of life altogether. It incorporated the desire to turn inventive genius, medicine, and science against the male self in an act of scientific self-torture, a hatred for and relinquishment of future male progress in favor of a return to the past, to childhood, and to woman. He wished, at some level, to give up the badge of male identity, and the success which the possessor of the penis could attain. Punished, cut, tortured, blinded, castrated, and reduced to a bleeding lump, he would at last be worthy to be received by a disembodied "angel of mercy," the apotheosis of the sainted female power that Gardner saw his mother embody. The agony his birth had brought her would be redeemed.

Such destruction was a preemptive defense against the destruction by which the man felt appropriately threatened by woman-as-mother. It was a defense because it was *self*-fulfilling, self-assertion by self-obliteration, ambiguous identification with the aggressor in frustrating her. It was maternal power that Gardner had presented quenching men in bloody prison murders, women who, he said, delighted in watching wild beasts consume men and who got pleasure from watching "capital executions." According to Gardner, it was mothers who, like cannons, fired their babies from them, turned them into lethal weapons, and launched them into careers of violence, doing these things perhaps in repayment for the agonies their sons' births had brought them and in turn becoming the victims of their sons' reciprocal violence.

Gardner's surgery expressed several interlocking attitudes which were, perhaps, variants of the birth-agony cycle of guilt, hostility, projection, and identification. It was an attempt to punish women for their expulsion of men into a horrifying world of robbing and killing. It was an attempt to control what Gardner perceived as frighteningly powerful and to prevent it from fulfilling its threat to extinguish him. To the extent that he identified with woman, it represented self-extinction, both as a defense and as an expression of his desire to opt out of the terrible and enslaving burden that possession of a penis conferred on him. Some of his operations, most obviously for the treatment of sterility in woman, represented his attempt to maintain the clear distinction between sex roles. But the psychology represented by the horse metaphors, embodying hostility toward and identification with women and hostility toward and identification with men, reflected a role confusion and role dissatisfaction that threatened the sexual distinction in the first place. So, too, the sentence: "We all know the feelings of the accoucheur to whom this grave accident has happened"—that is, the perineum ruptured by parturition. The woman's body stood for his own, as indeed it furnished material for the establishment of his professional, male identity. Gardner went on to repair the sufferer's body and, in doing so, to repair his own. He admitted in the same article, "We are apt to get our remembrances of the male and female perinæum somewhat jumbled."[30]

Obstetrics was another way in which Gardner could deal with woman's power and the cycle of guilt it evoked. The entire Briareus passage, from the first page of Gardner's *History of Midwifery*, illustrates his attitude toward childbirth.

> From the foundation of the world man has been born of woman; and notwithstanding that his inventive genius has discovered steam, the great Briareus of the nineteenth century, and harnessed him to his chariot, and sends lightning to do his bidding over the almost boundless extent of the world, yet we cannot hope that any change may be affected in this particular.

The natural implication of "we cannot hope" is that the same inventive genius would like to be able to make men independent of woman (and of guilt) for reproduction, in effect, to reproduce themselves; but the most man could do was to attempt to keep woman's jaded but explosive uterus reined in, harnessed to male ambition. Woman's capacity to give birth was the standard against which Gardner measured male achievements. Man could not do what God and woman could, that is, "originate power." What he could instead, said Gardner, was "avail himself of the latent energies of water and the electric fluid." He did so by way of "the greatest piece of mechanism . . . the human hand," greater, that is, than the natal mechanism, and actuated by the male prerogative and distinction, "the propelling agency of the will." Sims, Gardner said, had a "God inspired eye" and could "do anything . . . with a needle and a bit of silver wire." The vision is that of man's organizing of latent energies—proto-sublimation—and it existed as an expression of the male's envy of female creative power, and his desire both to emulate and to transcend it.[31]

Gardner associated the female supervision of parturition with darkness, grossness, and superstition, and male supervision with light, refinement, and science. In Gardner's view progress was in male hands, man's conquest of nature linked to his subordination of woman, which was, of course, a psychologically accurate connection. "At the present time there is a proposition mooted—springing from the same high source which advocates woman's rights, the Bloomer costume, and other similar nonsensical theories—to give again the portion of the healing art, if not the whole domain of medicine, to the females." Elevation of woman in any sphere was a reversal of historical and social sublimation, the placing of what Gardner regarded as dark appetite and nearly ungovernable natural instinct over will and civilization.

> The dark ages seem to be again reviving. Hand in hand with the infinitesimals and the water-work, comes the hard-faced midwife, tinctured with both theories. . . . We have lecturers and lecturesses and female colleges, where the very large and intelligent classes are taught how to get children, and especially how not to get them. The Woman's Rights Convention cannot see why women should bear children more than men and while waiting some plans to equalize this matter, they refuse to bear them themselves.

Expanding and defending his claim for the male control of obstetrics, Gardner betrayed his underlying project—to overcome the given distinction in the procreative powers of men and women—by attributing it to his rivals. Gardner must have found it especially galling that women were willing and able to refuse to perform that very function he devoted his life to emulate, if not to assume.[32]

Gardner believed men should control both gestation and parturition. Similarly, copulation and conception should be dictated by men according to their social purposes. If they copulated when either of their vital powers were at a low ebb, a husband and wife would produce feeble offspring.

> If we could trace back the history of these puny children, the "runts" as they are unkindly styled in families, the scrofulous, weakly, ex-sanguine, nervous, prematurely old, early dying children, to the time of their conception, we should find that the great majority of them, dated their initial origin to a day of languor—and disturbance of either body or mind, or both; at times when the prospect of failure was imminent, when harassed by previous habits, disagreement with a partner, defalcation with a clerk, an illness which confined one in the midst of a busy season at home, when the oldest son or the loved daughter had done something wrong, compromised themselves or their family: when some family misunderstanding existed, when the master of the house had come home much later than usual, and a "little worse" for his evening's entertainment, and twenty years more or less afterward, you complain of certain strange idiosyncrasies in your child, and say "there were no such tendencies in your family."

The undesirable results of unregulated copulation included damage to the propagators, as well as feeble offspring. One of the chief purposes of all of Gardner's work was to provide rules, techniques, and exhortation for the prevention of such results.[1]

In Gardner's view, nineteenth-century American life was nerve-racking and made enormous demands on a man's bodily economy.

On one hand there was that "carking care," the incessant experience of business anxiety and economic crises, and the lifelong prospect of imminent failure. "When a continued mental anxiety for a long period has driven 'sleep from the eyes and slumber from the eyelids,' such as is often noticed among business men in seasons of great financial disturbance, there is threatening disease, danger of some cerebral inflammatory action, or more serious disorganization, that may destroy the intellect." Under those conditions a man should not copulate. But on the other hand, there were the dangers of success; it created unnatural appetites.

> We are living in a hot-house, where our nervous energies are developed at the expense of our physique. Life in a city, with its imperfect aeration, where we live in the shadow of great houses and behind curtains deprived of the revivifying influences of the sunbeam, the great source of life and energy, where we have the exercise of but parts of our frame, where our food is stimulating and our daily life exciting, where we read little from the calm book of nature, but much from the sensuous and feverish one-sided portrayals of dramatic painters of love and passion—this side is not nature, nor are the mad feelings which possess us nature either. The lustful cravings of our pampered selves is no more nature than is the call for brandy a natural appetite!

These conditions, said Gardner, were the causes of "physical excess" in marital copulation, a danger of which "W" had warned thirty-five years earlier. In working toward success one should conserve one's energies: having attained it, one had to be eternally vigilant to avoid debilitating expenditure. Gardner shared the ancient belief he presented in *Conjugal Sins*. "In the warlike nations of antiquity, procreation was considered debilitating." At no time should Americans lose sight of these precepts. Sexual anxiety was as much a disease of the democratic temperament as other forms of the economy.[2]

Gardner said large families were evidence of the heedless copulation of young clergymen compensating for their previous hoarding of energy by overexpenditure. The net result was loss of energy and the capacity to "organize" it. The loss could be cumulative, since organization itself required energy to control energy. Young married couples should break themselves in slowly. The manual worker finds "the instrument blisters the unaccustomed hand, and works gently till time has gradually hardened the palm for the occupation." But in no sense, warns Gardner, did the analogy mean couples can ever copulate frequently or without heeding the rules he provided. Gardner also attributed "physical excess" to male fears about virility, by way of his lengthy quotation of Lallemand's *Les Pertes Séminales Involontaires* (3 volumes, 1836–42), which was published in 1853 in Philadelphia as *A Practical Treatise on the Causes, Symptoms and Treatment of Spermatorrhoea*. Gardner quoted Lallemand's argument that a man used the occasion of copulation to demonstrate his virile power: it was a question of "vanity." And "those who are least strong in this respect, most fear to allow their weakness to appear." Such men forced themselves to copulate when they did not really want to. Such reluctance could be masked very neatly by Gardner's rules about the ejaculation of sperm.[3]

So the American husband had to govern his copulation to preserve his own energies, his wife's future childbearing capacity, and the eugenic health of the race. He also had to protect his notion of his wife's belief about his virility,[4] even though all of the precautions demonstrated his anxiety about it. Above all, he had to deal with his wife's potentially explosive appetite by avoiding overstimulating her (and perhaps by avoiding stimulating her at all) and by making sure that the right amount of his magically appeasing sperm infused her otherwise insatiable genital organs, without expending more than his own system would bear.

Gardner allowed that married couples could copulate during the "safe" period (which he got wrong), but they had to reconcile that grudging permission with his view that the only legitimate aim of the pleasures of pure love was procreation. They could not copulate during menstruation. In the remaining part of the cycle, when conception was possible, Gardner advised "parents" to "sedulously avoid connections . . . at times of physical debility, when recovering from disease, worn by business cares, gloomy and despondent, or oppressed by grief." He went on to quote another authority to the effect that parents should not copulate at night and in bed. Nor should they copulate in the early morning, late afternoon or evening. They should "have this function [copulation] in active exercise when the sun is up in the heaven, so as to furnish electric states of body." The widest "departure from the law of health in regard to the propagation of offspring, in respect to their constitutional relations to life [was] to beget them when proper electrical currents were wanting." Gardner had already criticized city life's debilitation of "our physique" because people were deprived "of the sunbeam, the great source of life and energy." Sexual expenditure had to be in the presence of the sun. The copulators would be recharging their batteries even as they were discharging. The sun would back a man up, by imparting renewed life to him (from its independent source) even as he risked death by entering what Gardner regarded as the dark and deadly dungeon of woman's generative tract.[5]

Dr. Theophilus Parvin also argued that there should be "restraints upon lawful sexual indulgence." He quoted or paraphrased Plutarch, Jeremy Taylor, canon law, "Mahomed," Zoroaster, and Solon, the last four respectively suggesting intercourse be limited to three or four times a week, once a week (on Fridays), once in nine days, and once in ten. Some doctors recommended once a month, and the Reverend Sylvanus Stall once a week. Dr. Parvin's apparent preference was the English Dr. William Acton's recommendation that "an indulgence once in a week or in ten days may be the rule for strong, healthy men." Moreover, men should cease to copulate altogether after a certain age or they would hasten their death. Parvin warned against copulation during menstruation, "for it may then cause a urethritis in the male, and it may increase the normal monthly flow till it is a serious haemorrhage. . . ." Nor should it take place during "convalescence" after a spontaneous abortion or after parturition. Like Gardner he saw disease as punishment for sexual transgressions. "Injurious consequences" followed contraception, "for gross violation of nature's law brings punishment." Parvin subscribed to the functional, eugenic view of copulation. The rationale for Parvin's (and Gardner's) acceptance of Social Darwinism was the health of society conceived as a body. Parvin castigated those doctors who were, "by all science and art, endeavoring to set aside the great law given by Darwin, of the survival of the fittest, since their effort is to make the unfit survive."[6]

Having stated that sperm was "the purest extract of the blood," Gardner went on to argue the body's capacity to reabsorb it, an argument which goes a long way to explain how exactly energy and sperm came to be identified with each other in the popular imagination. "Nature in creating it [sperm] has intended it not only to communicate life, but also to nourish the individual life. In fact, the reabsorption of the fecundating liquid impresses upon the entire economy an entirely new energy and a virility which contributes to the prolongation of life." Women had no such magical substance.[7]

That reabsorptive effect suggested an additional reason for not copulating during business trials; in the first place, when things were going badly a man did not want to throw one more strain on his debilitated economy (because it could drive him mad or even kill him, and certainly would result in feeble offspring); but in the second place, because of this reabsorptive effect, saving his sperm would give a tremendous boost to a man's capacity to deal with business problems. It would pay off in times of prosperity as well as of failure. The "vigor, elasticity, and energy of the mental machinery is augmented, or depressed, as the blood is strong and powerful." There was no time at all when man undergoing constant and universal competition was unable to rationalize not copulating.[8]

Gardner's account of sperm and ova in *The Causes and Curative Treatment of Sterility* clearly reflected his view of the sexes. The "male affords a fructifying fluid," "the male life-giving principle," "the fecundating principle, the sperm, the spermatic fluid, or in scripture language, the seed," "the secretions of the testicles which last is the true spermatic, life-giving emanation." His words were as profuse as the sperm; its "power" was "immense." The apotheosis of his characterization of sperm was as "the Danaean shower" of godlike gold. (Todd also associated sperm with gold, and both with male energy.) In the same book (*Sterility*), woman's "ovum," "egg," or "germ" was never qualified by more than "the," as it resignedly awaited the "spermatozoa [which act] as if imbued with a knowledge of its duties, or pressed forward by instinct . . . prolonging its search [for] the ovum . . . already surrounded by the spermatozoa rapidly moving around it, and embracing it . . . the tail alone noticeable, quivering with evident vitality." The sperm had the quality of a Snowden pursuing a medical career or a Hall bringing the railroad to the otherwise virgin body of nature.[9]

The "powers of nature" worked through woman: her embodiment of "physical energies" culminated in a "perfected" being necessarily superior to its bearer. The quotation has additional significance:

> The germs of immortality struggling beneath that mother's breast, and the whole powers of nature are quickened, and developed, and exhausted to perfect this grandest of works—a labor wherein man and divinity work together—one which, oft repeated as it is, is still a constant miracle: one that calls down a constant blessing from heaven. To this work, where God does a part, man surely should give his best efforts—no immature defective offering—but the concentrated powers of his perfected nature.

Sperm was the concentrated powers of his "perfected" nature, equivalent then, at some level of Gardner's mind, to woman's baby;

ejaculation anticipated parturition. Given the sexually invidious conception of male and female throughout Gardner's work, and the very specifically male denotation of "man" in the last sentence of the last quotation, I think the earlier occurrence of "man" in the previous sentence must be read as potentially sex-specific too. Woman was simply man's agent in reproduction, as she was God's (and man God's representative). That was why a "proper" man could marry any woman: "A man may marry from love, and yet marry guided solely by reason. To a proper man any woman has the faculty to inspire him with the most ardent passion." The only proviso was that she be a healthy reproductive machine for the proper development of his seed. Man's reproductive "passion" should be devoted to the selection of good breeding stock.[10]

The proper man, said Gardner, was "an estimable christian gentleman and patriot." He required qualification as his sperm did, and as woman and ovum did not. He had to make proper investment of his Danaean gold: expenditure following lubricious thoughts was "unclean excretion," debasing sperm to the urine with which it had to share a vehicle.[11] The man's patriotism was necessary for the generating of a male child.

> So evident is this effect of the mind, and the physical condition of the body over the products of generation, that the sex of the children is capable of being determined by the spirit of the parents. Thus it has been noted, that a large proportion of the children born of truly patriotic parents, during the war of revolution, and during the revolution of France, were male, in answer to the interior longings of the parents, that new sons might be born to them to sustain the grand and glorious cause of freedom, to repulse the invaders, and bring consequent peace, plenty, and an advance in human rights. On the contrary, those nerveless, pusillanimous parents, guided by no higher aim than their own selfish desires, swayed more by fear than honor, constantly hoping that to them, would be given no children capable of fighting the battles for their country, freedom, and right; these were subsequent parents to female children in a large degree.

The passage left open the question of each sex's contribution to these results, despite the strong suggestion that the weaker sex fell into the same category as cowardice, pusillanimity, selfishness, fear, and lack of patriotism. A few pages further on he made it quite clear that the decisive contribution to the character of the child was the father's:

> . . . some of the nations of Europe, where constant and prolonged wars, which took the young and stalwart men as soldiers, and left

only the effeminate, the aged, sickly, and crippled at home to marry and propagate the race. The result, in some of these countries where war was very nigh perpetual, was to leave the people at the end of a century, puny in size, weak in body—and ill-formed to the last degree—and this, too, notwithstanding that one-half the elements employed—viz. the women—were not deteriorated by the sacrifices of war.

Man's contribution to procreation was more significant for the good of society than woman's. It was up to men to teach women the ideological and racial significance of reproduction.[12]

It should be recalled that Gardner, like Todd, saw American men in a constant state of virtual war, robbing and killing each other. Unless Gardner's copulative and other eugenic rules were followed, America was threatened with "national decay," and even worse. The alternative to God's intervention was "self-destruction and moral degradation."

> Let us hope that our present high state of civilization will not repeat the iniquities perpetrated in the corresponding Golden Age of barbarism, of which we read in our school books, *Roma fuit*, lest we may have inscribed, upon our national ruin, for succeeding races to read in the obsolete tongue of a forgotten people
>
> AMERICA WAS!

Nemesis would overtake the American empire, and the American people (especially the men), "careless of the rules of health, may rapidly degenerate, or even disappear, as the Indians are doing."[13]

So underlying the language describing the enfeebling effects of prolonged warfare on European peoples were Gardner's brittle hopes for a new, scientifically bred race of patriotic giants, hand in hand with his fears of lack of control, disease, degeneracy, and racial suicide. And again, responsibility for each outcome was male and female respectively. If women would submit themselves to men completely, and to Gardner's program for politic breeding, they would acknowledge in effect his premise that reproduction (like everything else) was man's sphere, and American society would go forward to act out man's procreative dream. If not, then American society would have been brought down by woman, her maternal threat to obliterate guilty men fulfilled.

Gardner's association of women's freedom with sexual and social anarchy was identical to Todd's. So, too, was his projection of his sexual preoccupations onto nature and the body politic. "We must insist, and satisfactorily prove, too, that the republic is our *mother* country: for within three months, she has brought into the world two states at a birth, and is already far gone with two more." Gardner construed the political actions of men as the reproductive action of a woman's body. The former was in emulation of the latter. A doctor was in a position to elaborate the metaphor: "money, after having circulated through the arteries of the State, will be returned by its thousand veins to the heart again in proper time, after giving growth in its progress, to the noble Croton Aqueduct." In the body politic, money took the place of blood, which generated babies by way of Danaean gold. Presumably the male population fathered heirs and states on the body of the republic by way of money, the extension of its spermatic power. If a man did not copulate very often, his spermatic power would be reabsorbed, to fertilize the mind which accordingly would give birth to social and political projects, aqueducts, and states, for example.[14]

The geography of America allowed Gardner to extend his physiological vision to the West. The settled state could be purged, leaving pure, healthy, and controllable blood to create the fine national physique. "We have no starving population, in this land of grain, high-paid labor. . . . There is always the west wanting to draw off, through the mighty sluices of our continental railway lines the superabundance of poverty, which in Europe stagnates into cesspools of abomination . . . which breed moral and physical pestilence, below the surface of these brilliant capitals." So the West and nature were at once the source of new vigor, which man, as Gardner pointed out, could draw up, from the ground, like Antaeus, and the place that could absorb his unclean excretion. Gardner also anthropomorphized it as a woman, according to the convention I have described.[15]

The men who went West to dig gold from the female body of the continent were like obstetricians. For Gardner compared gold mining to midwifery: he described midwives who came "with reckless adventure, not like our California adventurers, themselves to incur any perils for the sake of gold, but to allow the unfortunates who confide in them to run the risk, and to suffer any calamity which their temerity might cause." The parturitive process over which Gardner presided "gilded" a life. The chiffonier, too, was like the gold miner, and Gardner compared the activities of both to the obstetrician's. The chiffonier's job was to pick over the piles of dirt in the streets of Paris. "He seeks for hidden treasures." He could view "every heap of filth [as] a mine of unknown riches, which he is to open and work." He could also view it as an obstetrician viewed a woman's body. "Imagination takes him to the side of some extensive dirt heap, pregnant with the rich sweepings of a tailor's shop."[16]

The rich meanings of this pile of metaphors suggest that, like Todd, Gardner projected his view of woman onto the continent and identified his professional activities in settlement with the more heroic male activities out West (just as Sims saw himself as a "pioneer" when he was looking into a woman's generative tract). It suggests that he aggrandized woman's procreative activity as something to emulate, and feared it as something it was essential to control; that he devalued woman's body as earth and as a heap of filth, probably because it held the threat of death to Gardner. Amplifying his association between woman's clothing and her sexuality, Gardner had fantasized a tailor's artificial reproduction. "It is to be hoped . . . that [nature] will never go so far as to desert the regular and time-honored way of propagating men and women, the latter especially, and so permit the tailor and dressmaker to fabricate them entirely—as they already do to a startling degree of wood, hay, stubble, and any kind of bone except their own." The combination here of that fantasy with Gardner's identification with the chiffonier's use of the tailor's sweepings suggests that his assumption of the obstetrical function expressed the fantasy of giving birth himself, as the final escape from deadly dependence on stifling, imprisoning woman, and the guilt such an attitude reflected. The notion assumed that Gardner incorporated both filth and gold in himself, an idea borne out by his dual characterization of sperm (unclean excretion and Danaean shower) and by his adherence to proto-sublimation, which is again shown to be rooted in Gardner's apprehensions about maternal power. Transmuting oneself into something higher (or its projected equivalent in the refining of nature) was an enactment of the male self's escape from mother and the assimilation of her power to oneself. But its preoccupation with such an escape betrayed its fixation on and identification with woman's processes, the desire to become her and escape the horrifying burden of perpetually escaping selfhood.[17]

Gardner envisioned the obstetrician as the great mediator and transmuter, standing between the base and worthless powers of female nature and the valuable and civilized forms of wealth, pleasure, and progress. In *Old Wine* he let his own fancy play. "The transition is natural and easy, from the clergy to *good livings,* and

so to cookery, the most agreeable of all the sciences. . . ." He went
on to make a transparent comparison between the role of the French
chef and the role of the obstetrician, which Gardner regarded as
"doing that which pleased his taste, and afforded him more real
pleasure than the exercise of any recreation: and . . . he enters into
the science of treatment with gusto." The skilled chef could "convert
by his anxious alchemy a tough old ram, the *pater-familias* of many
generations into a delicate, plump saddle of venison." He deserved
the thanks of "generations yet unborn." His ability was "miracu-
lous." He could make something out of nothing, so he repudiated
the maxim "Ex nihilo nihil fit." Above all he could transform one
thing into another, old life into new, raw foodstuff into haute cuisine.
"Think of the immense productions of the earth, its millions of
bushels, its millions of pounds, and the incredible magnitude and
worth of the large portion of the whole, that must pass through the
hands of the cook on the way to the millions of mouths that stand
perpetually open." Gardner saw the cook's activity, and the obstetrician's for which it stood, as a paradigm of nineteenth-century male
Faustian conquest and conversion of natural resources into the
progress of civilization.

> Two mighty processes are thus going on in the world without
> ceasing.
> Nature is exhausting her energies in producing; man his life in
> consuming; while the cook stands between them, the great organ of
> communication from one to the other.

Like Gardner, the chef preserved such energies from waste, and as
Gardner fondly imagined of his own return, he deserved an eager
welcome from America. "What an important officer is he in the
general dissemination of pleasure, and the protection of so much
wealth from waste: Surely such an *artiste* must be welcomed with
eagerness among my countrymen in the New World." Such cooks
should, like Gardner, be "raised to the dignity of professors." Since
Gardner gave the name "alchemy" to this culinary "science," it
was equivalent in his view to the transmutation of base metals into
gold.[18]

Gardner presided over a process he viewed identically. He could
mediate the arena of American history. Nature stood to mankind as
woman stood to man. The two "mighty processes," exhaustion and
consumption, went on microcosmically in procreation. Gardner
guided a woman's pregnancy, as "the whole powers of nature" were

"exhausted" to "perfect this grandest of works." He also told man, emulating woman, how to "concentrate" his own resources, otherwise waste, and turn them into wealth, foreshadowing the "miracle" of the production of new life, which Gardner compared to riches and gold. Not only was such an office parallel to other heroic and manly enterprises, but it was one on which they depended for existence and perpetuation.

Men needed to "consume" women (or else be consumed), to "recruit" their "exhausted energies," and, Gardner went on, "redouble our strength at every fresh contact with our mother Earth," a process with which evidently Gardner, in one mood, identified. This was, I think, the general view of women that men would have liked to have had all the time, and it was manifested in the project of using their own unrefined resources in proto-sublimation, and vice versa, their treatment of women a projection of their treatment of themselves. Woman should be inexhaustible and undemanding resources. But that hope came with the guilty fear that men were dependent on women—indeed, hope and fear sprang from the same matrix. Men were dependent for power on that from which they wished to be independent. One effect of this bind (part of the burden of being male) was the fantasy of sex role reversal. That way women became insatiable consumers of male resources, such an apprehension reminding us that was the deeper belief anyway, and the reverse (men consuming women's resources) was simply wishful thinking, or projection. Women were insatiable consumers, and men's relationship with them a ceaseless expenditure that could drain them dry and make them unmanly, passive, and dependent, like women. So deep was this fear, and men's need to escape the role of which it was part, that men brought about that which they feared.

Gardner's fantasy of adopting a position between male and female immunized him from exhaustion and consumption. As a "great organ" which "disseminated pleasure" he could become a huge and perpetually replenished penis, even as he identified its function with parturition, as inexhaustible as Todd's fountain. He both funneled and delivered fetal resources, and eternally satisfied vaginas standing perpetually open, like the cook's customers' mouths.

At the same time, Gardner's own "taste" and preoccupation compelled him to daily contact not with mother earth but with real women's real generative organs and the fears they invoked. "Mine is but the common story of every physician—I have had unknown

women walk into my office, and inquire, 'Are you the doctor?' and
upon an affirmative reply, without further preface, say, 'I want you
to produce an abortion for me,' as coolly as if ordering a piece of beef
for dinner." Gardner confused sexual and oral appetite. In his
attempt to rival Sims, that is, in *his* "Rupture of the Perinaeum,"
Gardner reproduced the Simsian notion (common throughout gynecology) that the "position of the vulva is in fact as various as the
location of the mouth,—which is sometimes in the middle of the
face, and sometimes at the lowest portion, with scarcely a per-
ceptible chin below it." Gardner said that American mothers "fed"
on their sons. So his fantasy of being a cook scientifically and perpetually able to stuff mouths (as he had it parents "stuffed" their
children) was appropriate to a man confronting a world of demanding vaginas he saw as mouths. In a more violent variation of the
same consuming horror, Gardner lost control, the line between himself and women blurred, and his own being became a helpless mass
of mouths from which his bloody essence oozed, a sacrifice to his
hovering mother. "He cannot move. The blood oozes from a hundred
orifices, 'those poor dumb mouths.' . . ." His obstetrical and emotional identification with the fetus[19] explains, perhaps, why he could
be so appalled at a rich woman's ordering an abortion. She did so in
terms that Gardner confused with her cooking and eating the product of his relation with her, that is, the fetus. He was the reproductive cook, not she. He would have it that men take charge of
the consuming world. The confusion between alimentary processes
(absorption, conversion, and anal production) and reproduction,
between self-sufficient Faustian processes of proto-sublimation and
the female originating power they were intended to emulate, was
symptomatic of the sexual anxieties I have described.

This motif adds another dimension to our understanding of his
career. His metaphors for his own language represent the violence of
his obstetrical ambitions, to do to women what he feared they
wanted to do to him. He flung his books as well as his instruments
into the teeth of jaded but consuming woman. It was with an "old
saw" that he cut his way out of the imprisoning and fleshly crowd,
representing perhaps the way men experienced the press of democratic struggle, projecting its suffocating effects onto women. It was
with his words that he wanted to "harrow up" the sensibilities of
young New York ladies, that is, to apply to the fair portion of the
republic "a heavy frame of timber (or iron) set with iron teeth or
tines, which is dragged over ploughed land to break clods, pulverize
and stir the soil, root up weeds, or cover the seed."[20]

The cool, rich woman ordering an abortion, contraception, women living free of relentless childbearing—they all did away with what was central and necessary to Gardner, his vision of woman's agonizing, appalling birth pangs, and the guilty, aggressive psychology constructed around it, refracting in its many facets the identical and similar aspects of other nineteenth-century American men.

Notes to Chapters

Introduction

1. John Bowlby, *Attachment* (New York: Basic Books, 1969).
2. R. D. Laing, *The Divided Self* (Baltimore: Pelican, 1965), pp. 25, 17.
3. Elizabeth Janeway, *"Beyond Stonehenge," New York Times Book Review* (July 29, 1973).

Chapter 1: The American Man

1. Alexis de Tocqueville, *Journey to America,* ed. J. P. Mayer (London: Faber and Faber, 1959), pp. 321–27; Tocqueville, *Democracy in America,* ed. Phillips Bradley, 2 vols. (New York: Knopf, 1945), 1:306; Gustave de Beaumont, *Marie,* trans. and ed. Barbara Chapman (Stanford: Stanford University Press, 1958), *passim;* Tocqueville, *Journey to America,* p. 326.
2. Tocqueville, "Fortnight in the Wilderness," in George Wilson Pierson, *Tocqueville and Beaumont in America* (New York: Oxford University Press, 1938), pp. 236, 263, 266, 277.
3. *Ibid.,* p. 232; Henry David Thoreau, *The Writings of Henry David Thoreau,* 11 vols. (Boston: Riverside, 1893), 3:162.
4. Tocqueville, "Fortnight," pp. 234–35.
5. *Ibid.,* pp. 239, 249–50, 272–73.
6. *Ibid.,* pp. 243–44, 245; D. H. Lawrence, *Studies in Classic American Literature* (New York: Viking, 1964), p. 25; Hamlin Garland, *Other Main Travelled Roads* (New York: Harper, n.d. [copyright 1892]), p. 102; Benjamin Rush, *Medical Inquiries and Observations upon Diseases of the Mind* (New York: Hafner, 1962 [facsimile of 1812 ed.]), p. 59.
7. For Tocqueville's general account of American wives, see below, chs. 3 and 5; Tocqueville, "Fortnight," pp. 237, 244; Tocqueville, *Democracy,* 2:140, 141; "Fortnight," pp. 244, 243.
8. Tocqueville, "Fortnight," pp. 278, 282.

Chapter 2: The Arena

1. Lawrence, *Studies,* pp. 48–49; Arthur Moore, *The Frontier Mind* (New York: McGraw-Hill, 1963), p. 127; R. M. Dorson, *Jonathan Draws the Long*

Bow (Cambridge, Mass.: Harvard University Press, 1946), pp. 14–15; Henry Nash Smith, *Virgin Land* (New York: Vintage, 1950), bk. 2.

2. Lawrence, *Studies*, pp. 59, 61, 62.

3. James Fenimore Cooper, *Notions of the Americans*, 2 vols. (London: Henry Colburn, 1828), 1:vi, vii; by "autonomy" I mean the fantasy of total self-sufficiency, which ideally was experienced away from all other people.

4. *Ibid.*, 1:33, 34, 140.

5. *Ibid.*, 2:2, 71; Leslie Fiedler, *Love and Death in the American Novel*, rev. ed. (New York: Stein and Day, 1966), p. 26.

6. Ik Marvel [pseud.], *Reveries of a Bachelor*, 30th ed. (New York: Charles Scribner, 1859), p. vii; Frank L. Mott, *Golden Multitudes* (New York: Macmillan, 1947), p. 307; Mott's criterion for overall bestsellerdom is a sale of at least 225,000; Marvel, *Reveries*, preface and pp. 17, 78–79, 72, 82, 267, 144–45, 298.

7. Marvel, *Reveries*, pp. 19–21, 20, 31.

8. *Ibid.*, pp. 21, 24.

9. Quoted in Moore, *Frontier Mind*, p. 204.

10. Marvel, *Reveries*, p. 81; for the connection between reverie and masturbation, see below, p. 173.

11. *Ibid.*, p. 95; Herman Melville, *Moby Dick* (New York: Hendricks House, 1952), pp. 414–15; Marvel, *Reveries*, pp. 95, 31, 96, 133.

12. Marvel, *Reveries*, pp. 91, 66.

13. The analogy between the unsettled West and the sea was frequently remarked during the nineteenth century (Tocqueville, "Fortnight," p. 264), and it is a constant one in *Moby Dick*. One might bear in mind the folklore of sailors' sex lives when considering frontiersmen.

14. Cooper, *Notions*, 1:142–43.

15. Herbert Moller, "Sex Composition and Correlated Culture Patterns of Colonial America," *William and Mary Quarterly*, ser. 3, vol. 2 (1945), 114–22; J. R. Potter, "The Growth of Population in America, 1700–1860," in *Population in History*, ed. D. V. Glass and D. E. C. Eversley (London: Edward Arnold, 1965), p. 663; John Demos, *A Little Commonwealth* (New York: Oxford University Press, 1970), p. 151; Potter, "Growth," p. 649; Demos, "Families in Colonial Bristol, Rhode Island: An Exercise in Historical Demography," *William and Mary Quarterly*, ser. 3, vol. 25 (1968), 50, 51; Moore, *Frontier Mind*, ch. 1; Moller, "Sex Composition," p. 129; Potter, "Growth," pp. 680–81, 684–85.

16. Potter, "Growth," p. 681.

17. Demos, *Little Commonwealth*, pp. 77–79; Morgan, *Family*, pp. 27, 145–47; Demos, "Families," pp. 50–51; Potter, "Growth," pp. 651, 678 n. 94; Christopher Lasch, "Burned Over Utopia," *The New York Review of Books*, 8, no. 1 (Jan. 26, 1967), 18.

18. Cooper, *Notions*, 2:427; Tocqueville, *Democracy*, 2:166.

19. George Rogers Taylor, *The Transportation Revolution* (New York: Harper & Row, 1968), p. vii and *passim;* p. 394.

20. *Ibid.*, pp. 166–67, 153.

21. *Ibid.*, pp. 34, 36, 43, 52.

22. Harry N. Scheiber, *Ohio Canal Era: A Case Study of Government and the*

Economy (Athens: Ohio University Press, 1969), p. 283; Smith, *Virgin Land*, ch. 2; W. M. Hall, "Speech of July 7, 1847," included in Railroads, U.S. (TPR p.v. 20), New York Public Library; Marietta etc. Annual Report, quoted in Scheiber, *Ohio Canal Era*, pp. 286, 287.

23. Melville, *Moby Dick*, p. 166; Taylor, *Transportation Revolution*, p. 385.

24. Tocqueville, *Democracy*, 2:44.

25. Joseph A. Schumpeter, *Business Cycles*, 2 vols. (New York: McGraw-Hill, 1939), 1:295; Scheiber, *Ohio Canal Era*, pp. 343, 186.

Chapter 3: Work and Sex

1. Tocqueville, *Democracy*, 2:225.

2. *Ibid.*, 1:257.

3. *Ibid.*, 2:124, 1:315; Augustus K. Gardner, "The Physical Decline of American Women," *The Knickerbocker*, 55 no. 1 (Jan. 1860), 39; Amariah Brigham, *Remarks on the Influence of Mental Cultivation and Mental Excitement Upon Health*, 2d ed. (Boston: Marsh, Capen and Lyon, 1833 [1st ed. 1832]), pp. 52–53. See too Bernard Wishy, *The Child and the Republic* (Philadelphia: University of Pennsylvania Press, 1968), pp. 57–58.

4. Donald B. Meyer, *The Positive Thinkers* (Garden City, N.Y.: Doubleday, 1965), pp. 50–51; Richard C. Wade, *The Urban Frontier* (Chicago: University of Chicago Press, 1964), pp. 308–10; Alexander Mitscherlich, *Society Without the Father*, trans. E. Mosbacher (New York: Harcourt Brace Jovanovich, 1969), pp. 56–57, 150, 159; Max Weber, *The Protestant Ethic and the Spirit of Capitalism* (New York: Scribner, 1958), pp. 21–22 and *passim;* Aileen Kraditor, *Up from the Pedestal* (New York: Quadrangle Books, 1968), p. 14; Smith, *Virgin Land*, p. 43.

5. Meyer, *Positive Thinkers*, pp. 51, 48. Joan Thirsk implies that, in England, this change, from work to worklessness, represented a loss of independence for women, in terms which may be compared to Meyer, *Positive Thinkers*, ch. III: "Among the working classes women may have maintained their economic independence through toiling alongside their husbands, but middle-class women by the late eighteenth century were swooning, docile, dependent creatures" (Thirsk, "The Family," *Past and Present*, no. 27 [April 1964], 121). For evidence of male concern over "trend-setting" women see Anon., *Employment of Females as Practitioners in Midwifery* (Boston: Cummings and Hillard, 1820), pp. 14–15, 22; Cooper, *Notions*, 1:252–53; Gardner, "Decline," pp. 37–52; Marvin Meyers, *The Jacksonian Persuasion* (New York: Vintage, 1960), pp. 129–31.

6. Elizabeth F. Baker, *Technology and Woman's Work* (New York: Columbia University Press, 1964), pp. 53, 24, 21, 25, 52, 35, 42, 426.

7. Wishy, *The Child*, p. 72. In his picture of scientific advance in nineteenth-century America (which he calls profoundly disappointing), I. Bernard Cohen quotes the president of Harvard's annual explanation in the 1840s for the inability to fill the post of professor of engineering: engineers were too busily employed "in superintending the railroads and other public works in progress throughout the United States" to do something so relatively unimportant as teaching. "Science in the Nineteenth Century," in A. M. Schlesinger, Jr., and

Morton White, eds., *Paths of American Thought* (Boston: Houghton Mifflin, 1963), p. 173. Catherine Beecher quoted in Willystine Goodsell, ed., *Pioneers of Women's Education in the United States* (New York: McGraw-Hill, 1931), p. 173; Baker, *Technology*, p. 60.

8. Tocqueville, *Democracy*, 2:222–23, 140.

9. *Ibid.*, 219, 249; Charles M. Schwab had "seen more men fail in business through the attitude taken by their wives . . . than from all the vices put together. A nagging wife . . . is one of the worst handicaps he could have." Quoted in Irving Wyllie, *The Self-Made Man in America* (New York: Free Press, 1966), p. 31.

10. Tocqueville, *Democracy*, 1:315; Beaumont, *Marie*, p. 217; see also Wishy, *The Child*, p. 29.

11. Tocqueville, *Democracy*, 2:223.

Chapter 4: Democratic Fathers and Democratic Sons

1. Erik Erikson, *Young Man Luther* (New York: W. W. Norton, 1962), ch. 6; K. V. Thomas, "Women and the Civil War Sects," *Past and Present*, no. 13 (1958), 44–45, 46–47, 48, 54–55; Elizabeth Eisenstein, "Some Conjectures about the Impact of Printing on Western Society and Thought," *Journal of Modern History*, 40, no. 1 (March 1968), 20; R. H. Tawney, *Religion and the Rise of Capitalism* (London: Penguin, 1938), ch. V, *passim;* Weber, *Protestant Ethic*, pp. 68–78.

2. Levin L. Schücking, *The Puritan Family*, trans. Brian Battershaw (London: Routledge and Kegan Paul, 1969), pp. 5, 10, 12, 16; Ian Watt, *The Rise of the Novel* (Harmondsworth, Middx., England: Penguin, 1963), pp. 69, 170.

3. Perry Miller, *Jonathan Edwards* (Cleveland: World, 1959), p. 109; Louis Hartz, *The Founding of New Societies* (New York: Harcourt Brace Jovanovich, 1964), pp. 4–7; ch. 4; Schücking assumes that the concerns of Defoe and Richardson and their particular public were shaped directly by the Puritan tradition; *Family*, pp. xviii, xiv, ch. 6; Bernard Bailyn, *The Ideological Origins of the American Revolution* (Cambridge, Mass.: Belknap Press, Harvard University, 1967), pp. 34–54, ch. 3. For the idea of a connection between "autonomy" and Bailyn's book I am indebted to Donald Meyer.

4. Watt, *Rise*, pp. 66, 168, 145–46; Schücking, *Family*, p. 106; Erikson, *Luther, passim;* Philippe Ariès, *Centuries of Childhood*, trans. Robert Baldick (New York: Knopf, 1962), pp. 355–56; Norman O. Brown, *Life Against Death* (Middletown, Conn.: Wesleyan University Press, 1959); Meyer, *Positive Thinkers*, pp. 63–64.

5. Perry Miller, *Errand into the Wilderness* (New York: Harper & Row, 1964), pp. 48–98; William Bradford, *Of Plymouth Plantation*, ed. Samuel Eliot Morison (New York: Knopf, 1953), p. 25; Thomas Jefferson, *Notes on Virginia* (New York: Harper Torchbooks, 1964), pp. 114–15; Miller, *The New England Mind* (Boston: Beacon Press, 1961), 1:ch. 3; Meyer, *Positive Thinkers*, p. 130; Edmund S. Morgan, *The Puritan Family* (New York: Harper & Row, 1966), pp. 91–97, 105–106, 138–39, 166–68; Winthrop Jordan, *White over Black* (Baltimore: Penguin, 1969), *passim*. Bailyn, *Origins*, pp. 233–46.

6. Quoted in Morgan, *Family*, p. 43; see Demos, *Little Commonwealth*, p. 181.

7. Morgan, *Family*, p. 43; Schücking, *Family*, pp. 32–36.

8. Morgan, *Family*, pp. 14, 43–45, 17; Schücking, *Family*, pp. 112–13, 41–44, 51.

9. Schücking, *Family*, pp. 88–89, 48, 5.

10. Meyer, *Positive Thinkers*, p. 53; Hartz, *The Liberal Tradition in America* (New York: Harcourt Brace Jovanovich, 1955), pp. 3, 50–54; Ariès, *Centuries*, pp. 415, 414; Tocqueville, *Democracy*, 1:277, 2:239–40, 103.

11. Tocqueville, *Democracy*, 2:204, 205–6.

12. *Ibid.*, 205; Ariès, *Centuries*, p. 406; Tocqueville, *Democracy*, 2:202–3.

13. Mitscherlich, *Society Without the Father*, pp. 155, 161; Erik Erikson, *Childhood and Society* (New York: W. W. Norton, 1963 ed.), pp. 286, 291; Benjamin Franklin, *Autobiography* (New York: Washington Square, 1940), pp. 5–28.

14. Stanley Elkins, *Slavery* (Chicago: University of Chicago Press, 1959), ch. II, pt. 1; Daniel Boorstin, *The Genius of American Politics* (Chicago: University of Chicago Press, 1953); Henry James, *Hawthorne* (London: Macmillan, 1883), pp. 43–44; Tocqueville, *Democracy*, 2:259.

15. Edward Jarvis, "On the Supposed Increase of Insanity," *American Journal of Insanity*, 8 (1852), 360, 361; Beard quoted in Sigmund Diamond, ed., *The Nation Transformed* (New York: George Braziller, 1963), pp. 321–22.

16. Erikson, *Childhood and Society*, p. 312 (it is perhaps significant, in light of this diffusion of father ideal, that the Americans Harry Stack Sullivan and George Herbert Mead should conceptualize a generalized authority, whereas the European Freud should identify the power of Laius); Uri Bronfenbrenner, *Two Worlds of Childhood* (New York: Russell Sage Foundation, 1970), p. 104; Tocqueville, *Democracy*, 2:206, 219, 1:315.

17. Tocqueville, *Democracy*, 2:218–19; Demos, *Little Commonwealth*, p. 183.

18. William P. Dewees, *Treatise on the Physical and Medical Treatment of Children*, 7th ed. (Philadelphia: Carey, Lea and Blanchard, 1838), p. 213. Dewees, a protégé of Benjamin Rush, introduced copious bloodletting to the treatment of parturient women. An 1844 biographer claimed Dewees had "accomplished more for Obstetrics than any man in our country." Dewees also wrote a *System of Midwifery for the Use of Students and Practitioners* (1807) (based largely on current French expertise), *A Treatise on Diseases of Females* (1st ed. 1826), and *The Practice of Medicine* (1830) in addition to published lectures and pamphlets.

19. Robert Sunley, "Early Nineteenth-Century American Literature on Child Rearing," in Margaret Mead and Martha Wolfenstein, eds., *Childhood in Contemporary Cultures* (Chicago: University of Chicago Press, 1963), p. 159; Schücking, *Family*, ch. 2, and Morgan, *Family*, pp. 73, 78, 85, 90–108, describe fathers assuming the same relation to depraved though will-less children as God did toward fathers.

20. Sunley, "Child Rearing," p. 157; Dewees, *Treatise*, p. 245; Wishy, *The Child*, p. 40; Daniel R. Miller and Guy E. Swanson, *The Changing American Parent* (New York: John Wiley and Sons, 1958), p. 7; Dewees, *Treatise*, pp. 245–47, 249.

21. Sunley, "Child Rearing," p. 156; William H. Stokes, "Report of the Mount Hope Institution," *American Journal of Insanity*, 11 (1855), 265; "Report of

the Massachusetts General Hospital," *American Journal of Insanity,* 14 (1858), 378; George Cook, "Mental Hygiene," *American Journal of Insanity,* 15 (1859), 275, 278; see also Isaac Ray, *Mental Hygiene* (New York: Hafner reprint, 1968 [1st pub. 1863]), p. 143 and *passim.*

22. Stokes, "Report," p. 265; "Report of Mass. General," p. 278; Ray, *Mental Hygiene,* pp. 19–20; Cook, "Mental Hygiene"; see also Ruth B. Caplan, *Psychiatry and the Community in Nineteenth Century America* (New York: Basic Books, 1969), p. 17.

23. Brigham, *Remarks,* p. 16.

24. Ray, *Mental Hygiene,* pp. 246 (and ch. 4, *passim*), 58, 138, 287, 133; see also pp. 117–38, 287–91.

25. Brigham, *Remarks,* pp. 76, 14, 13, and Preface; Ray, *Mental Hygiene,* p. 54; I discuss the increase of insanity and its relation to females in Chapter 6.

26. Brigham, *Remarks,* pp. ix–x, 15, 36; Ray, *Mental Hygiene,* p. 106.

27. Brigham, *Remarks,* pp. 39–40, 65, 45–46.

28. Ray, *Mental Hygiene,* pp. 68, 307, 58, 20, 48, 89, 139, 140, 142, 243, 107, 275.

29. Sunley, "Child Rearing," pp. 151, 159, 165–66; see, e.g., Wishy's bibliography in *The Child,* and John L. Thomas, "Romantic Reform in America, 1815–1865," in David Brion Davis, ed., *Ante-Bellum Reform* (New York: Harper & Row, 1967), *passim.*

30. By "existential" I mean to do with human existence in the particular human's own terms; i.e., Erikson's definition in *Luther,* p. 22.

31. Dewees, *Treatise,* pp. 239, 260–61; Sunley, "Child Rearing," p. 160.

32. Wishy, *The Child,* pp. 26–29, 55–56; Cook, "Mental Hygiene," p. 277.

Chapter 5: Freedom of Intercourse

1. Tocqueville, *Democracy,* 2:209–10; Cooper, *Notions,* 1:36, 258.

2. Cooper, *Notions,* 1:261, 263–64, 232 (see also 1:255–56).

3. *Ibid.,* 41, 208, 258.

4. *Ibid.,* 260, 37.

5. *Ibid.,* 264; Tocqueville, *Democracy,* 2:225.

6. Cooper, *Notions,* 1:263–64; Isaac Ray, "The Insanity of Woman Produced by Desertion or Seduction," *American Journal of Insanity,* 23 (1866), 272, see Barbara Welter, "The Cult of True Womanhood," *American Quarterly,* 18, no. 2, pt. 1 (1966), 151–74.

7. Cooper, *Notions,* 1:265–66, 260.

8. *Ibid.,* 140; Tocqueville, *Democracy,* 2:216.

9. Cooper, *Notions,* 1:140–42; Meyer, *Positive Thinkers,* pp. 55–56.

10. Cooper, *Notions,* 1:141–42, 37.

11. Tocqueville, *Democracy,* 2:209–11, 179, 224, 212.

12. *Ibid.,* 219.

13. *Ibid.,* 213–14.

14. Tocqueville, *Journey,* p. 223.

15. Tocqueville, *Democracy,* 2:209, 224, 210, 219.

16. *Ibid.,* 212, 213.

17. *Ibid.,* 213, 212; Margaret Fuller, *Woman in the Nineteenth Century* (New

York: 'Norton, 1971 [1st ed. 1845]), pp. 25–37, 167, *passim;* Aileen Kraditor, *Means and Ends in American Abolitionism* (New York: Pantheon, 1967), ch. 3; Helen Papashvily, *All the Happy Endings* (New York: Harper & Row, 1956), pp. 73–74; Sidney Ditzion, *Marriage, Morals, and Sex in America* (New York: Bookman Associates, 1953), pp. 94, 260; William R. Taylor, *Cavalier and Yankee* (New York: George Braziller, 1961), pp. 172–76; Meyer, *Positive Thinkers*, pp. 52–53; Tocqueville, *Democracy*, 2:223–24.

18. Tocqueville, *Democracy*, 2:210.

19. *Ibid.*, 222, 224.

Chapter 6: Strong Men over Orderly Women

1. Tocqueville, *Democracy*, 2:154, 137; bk. 2, chs. 10, 13.

2. *Ibid.*, 1:315; 2:144–47, 167, 219, 140.

3. *Ibid.*, 1:315.

4. *Ibid.*, 315; 2:165, 145.

5. *Ibid.*, 1:303, 305; 2:165; 1:305, 306–7.

6. *Ibid.*, 337, 307, 308. Cooper called post-1830 New York a "social bivouac." Quoted in Meyers, *Jacksonian Persuasion*, p. 78.

7. Tocqueville, *Democracy*, 1:308, 315.

8. Ray, "Insanity," p. 273; Tocqueville, *Democracy*, 2:222, 223.

9. Tocqueville, *Democracy*, 2:218–19.

10. Baker, *Technology*, p. 159; Barbara Cross, ed., *The Educated Woman in America* (New York: Teachers College Press, 1965), pp. 1, 6–13, 51–101; Ditzion, *Marriage*, pp. 249–50; Mark Twain, *Huckleberry Finn*, in *The Portable Mark Twain* (New York: Viking, 1946), p. 539.

11. Smith, *Virgin Land*, ch. 20.

12. R. W. B. Lewis, *The American Adam* (Chicago: University of Chicago Press, 1958), p. 1.

13. Erikson, *Childhood and Society*, p. 286; Caplan, *Psychiatry*, p. 21; Jarvis, "Supposed Increase," pp. 354–55; Jay Leyda, *The Melville Log* (New York: Harcourt Brace Jovanovich, 1951), 1:51; Tocqueville, *Democracy*, 2:167 (and see 2:147).

14. Esquirol quoted in Jarvis, "Supposed Increase," p. 349 (and see Ray, *Mental Hygiene*, pp. 228–29, 284); Norman Dain, *Concepts of Insanity in the United States, 1789–1865* (New Brunswick, N.J.: Rutgers University Press, 1964), p. 89. In spite of changes of emphasis during the century, mental illness was always construed to combine both psychological ("moral") and physical ("somatic") elements. Mental sickness/health would affect/be affected by bodily sickness/health. Hence the associations I am describing had an inevitable physical counterpart.

15. Dain, *Concepts*, p. 212, n. 9; Caplan, *Psychiatry*, pp. 19, 21; Ray, *Mental Hygiene*, pp. 254–57; Cook, "Mental Hygiene," pp. 272, 277; Caplan, *Psychiatry*, p. 170. Ray is explicit about this necessity for men to run the danger of going mad. "I do not suppose that [insanity-inducing] excitement can be banished from every sphere of human activity, or that such a result would be desirable, if it could. It has its uses, and within certain limits it furnishes indispensable aid in realizing the purposes and aspirations of men." *Mental Hygiene*, p. 191.

16. Ray, *Mental Hygiene*, pp. 259–60; Dain, *Concepts*, pp. 85–86.

17. Dain, *Concepts*, p. 90; Nash, *Wilderness*, p. 74.

18. G. R. Taylor, *Transportation Revolution*, pp. 388, 392; R. H. Shryock, *Medicine and Society in America* (Ithaca, N.Y., Great Seal paperback ed., 1962), pp. 100, 128, 161; Shryock, *Medicine in America* (Baltimore: Johns Hopkins Press, 1966), pp. 15, 128; Shryock, *Medicine in America*, p. 14; Dewees, *Treatise*, p. 130; Augustus Kinsley Gardner, *Conjugal Sins* (New York: J. S. Redfield, 1870), p. 80; Todd, *The Moral Influence, Dangers and Duties Connected with Great Cities* (Northampton: J. H. Butler, 1841), *passim*.

19. Quoted in Caplan, *Psychiatry*, p. 81.

20. Ray, *Mental Hygiene*, pp. 293, 216, 219.

21. Brigham, *Remarks*, preface.

22. *Ibid.*, pp. 80–81, vii, 81.

23. *Ibid.*, pp. 66, 81–82, 82–83.

24. *Ibid.*, pp. 82, 86, 84–86.

25. *Ibid.*, p. 81.

26. *American Journal of Insanity*, 7 (1850), 142–71.

27. Jarvis, "Comparative Liability," pp. 156, 157, 158.

28. *Ibid.*, pp. 150, 156.

29. *Ibid.*, pp. 158, 154–55, 158, 155.

30. *Ibid.*, pp. 153, 162, 166.

Chapter 7: The Absence of Midwives from America

1. *Maternity Care in the World: Report of a Joint Group of the International Federation of Gynecology and Obstetrics and the International Confederation of Midwives* (London: Pergamon Press, 1966).

2. "An Appeal to the Medical Society of Rhode Island, in behalf of Woman to be Restored to her Natural Rights as 'Midwife,' and elevated by Education to be the Physician of her own Sex" (N.Y.P.L., n.p., 1851), p. 6.

3. Carl T. Javert, "James Platt White, a Pioneer in American Obstetrics and Gynecology," *Journal of Medicine and Allied Sciences*, 3, no. 4 (Autumn 1948), *passim*.

4. Abraham Flexner, *Medical Education in the United States and Canada: A Report to the Carnegie Foundation for the Advancement of Teaching*, Bulletin no. 4 (New York: Carnegie Foundation, 1910), p. 154; Shryock, *Medicine in America*, p. 31; Robert H. Wiebe, *The Search for Order, 1877–1920* (New York: Hill and Wang, 1968), pp. 112–13.

5. John V. D. Young, "The Midwife Problem in the State of New York," *New York State Journal of Medicine*, 15, no. 8 (1915), 292; Frances E. Kobrin, "The American Midwife Controversy: A Crisis of Professionalization," *Bulletin of the History of Medicine*, 40 (1966), 350–63.

6. Kobrin, "Midwife Controversy," pp. 352, 353, 359, 360; "Discussion," following Young, "Midwife Problem" (cited hereafter as "Discussion—Midwife Problem, 1915"), p. 300; Joseph B. De Lee, ed., *Obstetrics*, in *The Practical Medicine Series: Comprising Eight Volumes of the Year's Progress in Medicine and Surgery* (Chicago: The Year Book Publishers, 1926), pp. 300–1; Kobrin, "Midwife Controversy," pp. 354, 359; Flexner, *Report*, p. xiii; Young, "Midwife

Problem," p. 292; Kobrin, "Midwife Controversy," p. 360; A. B. Emmons and J. L. Huntington, "The Midwife: Her Future in the United States," *American Journal of Obstetrics and Diseases of Women and Children*, 65, no. 3 (1912), 393; Young, "Midwife Problem," pp. 292, 295.

7. Kobrin, "Midwife Controversy," p. 351; "Discussion—Midwife Problem, 1915," p. 299; Young, "Midwife Problem," p. 291; "Discussion—Midwife Problem, 1915," p. 300. One further line of attack on midwives was their investigation and prosecution by the Legal Bureau of the Medical Society of the County of New York. Young presents 99 cases of "criminal practice," the bald outline of which makes sad reading: "Midwife Problem," p. 293.

8. "Discussion—Midwife Problem, 1915," p. 300; Linsly Williams, "The Position of the New York State Department of Health Relative to the Control of Midwives," *New York State Journal of Medicine*, 15, no. 8 (1915), 299, 296, 297, 296, 298.

9. Kobrin, "Midwife Controversy," pp. 354–55; Shryock, *Medicine in America*, p. 187.

10. It was according to such rationale that Lilburn Merrill recommended the invasion of the immigrant family by social workers, to save the male child from the degeneracy and foreign habits of an un-American upbringing, to free him for individualism. Wishy, *The Child*, p. 135.

11. Emmons and Huntington, "The Midwife," p. 399.

12. "Discussion—Midwife Problem," p. 300; Flexner, *Report*, p. xiii; Gardner, *Our Children* (Hartford: Belknap and Bliss, 1872), *passim* (see discussion in pt. IV, below); George J. Engelmann, "The Increasing Sterility of American Women," *Transactions of the Section on the Diseases of Women of the American Medical Association* (1901), 271–95; Mark Haller, *Eugenics: Hereditarian Attitudes in American Thought* (New Brunswick: Rutgers University Press, 1963); John Higham, *Strangers in the Land* (New York: Atheneum, 1968), pp. 150–53.

13. Young, "Midwife Problem," pp. 291, 294; Kobrin, "Midwife Controversy," p. 363; Harold Speert, "Midwifery in Retrospect," in *The Midwife in the United States: Report of a Macy Conference* (New York: Josiah Macy, Jur. Foundation, 1968), pp. 176–77; Kobrin, "Midwife Controversy," pp. 350–51, 357; Williams, "Control of Midwives," pp. 296, 298; Kobrin, "Midwife Controversy," p. 353; Howard W. Haggard, *Devils, Drugs and Doctors* (New York: Pocket Books, 1959), p. 94.

14. Kobrin, "Midwife Controversy," p. 363; Kraditor, *The Ideas of the Woman Suffrage Movement, 1890–1920* (New York: Columbia University Press, 1965), ch. 6 *passim*.

15. Kobrin, "Midwife Controversy," pp. 350, 362, 363.

16. *Ibid.*, pp. 355–56, 351–52, 357, 355.

17. R. W. Holmes, "Fads and Fancies of Obstetrics," *Journal of the American Medical Association*, 77 (1921), 314; Kobrin, "Midwife Controversy," p. 353; W. H. Allport, "Tristram Shandy and Obstetrics," *American Journal of Obstetrics*, 65 (1912), 612–17; "Discussion—Midwife Problem, 1915," p. 301.

18. Kobrin, "Midwife Controversy," p. 362; Haggard, *Devils*, pp. 94–95; Flexner, *Report*, pp. 155, x, 10; Kobrin, "Midwife Controversy," p. 353; Flexner, *Report*, pp. x, 15; Haggard, *Devils*, pp. 11, 44–45; Kobrin, "Midwife Controversy," pp. 351–52; "Discussion—Midwife Problem, 1915," pp. 300, 301; Kobrin, "Midwife Controversy," p. 354; Williams, "Control of Midwives," p. 299.

19. De Lee, *Obstetrics*, pp. 301–2, 306; 301–17 *passim;* 324.

20. *Ibid.*, pp. 282, 284–85.

21. *Ibid.*, p. 290; the point of this paragraph is elaborated in the rest of pt. II and in pt. III below.

22. Sister M. T. Shoemaker, *History of Nurse-Midwifery in the United States* (Washington, D.C.: Catholic University Press, 1947), pp. 42–44, 51, 52, 58; Mary M. Roberts, *American Nursing* (New York: Macmillan, 1954), p. 243; Minnie Goodnow, *Nursing History*, 7th ed. (Philadelphia: W. B. Saunders, 1942), pp. 276–78.

23. Shoemaker, *Nurse-Midwifery*, pp. 6, 12–13, 30, 59; Roberts, *American Nursing*, pp. 239–40.

24. Hattie Hemschemeyer, "Midwifery in the Untied States," *American Journal of Nursing*, 39, no. 11 (1949), 1184; Goodnow, *Nursing History*, p. 276.

25. Haggard, *Devils*, p. 14; Dr. Nelson quoted in Stephen Schwartz, "A Holy War Rages over Natural Childbirth," *Potomac*, the magazine section of the Washington *Post* (Oct. 18, 1970), pp. 12, 37–43, 46, 47–53; Dr. Tucho Perrusi quoted in Judith Brister, "Traditional Childbirth Posture Is Unnatural," Washington *Evening Star* (Aug. 11, 1971), C. 10.

Chapter 8: Democratic Doctors

1. Meyer, *Positive Thinkers*, p. 23.

2. Dewees, *Treatise*, pp. xi, 21–24; review of Brigham quoted on first page of 2d ed. of *Remarks;* Cook, "Mental Hygiene," pp. 276, 282.

3. Ray, *Mental Hygiene*, pp. 15, 22, 53.

4. *Ibid.*, pp. 116, 262, 223.

5. *Ibid.*, pp. 247, 158, 206, 15; see, too, p. 290.

6. *Ibid.*, pp. 107–8, 205.

7. *Ibid.*, pp. 143–55, 220–21, 156–81, 157, 162, 164, 54, 165–74; the source of society's enervating passivity was "generally the softer sex," p. 165.

8. *Ibid.*, p. 105.

9. *Ibid.*, pp. 123–25.

10. *Ibid.*, pp. 56–58, 233–45, 266–77; 57, 234–35, 272–75; Evert A. and George L. Duyckinck, *Cyclopoedia of American Literature* (Philadelphia: William Rutter, 1880 [1st ed. 1867]), 1: iii; Gardner, *Conjugal Sins*, pp. 9–10; John Todd, *The Student's Manual* (Northampton: Hopkins, Bridgman, 1835), p. 147.

11. Shryock, *Medicine and Society*, pp. 22–31; Bridenbaugh, *Rebels and Gentlemen* (New York: Oxford University Press, 1965), ch. VIII *passim;* H. Thoms, *Chapters in American Obstetrics* (Springfield, Illinois: Charles C. Thomas, 1961), pp. 16–19, 35, 74–75; Shryock, *Medicine and Society*, p. 138; Shryock, *Medicine in America*, pp. 237–43; Bailyn, *Ideological Origins*, chs. III, V, and VI; Jack P. Greene, "Political Mimesis," *American Historical Review*, 75, no. 2 (1969), 344 and *passim*.

12. Meyer, *Positive Thinkers*, p. 165; Rush, *Medical Inquiries*, pp. 59–60, 249; Shryock, *Medicine in America*, p. 239 (and see p. 249); Rush, *Medical Inquiries*, pp. 32, 34, 184–91 and *passim* (and see Shryock, *Medicine and Society*, pp. 31–32); Rush, *Medical Inquiries*, pp. 347, 349.

13. Rush, *Medical Inquiries,* p. 125.

14. *Ibid.,* pp. 354, 353, 126, 127; 61–62 (see, too, pp. 351–52).

15. *Ibid.,* pp. 352; 347, 253; 255; for the surgical treatment of woman's desire, see ch. 11, below.

16. Shryock, *Medicine in America,* p. 242; J. R. Pole, *The Advance of Democracy* (New York: Harper & Row, 1967), pp. 1–12 and *passim;* David Hackett Fischer, *The Revolution of American Conservatism* (New York: Harper & Row, 1969), p. 191 and *passim;* Scheiber, *Ohio Canal Era, passim;* William Appleman Williams, *The Contours of American History* (New York: Quadrangle, 1966), pp. 75–245; Shryock, *Medicine and Society,* pp. 31–32; 20, 148–50; Kobrin, "Midwife Controversy," p. 358.

17. Shryock notes the "divorce between science and public affairs" after Rush's generation, in *Medicine in America,* p. 250; Perry Miller, *The Life of the Mind in America* (New York: Harcourt Brace Jovanovich, 1963), p. 325; for accounts of the competing medical theories see Shryock, *Empiricism vs. Rationalism,* in *American Medicine, 1650–1950,* reprinted from *Proceedings of the American Antiquarian Society* (Worcester, Mass., April 1969), and Edwin H. Ackerknecht, "Recurrent Themes in Medical Thought," *Scientific Monthly,* 69, no. 2 (1949).

18. Miller, *Life of the Mind,* pp. 325–26; Shryock, *Medicine in America,* pp. 5–6, 143, 144; Miller describes quacks as "empiricists gone mad, not necessarily dishonest," *Life of the Mind,* p. 326; Dain, *Concepts,* pp. 147, 164.

19. Bridenbaugh, *Rebels and Gentlemen,* pp. 266, 276–77; Flexner, *Report,* pp. ix–x, 3, 8–9; xi, 18–19; Shryock, *Medicine and Society,* p. 146; Shryock, *Medicine in America,* ch. VI.

20. Shryock, *Empiricism vs. Rationalism,* pp. 129–34; Tocqueville, *Democracy,* 1:43, 44; Gardner, "Thoughts on Health," *Frank Leslie's Illustrated Newspaper,* 34, no. 876 (July 13, 1872), 283; Dain, *Concepts,* p. 83; Haggard, *Devils,* p. 121; Dain, *Concepts,* pp. 80, 83; Tocqueville, *Democracy,* 2:11–13, 275–78; Shryock, *Medicine in America,* pp. 150–51.

21. The AMA was founded in 1847. In 1848 its Committee on Education had decided there were too many doctors—five times as many proportionately as in France. Morris Fishbein, *A History of the American Medical Association* (Philadelphia: W. B. Saunders, 1947), p. 47.

22. Newcomb quoted in I. Bernard Cohen, "Science in America: The Nineteenth Century," in A. M. Schlesinger, Jr., and Morton White, eds., *Paths of American Thought* (Boston: Houghton Mifflin, 1970), pp. 185, 186.

23. Shryock, *Empiricism vs. Rationalism,* pp. 103–4; Dewees, *Treatise,* p. 268; Miller, *Life of the Mind,* p. 324; Ackerknecht, "Recurrent Themes," p. 82. It should be pointed out that Rush's assertiveness rested in the context of the most flourishing of American medical schools (Philadelphia in the second half of the eighteenth century), which was itself very largely the outcropping of European medicine, since its founders all had found it essential to get their medical training in Europe. Bridenbaugh, *Rebels and Gentlemen,* ch. VIII *passim.*

24. Flexner, *Report,* p. 9; Caplan, *Psychiatry,* pp. 247; 134–35, 140, 172, 185, 202, 229, 248; Dain, *Concepts,* pp. 143–44; 63, 71, 136, 139, 56, 124; Caplan, *Psychiatry,* p. 200; John C. Burnham, "Psychoanalysis and American Medicine, 1894–1918: Medicine, Science and Culture," *Psychological Issues,* 5, no. 4 (1967), 48.

Chapter 9: The Rise of Gynecology

1. Harvey Graham, *Eternal Eve* (London: Hutchinson, 1960), pp. 160, 169, 177, 188.

2. Elizabeth Nihell quoted in *ibid.*, p. 159; Arthur H. Cash, "The Birth of Tristram Shandy: Sterne and Doctor Burton," in *Studies in the Eighteenth Century*, ed. R. F. Brissenden (Toronto: University of Toronto Press, 1968), pp. 135–36, 143, 144, 146.

3. Graham, *Eternal Eve*, p. 169; Thoms, *Chapters*, p. 12; Shryock, *Medicine in America*, p. 182; Graham, *Eternal Eve*, pp. 110, 128, 145, 164, 257; see also Speert, "Midwifery," pp. 163–64; Samuel Gregory, *Man-Midwifery Exposed and Corrected* (Boston: Houghton Mifflin, 1848).

4. Graham, *Eternal Eve*, ch. 12; Rhoda Truax, *The Doctors Warren of Boston* (Boston: Houghton Mifflin, 1968), p. 95; Graham, *Eternal Eve*, p. 195.

5. T. Gaillard Thomas, *A Practical Treatise on the Diseases of Women* (Philadelphia: H. C. Lea, 1868), Preface; Graham, *Eternal Eve*, chs. 15–18; Sims, *Life*, chs. 18, 17.

6. Flexner, *Medical Education*, p. 3; Shryock, *Medicine and Society in America*, pp. 23–24; Morris, *Encyclopedia*, p. 574; Shryock, *Medicine and Society in America*, p. 135; Fielding H. Garrison, *An Introduction to the History of Medicine*, 4th ed. (Philadelphia: W. B. Saunders, 1929 [1st ed., 1913]), p. 510.

7. Graham, *Eternal Eve*, pp. 223–25; George Bender, *Great Moments in Medicine* (Detroit: Parke-Davis, 1961), pp. 255, 264, 254; Arturo Castiglioni, *A History of Medicine*, trans. E. B. Krumbhaar (New York: Knopf, 1941), pp. 853–54; Garrison, *Introduction*, p. 509; James R. Chadwick, "Obstetric and Gynecological Literature, 1876–1881," *Transactions of the American Medical Association*, 32 (1881), 253–65.

8. Meigs, *Woman*, p. 54; Ray, "Insanity Produced by Seduction," p. 267.

9. Dain, *Concepts*, pp. 10, 26, 12, 65–66; Caplan, *Psychiatry*, p. 140; Meyer, *Positive Thinkers*, p. 56.

10. Dain, *Concepts*, pp. 132–43; Wiebe, *Search for Order*, pp. xiii, 1, 52, 5–6, 8; Augustus Kinsley Gardner, *History of the Art of Midwifery* (New York: Stringer and Townshend, 1852), p. 4.

11. Shryock, *Medicine in America*, pp. 189–90; *Medicine and Society*, p. 147.

12. Quoted in Fishbein, *History of the AMA*, pp. 82–83: all of the following quotations of Stillé are from those pages.

13. Smith, *Virgin Land*, ch. X.

14. Fishbein, *History of the AMA*, p. 85.

15. Gardner, "New York Medical College for Women," *Frank Leslie's Illustrated Newspaper*, 30, no. 759 (April 10, 1870), 71.

16. John Todd, *Woman's Rights* (Boston: Lee and Shephard, 1867); John Todd, *Serpents in the Dove's Nest* (Boston: Lee and Shephard, 1867), *passim;* Gardner, *Conjugal Sins*, dedication, p. 195.

17. Henry O. Marcy, "The Early History of Abdominal Surgery in America," *Transactions of the Section on Obstetrics and the Diseases of Women of the American Medical Association*, n.v. (1909), 251; *Transactions of the American Medical Association*, 10 (1857), 31; Gardner and Fordyce Barker, "Remarks on Puerperal Fever," *Transactions of the New York Academy of Medicine*, n.v.

(1858); Thomas, *Diseases of Women*, preface to 1st ed.; Gardner, *Conjugal Sins*, pp. 13–14.

18. Fishbein, *History of the AMA*, p. 150.

19. Horatio Robinson Storer, *The Causation, Course and Treatment of Reflex Insanity in Women* (Boston: Lee and Shephard, 1871), p. 79; Seale Harris, *Woman's Surgeon* (New York: Macmillan, 1950), *passim;* I describe these operations briefly in ch. 13, and at length in a forthcoming book, tentatively titled *Sexual Surgery*.

20. Garrison, *Introduction*, p. 509; James R. Chadwick, "Obstetric and Gynaecological Literature, 1876–1881," *Transactions of the American Medical Association*, 32 (1881), 255; Fishbein, *History of the AMA*, p. 1094; Harris, *Woman's Surgeon*, p. 308. In his eulogy at the time of Sims's death in 1883, W. O. Baldwin said of Sims's *Clinical Notes:* "There has been no work published on uterine surgery within the last century that has been as full of original thought and invention, or that has contributed so largely to the advance of gynecology as this book has done." Printed in Sims, *Life*, p. 433. Baldwin was president of the AMA in 1869.

21. Chadwick, "Obstetric Literature," pp. 255–61, 253–54; Sims, *Clinical Notes*, pp. 131–35, 206–7; and see Harris, *Woman's Surgeon*, p. 185.

Chapter 10: Architect of the Vagina

1. Emmett and Thomas quoted in Harris, *Woman's Surgeon*, pp. 372, 373; *ibid.*, pp. 373–74; Felix Martí-Ibanez, *Ariel: Essays in the Arts and the History and Philosophy of Medicine* (New York: M. D. Publications, 1962), p. 170. I have found Seale Harris's biography of Sims, *Woman's Surgeon*, indispensable. (Sims's autobiography, similarly indispensable, is not complete and does not touch the last twenty years of his life at all.)

2. Harris, *Woman's Surgeon*, chs. 10, 11; pp. 243, 225, 256–57; Arthur Selwyn-Brown, *The Physician Through the Ages* (New York: Capehart-Brown, 1928), p. 105; Marcy, "Abdominal Surgery," p. 260; Harris, *Woman's Surgeon*, pp. 270, 377–81, 358, 345–46; chs. 15, 16, 17; p. 392; Sims, *Life*, pp. 434, 436, and see pp. 435, 422.

3. Quoted in Harris, *Woman's Surgeon*, p. 373.

4. *Ibid.*, pp. 10, 17–18, 13–14, 9, 10, 51.

5. *Ibid.*, p. 66; Sims, *Life*, p. 192 (and see pp. 146–47); Stephen W. Williams, *American Medical Biography of Memoirs of Eminent Physicians* (New York: Milford House, 1967 [reprint of 1844 ed.]), p. 134.

6. Harris, *Woman's Surgeon*, pp. 73, 68, 72, ch. 8 *passim*.

7. Sims, *Life*, pp. 209, 231; Harris, *Woman's Surgeon*, pp. 84–85; J. Marion Sims, "Double Congenital Hare-lip, Absence of the Superior Incisors, and Their Portion of the Alveolar Process," *The American Journal of Dental Science*, 5 (1844), 54; Harris, *Woman's Surgeon*, pp. 160, 178.

8. Sims, *Clinical Notes*, pp. 11, 14, 16, 83, 160, 159, 154, 220, 18, 265.

9. Sims, "Double Congenital Hare-lip," pp. 51–52; George A. Bender, *Great Moments in Medicine* (Detroit: Parke-Davis, 1961), p. 259; Harris, *Woman's Surgeon*, pp. 83, 87, 88, 90, 132–33, 163, 172; Sims, "Double Congenital Hare-lip," pp. 55, 52.

10. Sims, *Life,* p. 231; Harris, *Woman's Surgeon,* pp. 84–85; Sims, *Life,* pp. 234, 435.

11. Harris, *Woman's Surgeon,* pp. 87, 88, 100, 102, 90–91, 99, 91–92; Sims, *Life,* pp. 243, 234–36; Selwyn-Brown, *Physician Through the Ages,* p. 105; Harris, *Woman's Surgeon,* pp. 195, 103.

12. *Woman's Surgeon,* pp. 123–24, 126, ch. 14 *passim,* pp. 305, 289–90, 321–22, 325–26, 382.

13. *Ibid.,* pp. 128–29; Thomas, *Diseases of Females,* p. 177 (for an account of both Sims's Operation and Bozeman's Operation, see their colleague Thomas, *Diseases of Females,* pp. 168–79); Harris, *Woman's Surgeon,* pp. 104, 110, 118, ch. 22 *passim,* pp. 198, 200, 257, 270–71, 310, 333–34, 343, 381–83.

14. Harris, *Woman's Surgeon,* pp. 129, 135, 288.

15. Sims, "The Discovery of Anaesthesia," *Virginia Medical Monthly,* 4, no. 2 (1877), 81–100; Harris, *Woman's Surgeon,* pp. 201–2, 203–4, 225–30. Sims's advocacy of southern priority in the discovery of anesthesia was a manifestation of the general competition among men (explained by Tocqueville as a function of democracy).

16. Haggard, *Devils,* pp. 101–7; Garrison, *Introduction,* p. 506; Sims, "Anaesthesia," pp. 94, 98–99 and *passim.*

17. Jarvis, "Supposed Increase," p. 360; Newton Arvin, *Herman Melville* (New York: Viking, 1957), pp. 20, 22; Thomas Melville quoted in *ibid.,* p. 23; Leyda, *log,* 1:51; Melville, *Moby Dick,* pp. 182, 183; Tocqueville, *Democracy,* 1:146, 147.

18. Harris, *Woman's Surgeon,* pp. 337, 339.

19. Sims, "Anaesthesia," p. 100; Harris, *Woman's Surgeon,* pp. 169, xvi–xvii, 152, 175, *passim.*

20. Harris, *Woman's Surgeon,* pp. 107, 298–307; "Patients' Memorandum" quoted in *ibid.,* p. 298.

21. Quoted in *ibid.,* p. 301.

22. *Ibid.,* pp. 79–80, 81, 100, 89.

23. *Ibid.,* pp. xvi, 87–88, 75, 99, 108–9, ch. 12 *passim.*

24. *Ibid.,* pp. 115–16, 133–34, 162, 157, 142, 144, chs. 14, 15, 16 *passim.*

25. *Ibid.,* pp. 156, 163–64, 162.

26. *Ibid.,* pp. 175–77, 158, 233, 222, 148, 188, 264, 267, 292, 293, 389.

27. *Ibid.,* p. 168.

28. *Ibid.,* p. 298; Harris quotes the "Memorial," pp. 170–72.

29. *Ibid.,* pp. 172–73, 168, 170–71, 173–74, 290.

30. *Ibid.,* pp. 272, 235; Sims, *Life,* pp. 328–69, ch. xix *passim,* title page, pp. 440–48; Harris, *Woman's Surgeon,* pp. 292–93, 335–36; see, too, pp. 257–59, 357, 365.

31. Sims, *Life,* pp. 234, 432; Harris, *Woman's Surgeon,* pp. 188, 63–64, 111, 105–6, 187, 117–18.

32. Sims, *Life,* pp. 373, 234; Harris, *Woman's Surgeon,* pp. 365–66.

33. Sims, *Life,* pp. 397–98.

34. *Ibid.,* p. 394.

35. *Ibid.,* p. 393; Harris, *Woman's Surgeon,* pp. 7, 55 (and see p. 11; xx, xvii); Sims, *Life,* p. 468.

36. Sims, *Life,* p. 447; Harris, *Woman's Surgeon,* p. 318; Sims, *Life,* pp. 246, 392.

37. *Ibid.*, pp. 392, 395; Sims, *Clinical Notes*, p. 241; Sims, *Life*, p. 509.

38. Sims, *Clinical Notes*, pp. 4–5, 115.

39. Harris, *Woman's Surgeon*, pp. 94, 340–41, 239–43.

40. Sims, *Clinical Notes*, pp. 231, 143, 116.

41. *Ibid.*, pp. 145, 151, 131–35, 206–7, 146.

42. *Ibid.*, pp. 162, 163, 4; Chadwick, "Obstetric Literature," p. 254.

43. Sims, *Clinical Notes*, pp. 168–69, 186–88; and see pp. 346–47.

44. *Ibid.*, pp. 192–93.

45. *Ibid.*, p. 401 (and see p. 105); "menorrhagia" was the name given to profuse menstruation; "dysmenorrhea" was the name for the equally vague, painful menstruation; Sims, *Life*, p. 234; Sims, *Clinical Notes*, pp. 42, 219–22.

46. Sims, *Clinical Notes*, pp. 178, 200, 189.

47. *Ibid.*, pp. 320, 322, 319.

48. *Ibid.*, pp. 330–31, 334.

49. Theophilus Parvin, "The Hygiene of the Sexual Function," *New Orleans Medical and Surgical Journal*, 11, n.s. (1883–84), 608.

50. Sims, *Clinical Notes*, p. 325; Parvin, "Sexual Function," p. 604; Gardner, *The Causes and Curative Treatment of Sterility* (New York: De Witt and Davenport, 1856), p. 111; Sims, *Clinical Notes*, p. 142.

51. Sims, *Clinical Notes*, pp. 321, 323–24, 330, 241; Henry Coe, "Is Disease of the Uterine Appendages as Frequent as It Has Been Represented?" *American Journal of Obstetrics*, 19, no. 6 (1886), 574.

52. Sims, *Clinical Notes*, pp. 20, 282, 301, 283.

53. *Ibid.*, pp. 145–46, 272, 277–79.

54. *Ibid.*, p. 360.

55. *Ibid.*, pp. 370, 369.

56. *Ibid.*, p. 354; Gardner's book is discussed in pt. IV, below.

57. Harris, *Woman's Surgeon*, p. 185; Morgan, *Family*, p. 34; Demos, *Commonwealth*, pp. 94, 95–96; Jefferson, *Notes*, p. 56.

58. Sims, *Clinical Notes*, pp. 105, 235, 311, 20, 42.

59. *Ibid.*, p. 373.

60. *Ibid.*

61. *Ibid.*, pp. 348, 16, 365.

Chapter 11: Sexual Surgery

1. This paragraph and the next two reflect the conclusions of Barker-Benfield, *Sexual Surgery*, forthcoming. Of course Sims and Gardner (the subject of pt. IV) illustrate the characteristics this paragraph mentions.

2. Isaac Baker Brown, *On the Curability of Certain Forms of Insanity, Epilepsy, Catalepsy* (London: Robert Hardwicke, 1866); "Meeting to Consider the Proposition of the Council for the Removal of Mr. I. Baker Brown," *British Medical Journal*, 1 (1867); Lawson Tait, "Masturbation," *The Medical News*, 53, no. 1 (July 7, 1888), 3. For an account of Baker Brown's theory, and of an American precursor, see Barker-Benfield, *Sexual Surgery*, ch. 2.

3. John Bunker, "Surgical Manpower: A Comparison of Operations and Surgeons in the United States and in England and Wales," *New England Journal of Medicine*, 282, no. 3 (1970); 135–44; Bunker, "When to Operate?" *Saturday Review* (Aug. 22, 1970), 30–31; Frances S. Norris, "We Need Women Doctors,"

letter to the editor, Washington *Evening Star* (Dec. 15, 1970); Robert P. Bolande, "Ritualistic Surgery—Circumcision and Tonsillectomy," *New England Journal of Medicine,* 280, no. 11 (March 13, 1969), 591–97; Judy Klemesrude, "Those Who Have Been There Aid Breast Surgery Patients," New York *Times* (Feb. 8, 1971); E. Weiss and O. Spurgeon English, *Psychosomatic Medicine,* 3d ed. (Philadelphia: W. B. Saunders, 1957), ch. 19 *passim.*

4. Abraham Myerson, James B. Ayer, Tracy J. Putnam, Clyde E. Keeler, Leo Alexander, *Eugenical Sterilization: A Reorientation of the Problem* (New York: Macmillan, 1936), *passim;* Caplan, *Psychiatry,* p. 301.

5. David T. Gilliam, "Oophorectomy for the Insanity and Epilepsy of the Female: A Plea for Its More General Adoption," *Transactions of the American Association of Obstetricians and Gynecologists,* 9 (1896), 320.

6. William Goodell, "Clinical Notes on the Extirpation of the Ovaries for Insanity," *American Journal of Insanity,* 38 (Jan.–April 1882), 295; Gardner, *Conjugal Sins,* p. 147; Gardner, *Our Children* (Hartford: Belknap and Bliss, 1872), p. 60.

7. Eleanor Flexner, *Century of Struggle* (New York: Atheneum, 1968), chs. 11, 12, 13, 15, 16, *passim;* Meyer, *Positive Thinkers,* pp. 52-54; Lydia Pinkham moved from political feminism before the Civil War to her famous medical response to women's disorders afterward; the scale of her dispensing of patent medicine to women was enormous; Jean Burton, *Lydia Pinkham Is Her Name* (New York: Farrar, Straus, 1949), pp. 17, 18; and R. C. Washburn, *The Life and Times of Lydia E. Pinkham* (New York: G. P. Putnam's Sons, 1931), pp. 168, 215, *passim;* Kraditor, *The Ideas of the Woman Suffrage Movement, 1890–1920* (New York: Doubleday, 1971), chs. 6, 7, *passim;* Higham describes WASP anxieties over "race suicide" in *Strangers in the Land,* pp. 143, 147–48; while Engelmann had castrated women (see Goodell, *Lessons in Gynecology* [Philadelphia: D. G. Brinton, 1879], p. 276), he ignored castration as a cause of sterility among WASP women in his article bewailing such a tendency, "The Increasing Sterility of American Women," *Transactions of the Section on the Diseases of Women and Children of the American Medical Association,* n.v. (1901), 271–95; the estimate of 150,000 castrated women in the U.S.A. in 1906 is in Ely Van de Warker, "The Fetich of the Ovary," *American Journal of Obstetrics and the Diseases of Women and Children,* 54 (July–Dec. 1906), 369; examples of the extensive involvement of parents, friends, and other doctors are Joseph Meyer, "A Case of Insanity, Caused by Diseased Ovaries, Cured by Their Removal—A Phenomenal Triumph for Operative Treatment," *Transactions of the American Association of Obstetricians and Gynecologists,* 7 (1894), 503–4; D. C. Brockman, "Oophorectomy for Grave Functional Nervous Diseases Occurring During Menstruation," *Transactions of the Western Surgical and Gynecological Association,* n.v. (1900), 104–10; a large number of the detailed case reports include reference to custodial relatives and encouraging friends.

8. A. Palmer Dudley, "Results of Ovarian Surgery," *Transactions of the Section on Obstetrics and Diseases of Women of the American Medical Association,* n.v. (1900), 187–88; Robert Battey, "Normal Ovariotomy," *Atlanta Medical and Surgical Journal,* 11, no. 1 (April 1873), 20–21; for the rationale of castrating an insane woman to prevent her bearing defective children, see the cases of Goodell and Gilliam, cited in notes 5 and 6 above.

9. For examples of the assumption of "positive amorous signs" as disorder or symptoms of disorder, see B. Sherwood Dunn, "Conservation of the Ovary," *Transactions of the American Association of Obstetricians and Gynecologists,* 10 (1897), 219, 220, 223; George Engelmann, "Cliterodectomy [*sic*]," *The American Practitioner,* 25 (1882), 3; "Transactions of the Woman's Hospital Society," *American Journal of Obstetrics and Gynecology,* 43 (1901), 721; Cushing and Carstens were discussants of Dunn's paper, "Conservation," pp. 224, 227; Cushing's earlier case, entitled "Melancholia, Masturbation; Cured by Removal of Both Ovaries," is part of the "Report of the Annual Meeting of the Gynecological Society of Boston," *Journal of the American Medical Association,* 8 (1887), 441–42; the final case quoted in this paragraph is A. J. Block, "Sexual Perversion in the Female," *New Orleans Medical and Surgical Journal,* 22, no. 1 (July 1894), 6.

10. Archibald Church, "Removal of Ovaries and Tubes in the Insane and Neurotic," *American Journal of Obstetrics and the Diseases of Women and Children,* 28 (1893), 494–95 (see, too, the "Discussion" of Church's paper in the same issue of the same journal, p. 573, where Church forcefully reiterated the need to castrate nymphomaniacs).

11. E. H. Pratt, "Circumcision of Girls," *Journal of Orificial Surgery,* 6, no. 9 (March 1898), 385–86; Dudley, "Results," p. 189; Dunn, "Conservation," p. 221; W. P. Manton, "The Legal Question in Operations on the Insane," *Transactions of the American Association of Obstetricians and Gynecologists,* 6 (1893), 246.

12. This is clear from the cases cited in the following notes; see, too, John Burnham, "Psychoanalysis and American Medicine: 1894–1918," *Psychological Issues* 5, no. 4 (1967); 73–81, *passim,* Meyer, *Positive Thinkers,* pp. 69–71, 96–98.

13. Dunn, "Conservation," *passim;* Allan Hamilton, "The Abuse of Oophorectomy in Diseases of the Nervous System," *New York Medical Journal,* 57 (1893), 180–83; Robert Edes, "Points in the Diagnosis and Treatment of Some Obscure Common Neuroses," *Journal of the American Medical Association,* 27 (1896), 1077–82; Edes, "The Relations of Pelvic and Nervous Diseases," *Journal of the American Medical Association,* 31 (1898), 1133–36.

14. E. Arnold Praeger, "Is So-Called Conservatism in Gynecology Conducive to the Best Results to the Patient?" *Transactions of the American Association of Obstetricians and Gynecologists,* 8 (1895), 322; Warner and Symington-Brown quoted in "Report of Gynecological Society of Boston," cited in note 9, above.

15. Hamilton, "Abuse," pp. 181, 182; Dunn, "Conservation," p. 213.

16. John Cokenower, "A Plea for Conservative Operations on the Ovaries," *Transactions of the Section on Obstetrics and Diseases of Women of the American Medical Association,* n.v. (1904), 298; Alfred Gordon, "Nervous and Mental Disturbances Following Castration in Women," *Journal of the American Medical Association,* 63 (1914), 1347 (this article and the discussion printed with it also provide evidence for the contemporary transplanting of ovaries, the early history of which I sketch in my *Sexual Surgery*).

17. Edes, "Relations," p. 1135; Church, "Removal," p. 494; W. J. Mayo, "Conservation of the Menstrual Function," *Journal of the American Medical Association,* 74, no. 25 (1920), 1685; Meyer, *Positive Thinkers,* pp. 72, 123, 93.

18. Dudley, "Results," p. 189.

19. Manton, "Mental Alienation in Women and Abdomino-Pelvic Disease," *Transactions of the Section on Obstetrics and Diseases of Women of the American Medical Association,* n.v. (1909), title.

20. "Report of Gynecological Society of Boston," p. 441.

21. This interpretation of Weir Mitchell's rest cure is based on his disciple's account, i.e., Henry T. Byford, *Manual of Gynecology,* 2d ed. (Philadelphia: P. Blakiston, 1897), pp. 180–85.

22. John O. Polak, "Final Results in Conservative Surgery of the Ovaries," *Transactions of the Section on Obstetrics and Diseases of Women of the American Medical Association,* n.v. (1909), 340; Goodell, *Lessons in Gynecology,* pp. 270–73.

23. Edes, "Relations," p. 1133; Dunn, "Conservation," pp. 233, 209–10.

24. For examples and meaning of sperm-sucking fantasies, see Barker-Benfield, "The Spermatic Economy," *Feminist Studies,* no. 1 (Summer 1972): 45–74; a slightly amended version was published in Michael Gordon, ed., *The American Family in Social-Historical Perspective* (New York: St. Martin's Press, 1973), pp. 336–372.

25. Dudley, "Results," p. 188; see, too, the letter Howard Kelly appended to his article "The Ethical Side of the Operation of Oophorectomy," *American Journal of Obstetrics,* 27 (1898), 207–8.

26. Cokenower, "Plea," p. 291; Van de Warker, "Fetich," p. 372; Edes, "Relations," p. 1134; D. MacLean, "Sexual Mutilation," *California Medical Journal,* 15 (1894), 382–84.

27. The phrase is Donald Meyer's, characterizing Erikson's account of Luther, in a review republished in Bruce Mazlish, ed., *Psychoanalysis and History* (Englewood Cliffs, N.J.: Prentice-Hall, 1963).

Chapter 12: The Reverend John Todd

1. *John Todd, The Story of His Life, Told Mainly by Himself,* compiled and ed. by Jonathan Edwards Todd (New York: Harper & Brothers, 1876), pp. 494, 496; Todd, *The Sunset Land* (Boston: Lee and Shephard, 1871), p. 245; Bancroft's recommendation is included in an advertisement for Todd's *Index Rerum* (Northampton: J. H. Butler, 1834) in the back of Todd's *The Moral Influence, Dangers and Duties, Connected with Great Cities* (Northampton: J. H. Butler, 1841); George Gissing, *The Odd Women* (New York: W. W. Norton, 1971), p. 154.

2. Todd, *Life,* pp. 471–72, 461.

3. Gardner, *Conjugal Sins,* pp. 69–70.

4. Todd, *Life,* pp. 20–23, 26, 27, 29, 33, 35.

5. *Ibid.,* pp. 29, 24, 28, 29, 459, 327. According to his son, Todd took to writing in Northampton in order to pay for his mother's keep; *ibid.,* p. 458.

6. Todd, *Student's Manual,* pp. 352–53.

7. Meyer, *Positive Thinkers,* pp. 53–54; John Scanzoni, *Sexual Bargaining* (Englewood Cliffs, N.J.: Prentice-Hall, 1972), pp. 36, 40.

8. Todd, *Life,* p. 118.

9. *Ibid.*, p. 108.

10. *Ibid.*, pp. 67–68.

11. *Ibid.*, p. 62; Clifford Clark, Jnr., "The Changing Nature of Protestantism in Mid-Nineteenth-Century America: Henry Ward Beecher's Seven Lectures to Young Men," *Journal of American History*, 57, no. 4 (March, 1971), p. 835; Weber, *Protestant Ethic*, p. 115; Todd, *Life*, p. 131.

12. Todd, *Life*, pp. 131, 312.

13. *Ibid.*, pp. 141, 139, 141, 215, 145, 146, 170, 157, 143, 167, 207.

14. *Ibid.*, pp. 231, 346, 280.

15. *Ibid.*, pp. 50, 134; Todd, *Sunset Land*, pp. 249, 250–51, 38–39, 292–94, 281, 283, 284; Meyer, *Positive Thinkers*, pp. 142–47; John Todd, *The Young Man, Hints Addressed to the Young Men of the United States* (Northampton: Hopkins, Bridgman, 1856 [1st ed., 1844]), p. 32.

16. Todd, *Woman's Rights*, pp. 20–22; Todd, *Sunset Land*, pp. 44–45; Todd, *Student's Manual*, pp. 149, 315.

17. Todd, *Life*, pp. 134, 354, 396; Todd, *A Sermon before the American Board of Commissioners for Foreign Missions at Pittsburgh, Pennsylvania, October 5, 1869* (Boston: T. R. Marvin and Son, 1869), p. 20.

18. Todd, *Sermon before . . . Commissioners*, pp. 6–7, 15, 10–11, and *passim*.

19. Todd, *Life*, pp. 257, 245.

20. *Ibid.*, pp. 258, 259.

21. *Ibid.*, pp. 259, 261–67, 287, 277–78, 301–2, 297, 299, 302, 293.

22. *Ibid.*, pp. 314, 140, 403–4, 409–10, 411, 417, 515–24. For clues to the connection between Melville and Todd see Egbert S. Oliver's "Explanatory Notes" to Melville's "The Lightning-Rod Man" in Melville, *Piazza Tales* (New York: Hendricks House, 1962), pp. 238–41.

23. Todd, *Life*, pp. 183, 187, 217, 501, 505, 216; Todd, *Student's Manual*, pp. 219–20.

24. Todd, *Life*, pp. 345, 511.

25. *Ibid.*, pp. 492, 307, 473, 282.

26. *Ibid.*, pp. 475, 481.

27. *Ibid.*, p. 480; Todd, "The Foot Lathe," in N. H. Baldwin, *Circular and Price List of Improved Portable Lathes and Fittings* (n.p., n.d.), p. 3.

28. My use of "phallic" may seem inconsistent with my remarks about the use of psychoanalytic theory in the introduction. In fact Todd himself was preoccupied with male masturbation and, *ipso facto*, its vehicle.

29. Todd, *Life*, pp. 488–90.

30. *Ibid.*, p. 373.

31. Todd, "Foot Lathe," pp. 2, 1; Todd, *Life*, p. 492.

32. Todd, *Life*, p. 492.

33. Todd, "Foot Lathe," pp. 1, 2, 4.

34. Todd, *Life*, pp. 484, 486, 482, 483, 482.

35. *Ibid.*, pp. 438, 439.

36. This and the next paragraph's quotations (apart from n. 37) are from Todd, *Life*, pp. 429–31. One wonders whether Todd was aware that the initials he gave his son spelled JET.

37. Todd, "Foot Lathe," p. 4.

Chapter 13: Primers for Anxiety

1. Todd, *Young Man*, pp. 113, 35.

2. *Ibid.*, p. 355; Todd, *Student's Manual*, p. 376; Todd, *Young Man*, pp. 119–20; Todd's response to urbanization was that it was essentially dangerous to the male character. In 1841 he published a book warning men of the damage a city would inflict on them unless they were shored up by religion. The titles of four of the book's six "Lectures" were "Temptations Peculiar to Christians in Great Cities," "Dangers Peculiar to Worldly Men Engaged in Business in Great Cities," and "Dangers Peculiar to Young Men in Great Cities" twice.

3. Todd, *Student's Manual*, pp. 372, 353; Tocqueville, *Democracy*, 2:105; Todd, *Student's Manual*, p. 372.

4. Todd, *Student's Manual*, pp. 284, 322; Todd, *The Daughter at School* (Northampton: Bridgman and Childs, 1868 [1st ed. 1853]), pp. 23, 31.

5. Todd, *Student's Manual*, pp. 309, 390, 326–27.

6. Irvin G. Wyllie, *The Self-Made Man in America: The Myth of Rags to Riches* (New York: The Free Press, 1966), ch. 4 *passim*; Todd, *Young Man*, p. 74; Todd, *Student's Manual*, p. 298; Tocqueville, *Democracy*, 2:22, 28–29, 138. Todd, *Student's Manual*, pp. 376, 304.

7. Todd, *Great Cities*, pp. 140, 142–43, 145–46.

8. Todd, *Daughter*, p. 112; Clark, "Changing Nature of Protestantism," pp. 837, 836.

9. Todd, *Student's Manual*, pp. 168, 184, 192.

10. *Ibid.*, pp. 223, 197.

11. *Ibid.*, p. 200; Todd, *Life*, pp. 503, 500.

12. Todd, *Student's Manual*, pp. 114, 321, 311.

13. Todd, *Student's Manual*, p. 309; Todd, *Life*, p. 373; Todd, *Student's Manual*, pp. 315–16. The similarity to Freud's account of superego and id is obvious.

14. Meyer, *Positive Thinkers*, p. 133; Tocqueville, *Democracy*, 2:104–5.

Chapter 14: Todd's Masturbation Phobia

1. Todd, *Student's Manual*, p. 165.

2. René Spitz, "Authority and Masturbation," *Psychoanalytic Quarterly*, 21 (1952), 490–577; E. H. Hare, "Masturbatory Insanity: The History of an Idea," *Journal of Mental Science*, 108, no. 452 (Jan. 1962), 1–21; Robert H. MacDonald, "The Frightful Consequences of Onanism: Notes on the History of a Delusion," *Journal of the History of Ideas*, 28, no. 3 (1967), 423–24. Spitz points out that Onan's sin (Gen. 38:9) was not masturbation but coitus interruptus. The circumstance common to both was what was held to be a waste of semen.

3. Watt, *Rise of the Novel*, pp. 52–53, 147–65 *passim*; Maximillian Novak, "Introduction" to Daniel Defoe, *Conjugal Lewdness* (Gainesville, Florida: Scholars' Facsimiles and Reprints [facsimile reprod. of 1727 ed.], 1967); MacDonald, "Onanism," pp. 424–25.

4. Watt, *Rise of the Novel*, pp. 51, 152, and *passim*; MacDonald, "Onanism," p. 425.

5. Spitz, "Authority," pp. 496–97; Watt, *Rise of the Novel*, pp. 81, 79.

6. Spitz, "Authority," pp. 494–95; see, too, MacDonald, "Onanism," p. 426, and Hare, "Masturbatory Insanity," pp. 2, 4.

7. Rush, *Medical Inquiries*, pp. 348–50; Todd, *Student's Manual*, p. 147; Woodward's letter to the editor included in "Deslandes Essay," *Boston Medical and Surgical Journal*, 19, no. 22 (Jan. 1839), 348–49; W, "Remarks on Masturbation," *Boston Medical and Surgical Journal*, 12, no. 6 (March 1835), 94–97; W, "Effects of Masturbation, with Cases," *Boston Medical and Surgical Journal*, 12, no. 9 (April 1835), 138–41.

8. W, "Remarks on Masturbation," p. 95; Shryock, "The Beginnings: From Colonial Days to the Foundation of the American Psychiatric Association," in J. K. Hall and Gregory Zilboorg, eds., *One Hundred Years of American Psychiatry* (New York: Columbia University Press, 1944), p. 25; Eric Dingwall, *The American Woman* (London: Gerald Duckworth, 1956), pp. 53, 75, n. 1; Spitz, "Authority and Masturbation," p. 507.

9. Todd, *Student's Manual*, ch. IV; Ray, *Mental Hygiene*, pp. 274–75. Eighteenth-century English masturbation phobia may have been associated with public anxiety over reading habits. After 1740 the new circulating libraries made novels accessible to poorer people and were said to have "debauched the minds of schoolboys." Reading then, as in Todd's day, depended on an increase in privacy, leisure, and income for purchasing or borrowing reading material and for the light to read by before or after work. Watt, *Rise of the Novel*, p. 44; Jarvis, "Comparative Liability," pp. 157, 161.

10. Todd, *Student's Manual*, pp. 166, 165.

11. *Ibid.*, pp. 147–48.

12. *Ibid.*, p. 145; Todd, *Young Man*, pp. 133–34.

13. Todd, *Student's Manual*, pp. 145–46, 148.

14. *Ibid.*, pp. 312–13, 152, 148.

15. T. W. Shannon, *Eugenics: or the Laws of Sex Life and Heredity* (Garden City, N.Y.: Doubleday, 1970 [replica of 1917 ed.]), p. 262; Todd, *Student's Manual*, pp. 146–47; Tocqueville, *Democracy*, 2:219.

16. Todd, *Student's Manual*, pp. 146, 154.

17. *Ibid.*, p. 146.

Chapter 15: The Spermatic Economy and Proto-Sublimation

1. W, "Remarks on Masturbation," p. 95.

2. Theophilus Parvin, "The Hygiene of the Sexual Function," *New Orleans Medical and Surgical Journal*, 11, n.s. (1883–84), 604; Anonymous, "Legislative Control of Prostitution," *New Orleans Medical and Surgical Journal*, 11 (March 1855), 704.

3. Todd, *Student's Manual*, p. 139.

4. Editorial, "Masturbation," *Boston Medical and Surgical Journal*, 19, no. 22 (Jan. 1839), 336; W, "Effects of Masturbation," p. 139; W, "Effects of Masturbation," p. 95 (and see p. 96).

5. Kai Erikson, *Wayward Puritans: A Study in the Sociology of Deviance* (New York: John Wiley, 1966), p. 20; see, e.g., Ditzion, *Marriage, Morals, and Sex, passim;* Alice Felt Tyler, *Freedom's Ferment* (New York: Harper & Row, 1962); ch. 13 and *passim;* two unpublished papers by students in the History Department, The American University, Washington, D.C.: Janet E. Kaufman, "Warning: Smoking May Be Hazardous to Your Health: The Anti-Tobacco

Crusade, 1830–1860" (1971), and Pauline B. Vivette, "The Psychology of Advertising Patent Medicines in the Late Nineteenth Century: Patterns of Appeals to the American Family" (1971). Todd, "My Workshop," *The Herald of Health and Journal of Physical Culture*, 53, o.s. (19, n.s.) (1872), 123–24.

6. Todd, *Student's Manual*, pp. 262, 276, 277, 292.

7. W, "Remarks on Masturbation," p. 96; Todd, *Life*, pp. 503, 268; W, "Remarks on Masturbation," p. 96.

8. W, "Insanity, Produced by Masturbation," *Boston Medical and Surgical Journal*, 12, no. 7 (March 1835), 110.

9. Conway Zirkle, "The Early History of the Inheritance of Acquired Characters and of Pangenesis," *Transactions of the American Philosophical Society*, 35, pt. 2 (1946), 141, 146. The history of ideas about sperm is complicated; it can be approached by way of Elizabeth Gasking, *Investigations of Generation, 1651–1828* (London: Hutchinson, 1967). See, too, B. Seeman, *The River of Life* (New York: W. W. Norton, 1961), pp. 26, 27, 31.

10. Gardner, *Our Children*, pp. 51, 162–63.

11. J. H. Walters, "Report on the Doctrine of Force, Physical and Vital," *Transactions of the American Medical Association*, 21 (1870), 273; Todd, *Serpents*, p. 10.

12. Sigmund Freud, "Three Contributions to the Theory of Sex" in *Basic Writings*, trans. and ed. A. A. Brill (New York: Modern Library, 1938), p. 611.

13. Henry David Thoreau, *Walden* (New York: New American Library, 1960), p. 149; Gardner, *Conjugal Sins*, pp. 182, 85; Parvin, "Sexual Hygiene," p. 607; see too Wyllie, *Self-Made Man*, p. 50.

14. Erikson, *Young Man Luther*, p. 253.

15. Todd, *Student's Manual*, pp. 375–76.

16. *Ibid.*, pp. 154, 150–51; according to Ray, masturbation put a man in the "loathesome prison house of the flesh," *Mental Hygiene*, p. 276.

17. Todd, *Student's Manual*, p. 141; Todd, *Daughter*, p. 110; Todd, *Student's Manual*, p. 146.

18. Todd, *Great Cities*, pp. 128–29.

19. Todd, *Student's Manual*, p. 356.

20. *Ibid.*, p. 358.

Chapter 16: Men Earn—Women Spend

1. See pt. IV below; see also Michael Gordon, "From Procreation to Recreation: Changes in Sexual Ideology, 1830–1940," presented at the 1970 meeting of the American Sociological Association, Washington, D.C.; Michael Bliss, "Pure Books on Avoided Subjects: Pre-Freudian Sexual Ideas in Canada," presented to the Canadian Historical Association, June 4, 1970. (According to Bliss the ideas he discusses were derived almost entirely from the United States); Wayland Young, *Eros Denied, Sex in Western Society* (New York: Grove Press, 1966), ch. 20.

2. See Ch. 13 n. 4.

3. Subtitle of Todd, *The Young Man*.

4. See Ch. 9, n. 16.

5. Meyer, *Positive Thinkers*, p. 57.

6. Todd, *Serpents*, pp. 9, 5, 18, 9; Todd, *Woman's Rights*, pp. 10, 9. Ch. III, "The Troubled Souls of Females," in Meyer, *Positive Thinkers*, casts a great deal of light on the subject of this paragraph.

7. Todd, *Daughter*, pp. 43, 49, 42.

8. Todd, *Woman's Rights*, pp. 14–15.

9. Meyer, *Positive Thinkers*, pp. 49, 50, 53, 58.

10. *Ibid.*, p. 51; Todd, *Woman's Rights*, pp. 17, 15, 10, 7, 13, 11, 17–18.

11. Todd, *Great Cities*, pp. 113–14; in asking women to "brace up and bear" his exposure of their sexuality, Todd evoked his relation with his own wife, whose unmarried name was Brace.

12. Todd, *Great Cities*, pp. 114–15.

13. *Ibid.*, p. 112.

14. Meyer, *Positive Thinkers*, p. 125 and ch. XI *passim*.

15. Todd, *Student's Manual*, pp. 378–79.

Chapter 17: Woman's Refinement

1. Todd, *Daughter*, pp. 21, 207–8, 212.

2. *Ibid.*, pp. 19–20, 68–69, 232, 235, 240, 242, 205–6.

3. *Ibid.*, p. 246; Todd, *Life*, p. 103.

4. Todd, *Serpents*, pp. 20, 3.

5. Todd, *Student's Manual*, p. 283.

6. Todd, *Serpents*, p. 10; Todd, *Woman's Rights*, pp. 8, 25, 11–12.

7. Todd, *Daughter*, p. 15.

8. Calvin Pease quoted in Miller, *Life of the Mind*, p. 65.

Chapter 18: Sex and Anarchy

1. Todd, *Serpents*, pp. 24, 16.

2. Press reviews of Storer's book appended to *ibid.*

3. *Ibid.*, pp. 3–4, 5; Todd, *Life*, p. 495; Gardner, "Report on Cases of Operative Midwifery, with the Particulars of a Novel Operation," *American Journal of Medical Sciences*, 47 (July 1852), title page.

4. Todd, *Serpents*, pp. 15–16, 19, 17; Norman Himes, *Medical History of Contraception* (New York: Schocken Books, 1970), pp. 287–301.

5. Todd, *Serpents*, pp. 9, 6–7, 7–9; Todd, *Woman's Rights*, p. 18.

6. Kraditor, *Up*, p. 184; Todd, *Woman's Rights*, pp. 12, 5–6; Camilla was a nearly unbeatable female warrior in Virgil's *Aeneid*, called an "intolerable scourge" and killed by treachery.

7. Meyer, *Positive Thinkers*, p. 52; John Todd, *Letter to New York Weekly Anglo-African* (Jan. 11, 1862). I am grateful to Dr. Ronald T. Takaki for this reference. On the first page of his *Life*, Todd said that as a child he slept in the same bed with blacks. His uncle, the Reverend Jonathan Todd, was a slave-owner. For the relation between abolitionism and the woman's rights movement see Kraditor, *Means and Ends in American Abolitionism* (New York: Pantheon, 1967), ch. 3, "The Woman Question."

8. Todd, *Woman's Rights*, pp. 17, 26; Todd, *Serpents*, pp. 12, 25.

9. Todd, *Young Man*, p. 278; see, too, pp. 278–79.

10. Sigmund Freud, *Civilization and Its Discontents,* trans. James Strachey (New York: W. W. Norton, 1962), p. 51; Karl Marx and Friedrich Engels, *Manifesto of the Communist Party* (New York: International Publishers, 1948 [1st ed. 1848]), p. 27.

11. Cf. Aileen Kraditor, *The Ideas of the Woman Suffrage Movement 1890–1920* (Garden City, N.Y.: Anchor, 1971), p. 76.

12. Todd, *Daughter,* p. 75; Todd, *Woman's Rights,* pp. 16–17.

13. Todd, *Woman's Rights,* pp. 14–16.

14. Todd, *Serpents,* p. 23.

15. Todd, *Woman's Rights,* pp. 14, 18, 8.

16. Tocqueville, *Democracy,* 2:28, 144–45.

Chapter 19: From Mother to Mother Earth

1. Todd, *Woman's Rights,* pp. 6, 8, 13; Meyer, *Positive Thinkers,* p. 56.

2. Todd, *Daughter,* pp. 214, 208–9; in 1870 Gardner referred to the "common use of cold ablutions and astringent infusions and variously medicated washes" (*Conjugal Sins,* pp. 107–8); Todd, *Woman's Rights,* p. 27; Todd, *Life,* p. 245.

3. Todd, *Daughter,* pp. 16–17, 133–34.

4. *Ibid.,* pp. 68–69, 6.

5. Todd, *Sunset Land,* pp. 65, 124, 27–28, 66–67; Todd, *Daughter,* p. 7; Todd, *Serpents,* pp. 7–8.

6. Ralph Waldo Emerson, *Five Essays on Man and Nature* (New York: Appleton-Century-Crofts, 1954), pp. 30, 28, 73.

7. Todd, *Life,* p. 346.

8. Smith, *Virgin Land,* pp. 35, 43.

9. Todd, *Sunset Land,* pp. 253–54, 245. For an accessible picture of Todd at the Mountain Wedding, see Louis B. Wright, *The American Frontier* (New York: Capricorn Books, 1971), p. 206. Todd is the tall, white-haired man in profile in the left center foreground of the picture; he is dressed in black with a book (the Bible) in his hand. His portrait hangs in the Jonathan Edwards Church in Pittsfield; Emerson, *Essays,* p. 13.

10. Todd, *Sunset Land,* p. 260.

11. *Ibid.,* p. 257; Gilpin quoted in Smith, *Virgin Land,* p. 40; Todd, *Sunset Land,* pp. 268–69.

12. Gardner, *Our Children,* pp. 36, 37.

13. Speech of Samuel Sullivan Cox, "Emancipation and Its Results—Is Ohio to Be Africanized?" delivered in the House of Representatives, June 6, 1862. Quoted in Stanley Feldstein, ed., *The Poisoned Tongue: A Documentary History of American Racism and Prejudice* (New York: William Morrow, 1972), pp. 144–45.

14. Todd, *Student's Manual,* p. 150.

15. Todd, *Life,* pp. 429–31; Todd, *Daughter,* pp. 214–15.

Chapter 20: Dr. Gardner's Education

1. S. W. Francis, "Biographical Sketches of Distinguished Living New York Physicians: VIII Augustus Kinsley Gardner," *Medical and Surgical Reporter,* 15 (1866), 313; Gardner, *History of the Art of Midwifery* (New York: Stringer and Townshend, 1852), dedication; Duyckinck, *Cyclopoedia,* 1:799, 824.

2. Francis, "Gardner," p. 315; Harris, *Woman's Surgeon,* pp. 134, 143; Gardner, *Midwifery,* p. 10; Harris, *Woman's Surgeon,* pp. 168, 237. Gardner delivered his "Eulogy on John W. Francis" before the New York Medico-Chirurgical College, March 7, 1861. Harris, *Woman's Surgeon,* pp. 134, 168, 172, 174.

3. Francis, "Gardner," p. 313; Higham, *Strangers in the Land,* pp. 236–37; Richard Hofstadter, *The Age of Reform: From Bryan to F.D.R.* (New York: Vintage, 1955), pp. 138–39, n. 8; Wilbur J. Cash, *The Mind of the South* (New York: Vintage, 1941), p. 118; for the nationalization of this pattern, see Lawrence J. Friedman, *The White Savage: Racial Fantasies in the Postbellum South* (Englewood Cliffs, N.J.: Prentice-Hall, 1970), chs. 3, 4, 8, and for feminism's assumption of it, see Kraditor, *Woman Suffrage Movement,* ch. 7.

4. Gardner, *Our Children,* pp. 37, 19; Gardner, *Old Wine,* p. 223; Gardner, *Our Children,* p. 37.

5. Gardner, *Our Children,* pp. 37, 51; Gardner, *Conjugal Sins,* p. 192; Gardner, *Our Children,* p. 44.

6. Gardner, *Old Wine,* pp. 99–100; Francis, "Gardner," pp. 313–14; Gardner, *Conjugal Sins,* p. 70.

7. Francis, "Gardner," p. 314.

8. Gardner, *Our Children,* p. 105.

9. *Ibid.,* pp. 106, 107.

10. *Ibid.,* p. 107.

11. *Ibid.,* p. 108.

12. *Ibid.,* pp. 110–11; Gardner, *Conjugal Sins,* p. 67; Gardner, *Our Children,* p. 125.

13. Francis, "Gardner," p. 314.

14. *Ibid.*

15. Obituary notice, newspaper clipping, no citation, in New York Academy of Medicine; Gardner, *Old Wine,* preface to 1st ed., pp. 28–29, 15, 242.

16. Gardner, *Old Wine,* pp. 223, 197, 144–45, 142.

17. *Ibid.,* pp. 105–6; Gardner, "Treatise on Uterine Haemorrhage," *American Medical Monthly* (June 1855), 1; Gardner, *Old Wine,* p. 99.

18. Gardner, *Old Wine,* pp. 224, 273.

19. *Ibid.,* pp. 322, 56, 137, 221.

20. *Ibid.,* pp. 305–6.

21. *Ibid.,* p. 125; Gardner, *Our Children,* p. 151.

22. Gardner, "The Physical Decline of American Women," pp. 217, 208, 221, 225, 215, 223. This article was published in *The Knickerbocker,* 55, no. 1 (Jan. 1860), 37–52, and as Appendix A in Gardner's *Conjugal Sins,* pp. 199–238; my notes refer to the latter.

23. Gardner, *Our Children,* pp. 199–200, 184.

24. Gardner, "Physical Decline," pp. 218, 234.

25. *Ibid.,* pp. 214, 215.

26. *Ibid.,* pp. 210, 220; Gardner, *Conjugal Sins,* ch. IX; Gardner, *Our Children,* p. 45.

27. In 1848 he had said that the poor in France were unable to marry because money was a "requisite for matrimony." In America, the question whether to marry or not was free of "the Almighty Dollar" (*Old Wine,* p. 83). Twenty-two years later, in *Conjugal Sins,* Gardner believed it was indeed money that deter-

mined whether or not Americans could marry (pp. 60–61). Gardner had no answer for poor women, except that they should go against nature by being celibate, denying themselves what Gardner regarded as their sweetest "interior satisfaction," i.e., motherhood. He told the readers of *Conjugal Sins* that they should copulate only to have children and have children only when they could afford it, and, of course, marry only when they could afford to have children.

28. Blackwood quoted by Himes, *Medical History of Contraception*, p. 280.

29. Gardner, *Old Wine*, pp. 157–60; Gardner, *Our Children*, p. 201.

30. Gardner, *Old Wine*, p. 164; Gardner, *Our Children*, p. 22.

31. Gardner, *Our Children*, p. 16.

Chapter 21: Gardner's Career

1. Augustus Kinsley Gardner, "Gonorrhoea; A Non-Specific Disease," reprinted from *The Medical Independent* (1864), 7.

2. Gardner, "Eulogy on John Snowden," "Obituaries of Members of New York Academy of Medicine" (handwritten, 1848).

3. Gardner, *Old Wine*, p. 181; Francis, "Gardner," p. 315; Gardner, "Flags Which Have Waved Over New York City," printed in the New York *Daily Tribune*, May 15, 1861. I am grateful to Mr. James J. Heslin of the New-York Historical Society for letting me have a copy of this article.

4. Gardner, *Our Children*, p. 21.

5. *Ibid.*, pp. 167, 166.

6. Francis, "Gardner," p. 315; clipping from *The Home Journal*, Feb. 2, 1876, in the NYAM; Gardner's poem is in the Duyckinck Collection, New York Public Library; Gardner, *Our Children*, pp. 175–76.

7. Gardner, "Uterine Haemorrhage," signature; Gardner, "Eulogy on John W. Francis," title page; Gardner, "Gonorrhoea," title page reads "Ex-Professor" etc.; Francis, "Gardner," pp. 314–15.

8. Gardner, "Gonorrhoea," signature; Gardner, *Conjugal Sins*, signature to preface; Leyda, *Log*, 1:xvi; the houses no longer exist.

9. Gardner, "Eulogy on Richard Sharp Kissam," read before the New York Academy of Medicine, December 3, 1862 (New York: C. W. Alvord, 1863); Francis, "Gardner," p. 315, n.

10. Francis, "Gardner," p. 315; Gardner, *Our Children*, p. 37.

11. Leyda, *Log*, 1:xxvi; Gardner, letter to Evert Duyckinck, Jan. 17, 1862, Duyckinck Collection, New York Public Library; "Medicus," letter to New York *Times*, Nov. 1, 1867.

12. Gardner, *Old Wine*, p. 160; New York *Times*, Oct. 18, 1867.

13. "Medicus," letter, *loc. cit.*

14. Augustus Kinsley Gardner, *The Causes and Curative Treatment of Sterility* (New York: De Witt and Davenport, 1856), p. 60; Augustus Kinsley Gardner, "The Rupture of the Perinaeum," *Medical Union* (1874), 108.

15. Gardner, *Our Children*, p. 204; Gardner, *Conjugal Sins*, pp. 130, 131; Gardner was a Unitarian; sexual ideology cut across all kinds of sectarian ideology, even if it was a cause of sectarianism.

16. Gardner, *Sterility*, p. 91; Gardner, *Our Children*, p. 226; Gardner, *Conjugal Sins*, p. 86.

17. Sims, *Clinical Notes*, pp. 4, 145, 262.

18. Gardner, *Conjugal Sins*, p. 9; Todd's letter to Gardner is published at the end of the 1874 edition (New York: G. J. Moulton, 1874) under "Endorsements and Opinions."

19. Reviews quoted in 1923 edition of *Conjugal Sins*.

20. Preface to 1874 edition; *The Home Journal*, Feb. 27, 1876.

21. Gardner, *Our Children*, p. 57.

22. W. Tyler Smith, *The Modern Practice of Midwifery*, ed. A. K. Gardner (New York: Robert M. De Witt, 1852); Sims, *Clinical Notes*, pp. 385, 397; Thomas, *A Practical Treatise on the Diseases of Women* (Philadelphia: H. C. Lea, 1878), pp. 182, 184.

Chapter 22: The Physical Decline of American Women

1. Gardner, "Physical Decline," p. 199.

2. *Ibid.*, pp. 200, 203–4.

3. *Ibid.*, pp. 204–5.

4. Abraham Jacobi, "On Masturbation and Hysteria in Young Children," *American Journal of Obstetrics and Diseases of Women and Children*, 8 (1875) and 9 (1876), 8, 599.

5. Gardner, "Physical Decline," pp. 206, 207.

6. *Ibid.*, p. 207.

7. *Ibid.*

8. *Ibid.*, pp. 208–9 (see, too, Gardner, *Conjugal Sins*, p. 180); Marion Harland, *Breakfast, Luncheon and Tea* (New York: Scribner, Armstrong, 1875), p. 5.

9. Gardner, "Physical Decline," pp. 207, 237, 204; Gardner, *Midwifery*, p. 28.

10. Gardner, "Physical Decline," pp. 212, 217, 215, 220, 224, 225, 229.

11. *Ibid.*, pp. 230, 236, 237; Gardner, *Conjugal Sins*, pp. 73–74.

12. Gardner, "Physical Decline," p. 237; Gardner, *Our Children*, p. 21.

13. Gardner, "Physical Decline," p. 204.

14. *Ibid.*, p. 210; Gardner, *Our Children*, p. 180.

15. Marvin Meyers, *The Jacksonian Persuasion: Politics and Belief* (New York: Vintage, 1960), p. 31; Gardner, *Our Children*, pp. 79–80.

16. Gardner, *Our Children*, pp. 8, 203.

17. *Ibid.*, pp. 203–4.

18. *Ibid.*, pp. 199–200, 125, 65.

19. Gardner, "Physical Decline," p. 216; Gardner, *Midwifery*, p. 31; Gardner, *Our Children*, p. 96; Gardner, "Physical Decline," p. 219; Gardner, *Conjugal Sins*, p. 177; e.g. Joachim C. Fest, *The Face of the Third Reich* (New York: Ace Books, 1970); see the chapter entitled "German Wife and Mother: The Role of Women in the Third Reich."

20. Lawrence Lader, *Abortion* (Indianapolis: Bobbs-Merrill, 1966), pp. 75, 78, 85–86, 81, 91, 87, 92.

21. Gardner, "Physical Decline," pp. 223, 224; Gardner, *Our Children*, p. 64.

22. Gardner, *Conjugal Sins*, p. 118.

23. Gardner, "Physical Decline," p. 228.

24. Gardner, *Conjugal Sins*, p. 85.

25. *Ibid.*, pp. 86–87, 108, 109.

26. Gardner, "Physical Decline," p. 231; Gardner, *Conjugal Sins*, p. 31; Herrick quoted in Himes, *Contraception*, p. 287.

27. Gardner, *Conjugal Sins*, p. 109.

28. Gardner, *Sterility*, p. 162; Kraditor, *Woman's Suffrage*, p. 92.

29. Gardner, *Conjugal Sins*, pp. 110, 108.

30. *Ibid.*, pp. 102–3, 99.

31. Gardner, "Perinaeum," p. 5; Gardner, *Conjugal Sins*, pp. 101–2, 89–90.

32. Gardner, "Physical Decline," pp. 222, 220.

33. *Ibid.*, pp. 221–22.

34. Gardner, *Conjugal Sins*, pp. 72, 14.

35. Gardner, *Our Children*, p. 109.

36. Gardner, *Conjugal Sins*, p. 70; Gardner, *Our Children*, p. 109.

Chapter 23: Punishing Women

1. Gardner, *Sterility*, pp. 111, 49.

2. Gardner, *Our Children*, pp. 200–1; Gardner, *Conjugal Sins*, pp. 216, 217.

3. Gardner, *Conjugal Sins*, p. 82.

4. Ilza Veith, *Hysteria: The History of a Disease* (Chicago: Phoenix, 1970), p. 172; Gardner, *Our Children*, p. 120.

5. Gardner, *Conjugal Sins*, pp. 173, 172.

6. Gardner, "Gonorrhoea," pp. 10–11; Gardner, *Sterility*, p. 17.

7. Elaine and English Showalter, "Victorian Women and Menstruation," *Victorian Studies*, 14 (1970), 83–89. Gardner, *Conjugal Sins*, ch. IX, pp. 133–34.

8. Gardner, *Conjugal Sins*, pp. 143–44, 145, 146.

9. *Ibid.*, pp. 147–48.

10. *The Autobiography of Bertrand Russell*, vol. 1, 1872–1914 (Boston: Little, Brown, 1967), p. 183.

11. Gardner, *Old Wine*, pp. 226, 190; Gardner, *Our Children*, p. 51.

12. Gardner, "Uterine Haemorrhage," p. 1.

13. Gardner, "Thoughts on Health," p. 283; Gardner, *Our Children*, pp. 33, 8–9.

14. Gardner, *Our Children*, pp. 29–30.

15. Gardner, *Old Wine*, pp. 22–23.

16. Gardner, *Conjugal Sins*, p. 19.

17. Gardner, *Our Children*, pp. 250–51.

18. Meyer, *Positive Thinkers*, pp. 58–59.

19. Gardner, *Our Children*, p. 59.

20. Gardner, *Old Wine*, pp. 210, 166.

21. Gardner, *Sterility*, p. 60; Gardner, *Our Children*, p. 250.

22. Gardner, "Perinaeum," pp. 103, 102, 104, 103, 111.

23. *Ibid.*, pp. 104, 102.

24. *Ibid.*, pp. 103, 104.

25. Todd, *Student's Manual*, p. 123; D. H. Lawrence used the same metaphor for the inflexibility of male purpose, Gerald Crich forcing his beautiful, rearing mare to stand as a train went past a crossing in *Women in Love*, ch. IX.

26. Gardner, *Old Wine*, p. 304; Augustus Kinsley Gardner, *Report of a Committee Appointed by the Academy of Medicine Upon the Comparative Value of*

Milk (New York: Craighead, 1851), p. 2; Gardner, *Midwifery,* p. 28. Briareus was "a giant with fifty heads and a hundred hands. . . . He was the offspring of Heaven and Earth and was of the race of Titans, with whom he fought in the war against Zeus" (Brewer's *Dictionary of Phrase and Fable*). He became a metaphor for prodigious activity, because of his many-handedness.

27. Gardner, *Old Wine,* p. 225.

28. *Ibid.,* pp. 221–22.

29. *Ibid.,* p. 46; Gardner, *Sterility,* p. 140.

30. Gardner, "Perinaeum," pp. 103, 105.

31. Gardner, *Old Wine,* p. 214; Gardner, "Perinaeum," p. 108; Gardner, *Midwifery,* p. 20.

32. Gardner, *Midwifery,* pp. 28, 31–32.

Chapter 24: The Great Organ of Communication

1. Gardner, *Our Children,* pp. 53–54.

2. *Ibid.,* p. 323; Gardner, *Conjugal Sins,* pp. 80, 29; Tocqueville, *Democracy,* 2:219.

3. Gardner, *Conjugal Sins,* pp. 78, 79, 81.

4. *Ibid.,* p. 81.

5. *Ibid.,* pp. 190, 191, 80.

6. Parvin, "Sexual Function," pp. 609–610; Bliss, "Pure Books," p. 5; Parvin, "Sexual Function," pp. 610–12, and see Bliss, "Pure Books," p. 9.

7. Gardner, *Conjugal Sins,* p. 163.

8. Gardner, *Our Children,* p. 140.

9. Gardner, *Sterility,* pp. 22, 35, 26, 27, 28, 29, 46.

10. Gardner, *Our Children,* pp. 51, 45.

11. *Ibid.,* p. 114; for Gardner's associating sperm with urine, see *Our Children,* p. 102, and *Old Wine,* p. 22.

12. Gardner, *Our Children,* pp. 39, 48–49.

13. *Ibid.,* p. 57; Gardner, *Conjugal Sins,* dedication, pp. 130, 131, 195; Gardner, *Our Children,* p. 34. This vision of a regression to barbarism has been traditional in American history, and, I suspect, reflects one of the deepest apprehensions of European peoples, leaving the civilization established by an eon of forebears to settle in what they regarded as void or barbaric lands. The emigrants tried to ward off such a danger by destroying the reminders of "barbarism" around them, that is the indigenes of the non-European continents; such destruction thereby brought about the very condition it was designed to prevent (see Ian D. MacCrone, *Race Attitudes in South Africa: Historical, Experimental, and Psychological Studies* [Johannesburg: Witwatersrand University Press, 1957], Part I, and Jordan, *White over Black,* ch. 1); Brigham was one example of such an apprehension in America; for examples in the Revolutionary era see Bailyn, *Ideological Origins,* p. 84, and Williams, *Contours,* pp. 107–8; of course it was part of the Puritan world view (see, e.g., Lawrence Cremin, *American Education: The Colonial Experience, 1607–1783* [New York: Harper & Row, 1970], p. 177), intimately connected to the apocalyptism of the Reformation (see W. Lamont, *Godly Rule* [London: Macmillan, 1969], *passim*).

14. Gardner, *Old Wine,* pp. 154, 211.

15. Gardner, *Our Children,* pp. 36–37.

16. Gardner, *Midwifery,* p. 31; Gardner, *Old Wine,* p. 152.

17. Gardner, *Old Wine,* p. 137.

18. *Ibid.,* pp. 290–92.

19. Gardner, *Conjugal Sins,* p. 111.

20. *Ibid.,* pp. 130–31; Gardner, "Perinæum," p. 104; *Oxford English Dictionary.*

Index

Abbott, Benjamin, 231
abortion, 88, 122, 190, 204–5
  anti-abortion legislation, 265
  midwives and, 204, 265
  physical decline of women and, 260,
    265–6
acquisitiveness and ambition (*see also*
    Competitiveness; Success, pursuit
    of), 5–6, 15, 45–7, 78, 92, 262
  insanity and, 50–1
  mental hygiene and, 73–4
Acton, William, 298
adolescence, 28–31, 232–3
Ahab, in *Moby Dick* (Melville), 17, 99
Alger, Horatio, 212
Allport, W. H., 68
American Board of Foreign Missions, 144
American Common Schools System, 231
American Gynecological Society, 67–8,
    89, 97
American Journal of Insanity, 82
*American Journal of Obstetrics and
    Diseases of Women and Children*,
    89
American Medical Association, 62, 85,
    87–9, 97–8
  Code of Ethics, 98
Amour, L' (Debreyne), 278
Aristotle, 181
Astor, John Jacob, 105
Athon, James, 52
Atlee brothers, 83
Atlee, John, 105

Autobiography (Franklin), 29
autonomy
  bachelorhood vs. marriage, 8–18
  fear of dependence on women and, 215
  ideal, cultural, 27
  mobility and, 13–18
  orderliness and, 49–50
  politics and, 24–5
  Protestantism, 23–5
  sexual, masturbation and, 223–6
  uniformity and, 30

bachelorhood
  mobility, 9–10, 13–18
  theme in literature of frontier, 8–18
"Bachelor's Soliloqy, The," 164–5
Bailyn, Bernard, 24, 25, 75
Baker, Josephine, 65
Baldwin, W. O., 92, 95, 106
Bancroft, George, 135
Barker, Fordyce, 88
Bartlett, Dr., 249–50
Battey, Robert, 89, 97, 124, 127, 128, 276
Beard, George, 30
Beaumont, Charles de, 3, 5, 22, 29, 38, 40
Beecher, Catherine, 21, 49
Beecher, Henry Ward, 141, 159–60
Beecher, Lyman, 146
Beekman, James, 103
behavior, sex roles and, 41–4
  gynecology and, 122–6
Bellevue School for Midwives, 63
Benedict, E. C., 105